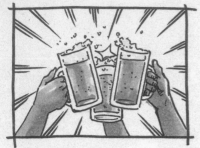

岸本斉史

I've recently starting going out to eat with my assistants after work. Once we get our drinks I always end up leading the toast... but my assistants' eyes seem to be stating that simply saying "thanks for your hard work today" is somewhat insufficient... Ah, but there ain't much variation that can be had there!!!

—Masashi Kishimoto, 2013

Author/artist Masashi Kishimoto was born in 1974 in rural Okayama Prefecture, Japan. After spending time in art college, he won the Hop Step Award for new manga artists with his manga **Karakuri** (Mechanism). Kishimoto decided to base his next story on traditional Japanese culture. His first version of **Naruto**, drawn in 1997, was a one-shot story about fox spirits; his final version, which debuted in **Weekly Shonen Jump** in 1999, quickly became the most popular ninja manga in Japan.

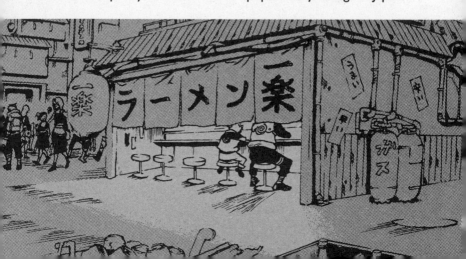

NARUTO VOL. 65
SHONEN JUMP Manga Edition

STORY AND ART BY MASASHI KISHIMOTO

Translation/Mari Morimoto
Touch-up Art & Lettering/John Hunt
Design/Sam Elzway
Editor/Alexis Kirsch

Printed in the U.S.A.

Published by VIZ Media, LLC
P.O. Box 77010
San Francisco, CA 94107

10 9 8 7 6 5 4 3 2 1
First printing, April 2014

SHONEN JUMP MANGA EDITION

NARUTO

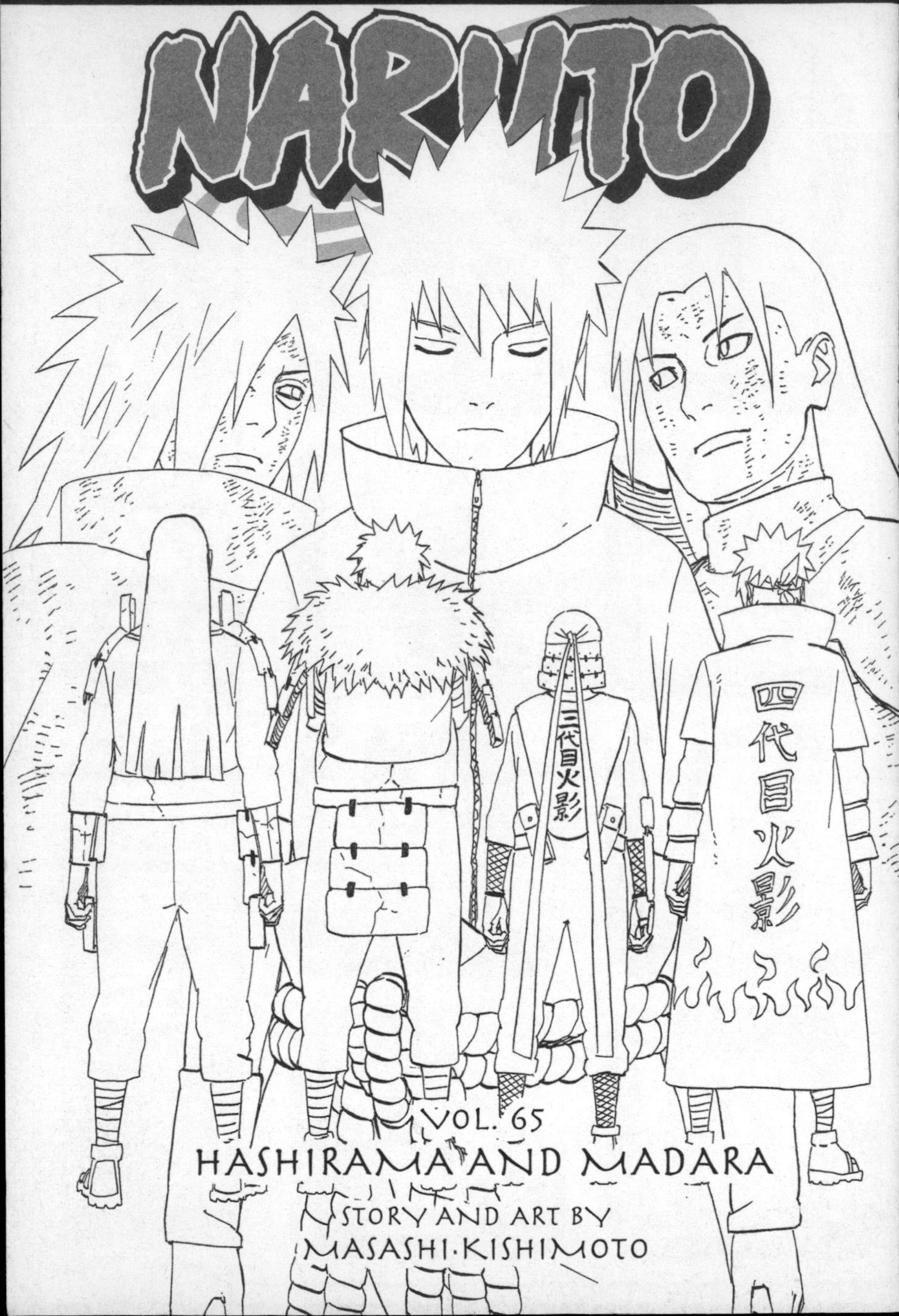
三代目火影
四代目火影

VOL. 65

HASHIRAMA AND MADARA

STORY AND ART BY
MASASHI KISHIMOTO

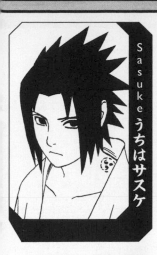

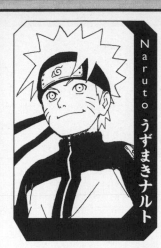

うちはサスケ Sasuke

うずまきナルト Naruto

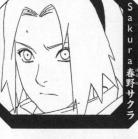

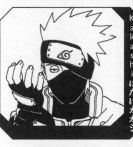

春野サクラ Sakura

はたけカカシ Kakashi

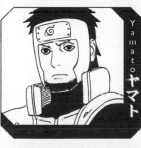

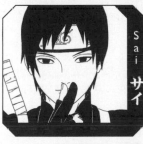

ヤマト Yamato

サイ Sai

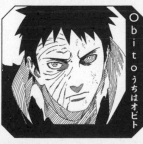

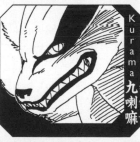

うちはオビト Obito

九喇嘛 Kurama

CHARACTERS

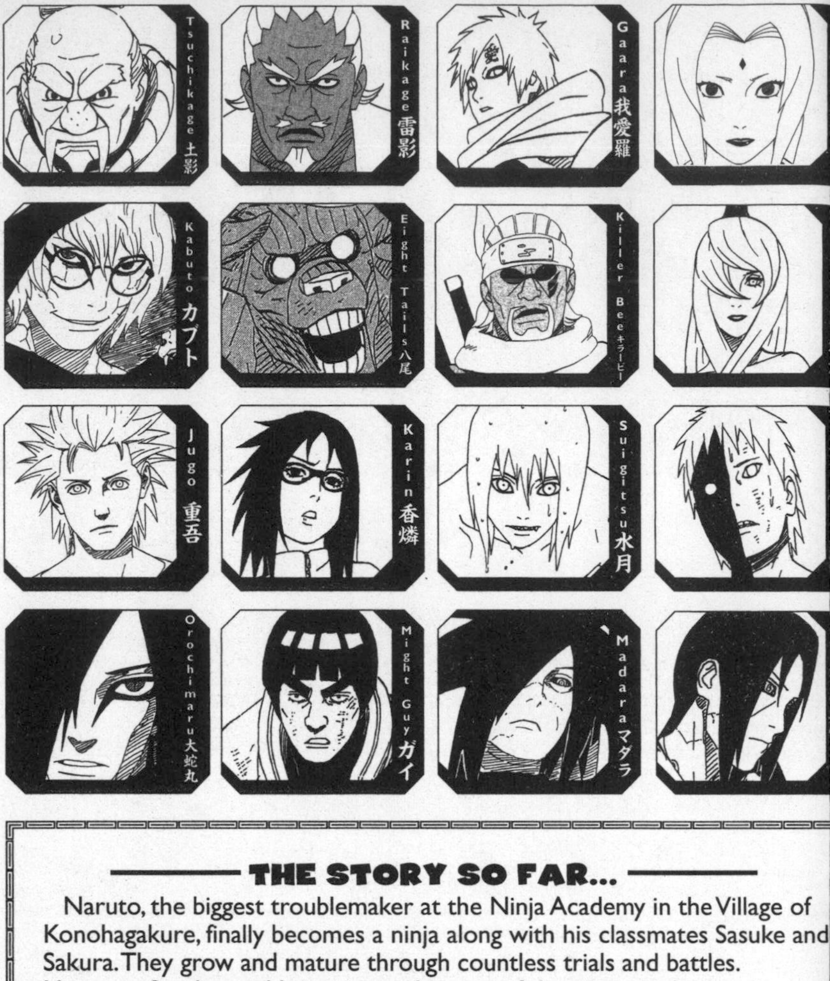
Gaara 我愛羅
Raikage 雷影
Tsuchikage 土影
Killer Bee キラービー
Eight Tails 八尾
Kabuto カブト
Suigetsu 水月
Karin 香燐
Jugo 重吾
Madara マダラ
Might Guy ガイ
Orochimaru 大蛇丸

THE STORY SO FAR...

Naruto, the biggest troublemaker at the Ninja Academy in the Village of Konohagakure, finally becomes a ninja along with his classmates Sasuke and Sakura. They grow and mature through countless trials and battles. However, Sasuke, unable to give up his quest for vengeance, leaves Konohagakure to seek Orochimaru and his power…

Two years pass. Naruto grows up and engages in fierce battles against the Tailed Beast-targeting Akatsuki. Elsewhere, after winning the heroic battle against Itachi and learning his older brother's true intentions, Sasuke allies with the Akatsuki and sets out to destroy Konoha.

The Fourth Great Ninja War against the Akatsuki begins. Having stopped the Edotensei jutsu with the help of his brother, Sasuke now heads off with Orochimaru to fullfil a new objective. Meanwhile, Naruto and his allies try to stop Obito and Madara from reviving Ten Tails. And what will Sasuke's next move be?!

NARUTO

VOL. 65
HASHIRAMA AND MADARA

CONTENTS

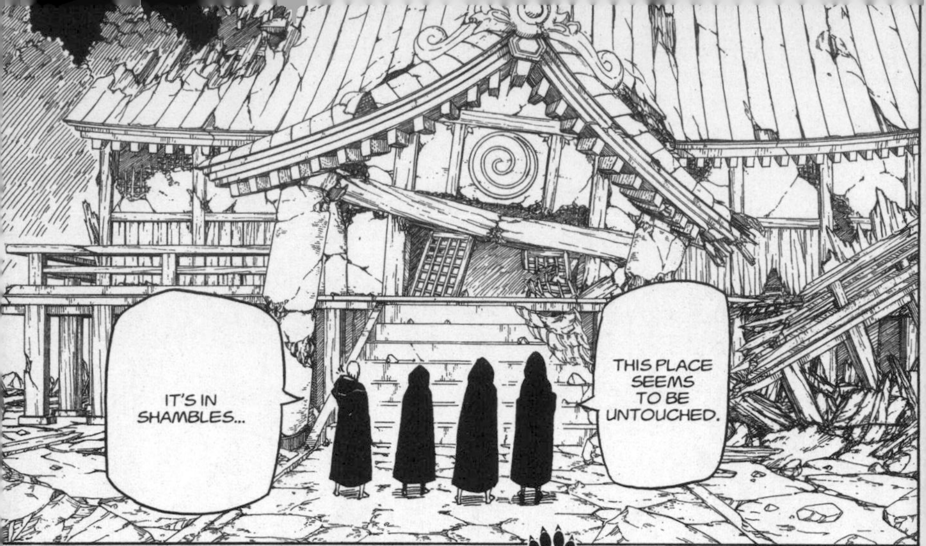
THIS PLACE SEEMS TO BE UNTOUCHED.
IT'S IN SHAMBLES...

Number 618: The All-Knowing

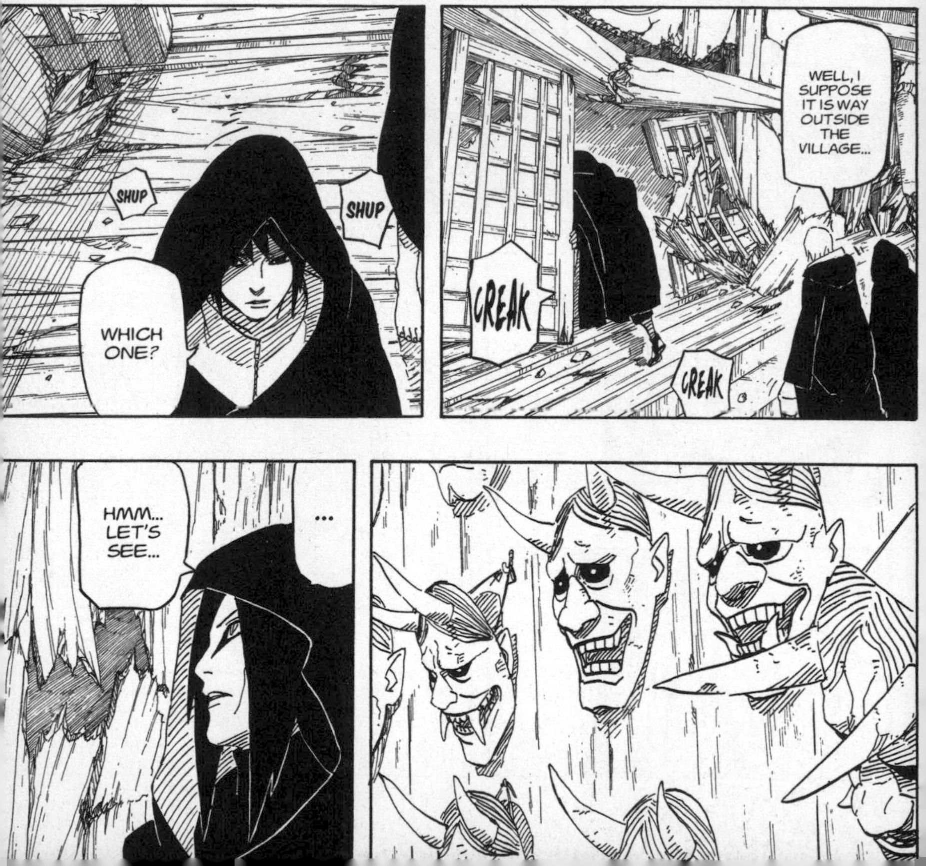
WELL, I SUPPOSE IT IS WAY OUTSIDE THE VILLAGE...
CREAK
CREAK
SHUP
SHUP
WHICH ONE?
...
HMM... LET'S SEE...

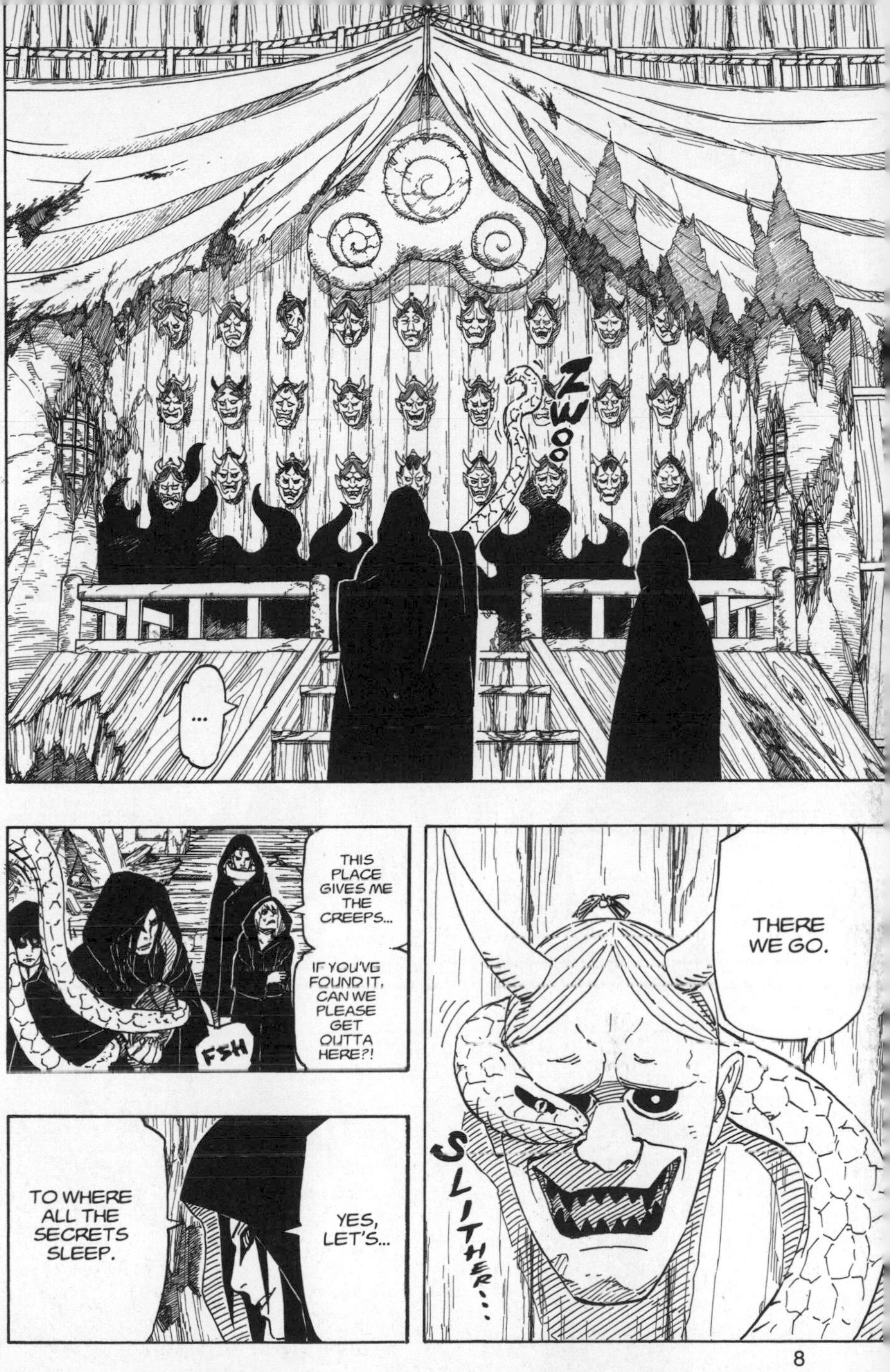
ZWOO
...
THERE WE GO.
SLITHER...
THIS PLACE GIVES ME THE CREEPS...
IF YOU'VE FOUND IT, CAN WE PLEASE GET OUTTA HERE?!
FSH
YES, LET'S...
TO WHERE ALL THE SECRETS SLEEP.

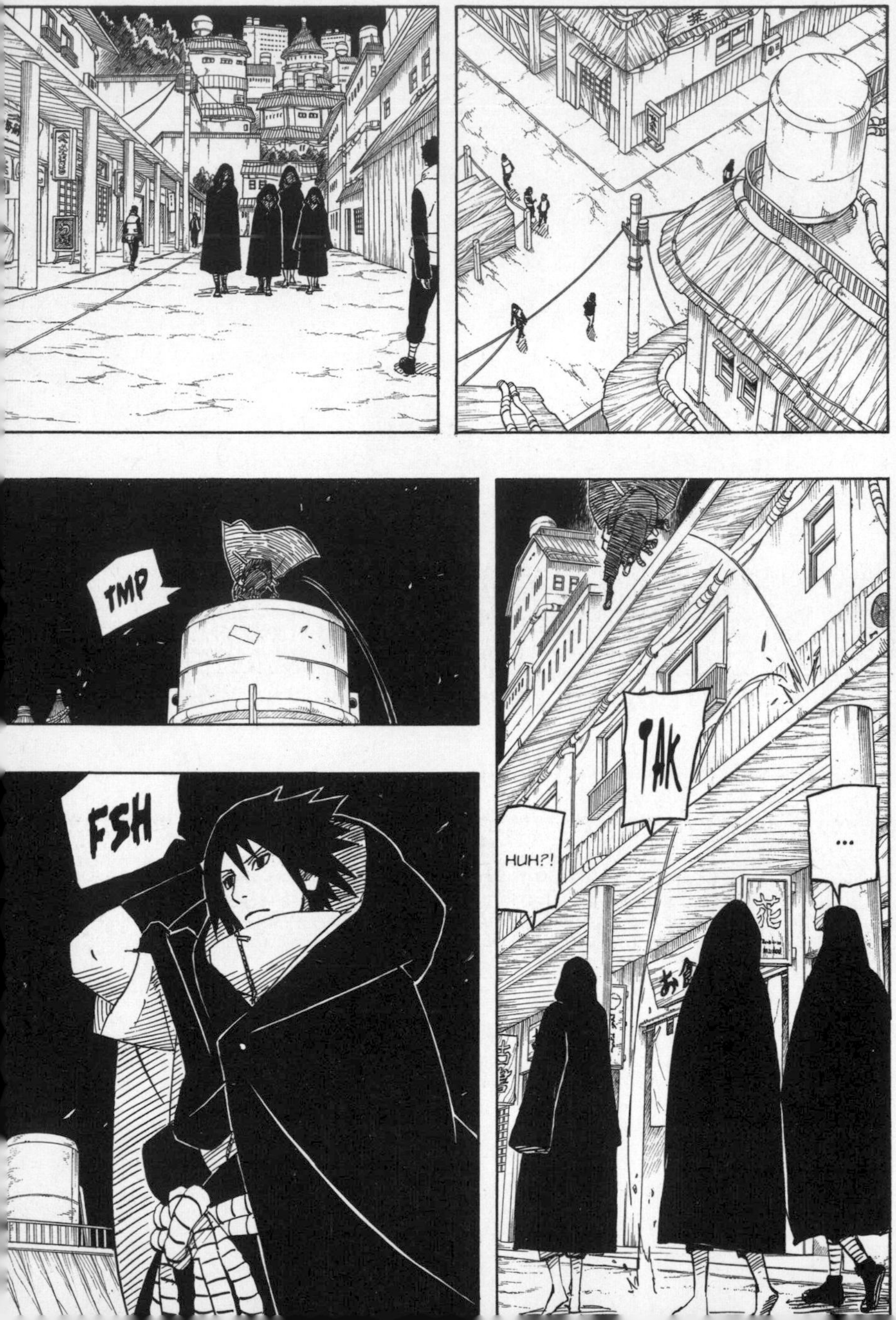
TAK
...
HUH?!
TMP
FSH

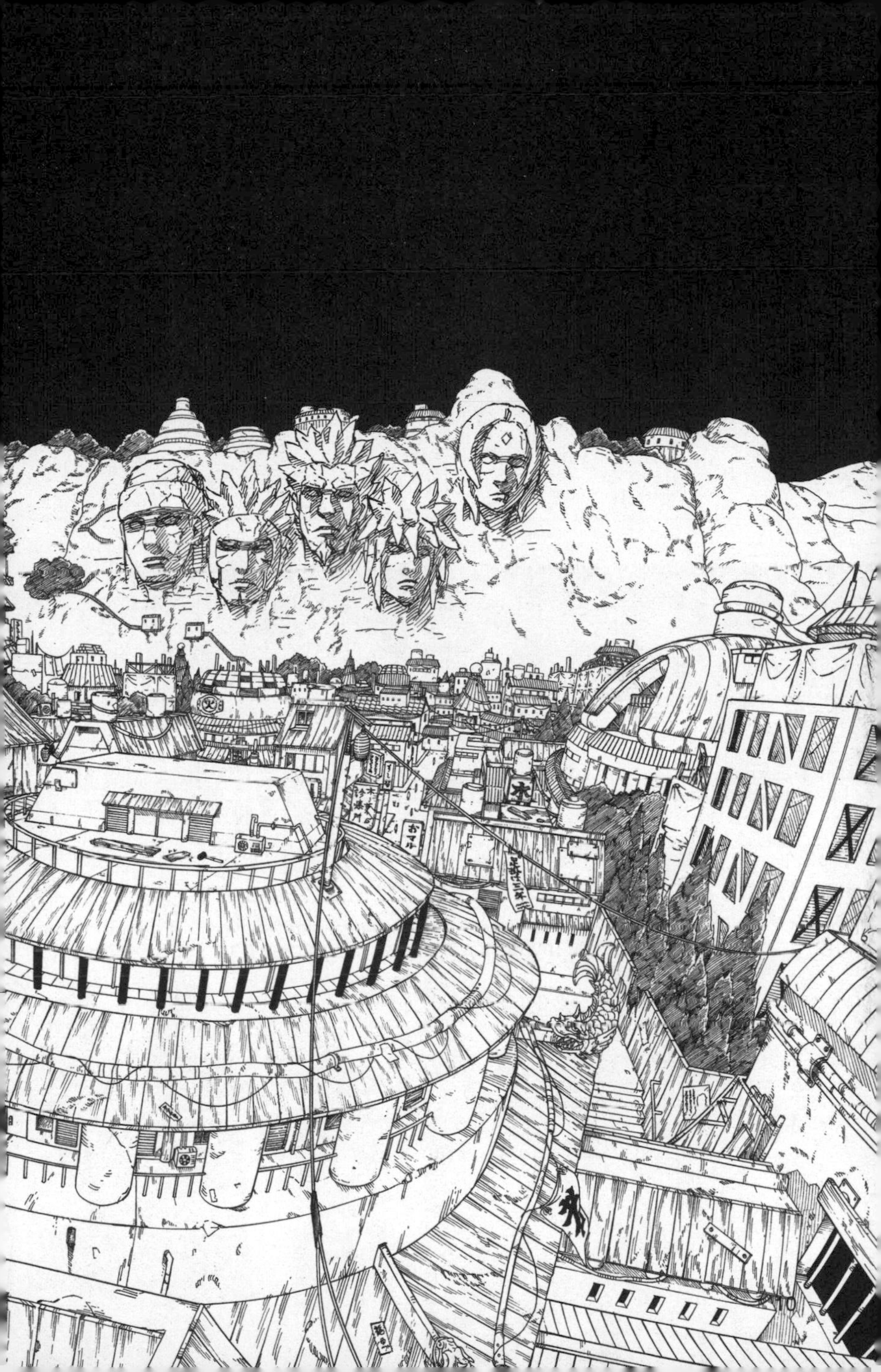

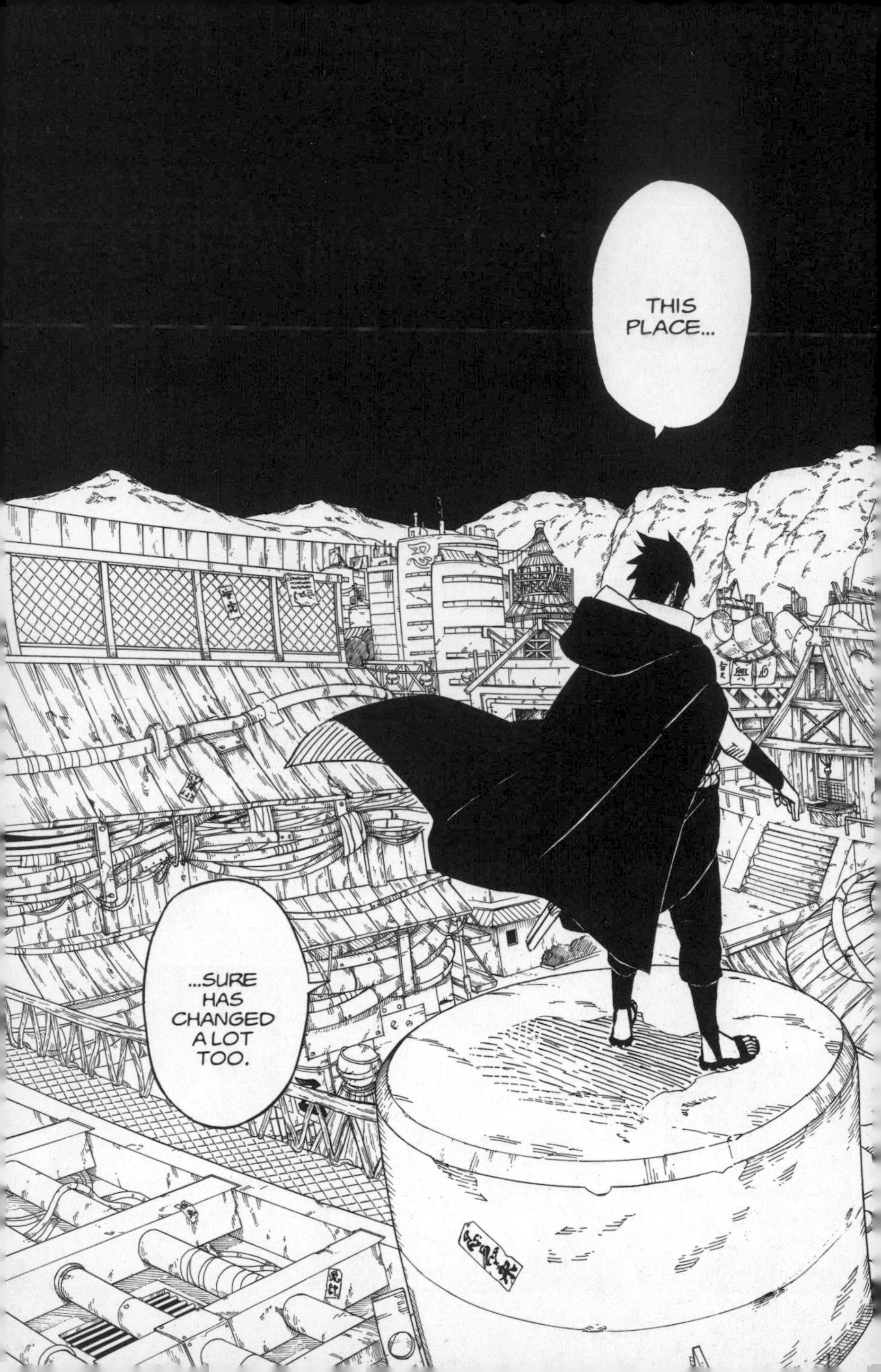
THIS PLACE...
...SURE HAS CHANGED A LOT TOO.

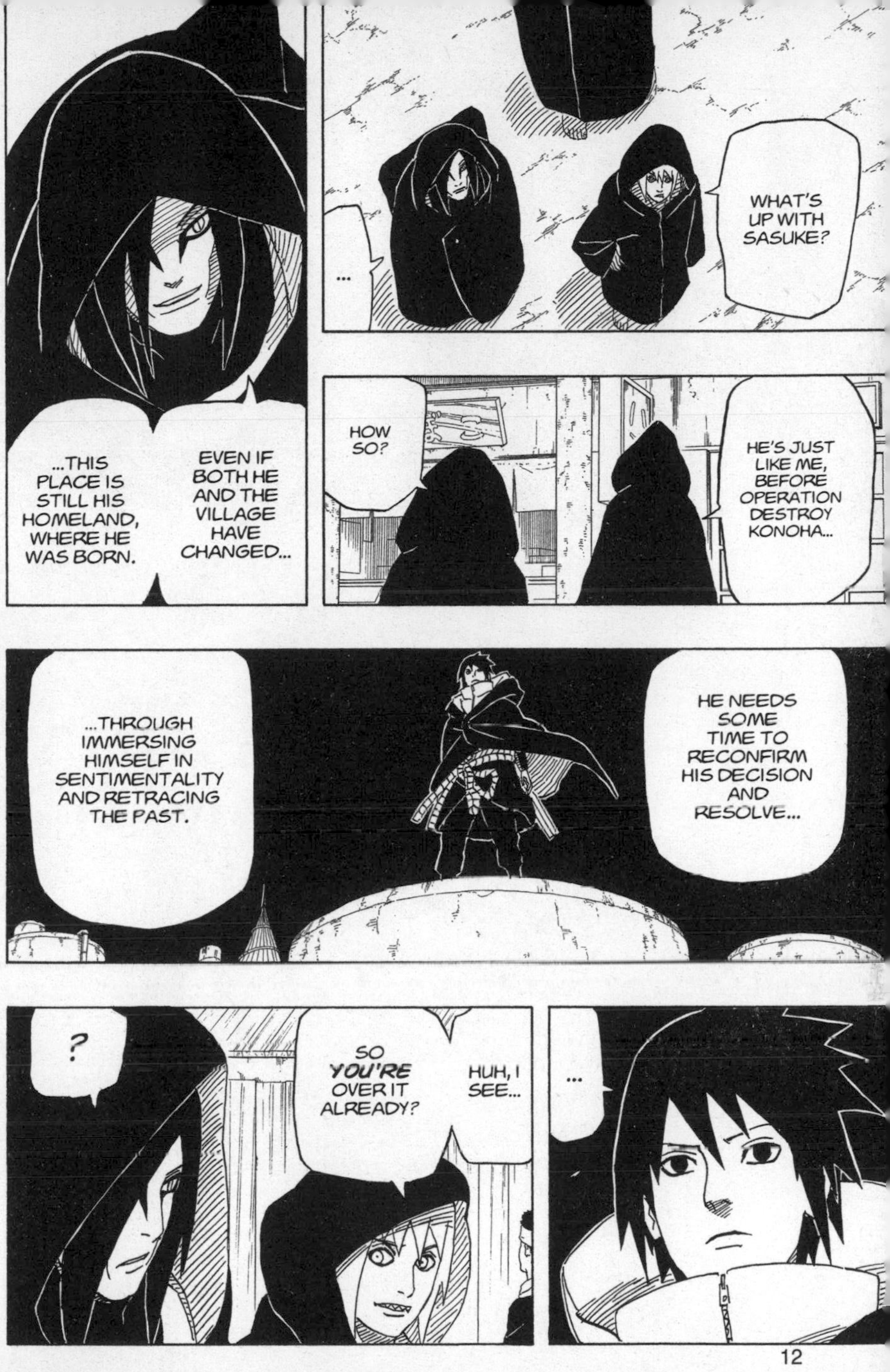
WHAT'S UP WITH SASUKE?
...
HE'S JUST LIKE ME, BEFORE OPERATION DESTROY KONOHA...
HOW SO?
EVEN IF BOTH HE AND THE VILLAGE HAVE CHANGED...
...THIS PLACE IS STILL HIS HOMELAND, WHERE HE WAS BORN.
HE NEEDS SOME TIME TO RECONFIRM HIS DECISION AND RESOLVE...
...THROUGH IMMERSING HIMSELF IN SENTIMENTALITY AND RETRACING THE PAST.
...
HUH, I SEE...
SO YOU'RE OVER IT ALREADY?
?

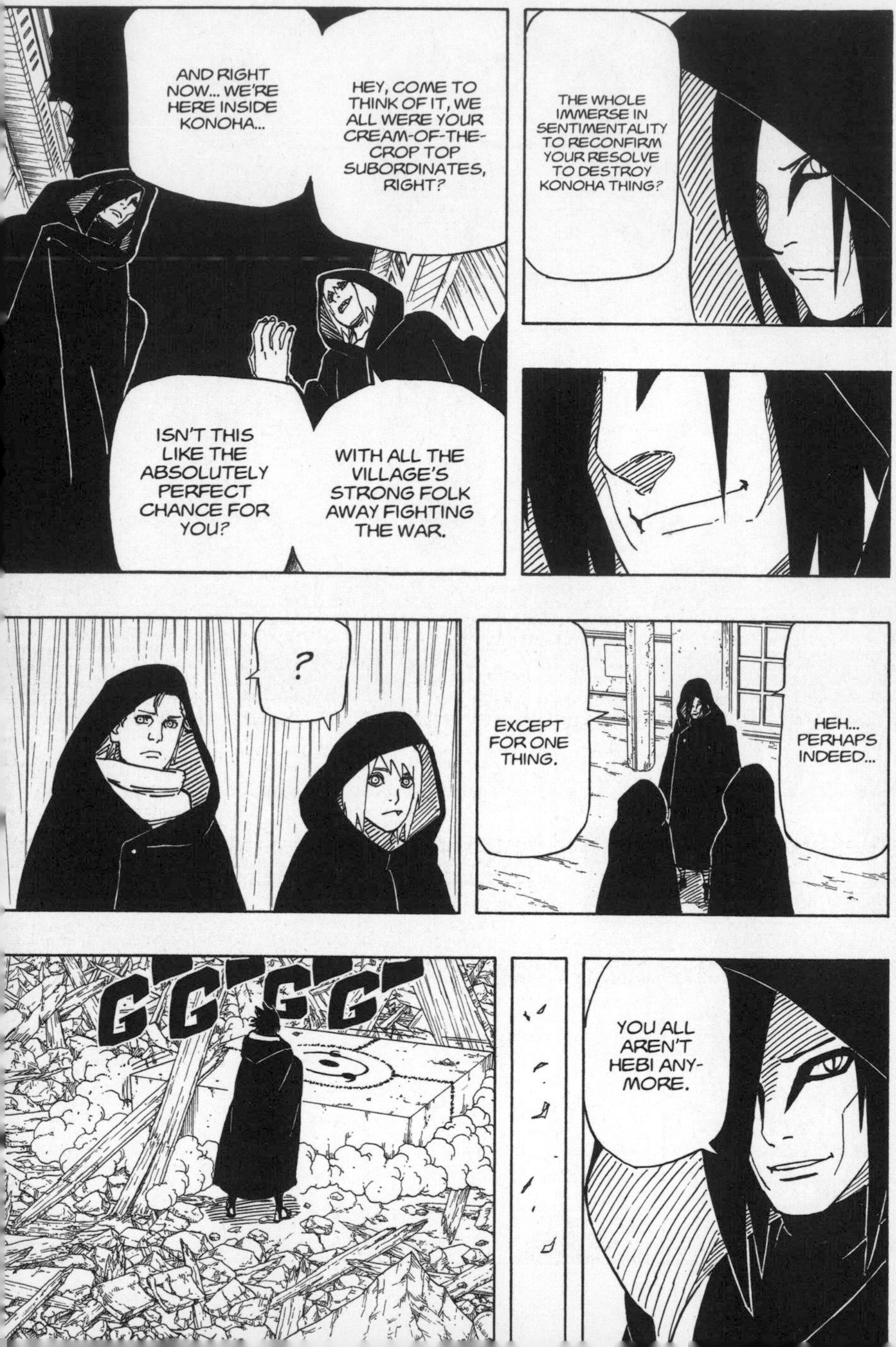
THE WHOLE IMMERSE IN SENTIMENTALITY TO RECONFIRM YOUR RESOLVE TO DESTROY KONOHA THING?
HEY, COME TO THINK OF IT, WE ALL WERE YOUR CREAM-OF-THE-CROP TOP SUBORDINATES, RIGHT?
AND RIGHT NOW... WE'RE HERE INSIDE KONOHA...
WITH ALL THE VILLAGE'S STRONG FOLK AWAY FIGHTING THE WAR.
ISN'T THIS LIKE THE ABSOLUTELY PERFECT CHANCE FOR YOU?
HEH... PERHAPS INDEED...
EXCEPT FOR ONE THING.
?
YOU ALL AREN'T HEBI ANY-MORE.
GGGG

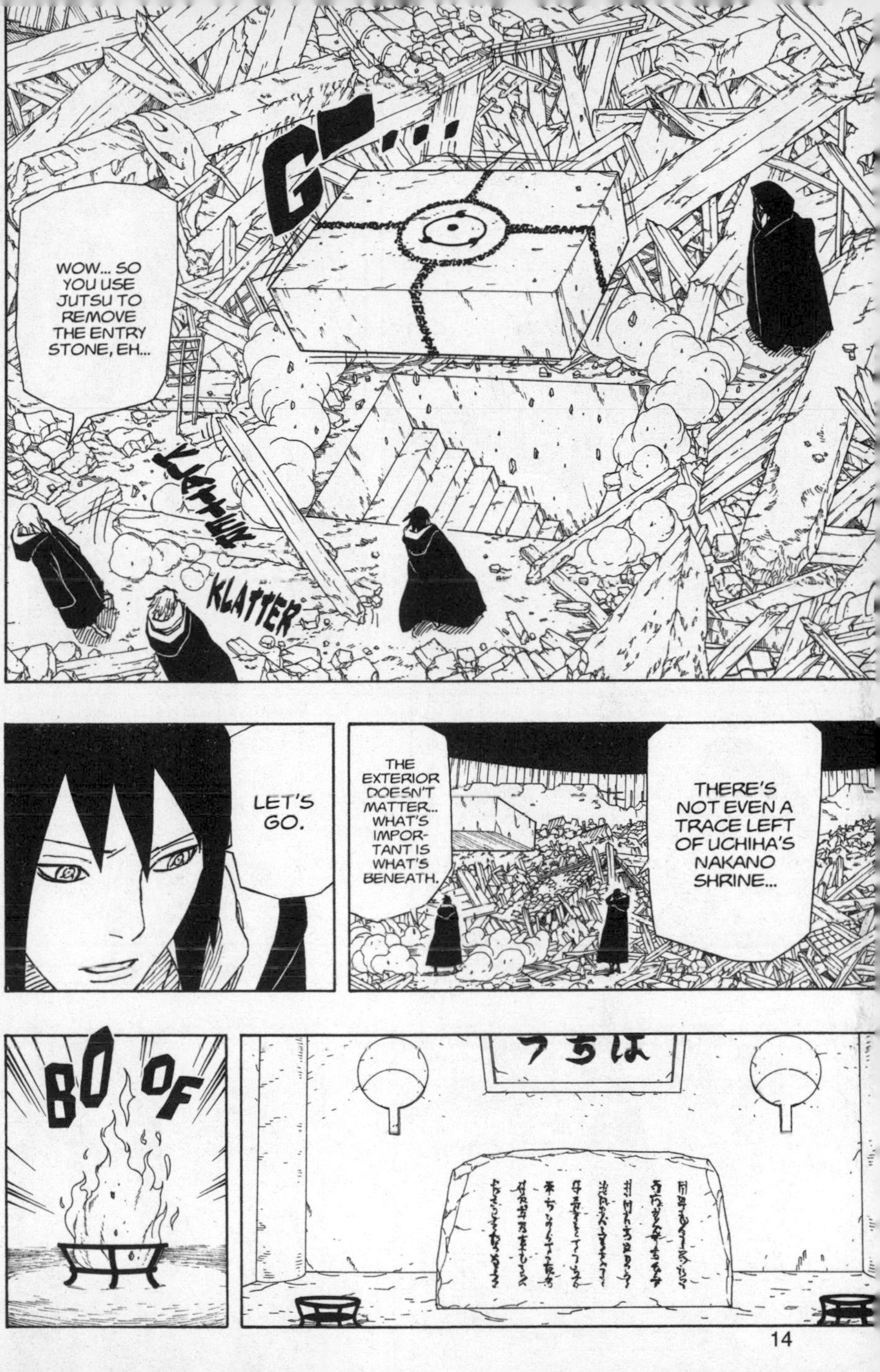
WOW... SO YOU USE JUTSU TO REMOVE THE ENTRY STONE, EH...
KLATTER
KLATTER
THERE'S NOT EVEN A TRACE LEFT OF UCHIHA'S NAKANO SHRINE...
THE EXTERIOR DOESN'T MATTER... WHAT'S IMPORTANT IS WHAT'S BENEATH.
LET'S GO.
うちは
BOOF

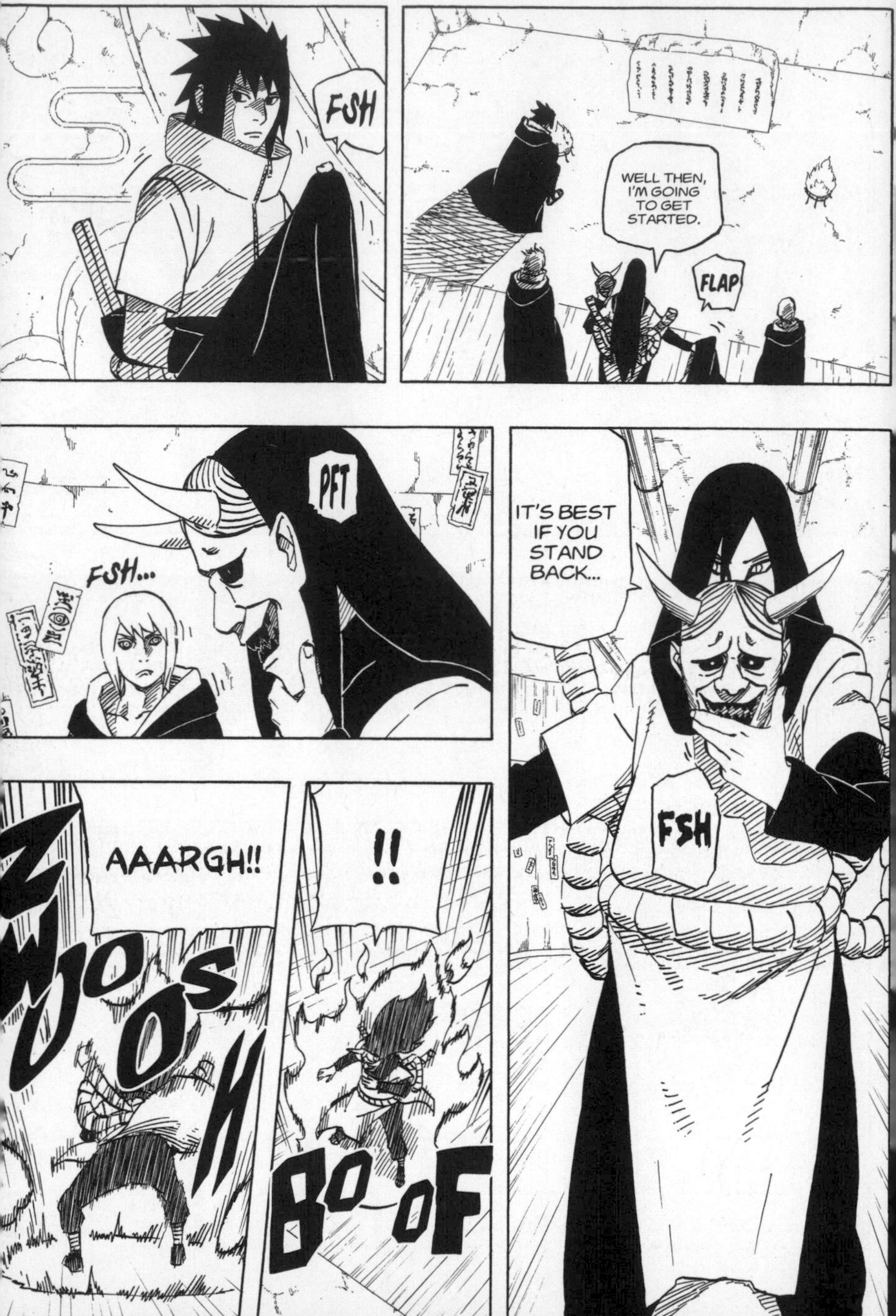
WELL THEN, I'M GOING TO GET STARTED.
FLAP
FSH
IT'S BEST IF YOU STAND BACK...
FSH
PFT
FSH...
!!
BOOF
AAARGH!!
WHOOSH

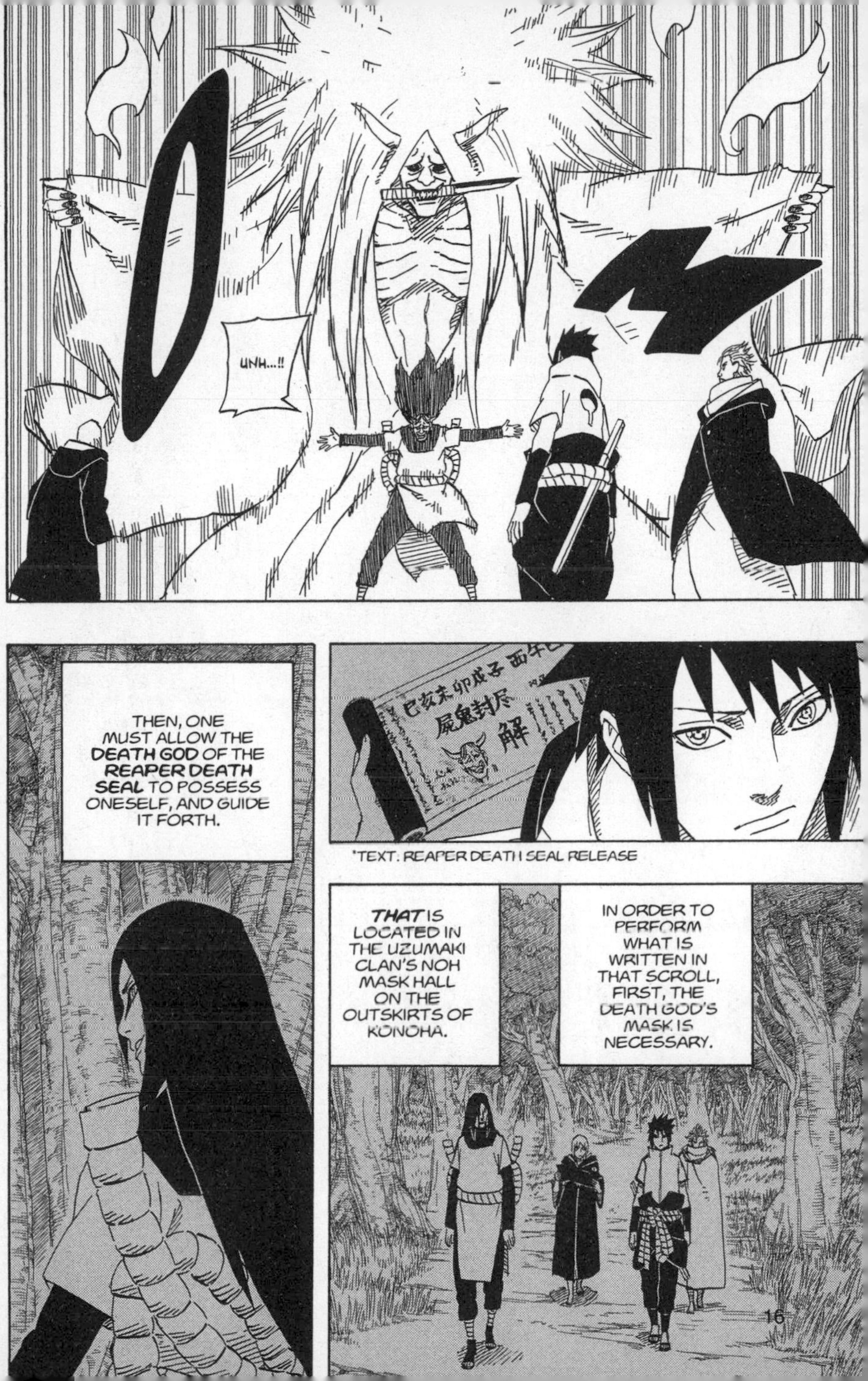
UNH...!!
*TEXT: REAPER DEATH SEAL RELEASE
IN ORDER TO PERFORM WHAT IS WRITTEN IN THAT SCROLL, FIRST, THE DEATH GOD'S MASK IS NECESSARY.
THAT IS LOCATED IN THE UZUMAKI CLAN'S NOH MASK HALL ON THE OUTSKIRTS OF KONOHA.
THEN, ONE MUST ALLOW THE DEATH GOD OF THE REAPER DEATH SEAL TO POSSESS ONESELF, AND GUIDE IT FORTH.

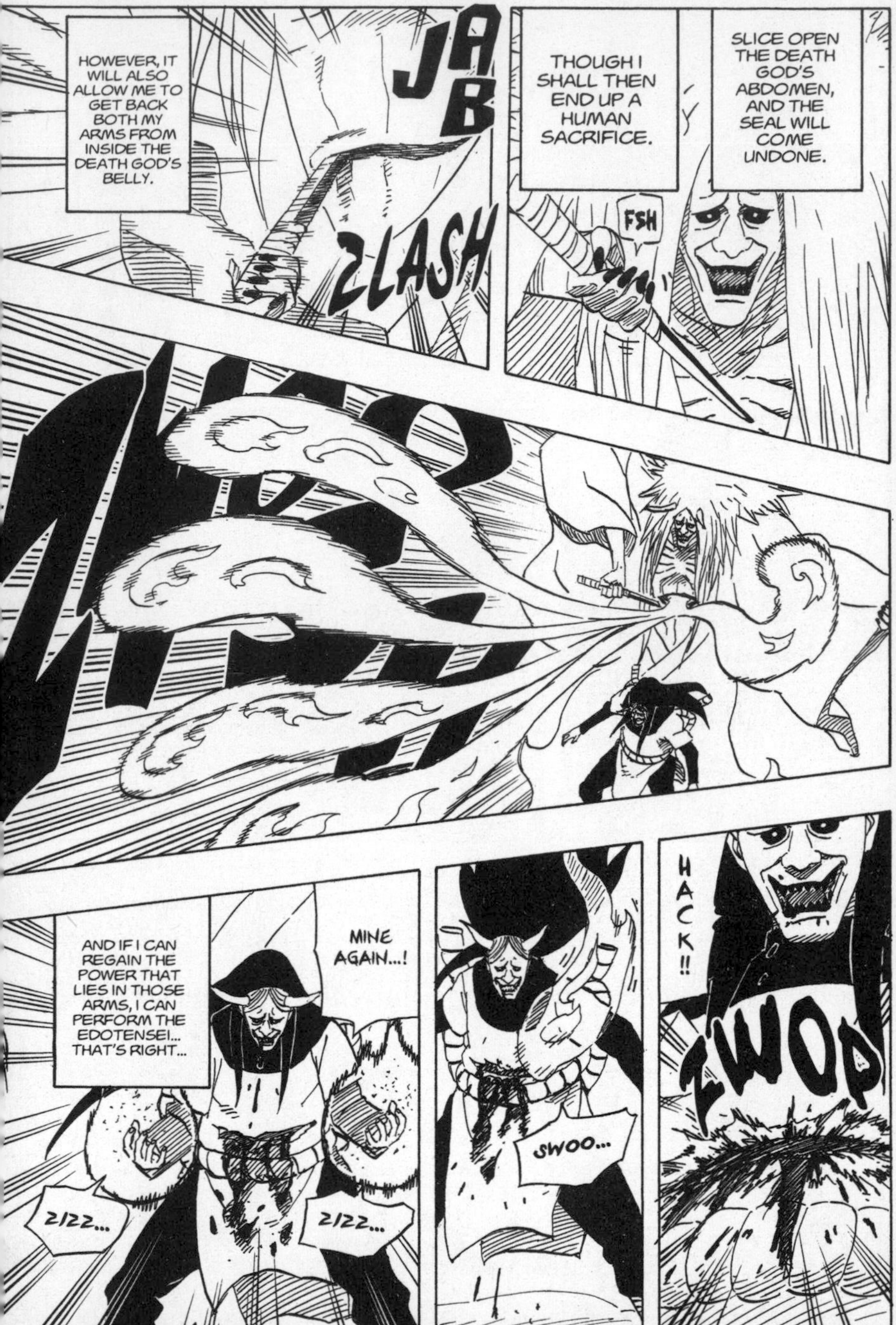
SLICE OPEN THE DEATH GOD'S ABDOMEN, AND THE SEAL WILL COME UNDONE.
THOUGH I SHALL THEN END UP A HUMAN SACRIFICE.
FSH
HOWEVER, IT WILL ALSO ALLOW ME TO GET BACK BOTH MY ARMS FROM INSIDE THE DEATH GOD'S BELLY.
JAB
ZLASH
HACK!!
ZWOP
SWOO...
MINE AGAIN...!
AND IF I CAN REGAIN THE POWER THAT LIES IN THOSE ARMS, I CAN PERFORM THE EDOTENSEI... THAT'S RIGHT...
ZIZZ...
ZIZZ...

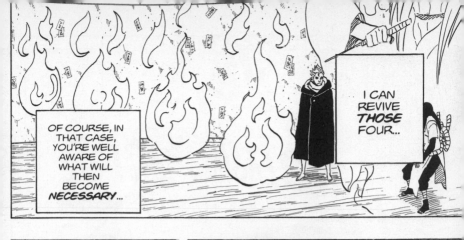

I CAN REVIVE THOSE FOUR...
OF COURSE, IN THAT CASE, YOU'RE WELL AWARE OF WHAT WILL THEN BECOME NECESSARY...
AHHH!! YOU'RE PLANNING TO USE US AS SACRIFICIAL LAMBS FOR THE EDOTENSEI!!
HO HO... THAT'S NOT SUCH A BAD IDEA, BUT...
WE'VE ACTUALLY GOT SOMETHING EVEN BETTER THAN YOU GUYS...
THOUGH IT'S STILL INVISIBLE TO YOU YET...
FSH
JUGO, SASUKE, SUIGETSU... GET READY!!
ROGER!
FSH

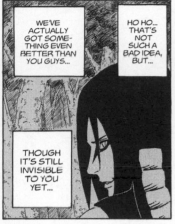

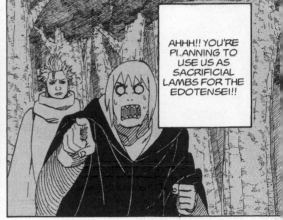

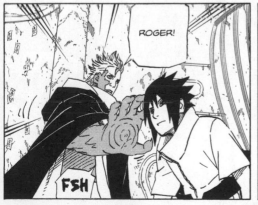

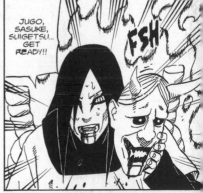

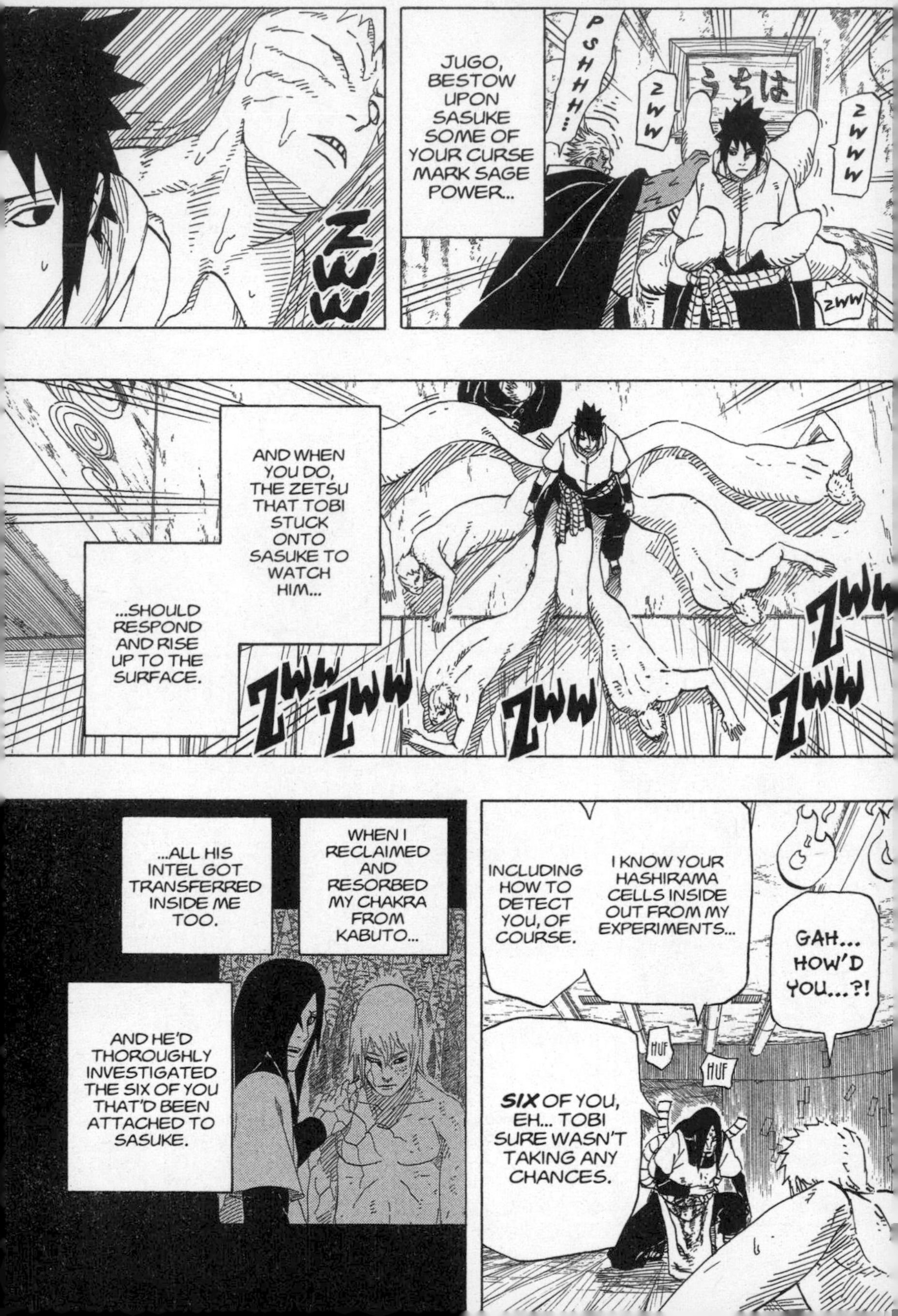
JUGO, BESTOW UPON SASUKE SOME OF YOUR CURSE MARK SAGE POWER...
PSHHH...
ZWW
ZWWW
ZWW
ZWW
AND WHEN YOU DO, THE ZETSU THAT TOBI STUCK ONTO SASUKE TO WATCH HIM...
...SHOULD RESPOND AND RISE UP TO THE SURFACE.
ZWW
ZWW
ZWW
ZWW
ZWW
ZWW
GAH... HOW'D YOU...?!
I KNOW YOUR HASHIRAMA CELLS INSIDE OUT FROM MY EXPERIMENTS...
INCLUDING HOW TO DETECT YOU, OF COURSE.
HUF
HUF
SIX OF YOU, EH... TOBI SURE WASN'T TAKING ANY CHANCES.
WHEN I RECLAIMED AND RESORBED MY CHAKRA FROM KABUTO...
...ALL HIS INTEL GOT TRANSFERRED INSIDE ME TOO.
AND HE'D THOROUGHLY INVESTIGATED THE SIX OF YOU THAT'D BEEN ATTACHED TO SASUKE.

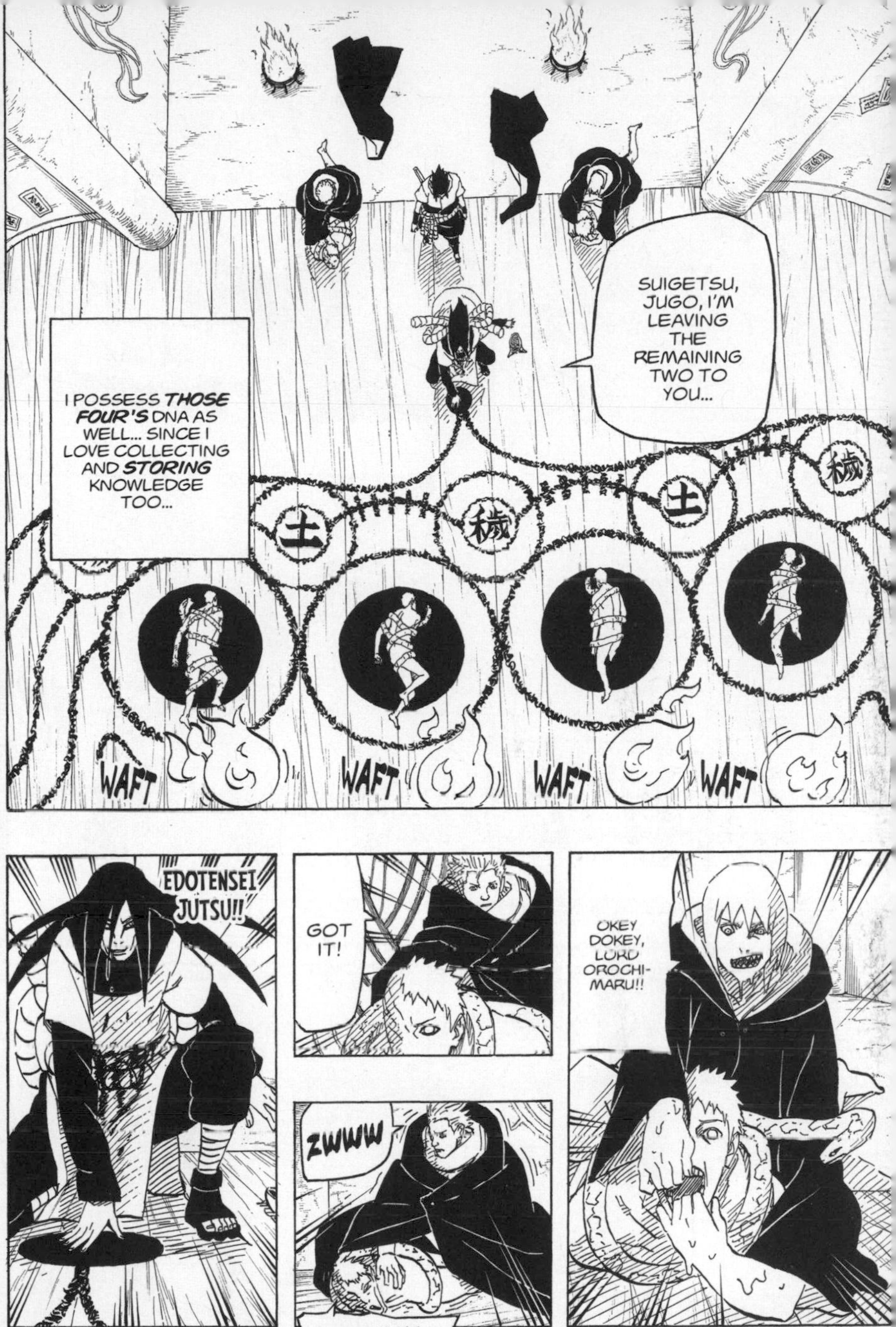

SUIGETSU, JUGO, I'M LEAVING THE REMAINING TWO TO YOU...
I POSSESS THOSE FOUR'S DNA AS WELL... SINCE I LOVE COLLECTING AND STORING KNOWLEDGE TOO...
WAFT
WAFT
WAFT
WAFT
OKEY DOKEY, LORD OROCHI-MARU!!
GOT IT!
ZWWW
PSHHH...
EDOTENSEI JUTSU!!

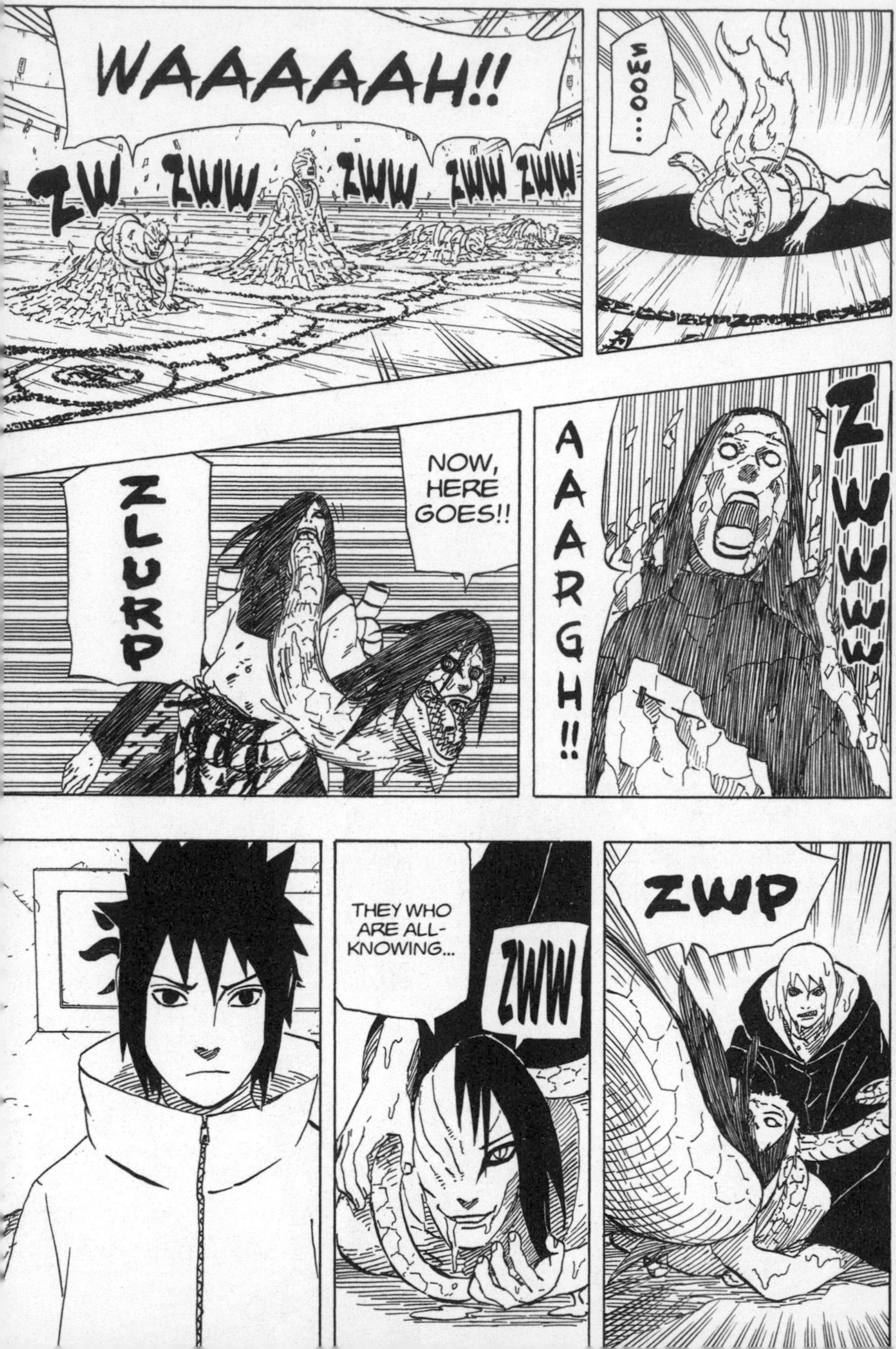
SWOO...
WAAAAAH!!
ZW ZWW ZWW ZWW ZWW
AAARGH!!
ZWWWWW
NOW, HERE GOES!!
ZLURP
ZWP
THEY WHO ARE ALL-KNOWING...
ZWW

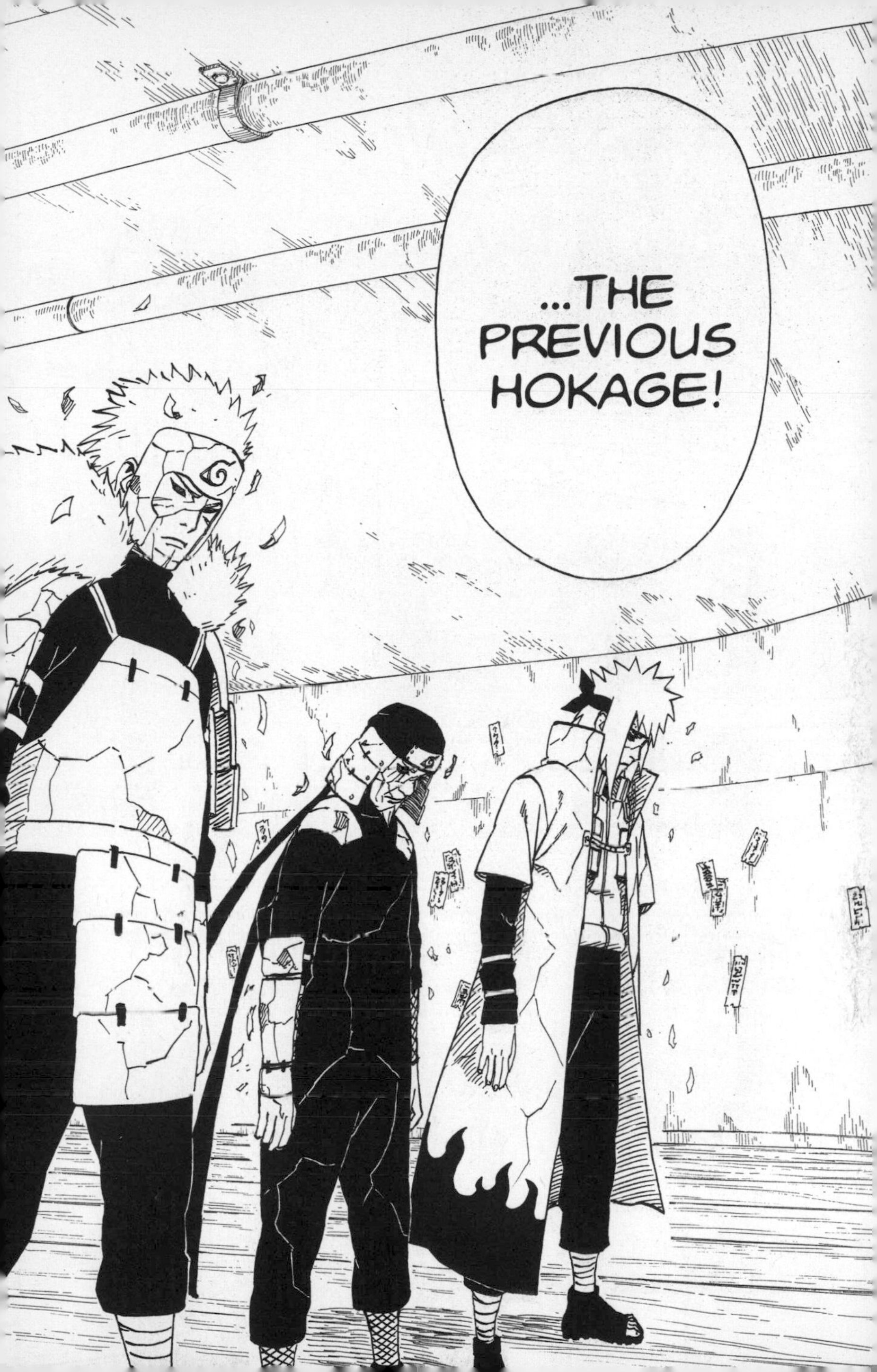
...THE PREVIOUS HOKAGE!

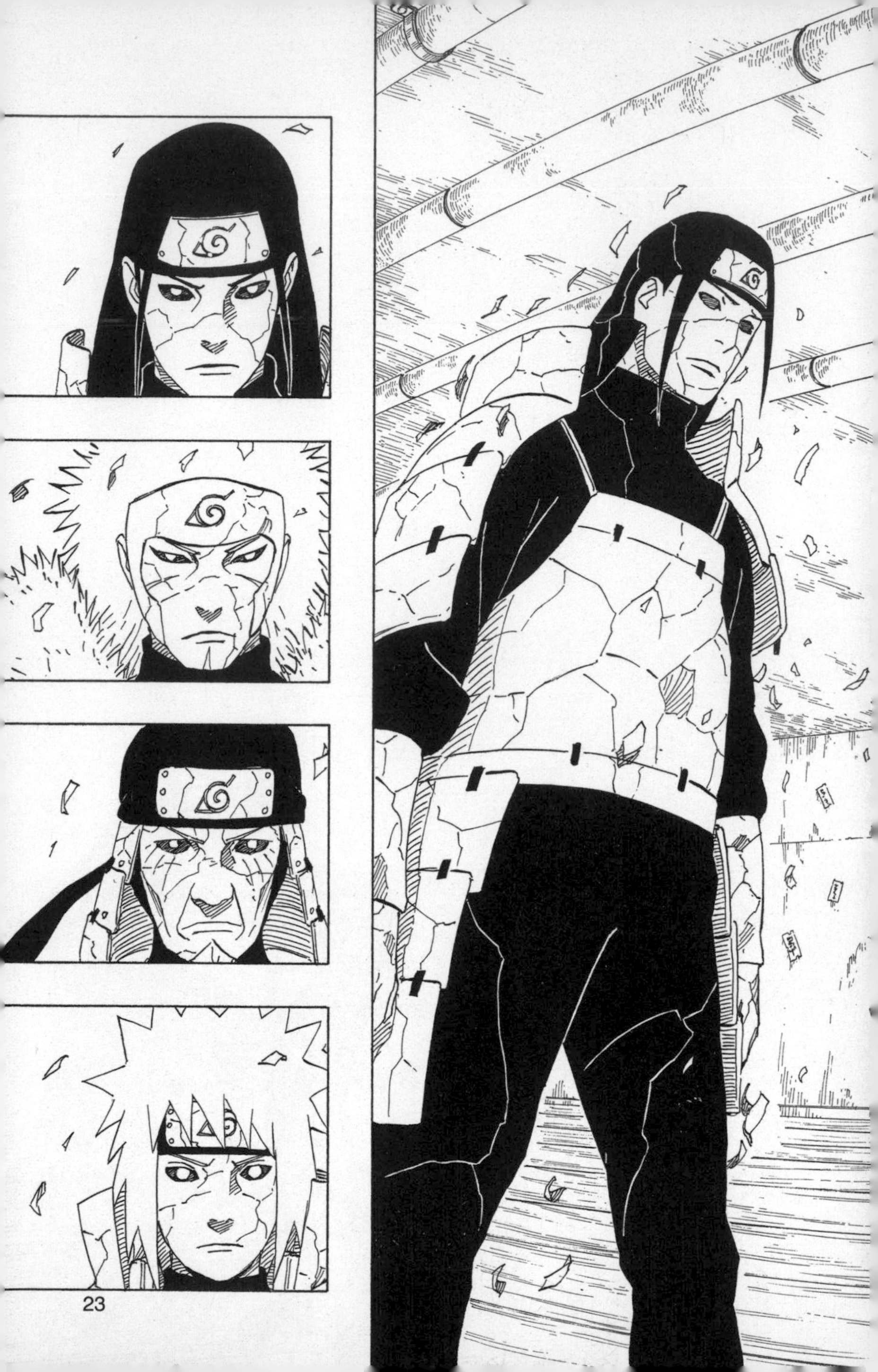

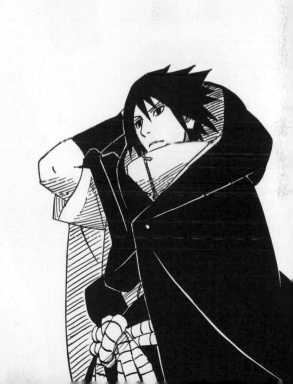

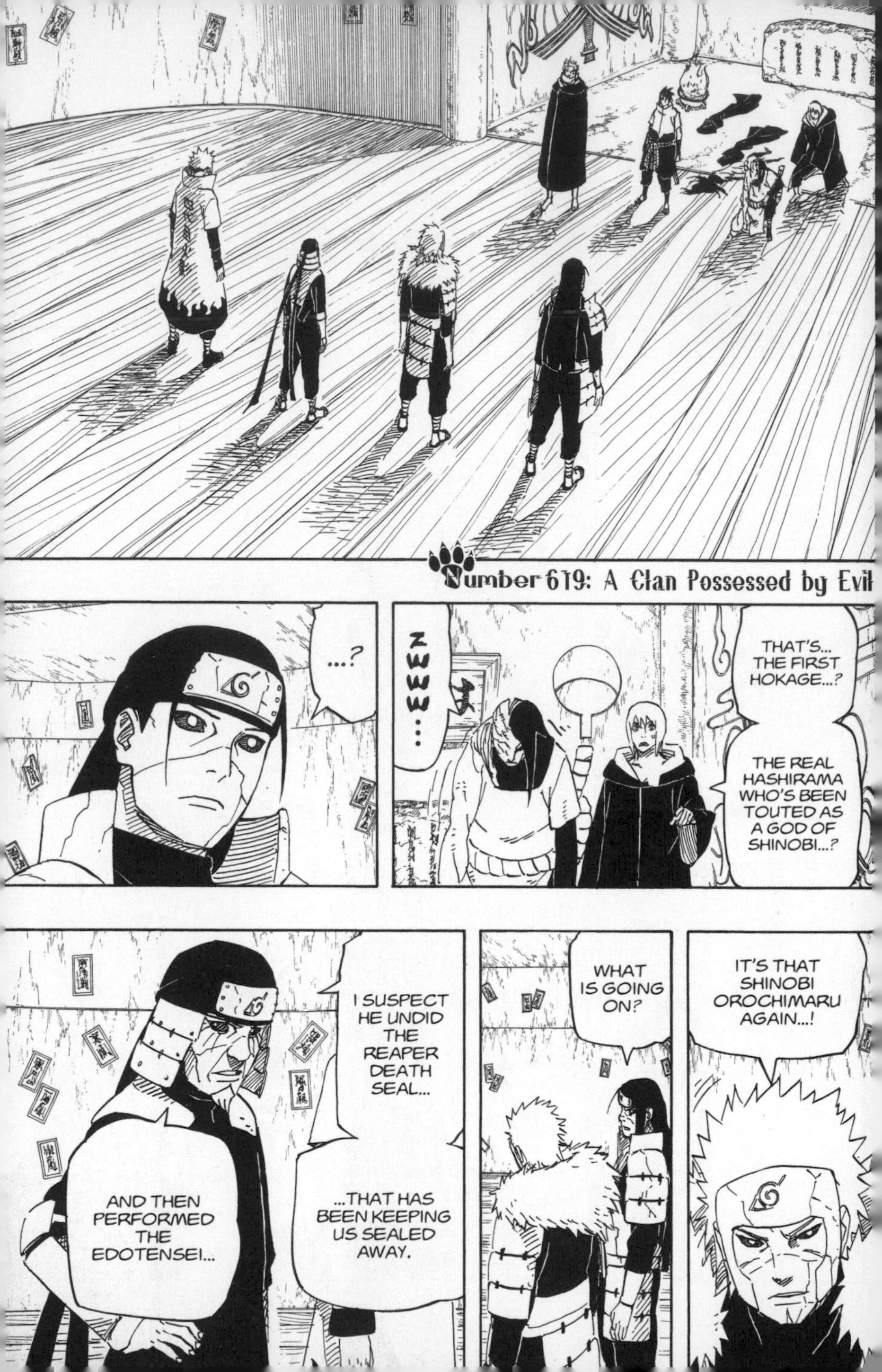
Number 619: A Clan Possessed by Evil
THAT'S... THE FIRST HOKAGE...?
THE REAL HASHIRAMA WHO'S BEEN TOUTED AS A GOD OF SHINOBI...?
ZWWW...
...?
IT'S THAT SHINOBI OROCHIMARU AGAIN...!
WHAT IS GOING ON?
I SUSPECT HE UNDID THE REAPER DEATH SEAL...
...THAT HAS BEEN KEEPING US SEALED AWAY.
AND THEN PERFORMED THE EDOTENSEI...

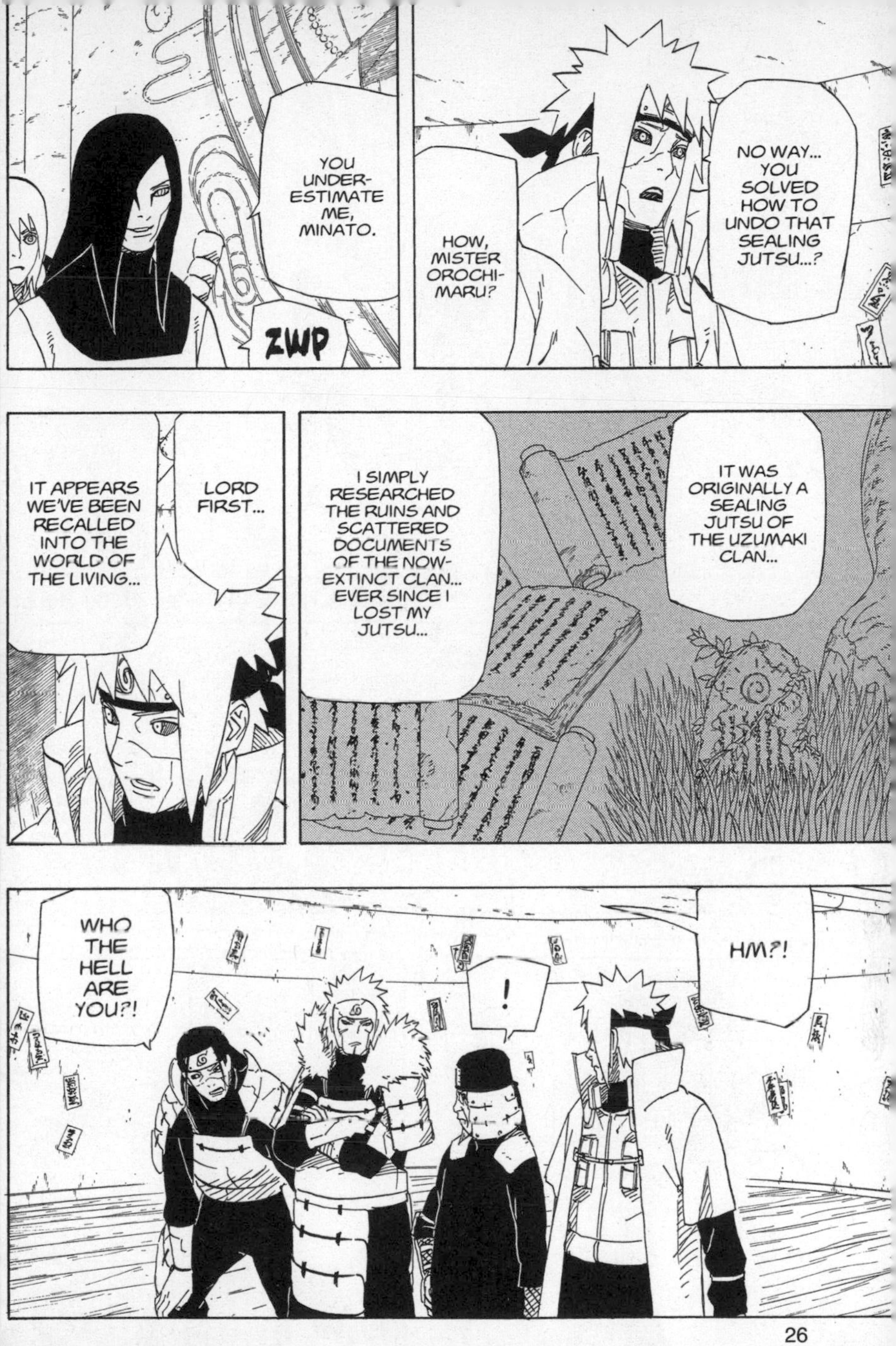
NO WAY... YOU SOLVED HOW TO UNDO THAT SEALING JUTSU...?
HOW, MISTER OROCHI-MARU?
YOU UNDER-ESTIMATE ME, MINATO.
ZWP
IT WAS ORIGINALLY A SEALING JUTSU OF THE UZUMAKI CLAN...
I SIMPLY RESEARCHED THE RUINS AND SCATTERED DOCUMENTS OF THE NOW-EXTINCT CLAN... EVER SINCE I LOST MY JUTSU...
LORD FIRST...
IT APPEARS WE'VE BEEN RECALLED INTO THE WORLD OF THE LIVING...
HM?!
!
WHO THE HELL ARE YOU?!

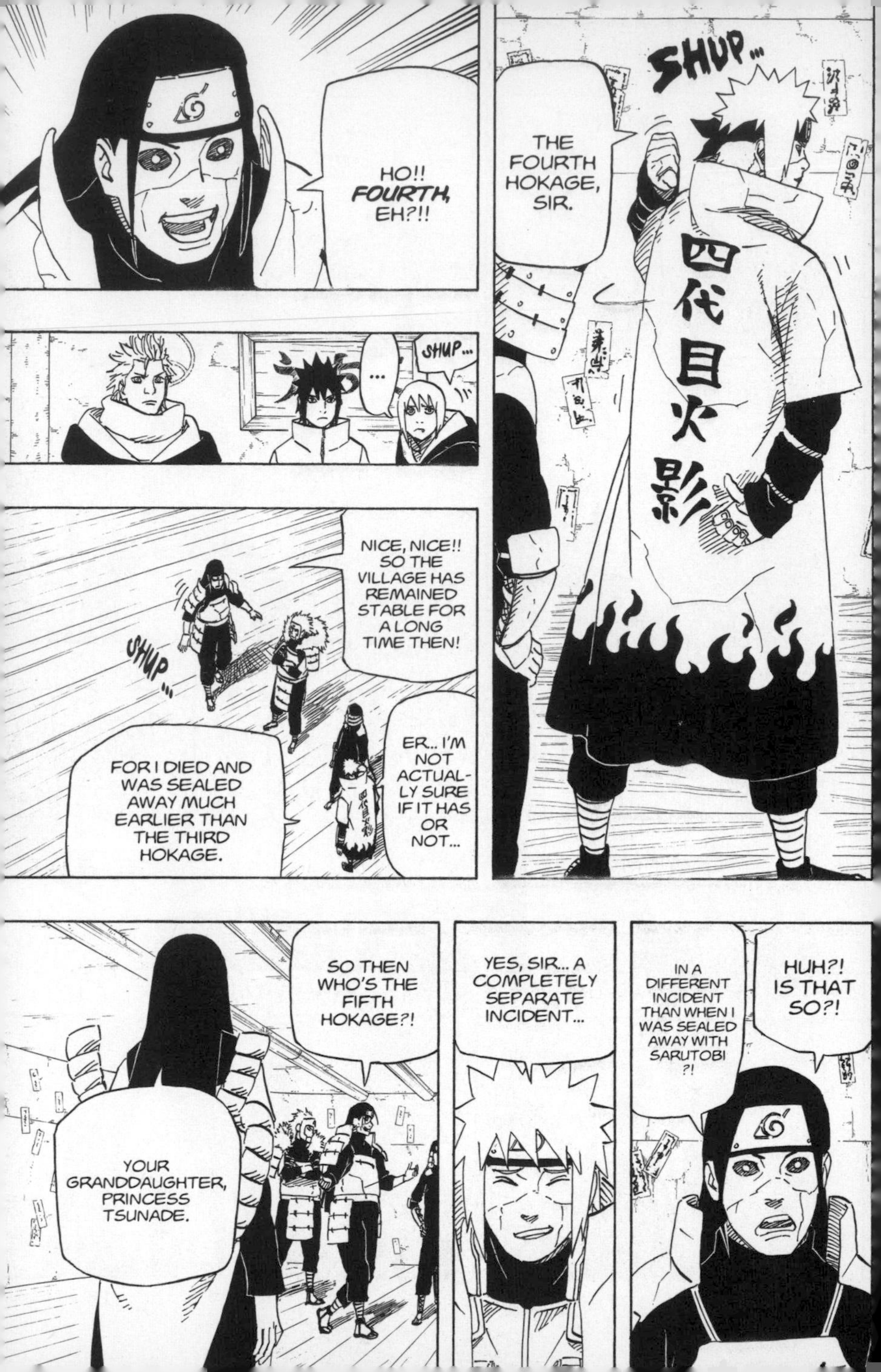
SHUP...
THE FOURTH HOKAGE, SIR.
四代目火影
HO!! FOURTH, EH?!!
SHUP...
...
NICE, NICE!! SO THE VILLAGE HAS REMAINED STABLE FOR A LONG TIME THEN!
SHUP...
ER... I'M NOT ACTUAL-LY SURE IF IT HAS OR NOT...
FOR I DIED AND WAS SEALED AWAY MUCH EARLIER THAN THE THIRD HOKAGE.
HUH?! IS THAT SO?!
IN A DIFFERENT INCIDENT THAN WHEN I WAS SEALED AWAY WITH SARUTOBI?!
YES, SIR... A COMPLETELY SEPARATE INCIDENT...
SO THEN WHO'S THE FIFTH HOKAGE?!
YOUR GRANDDAUGHTER, PRINCESS TSUNADE.

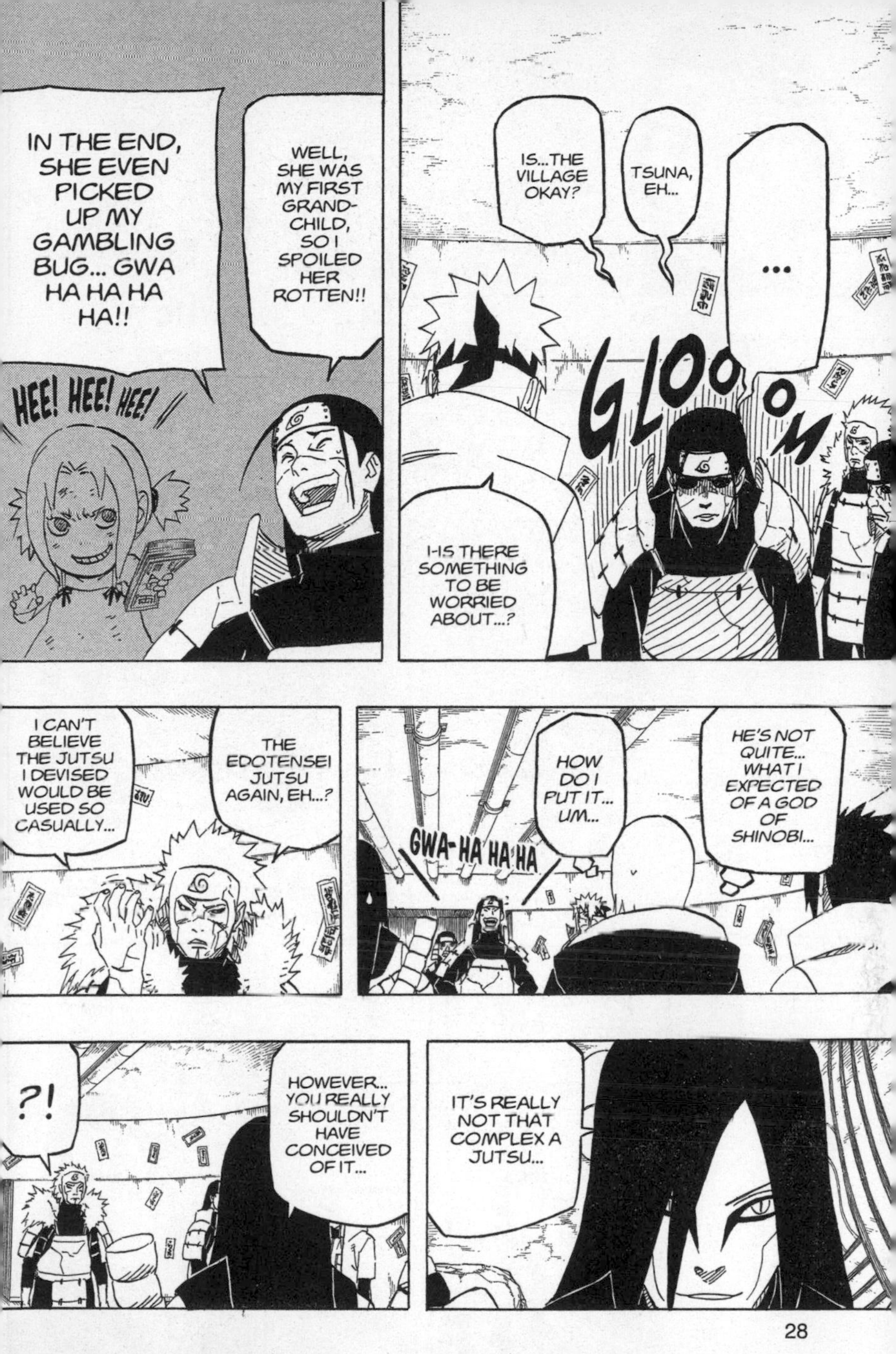
...
TSUNA, EH...
IS...THE VILLAGE OKAY?
GLOOOOM
I-IS THERE SOMETHING TO BE WORRIED ABOUT...?
WELL, SHE WAS MY FIRST GRAND-CHILD, SO I SPOILED HER ROTTEN!!
IN THE END, SHE EVEN PICKED UP MY GAMBLING BUG... GWA HA HA HA HA!!
HEE! HEE! HEE!
HE'S NOT QUITE... WHAT I EXPECTED OF A GOD OF SHINOBI...
HOW DO I PUT IT... UM...
GWA-HA HA HA
THE EDOTENSEI JUTSU AGAIN, EH...?
I CAN'T BELIEVE THE JUTSU I DEVISED WOULD BE USED SO CASUALLY...
IT'S REALLY NOT THAT COMPLEX A JUTSU...
HOWEVER... YOU REALLY SHOULDN'T HAVE CONCEIVED OF IT...
?!

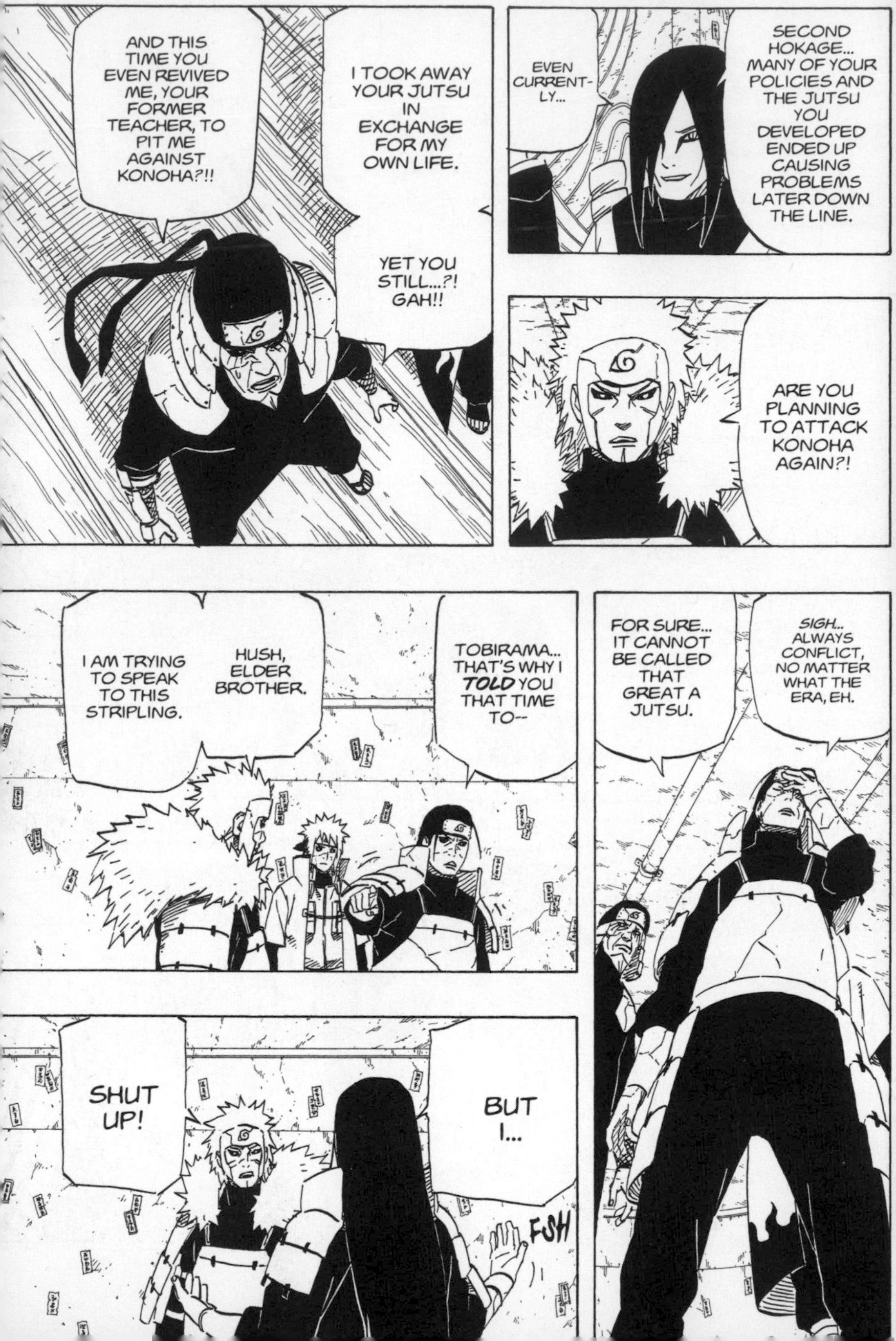
SECOND HOKAGE... MANY OF YOUR POLICIES AND THE JUTSU YOU DEVELOPED ENDED UP CAUSING PROBLEMS LATER DOWN THE LINE.
EVEN CURRENTLY...
ARE YOU PLANNING TO ATTACK KONOHA AGAIN?!
I TOOK AWAY YOUR JUTSU IN EXCHANGE FOR MY OWN LIFE.
AND THIS TIME YOU EVEN REVIVED ME, YOUR FORMER TEACHER, TO PIT ME AGAINST KONOHA?!!
YET YOU STILL...?! GAH!!
SIGH... ALWAYS CONFLICT, NO MATTER WHAT THE ERA, EH.
FOR SURE... IT CANNOT BE CALLED THAT GREAT A JUTSU.
TOBIRAMA... THAT'S WHY I *TOLD* YOU THAT TIME TO--
HUSH, ELDER BROTHER.
I AM TRYING TO SPEAK TO THIS STRIPLING.
BUT I...
SHUT UP!
FSH

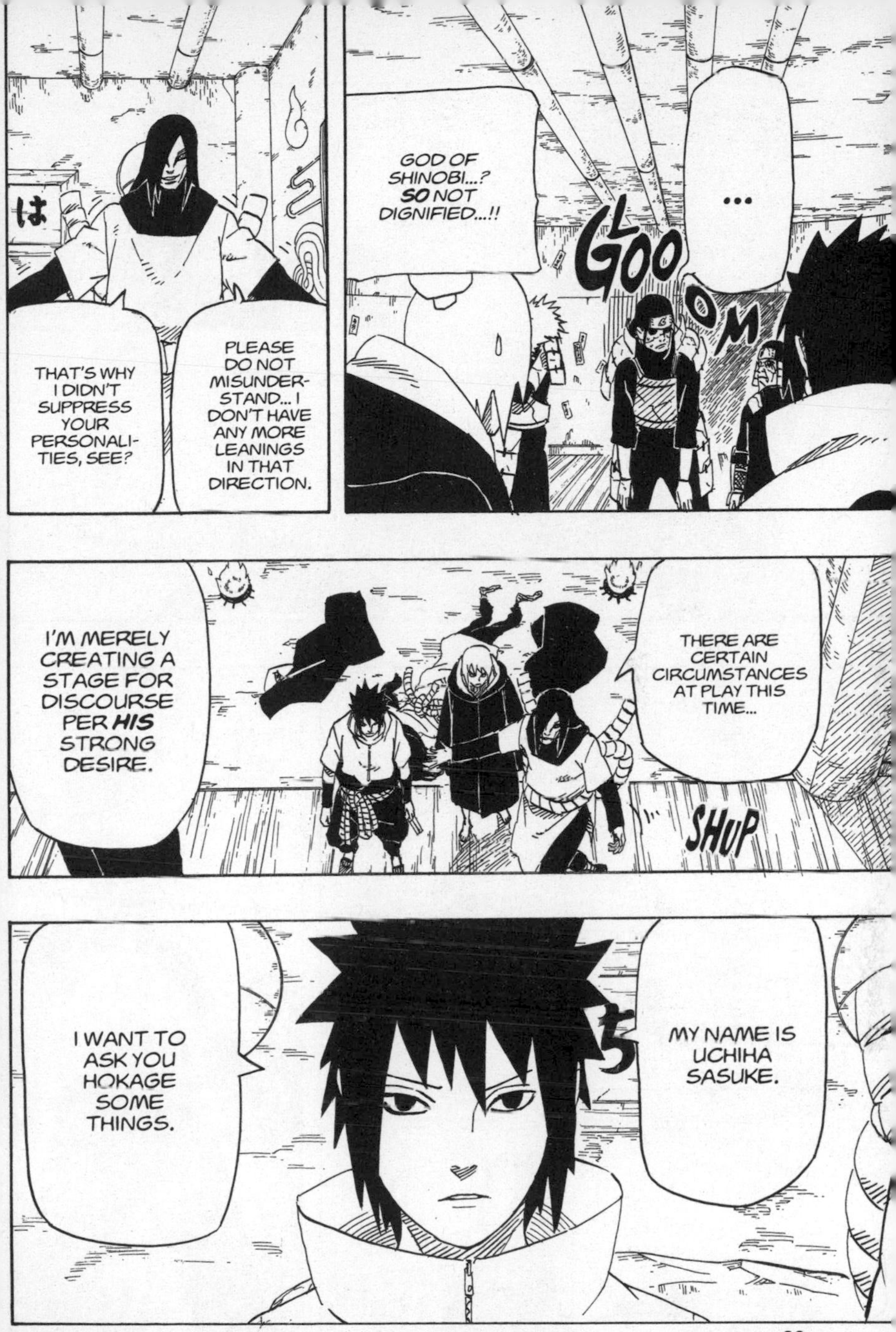
...
GOD OF SHINOBI...? SO NOT DIGNIFIED...!!
GOOOM
PLEASE DO NOT MISUNDERSTAND... I DON'T HAVE ANY MORE LEANINGS IN THAT DIRECTION.
THAT'S WHY I DIDN'T SUPPRESS YOUR PERSONALITIES, SEE?
THERE ARE CERTAIN CIRCUMSTANCES AT PLAY THIS TIME...
SHUP
I'M MERELY CREATING A STAGE FOR DISCOURSE PER HIS STRONG DESIRE.
MY NAME IS UCHIHA SASUKE.
I WANT TO ASK YOU HOKAGE SOME THINGS.

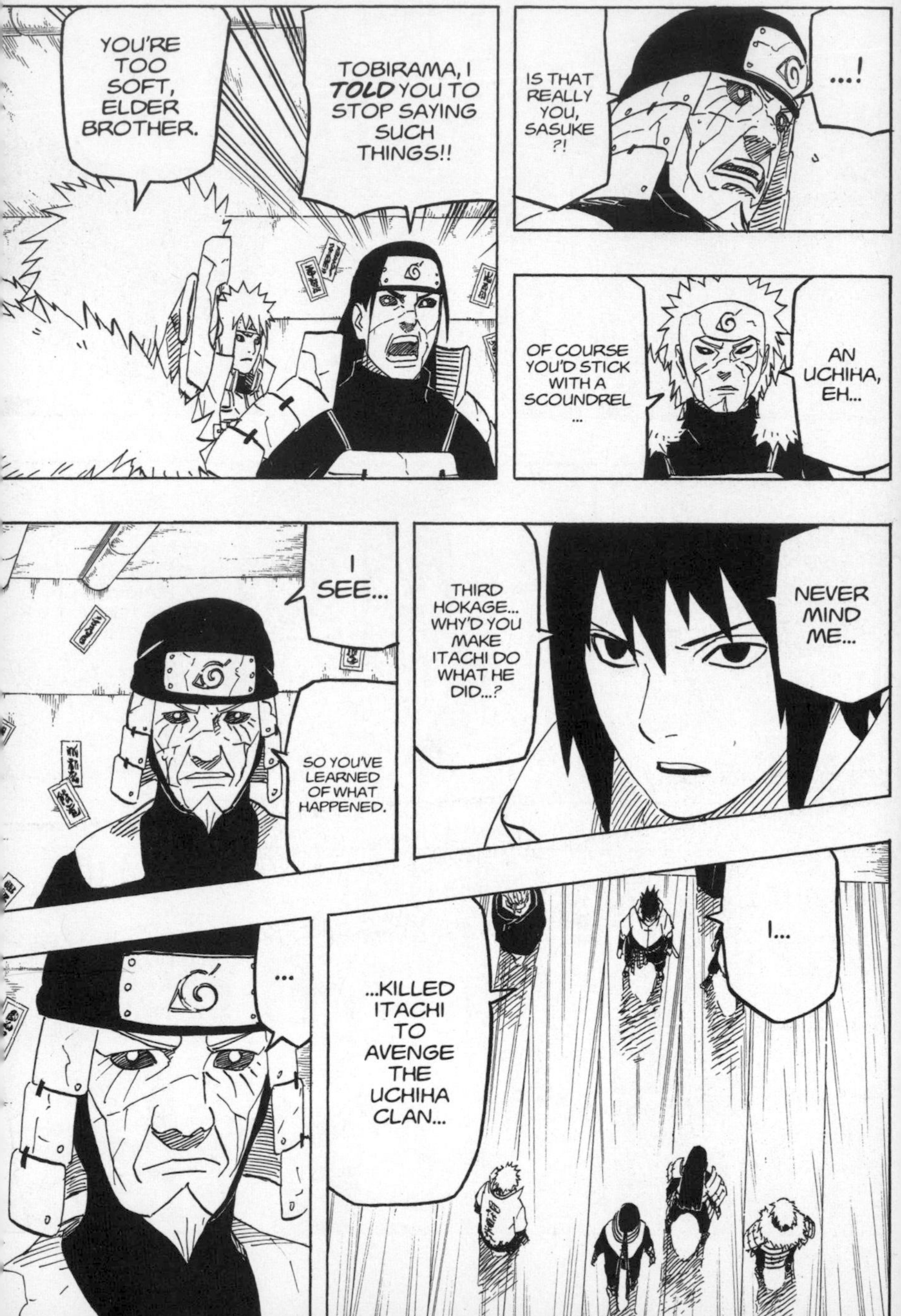
...!
IS THAT REALLY YOU, SASUKE ?!
AN UCHIHA, EH...
OF COURSE YOU'D STICK WITH A SCOUNDREL ...
TOBIRAMA, I **TOLD** YOU TO STOP SAYING SUCH THINGS!!
YOU'RE TOO SOFT, ELDER BROTHER.
NEVER MIND ME...
THIRD HOKAGE... WHY'D YOU MAKE ITACHI DO WHAT HE DID...?
I SEE...
SO YOU'VE LEARNED OF WHAT HAPPENED.
I...
...KILLED ITACHI TO AVENGE THE UCHIHA CLAN...
...

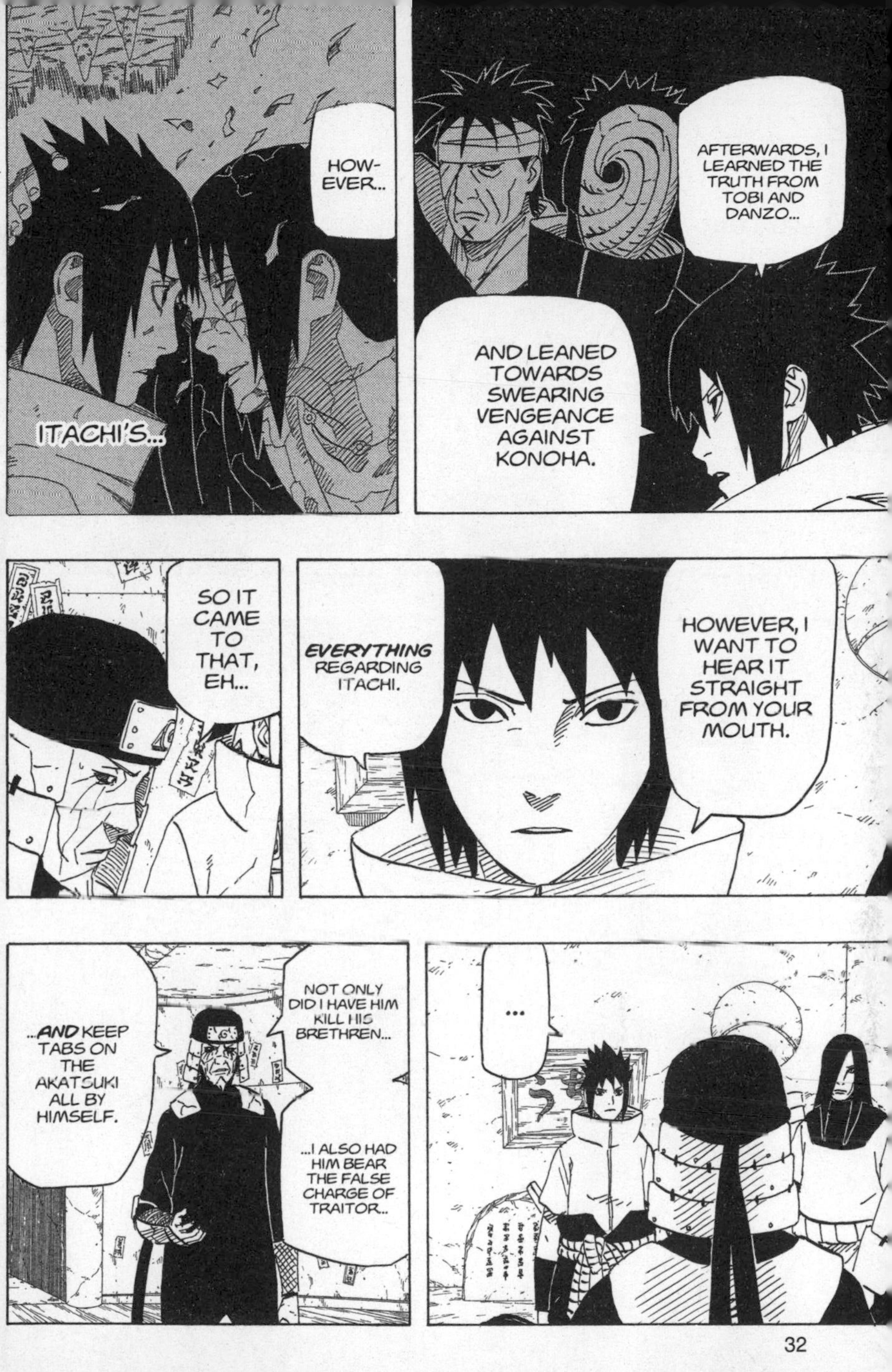
AFTERWARDS, I LEARNED THE TRUTH FROM TOBI AND DANZO...
AND LEANED TOWARDS SWEARING VENGEANCE AGAINST KONOHA.
HOW-EVER...
ITACHI'S...
HOWEVER, I WANT TO HEAR IT STRAIGHT FROM YOUR MOUTH.
EVERYTHING REGARDING ITACHI.
SO IT CAME TO THAT, EH...
...
NOT ONLY DID I HAVE HIM KILL HIS BRETHREN...
...I ALSO HAD HIM BEAR THE FALSE CHARGE OF TRAITOR..
...*AND* KEEP TABS ON THE AKATSUKI ALL BY HIMSELF.

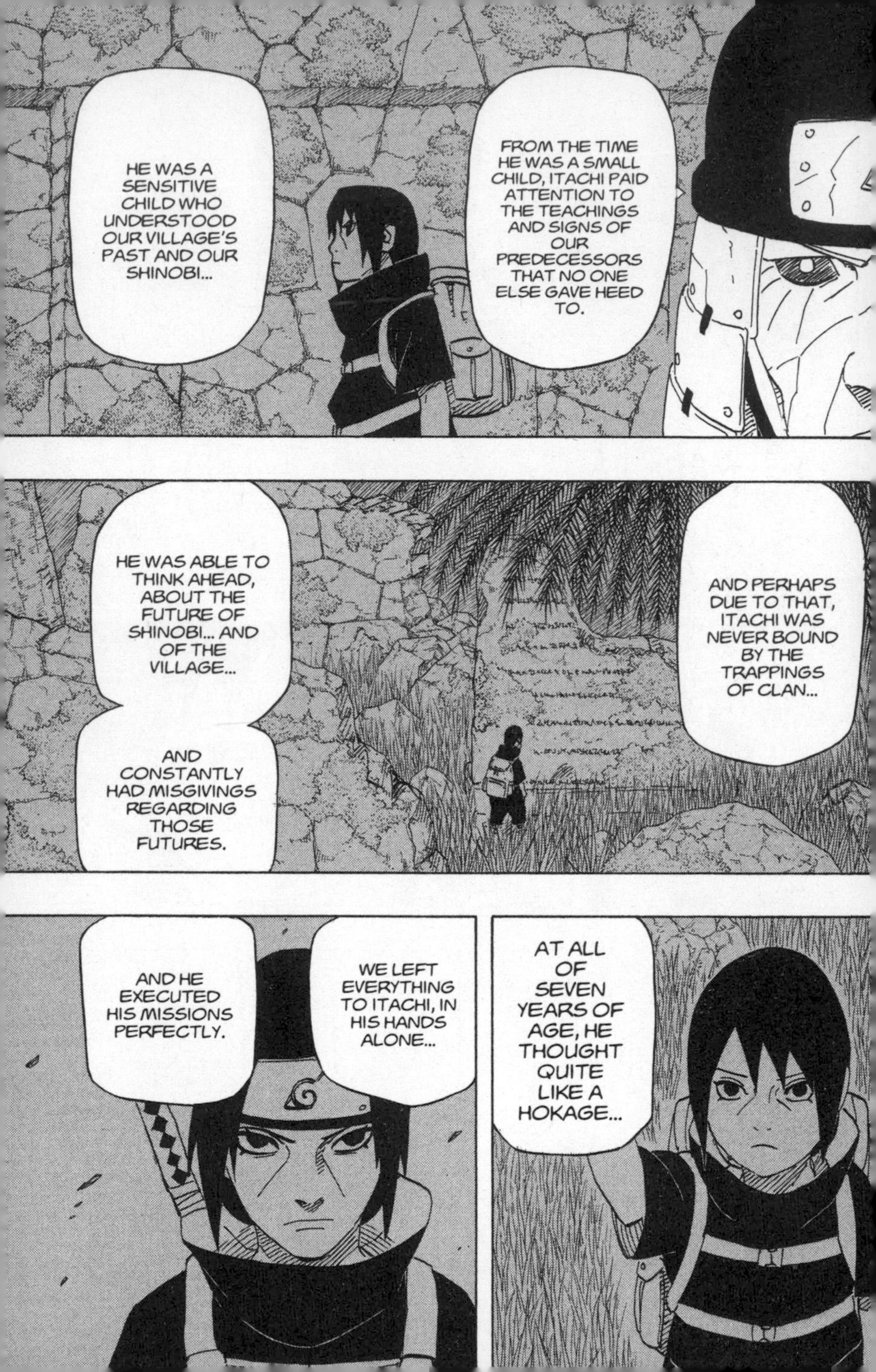
FROM THE TIME HE WAS A SMALL CHILD, ITACHI PAID ATTENTION TO THE TEACHINGS AND SIGNS OF OUR PREDECESSORS THAT NO ONE ELSE GAVE HEED TO.
HE WAS A SENSITIVE CHILD WHO UNDERSTOOD OUR VILLAGE'S PAST AND OUR SHINOBI...
HE WAS ABLE TO THINK AHEAD, ABOUT THE FUTURE OF SHINOBI... AND OF THE VILLAGE...
AND CONSTANTLY HAD MISGIVINGS REGARDING THOSE FUTURES.
AND PERHAPS DUE TO THAT, ITACHI WAS NEVER BOUND BY THE TRAPPINGS OF CLAN...
AT ALL OF SEVEN YEARS OF AGE, HE THOUGHT QUITE LIKE A HOKAGE...
WE LEFT EVERYTHING TO ITACHI, IN HIS HANDS ALONE...
AND HE EXECUTED HIS MISSIONS PERFECTLY.

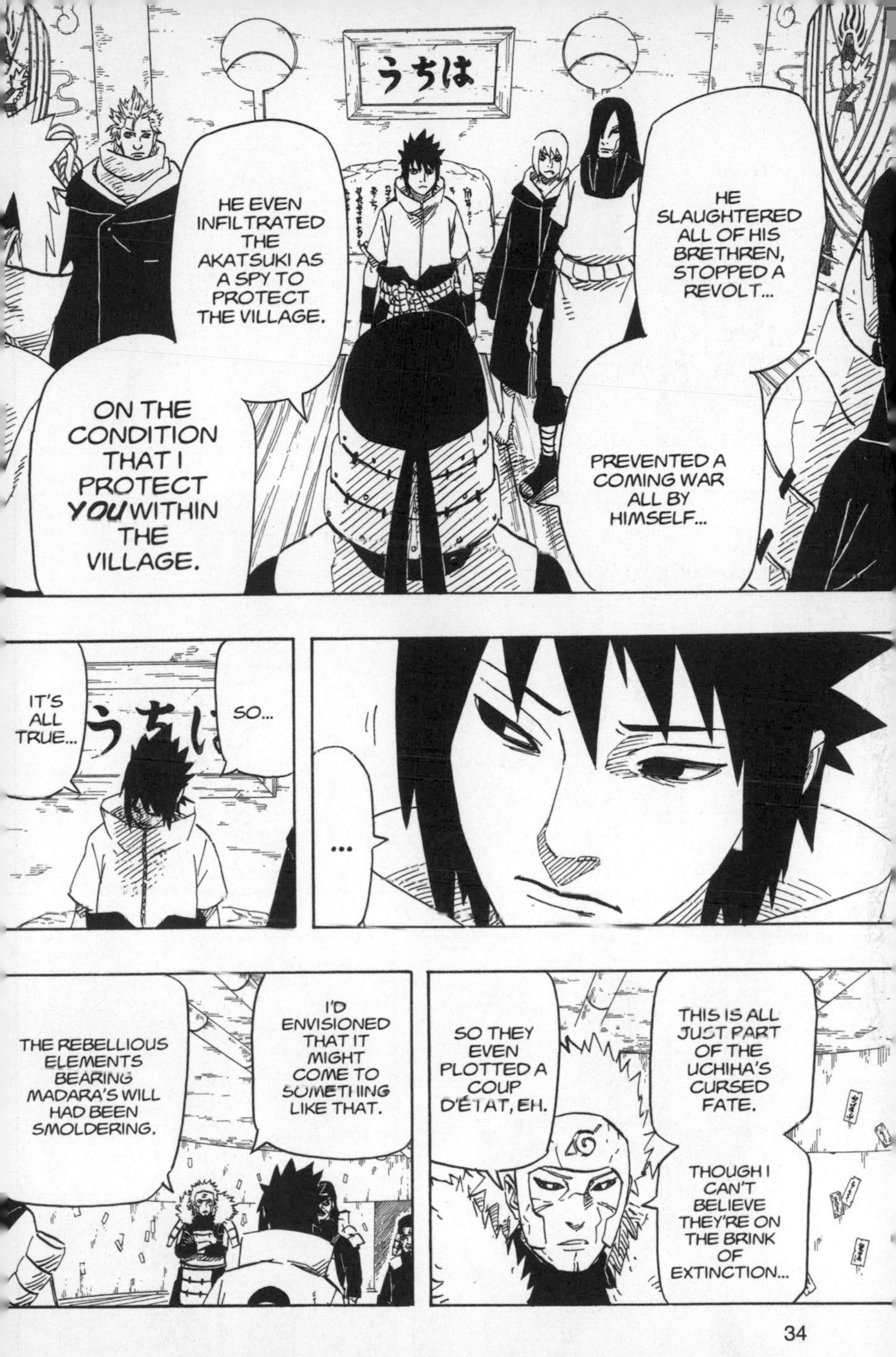
うちは
HE SLAUGHTERED ALL OF HIS BRETHREN, STOPPED A REVOLT...
PREVENTED A COMING WAR ALL BY HIMSELF...
HE EVEN INFILTRATED THE AKATSUKI AS A SPY TO PROTECT THE VILLAGE.
ON THE CONDITION THAT I PROTECT ***YOU*** WITHIN THE VILLAGE.
...
SO...
IT'S ALL TRUE...
THIS IS ALL JUST PART OF THE UCHIHA'S CURSED FATE.
SO THEY EVEN PLOTTED A COUP D'ÉTAT, EH.
THOUGH I CAN'T BELIEVE THEY'RE ON THE BRINK OF EXTINCTION...
I'D ENVISIONED THAT IT MIGHT COME TO SOMETHING LIKE THAT.
THE REBELLIOUS ELEMENTS BEARING MADARA'S WILL HAD BEEN SMOLDERING.

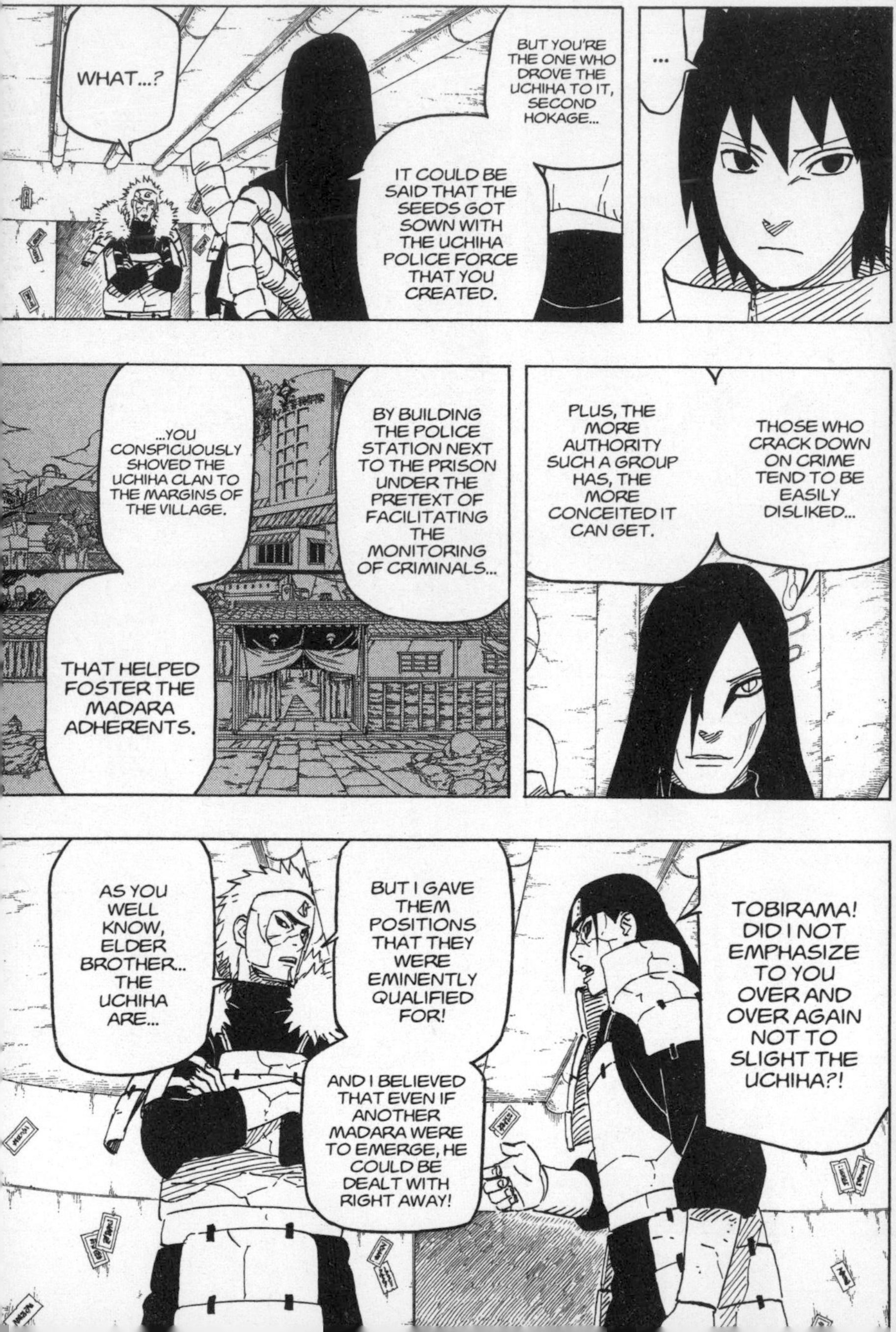
...
BUT YOU'RE THE ONE WHO DROVE THE UCHIHA TO IT, SECOND HOKAGE...
IT COULD BE SAID THAT THE SEEDS GOT SOWN WITH THE UCHIHA POLICE FORCE THAT YOU CREATED.
WHAT...?
THOSE WHO CRACK DOWN ON CRIME TEND TO BE EASILY DISLIKED...
PLUS, THE MORE AUTHORITY SUCH A GROUP HAS, THE MORE CONCEITED IT CAN GET.
BY BUILDING THE POLICE STATION NEXT TO THE PRISON UNDER THE PRETEXT OF FACILITATING THE MONITORING OF CRIMINALS...
...YOU CONSPICUOUSLY SHOVED THE UCHIHA CLAN TO THE MARGINS OF THE VILLAGE.
THAT HELPED FOSTER THE MADARA ADHERENTS.
TOBIRAMA! DID I NOT EMPHASIZE TO YOU OVER AND OVER AGAIN NOT TO SLIGHT THE UCHIHA?!
AS YOU WELL KNOW, ELDER BROTHER... THE UCHIHA ARE...
BUT I GAVE THEM POSITIONS THAT THEY WERE EMINENTLY QUALIFIED FOR!
AND I BELIEVED THAT EVEN IF ANOTHER MADARA WERE TO EMERGE, HE COULD BE DEALT WITH RIGHT AWAY!

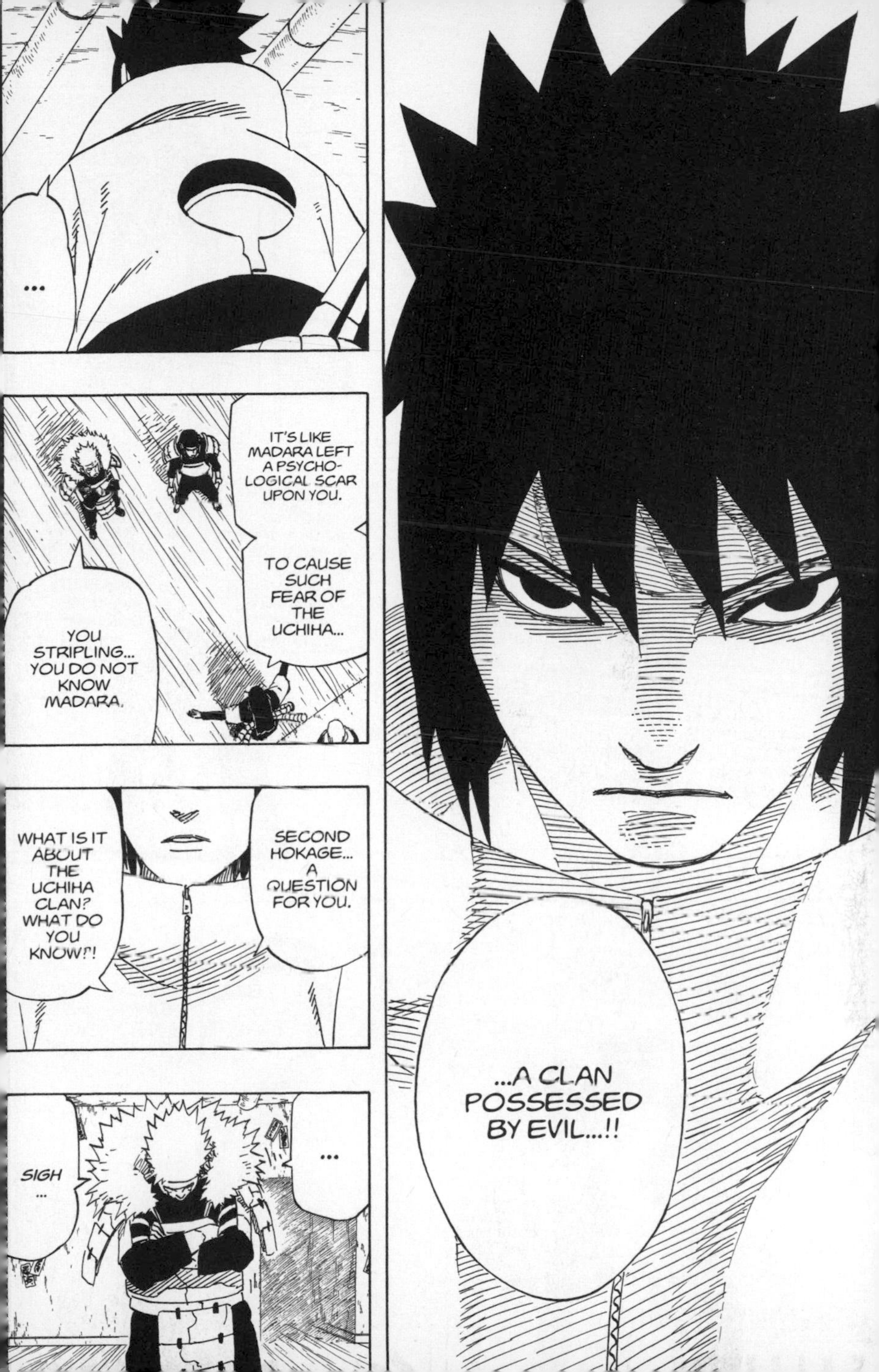
...A CLAN POSSESSED BY EVIL...!!
...
IT'S LIKE MADARA LEFT A PSYCHOLOGICAL SCAR UPON YOU.
TO CAUSE SUCH FEAR OF THE UCHIHA...
YOU STRIPLING... YOU DO NOT KNOW MADARA.
SECOND HOKAGE... A QUESTION FOR YOU.
WHAT IS IT ABOUT THE UCHIHA CLAN? WHAT DO YOU KNOW?!
...
SIGH ...

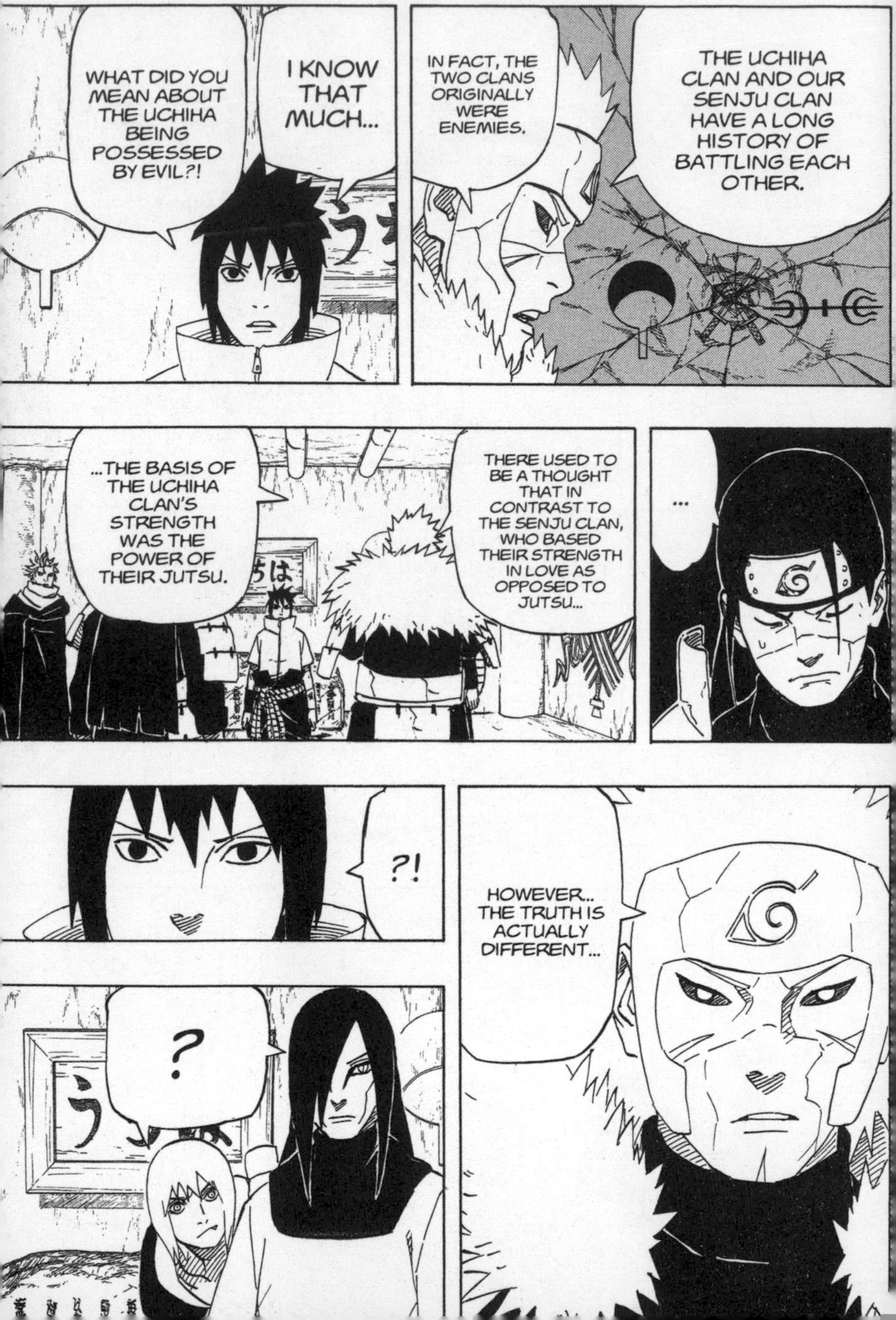
THE UCHIHA CLAN AND OUR SENJU CLAN HAVE A LONG HISTORY OF BATTLING EACH OTHER.
IN FACT, THE TWO CLANS ORIGINALLY WERE ENEMIES.
I KNOW THAT MUCH...
WHAT DID YOU MEAN ABOUT THE UCHIHA BEING POSSESSED BY EVIL?!
...
THERE USED TO BE A THOUGHT THAT IN CONTRAST TO THE SENJU CLAN, WHO BASED THEIR STRENGTH IN LOVE AS OPPOSED TO JUTSU...
...THE BASIS OF THE UCHIHA CLAN'S STRENGTH WAS THE POWER OF THEIR JUTSU.
HOWEVER... THE TRUTH IS ACTUALLY DIFFERENT...
?!
?

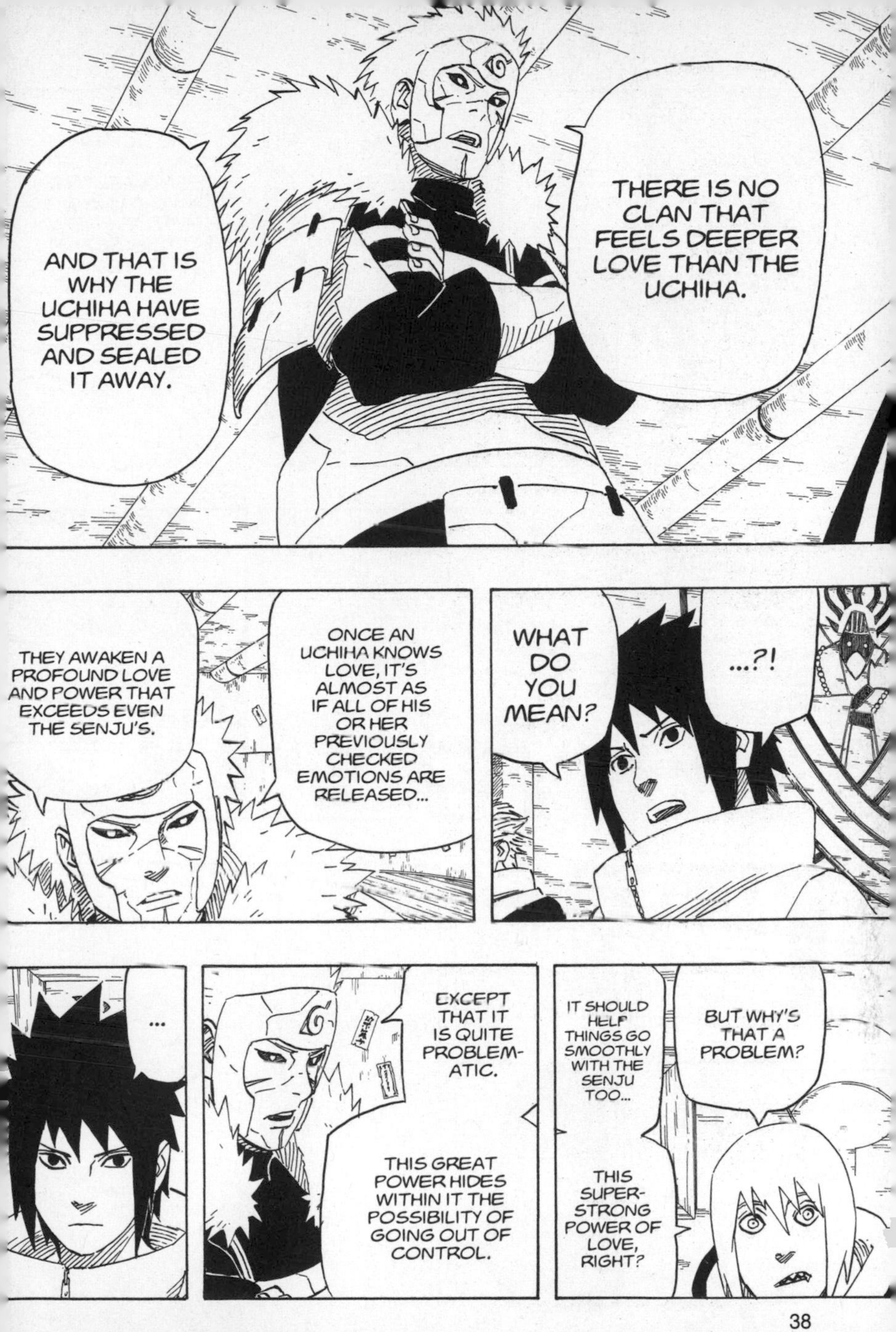

THERE IS NO CLAN THAT FEELS DEEPER LOVE THAN THE UCHIHA.
AND THAT IS WHY THE UCHIHA HAVE SUPPRESSED AND SEALED IT AWAY.
...?!
WHAT DO YOU MEAN?
ONCE AN UCHIHA KNOWS LOVE, IT'S ALMOST AS IF ALL OF HIS OR HER PREVIOUSLY CHECKED EMOTIONS ARE RELEASED...
THEY AWAKEN A PROFOUND LOVE AND POWER THAT EXCEEDS EVEN THE SENJU'S.
BUT WHY'S THAT A PROBLEM?
IT SHOULD HELP THINGS GO SMOOTHLY WITH THE SENJU TOO...
THIS SUPER-STRONG POWER OF LOVE, RIGHT?
EXCEPT THAT IT IS QUITE PROBLEM-ATIC.
THIS GREAT POWER HIDES WITHIN IT THE POSSIBILITY OF GOING OUT OF CONTROL.
...

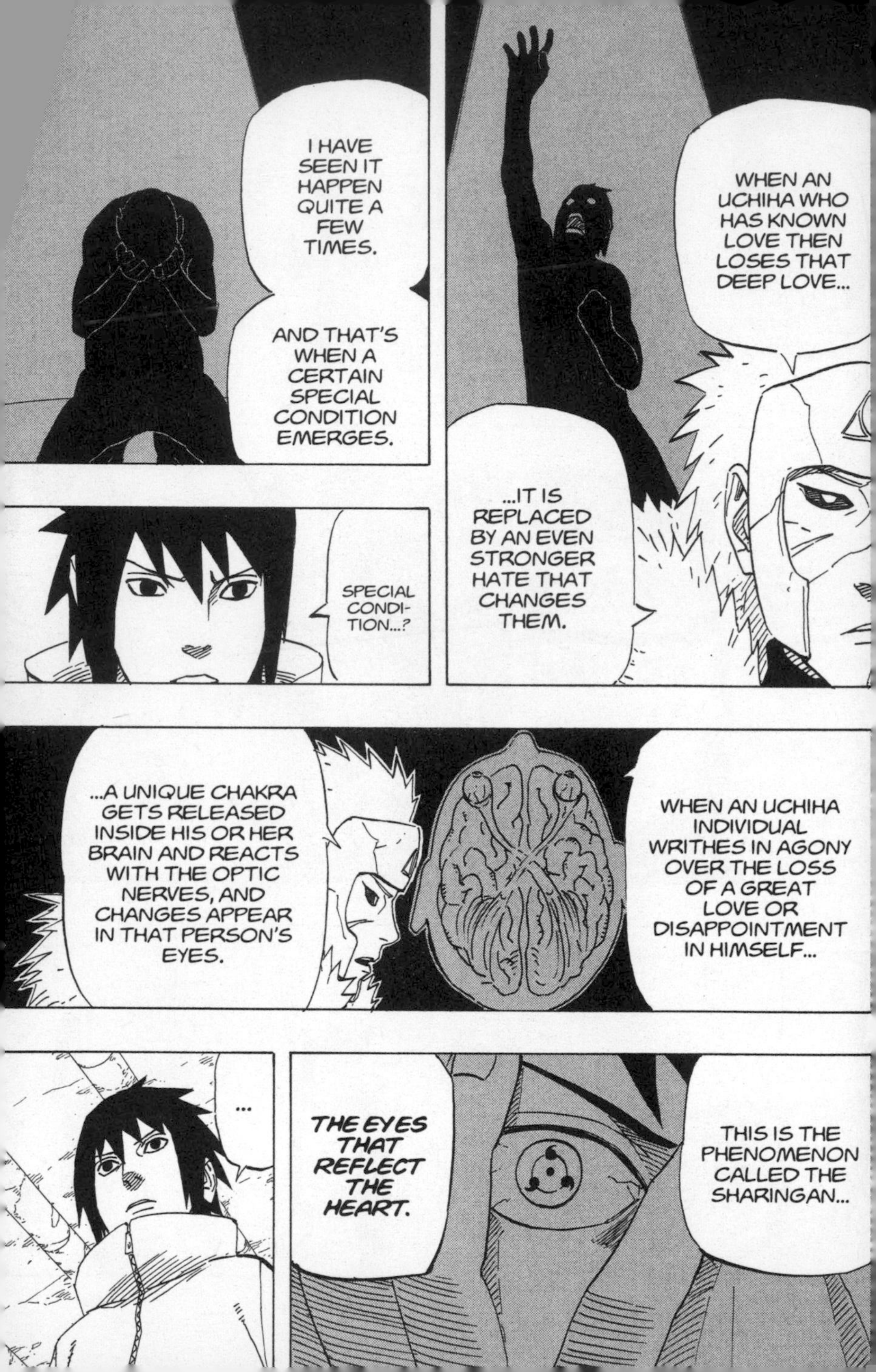

WHEN AN UCHIHA WHO HAS KNOWN LOVE THEN LOSES THAT DEEP LOVE...
...IT IS REPLACED BY AN EVEN STRONGER HATE THAT CHANGES THEM.
I HAVE SEEN IT HAPPEN QUITE A FEW TIMES.
AND THAT'S WHEN A CERTAIN SPECIAL CONDITION EMERGES.
SPECIAL CONDITION...?
WHEN AN UCHIHA INDIVIDUAL WRITHES IN AGONY OVER THE LOSS OF A GREAT LOVE OR DISAPPOINTMENT IN HIMSELF...
...A UNIQUE CHAKRA GETS RELEASED INSIDE HIS OR HER BRAIN AND REACTS WITH THE OPTIC NERVES, AND CHANGES APPEAR IN THAT PERSON'S EYES.
THIS IS THE PHENOMENON CALLED THE SHARINGAN...
THE EYES THAT REFLECT THE HEART.
...

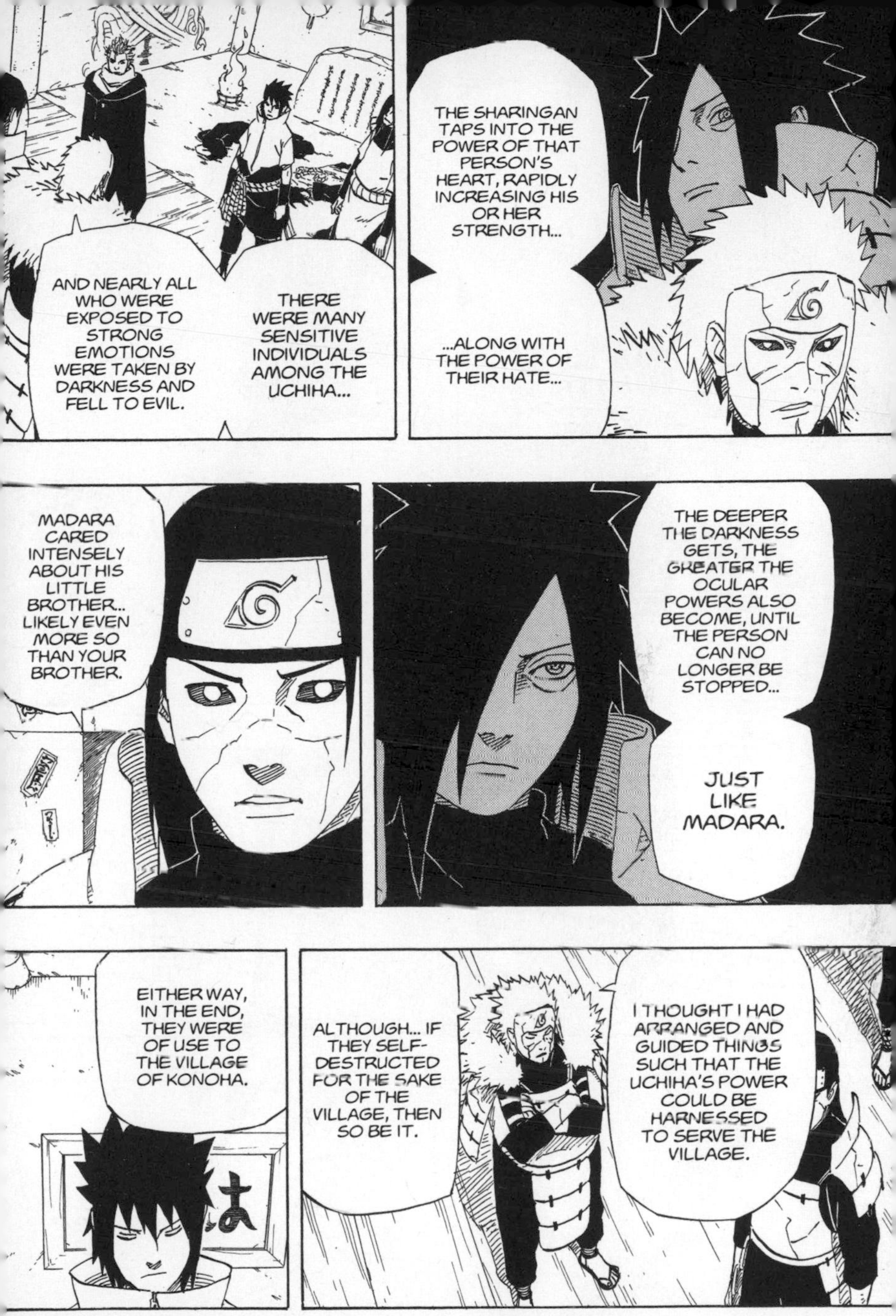
THE SHARINGAN TAPS INTO THE POWER OF THAT PERSON'S HEART, RAPIDLY INCREASING HIS OR HER STRENGTH...
...ALONG WITH THE POWER OF THEIR HATE...
THERE WERE MANY SENSITIVE INDIVIDUALS AMONG THE UCHIHA...
AND NEARLY ALL WHO WERE EXPOSED TO STRONG EMOTIONS WERE TAKEN BY DARKNESS AND FELL TO EVIL.
THE DEEPER THE DARKNESS GETS, THE GREATER THE OCULAR POWERS ALSO BECOME, UNTIL THE PERSON CAN NO LONGER BE STOPPED...
JUST LIKE MADARA.
MADARA CARED INTENSELY ABOUT HIS LITTLE BROTHER... LIKELY EVEN MORE SO THAN YOUR BROTHER.
I THOUGHT I HAD ARRANGED AND GUIDED THINGS SUCH THAT THE UCHIHA'S POWER COULD BE HARNESSED TO SERVE THE VILLAGE.
ALTHOUGH... IF THEY SELF-DESTRUCTED FOR THE SAKE OF THE VILLAGE, THEN SO BE IT.
EITHER WAY, IN THE END, THEY WERE OF USE TO THE VILLAGE OF KONOHA.

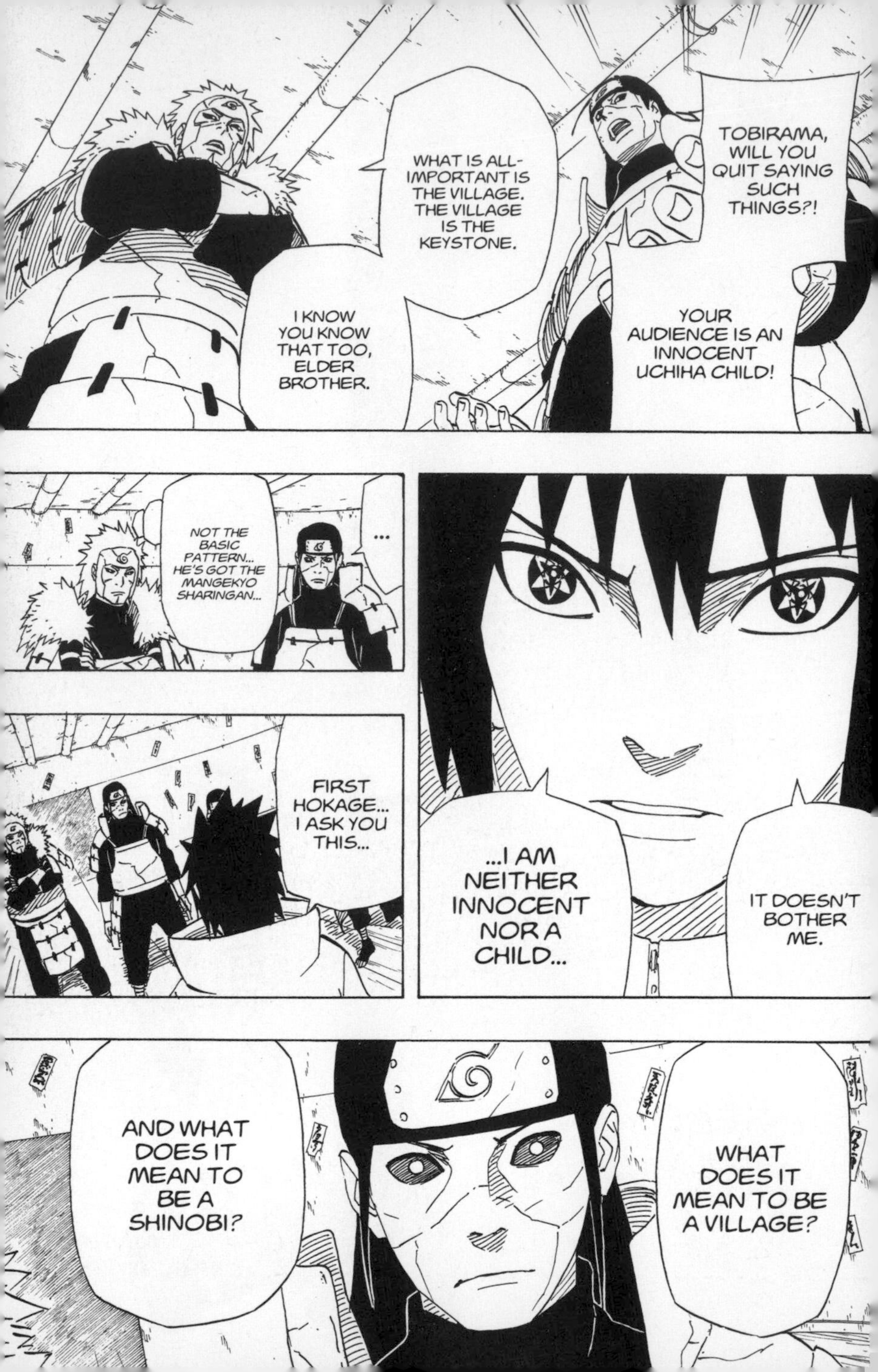

TOBIRAMA, WILL YOU QUIT SAYING SUCH THINGS?!
YOUR AUDIENCE IS AN INNOCENT UCHIHA CHILD!
WHAT IS ALL-IMPORTANT IS THE VILLAGE. THE VILLAGE IS THE KEYSTONE.
I KNOW YOU KNOW THAT TOO, ELDER BROTHER.
IT DOESN'T BOTHER ME.
...I AM NEITHER INNOCENT NOR A CHILD...
...
NOT THE BASIC PATTERN... HE'S GOT THE MANGEKYO SHARINGAN...
FIRST HOKAGE... I ASK YOU THIS...
WHAT DOES IT MEAN TO BE A VILLAGE?
AND WHAT DOES IT MEAN TO BE A SHINOBI?

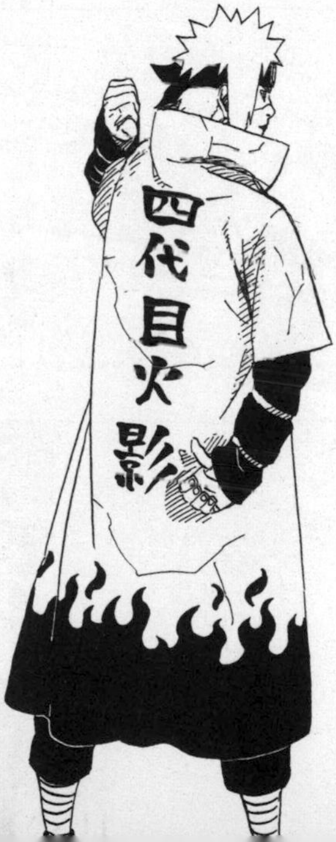
四代目火影

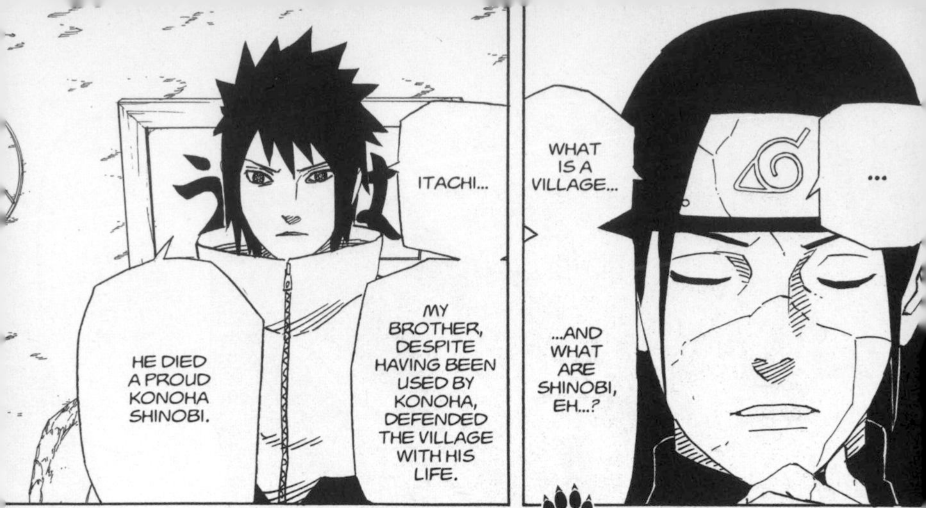
...
WHAT IS A VILLAGE...
...AND WHAT ARE SHINOBI, EH...?
ITACHI...
MY BROTHER, DESPITE HAVING BEEN USED BY KONOHA, DEFENDED THE VILLAGE WITH HIS LIFE.
HE DIED A PROUD KONOHA SHINOBI.

Number 620: Senju Hashirama

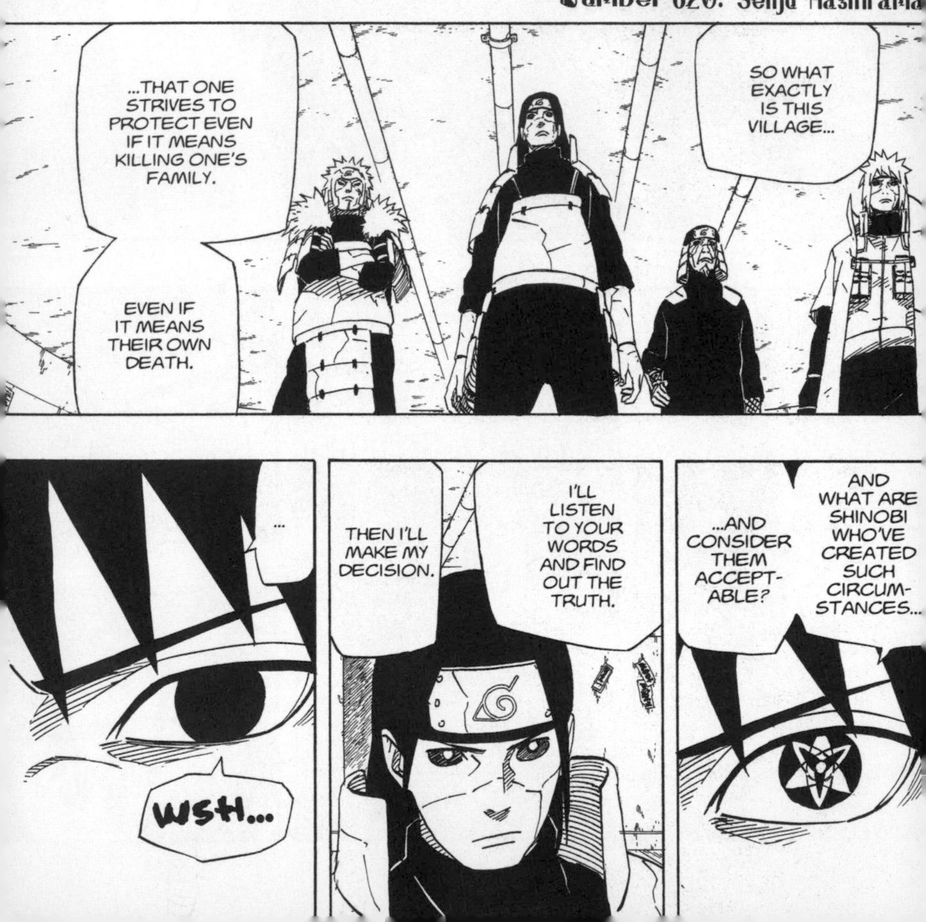
SO WHAT EXACTLY IS THIS VILLAGE...
...THAT ONE STRIVES TO PROTECT EVEN IF IT MEANS KILLING ONE'S FAMILY.
EVEN IF IT MEANS THEIR OWN DEATH.
AND WHAT ARE SHINOBI WHO'VE CREATED SUCH CIRCUM-STANCES...
...AND CONSIDER THEM ACCEPT-ABLE?
I'LL LISTEN TO YOUR WORDS AND FIND OUT THE TRUTH.
THEN I'LL MAKE MY DECISION.
...
WSH...

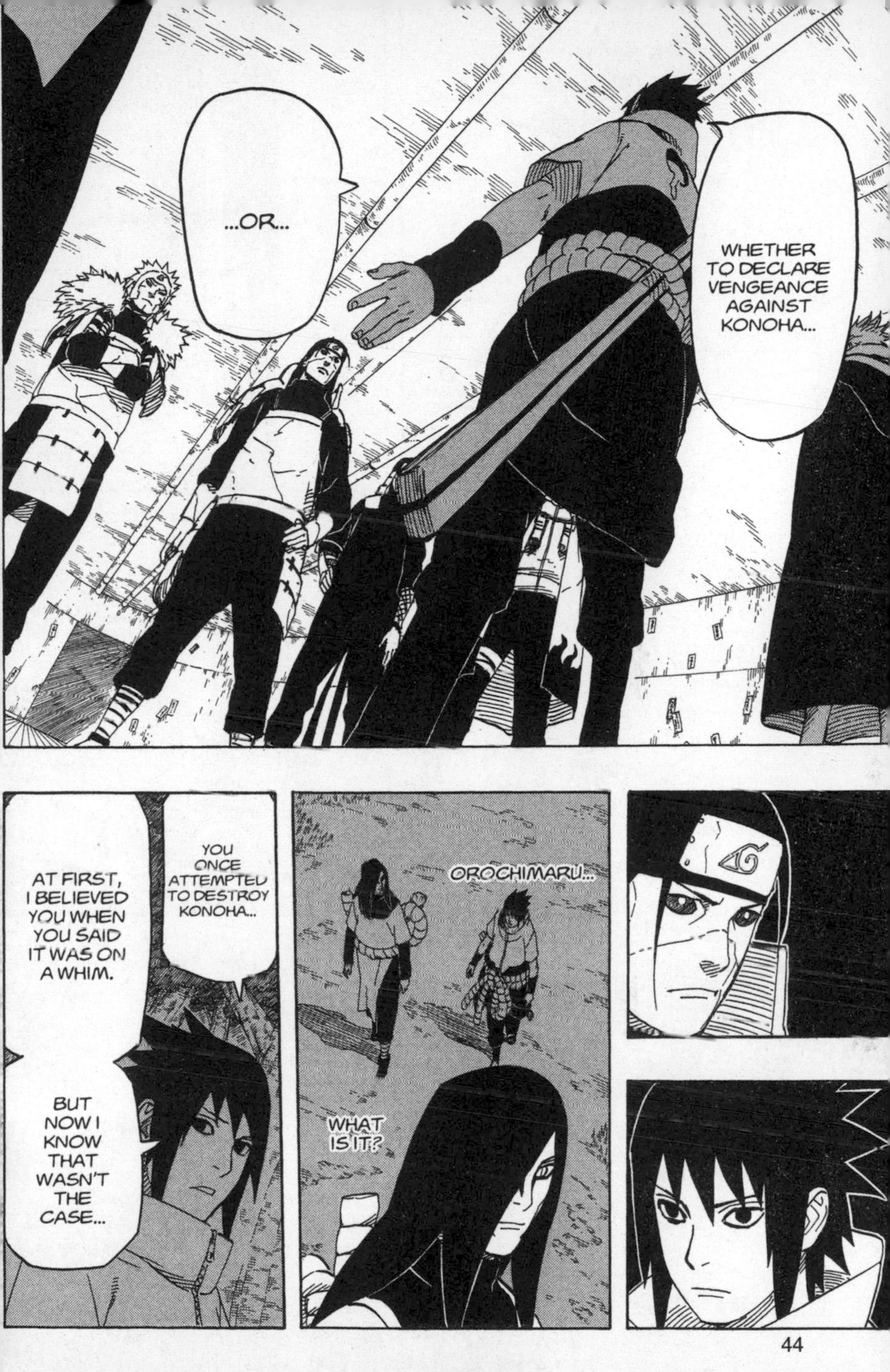
WHETHER TO DECLARE VENGEANCE AGAINST KONOHA...
...OR...
OROCHIMARU...
WHAT IS IT?
YOU ONCE ATTEMPTED TO DESTROY KONOHA...
AT FIRST, I BELIEVED YOU WHEN YOU SAID IT WAS ON A WHIM.
BUT NOW I KNOW THAT WASN'T THE CASE...

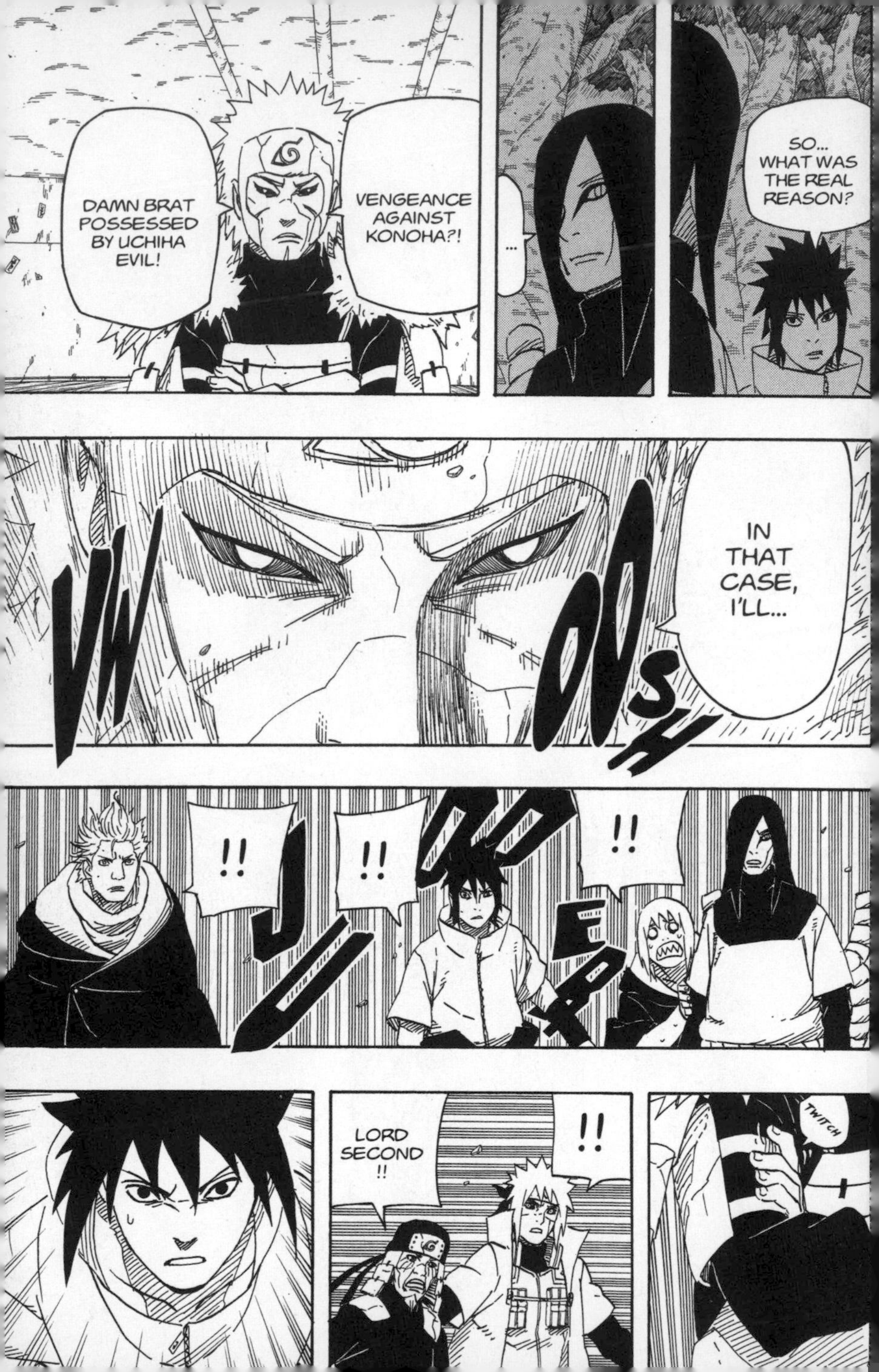
SO... WHAT WAS THE REAL REASON?
...
VENGEANCE AGAINST KONOHA?!
DAMN BRAT POSSESSED BY UCHIHA EVIL!
IN THAT CASE, I'LL...
VWOOSH
!!
!!
!!
TWITCH
!!
LORD SECOND !!

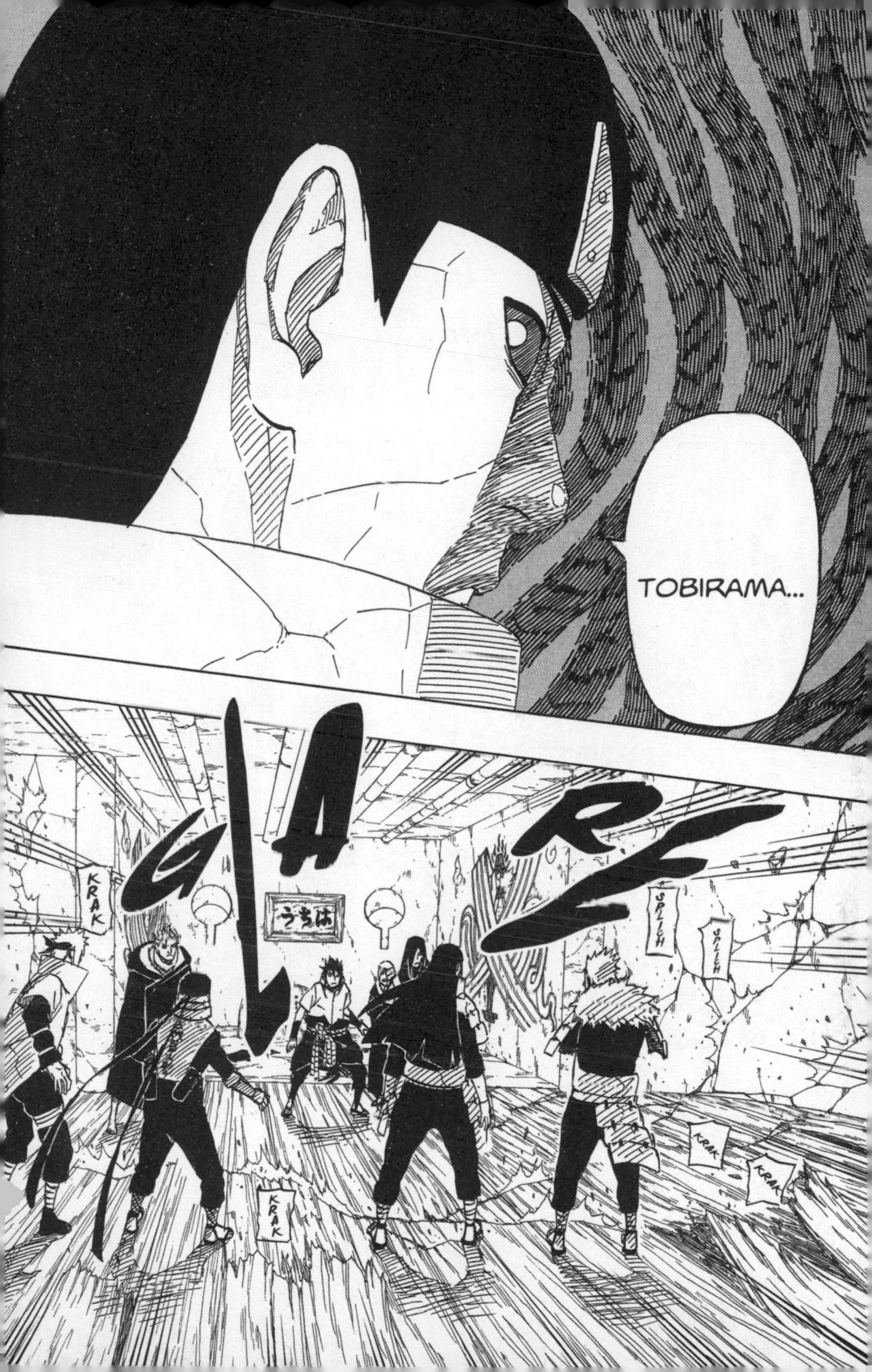
TOBIRAMA...
SPLICH
SPLICH
KRAK
KRAK
うちは
KRAK
KRAK

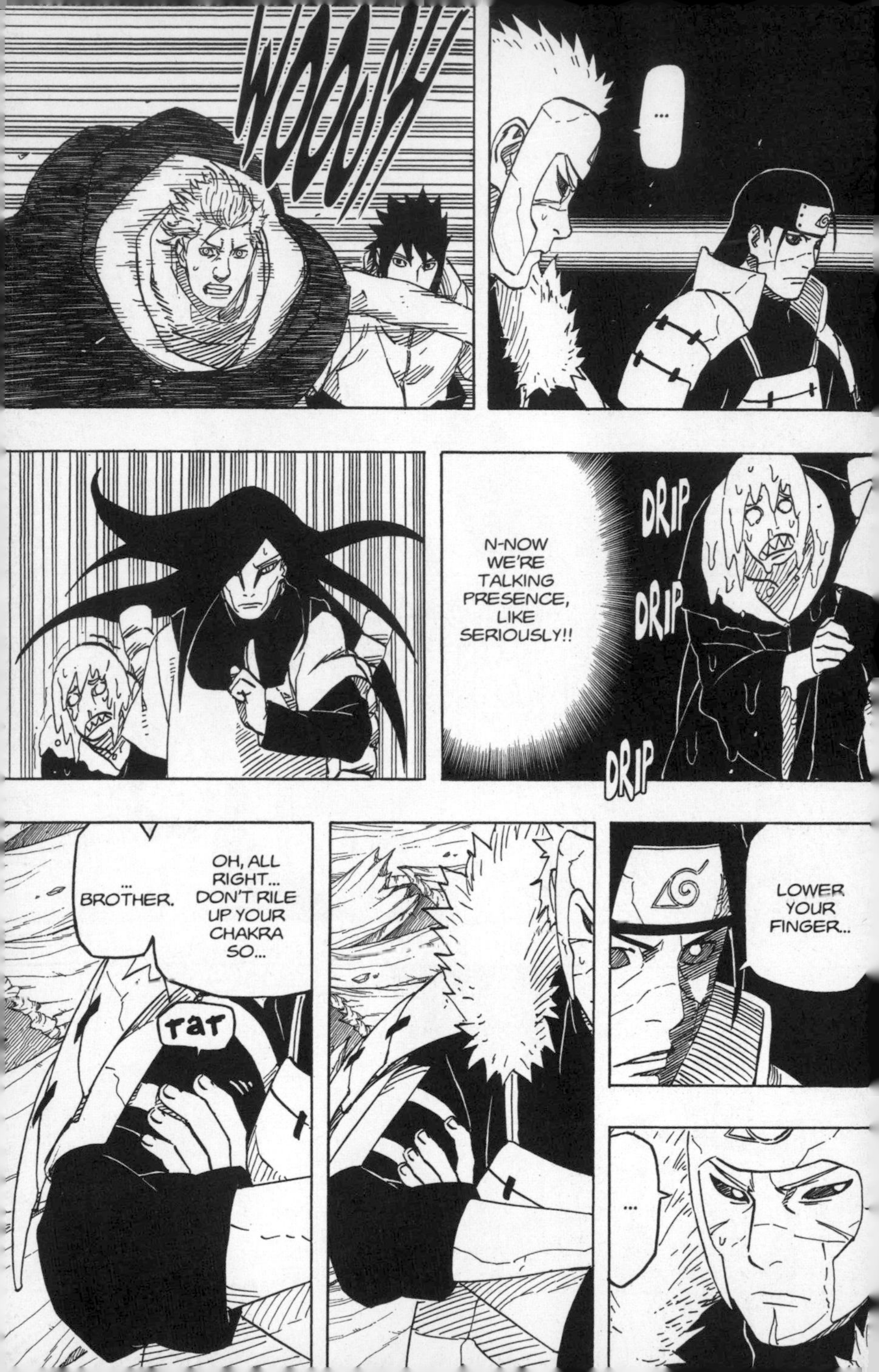
...
WOOSH
N-NOW WE'RE TALKING PRESENCE, LIKE SERIOUSLY!!
DRIP
DRIP
DRIP
LOWER YOUR FINGER...
...
OH, ALL RIGHT... DON'T RILE UP YOUR CHAKRA SO...
... BROTHER.
TAT

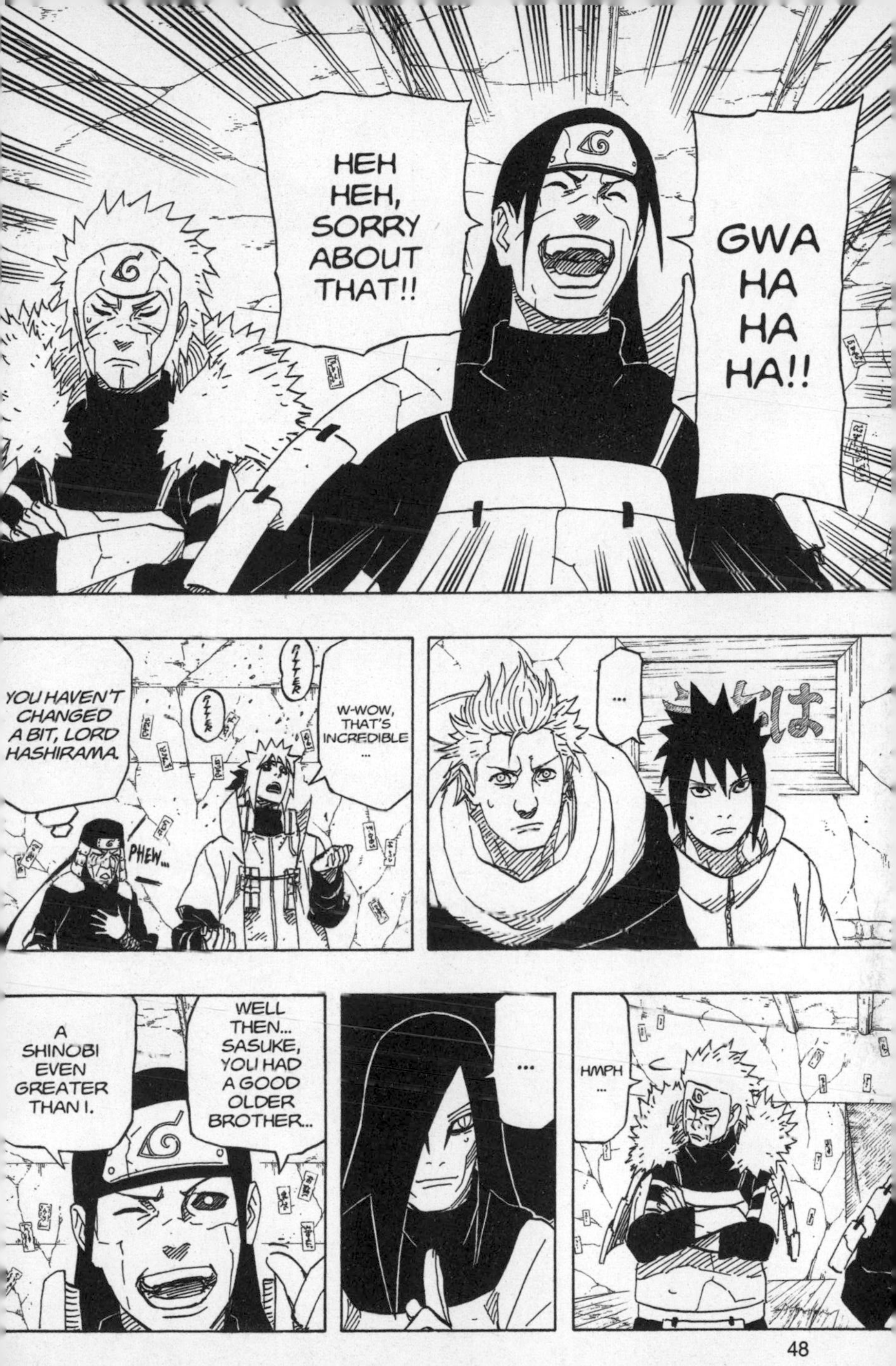
GWA HA HA HA!!
HEH HEH, SORRY ABOUT THAT!!
...
PITTER
PITTER
W-WOW, THAT'S INCREDIBLE...
YOU HAVEN'T CHANGED A BIT, LORD HASHIRAMA.
PHEW...
HMPH...
...
WELL THEN... SASUKE, YOU HAD A GOOD OLDER BROTHER...
A SHINOBI EVEN GREATER THAN I.

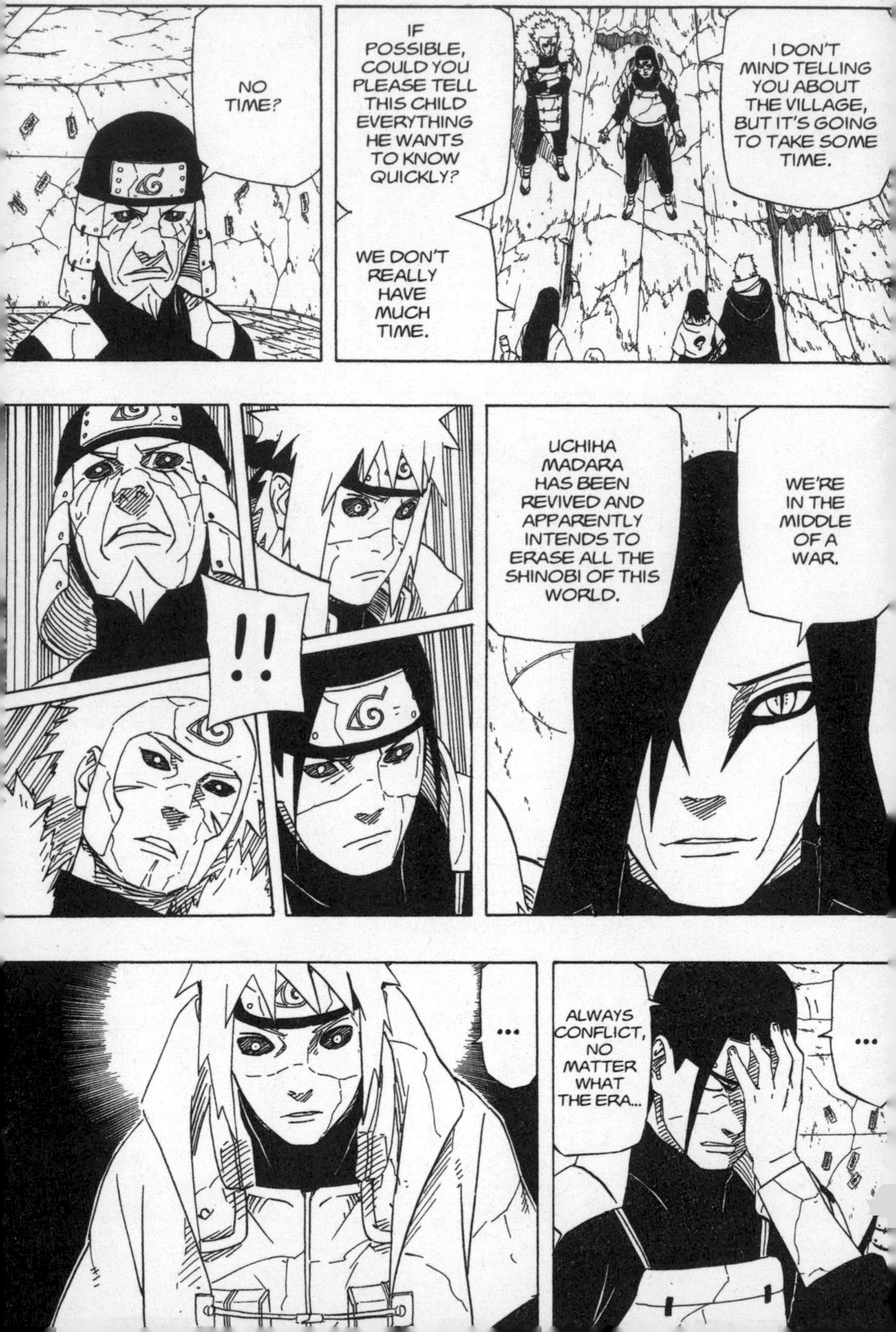
I DON'T MIND TELLING YOU ABOUT THE VILLAGE, BUT IT'S GOING TO TAKE SOME TIME.
IF POSSIBLE, COULD YOU PLEASE TELL THIS CHILD EVERYTHING HE WANTS TO KNOW QUICKLY?
WE DON'T REALLY HAVE MUCH TIME.
NO TIME?
WE'RE IN THE MIDDLE OF A WAR.
UCHIHA MADARA HAS BEEN REVIVED AND APPARENTLY INTENDS TO ERASE ALL THE SHINOBI OF THIS WORLD.
!!
...
ALWAYS CONFLICT, NO MATTER WHAT THE ERA...
...

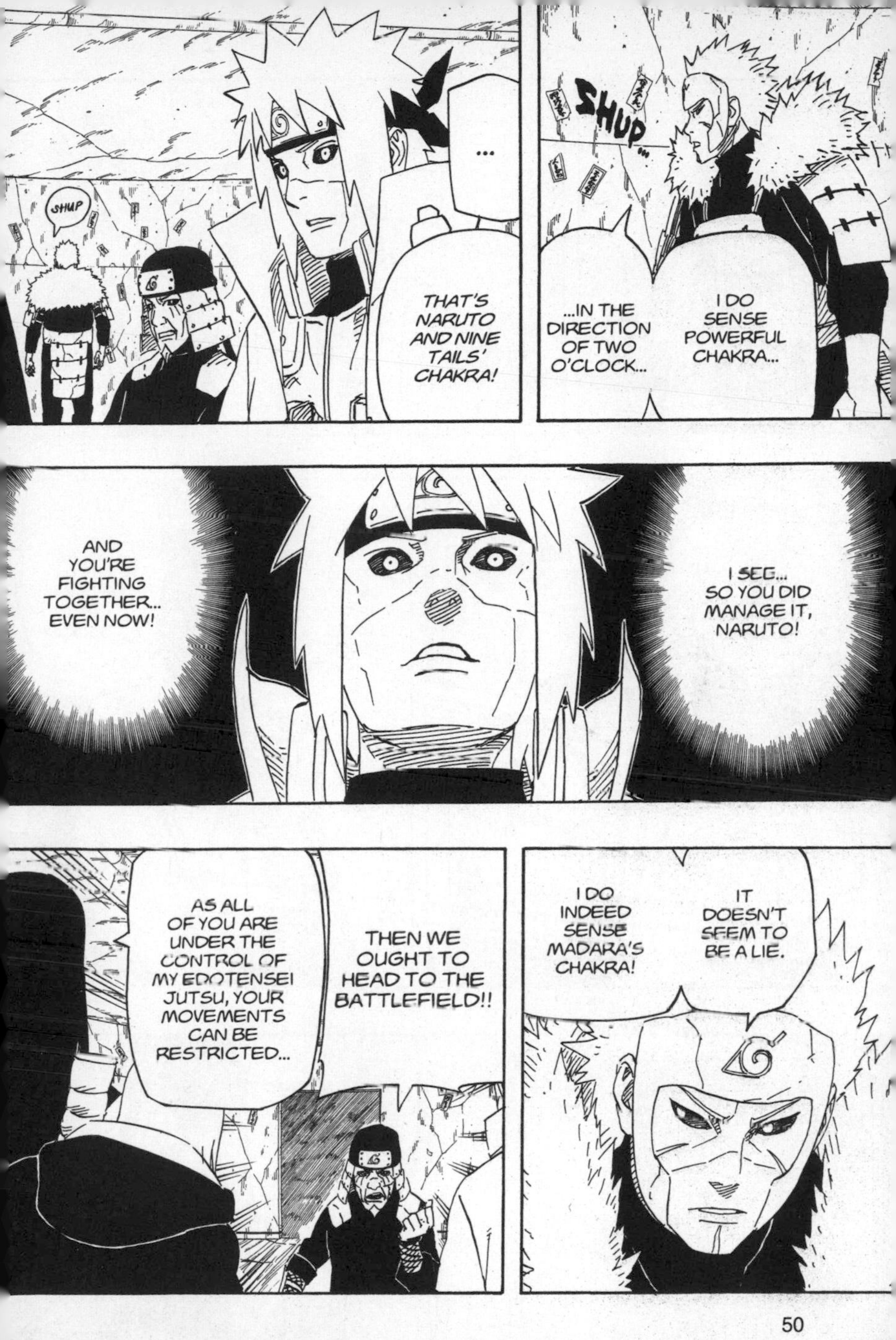
SHUP...
I DO SENSE POWERFUL CHAKRA...
...IN THE DIRECTION OF TWO O'CLOCK...
...
SHUP
THAT'S NARUTO AND NINE TAILS' CHAKRA!
I SEE... SO YOU DID MANAGE IT, NARUTO!
AND YOU'RE FIGHTING TOGETHER... EVEN NOW!
IT DOESN'T SEEM TO BE A LIE.
I DO INDEED SENSE MADARA'S CHAKRA!
THEN WE OUGHT TO HEAD TO THE BATTLEFIELD!!
AS ALL OF YOU ARE UNDER THE CONTROL OF MY EDOTENSEI JUTSU, YOUR MOVEMENTS CAN BE RESTRICTED...

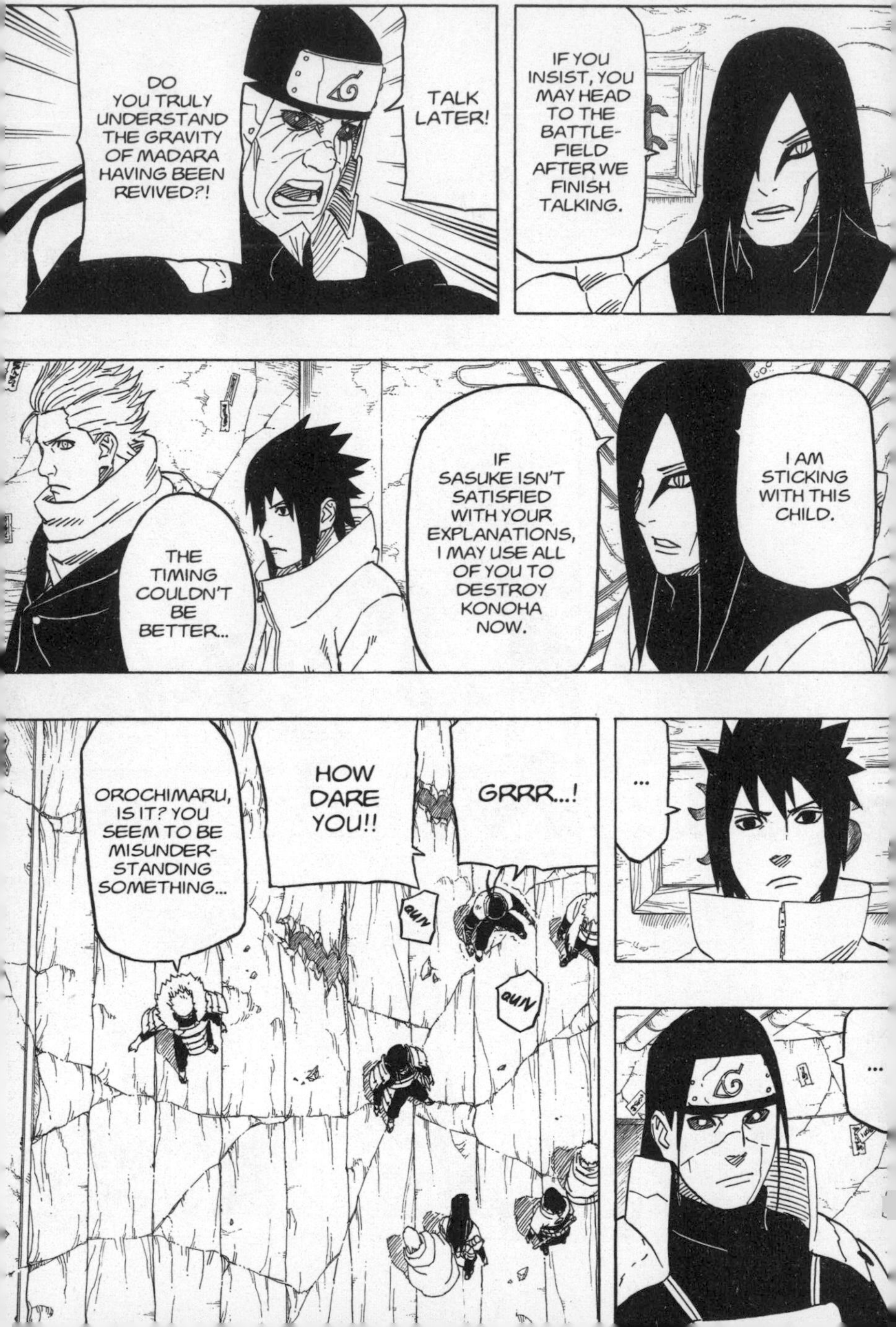
IF YOU INSIST, YOU MAY HEAD TO THE BATTLE-FIELD AFTER WE FINISH TALKING.
TALK LATER!
DO YOU TRULY UNDERSTAND THE GRAVITY OF MADARA HAVING BEEN REVIVED?!
I AM STICKING WITH THIS CHILD.
IF SASUKE ISN'T SATISFIED WITH YOUR EXPLANATIONS, I MAY USE ALL OF YOU TO DESTROY KONOHA NOW.
THE TIMING COULDN'T BE BETTER...
...
...
GRRR...!
HOW DARE YOU!!
QUIV
QUIV
OROCHIMARU, IS IT? YOU SEEM TO BE MISUNDER-STANDING SOMETHING...

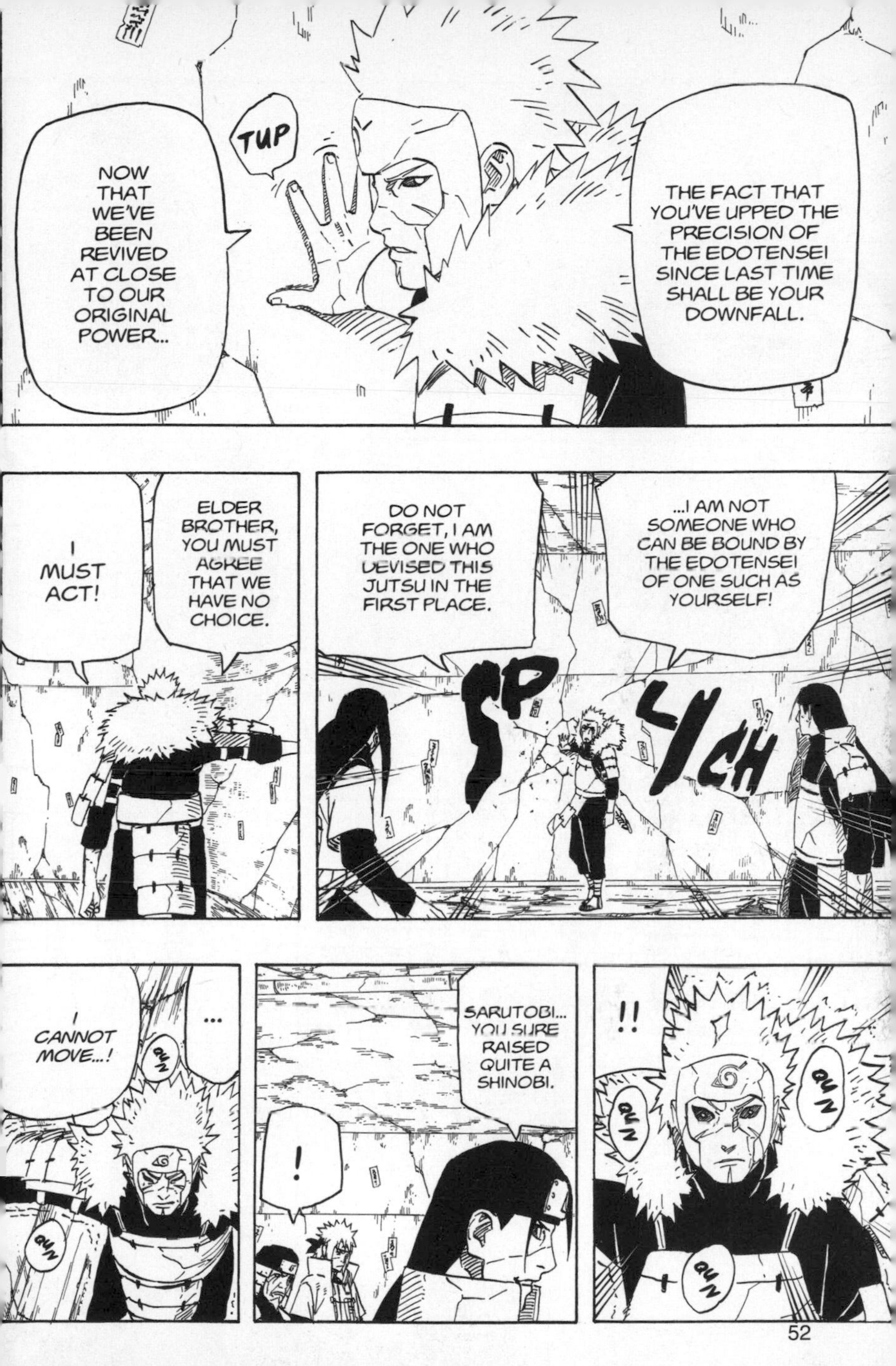

THE FACT THAT YOU'VE UPPED THE PRECISION OF THE EDOTENSEI SINCE LAST TIME SHALL BE YOUR DOWNFALL.
TUP
NOW THAT WE'VE BEEN REVIVED AT CLOSE TO OUR ORIGINAL POWER...
...I AM NOT SOMEONE WHO CAN BE BOUND BY THE EDOTENSEI OF ONE SUCH AS YOURSELF!
DO NOT FORGET, I AM THE ONE WHO DEVISED THIS JUTSU IN THE FIRST PLACE.
SPLICH
ELDER BROTHER, YOU MUST AGREE THAT WE HAVE NO CHOICE.
I MUST ACT!
!!
QUN
QUN
QUN
SARUTOBI... YOU SURE RAISED QUITE A SHINOBI.
!
...
I CANNOT MOVE...!
QUN
QUN

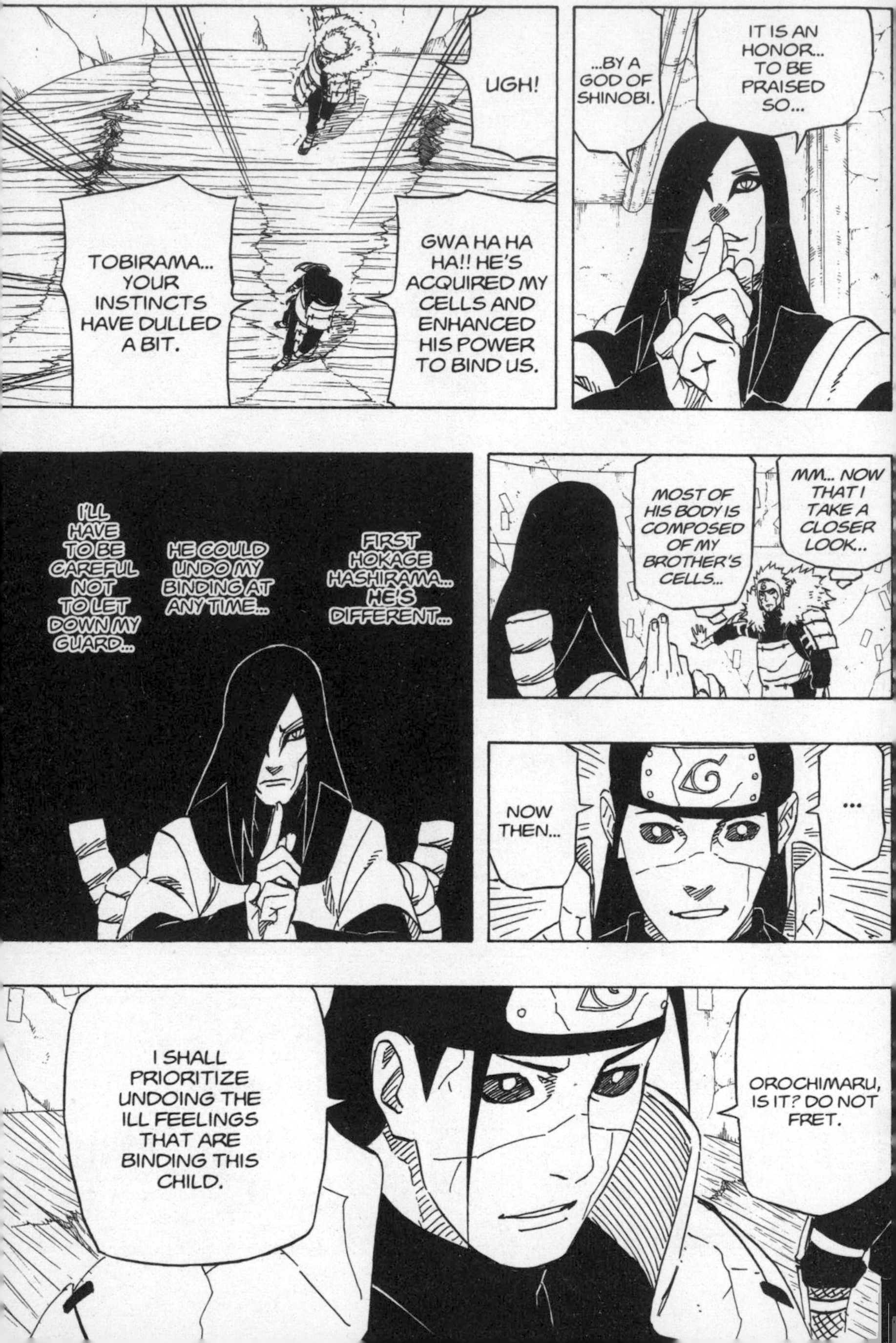
IT IS AN HONOR... TO BE PRAISED SO...
...BY A GOD OF SHINOBI.
UGH!
GWA HA HA HA!! HE'S ACQUIRED MY CELLS AND ENHANCED HIS POWER TO BIND US.
TOBIRAMA... YOUR INSTINCTS HAVE DULLED A BIT.
MM... NOW THAT I TAKE A CLOSER LOOK...
MOST OF HIS BODY IS COMPOSED OF MY BROTHER'S CELLS...
...
NOW THEN...
FIRST HOKAGE HASHIRAMA... HE'S DIFFERENT...
HE COULD UNDO MY BINDING AT ANY TIME...
I'LL HAVE TO BE CAREFUL NOT TO LET DOWN MY GUARD...
OROCHIMARU, IS IT? DO NOT FRET.
I SHALL PRIORITIZE UNDOING THE ILL FEELINGS THAT ARE BINDING THIS CHILD.

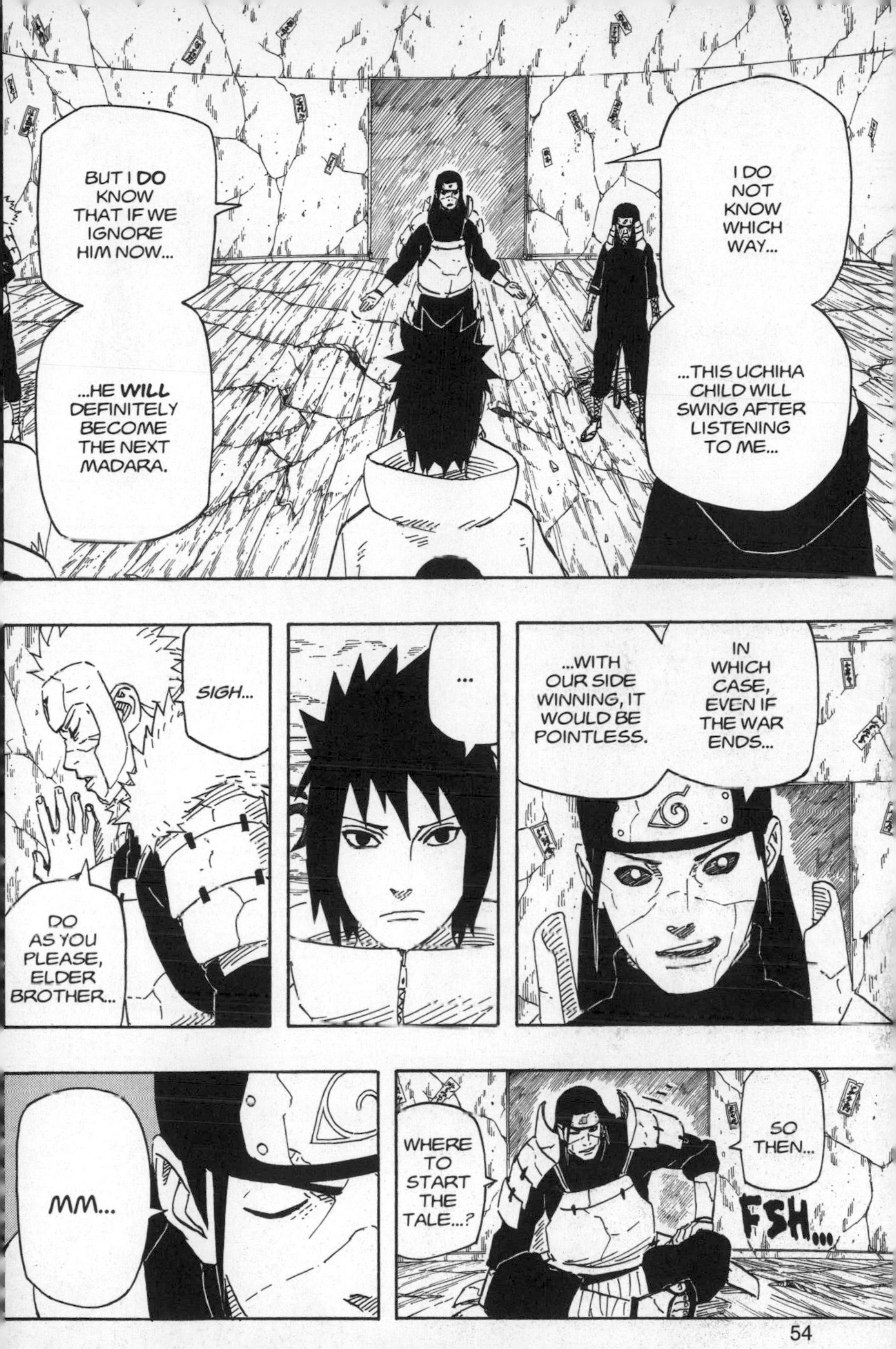
I DO NOT KNOW WHICH WAY...
...THIS UCHIHA CHILD WILL SWING AFTER LISTENING TO ME...
BUT I DO KNOW THAT IF WE IGNORE HIM NOW...
...HE WILL DEFINITELY BECOME THE NEXT MADARA.
IN WHICH CASE, EVEN IF THE WAR ENDS...
...WITH OUR SIDE WINNING, IT WOULD BE POINTLESS.
...
SIGH...
DO AS YOU PLEASE, ELDER BROTHER...
SO THEN...
FSH...
WHERE TO START THE TALE...?
MM...

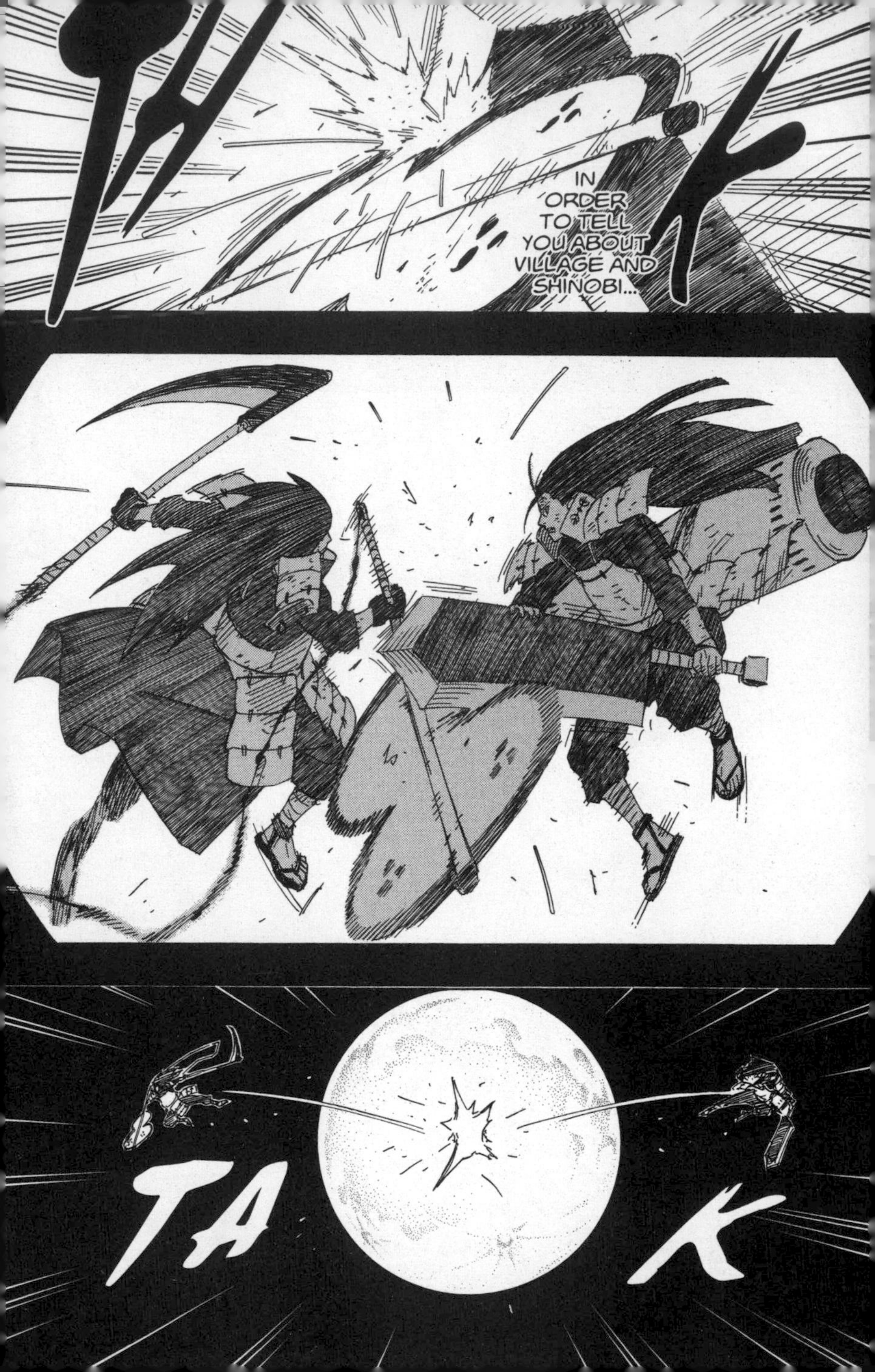
THWK
IN ORDER TO TELL YOU ABOUT VILLAGE AND SHINOBI...
TAK

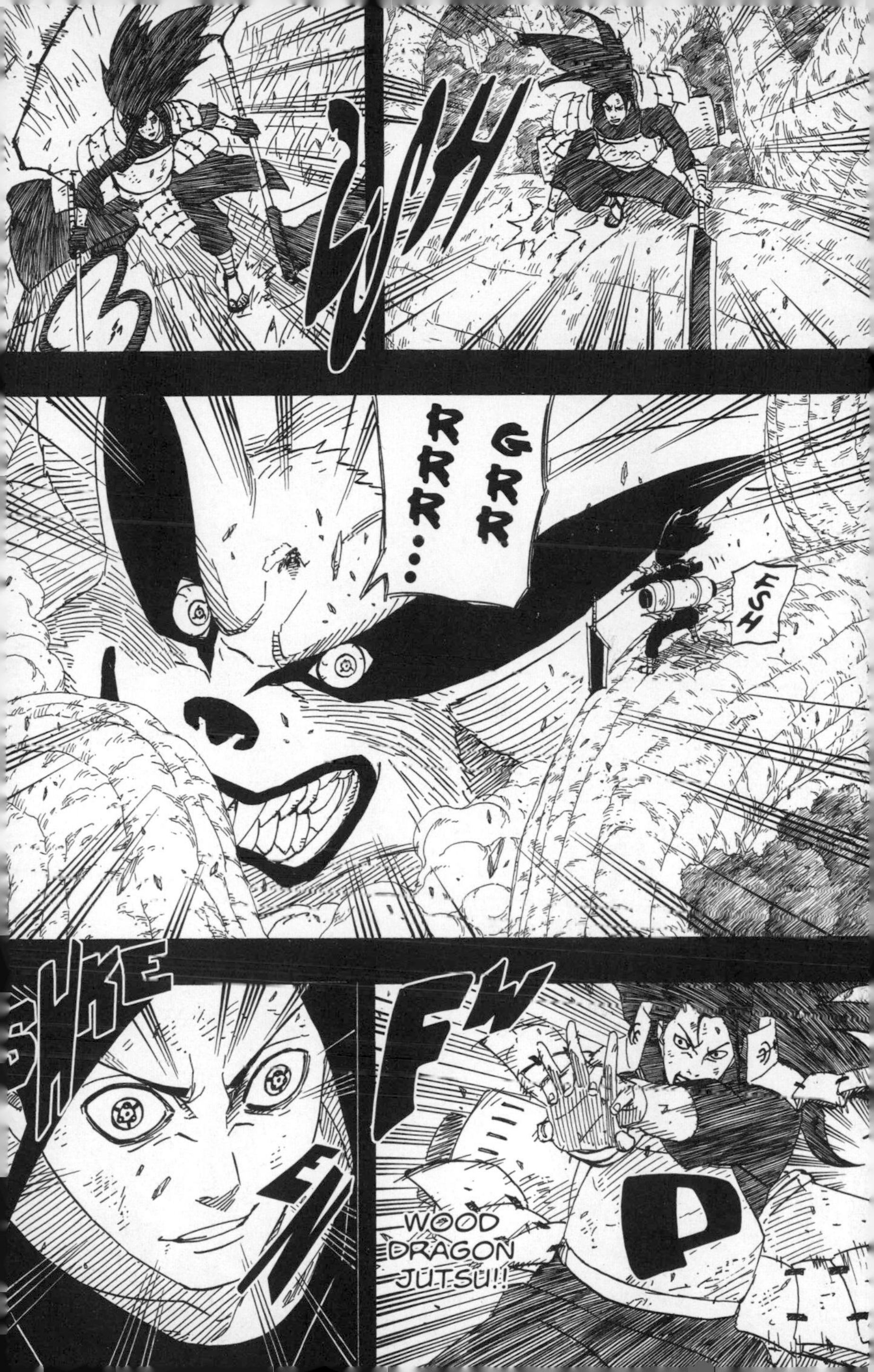
GRRR
RRR...
FSH
FW
P
WOOD DRAGON JUTSU!!

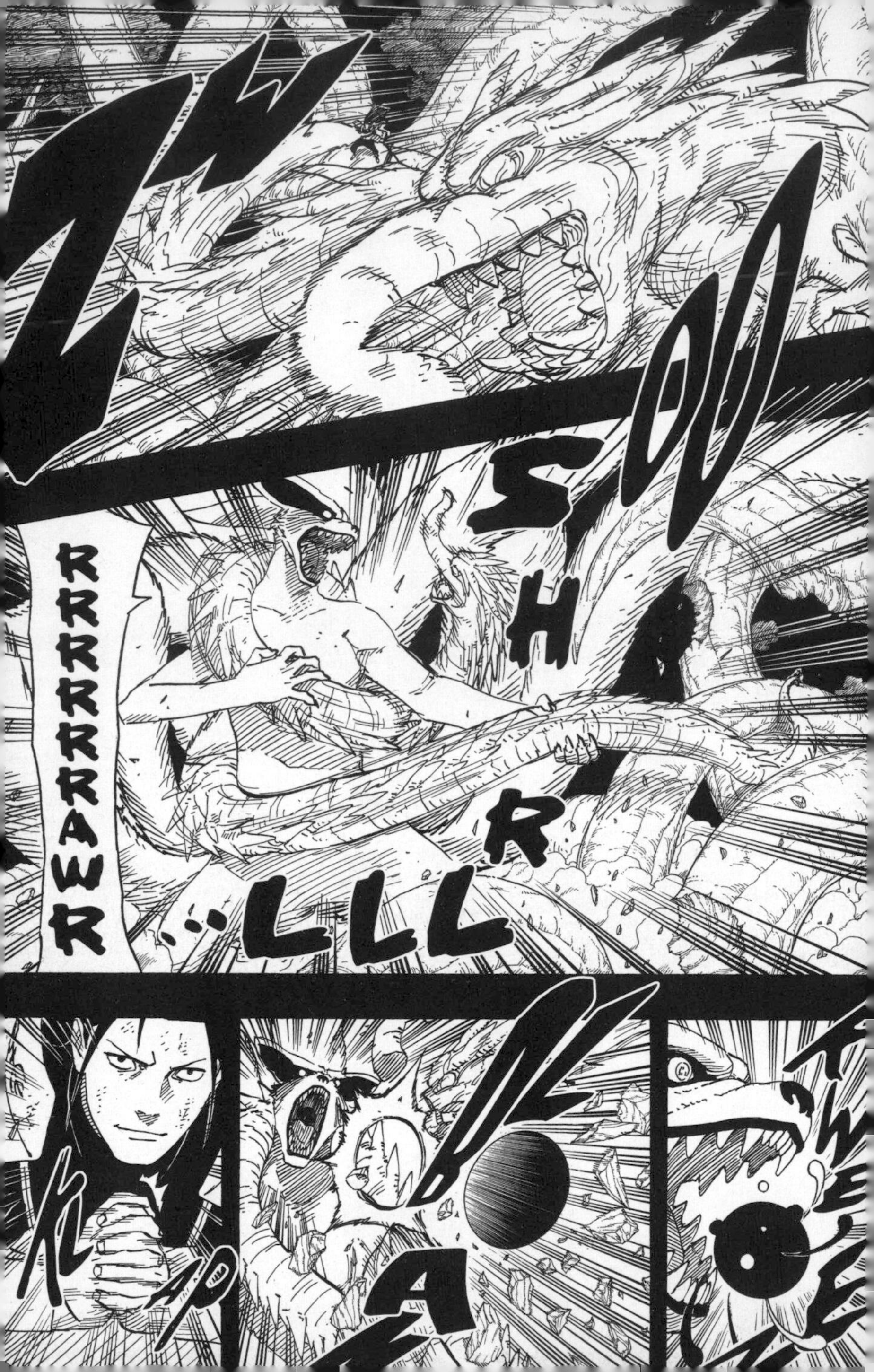
RRRRRRRAWR
KLAP

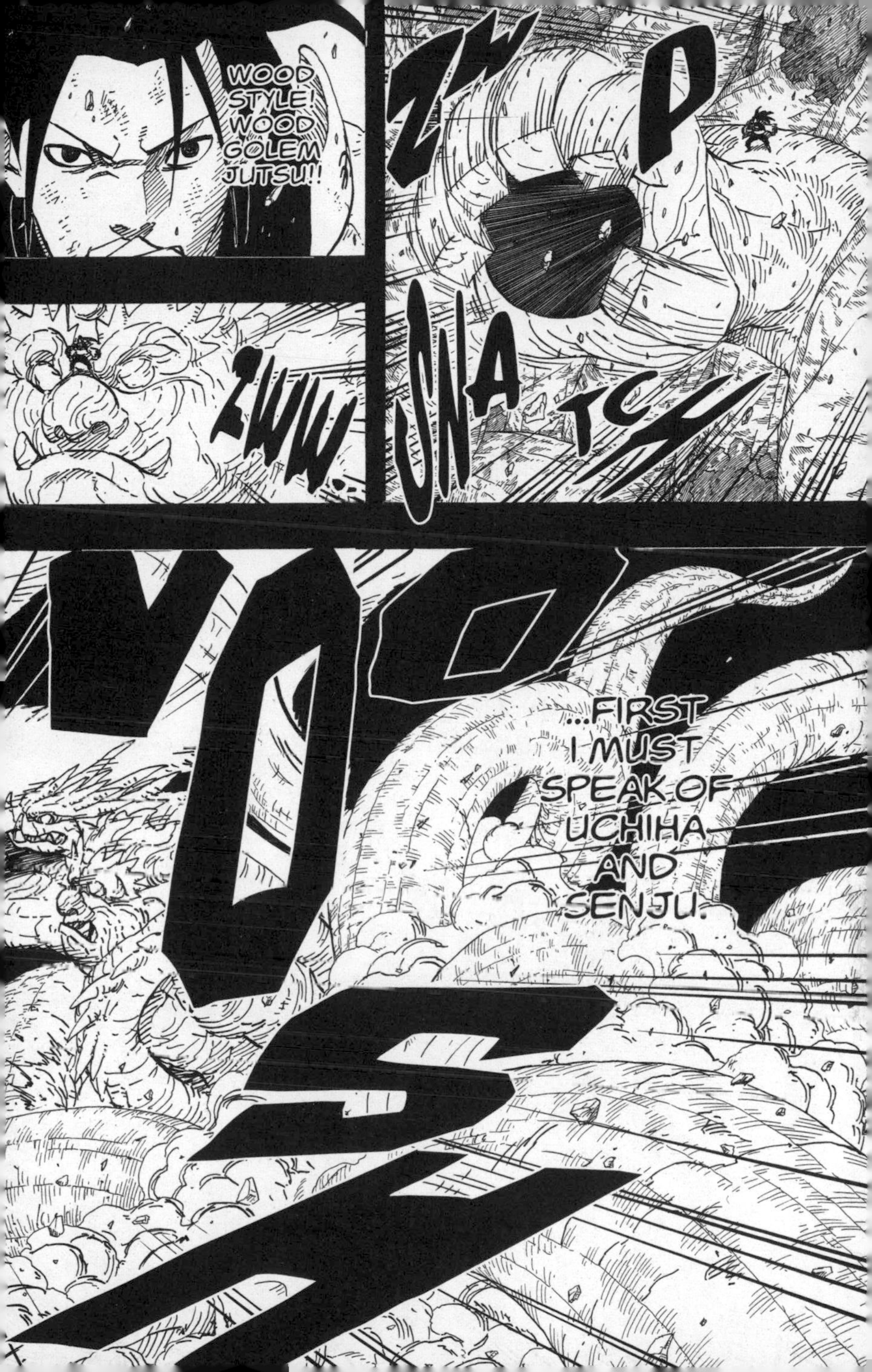
ZZZZP
WOOD STYLE! WOOD GOLEM JUTSU!!
SNATCH
ZWWW
...FIRST I MUST SPEAK OF UCHIHA AND SENJU.
WOOSH

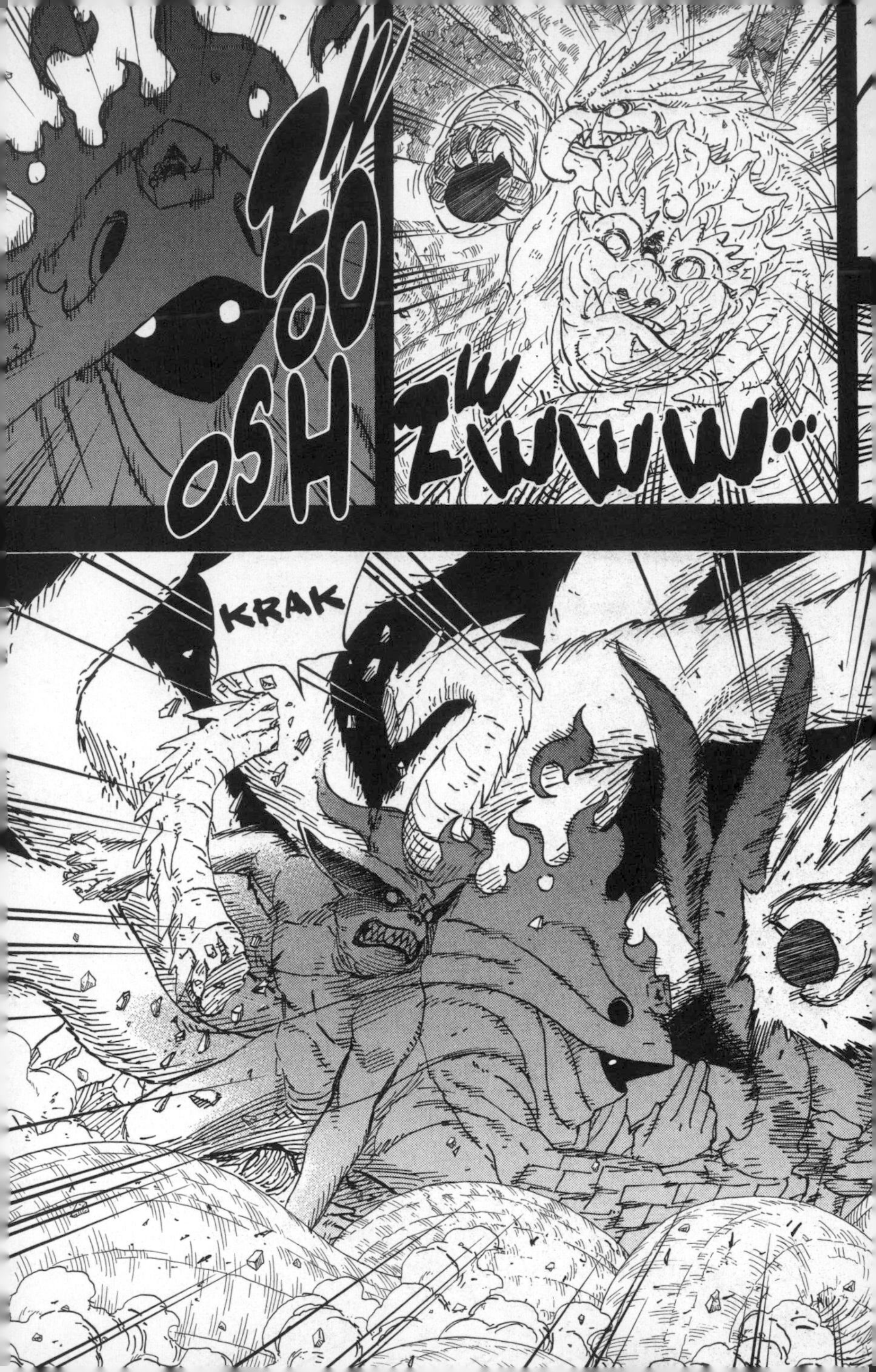
KRAK

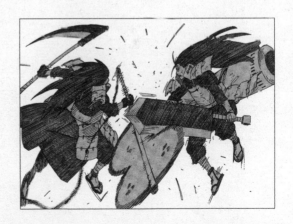

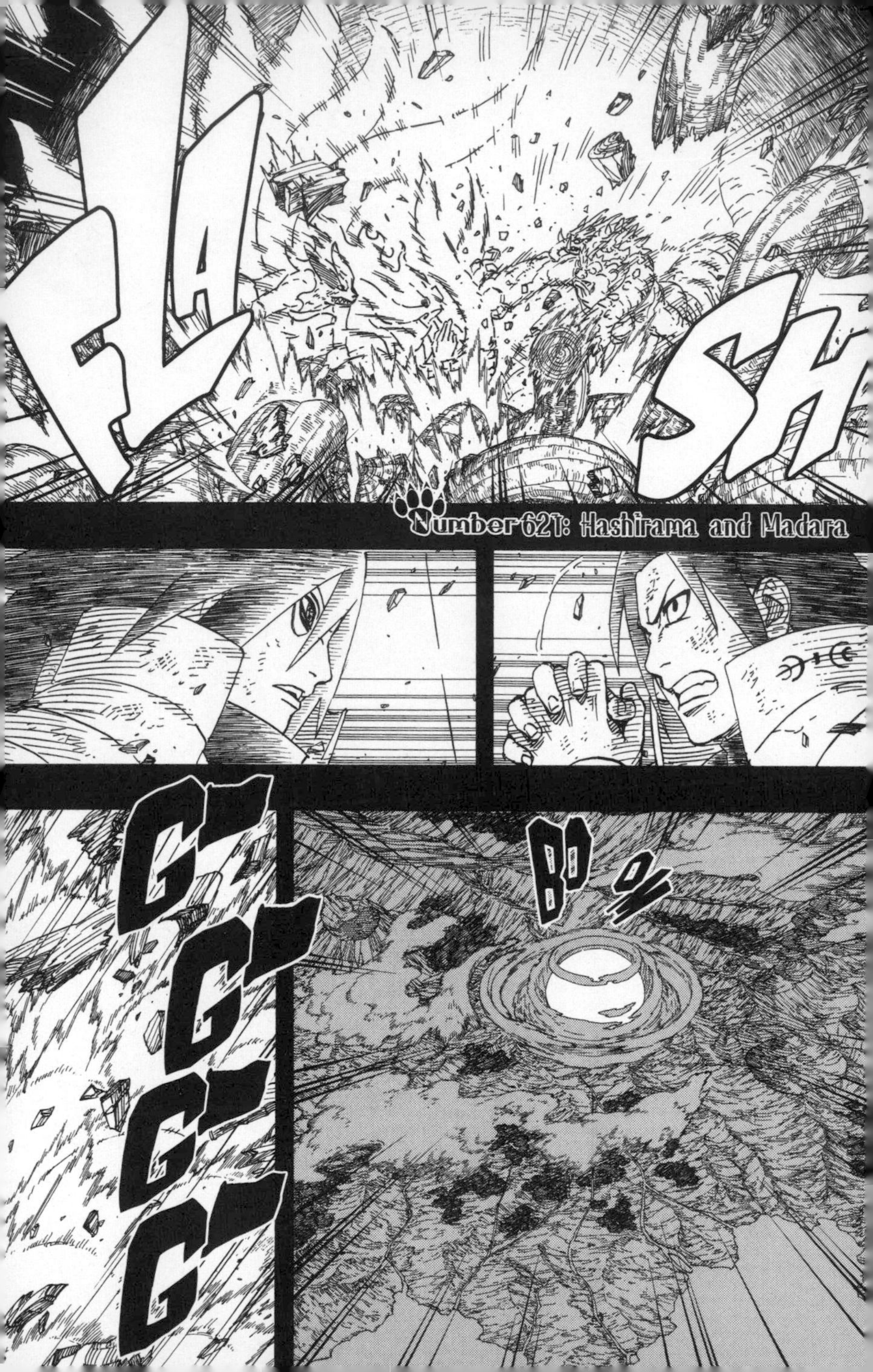
FLASH
Number 621: Hashirama and Madara
BOOM
GGGG

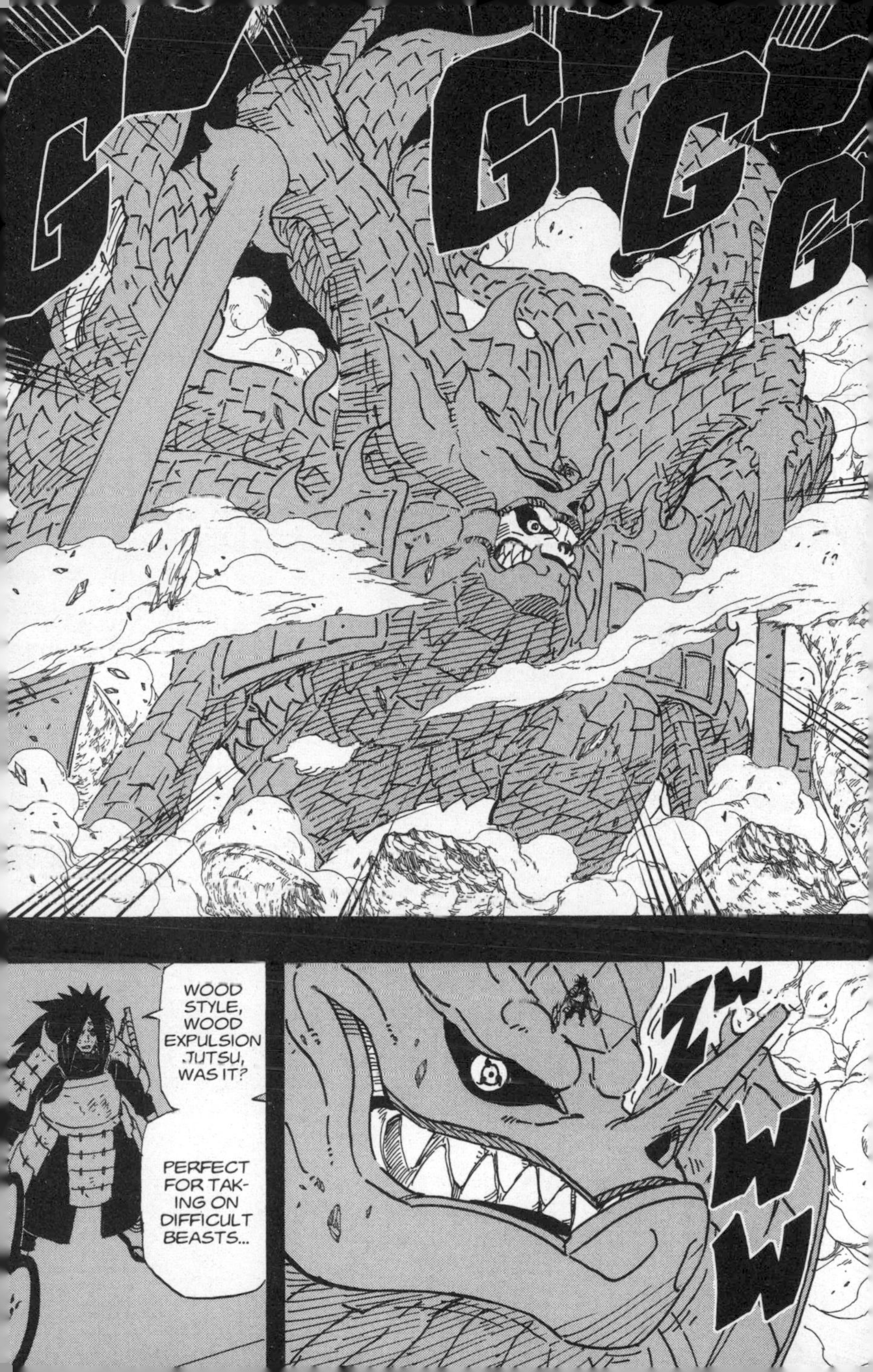
WOOD STYLE, WOOD EXPULSION JUTSU, WAS IT?
PERFECT FOR TAKING ON DIFFICULT BEASTS...

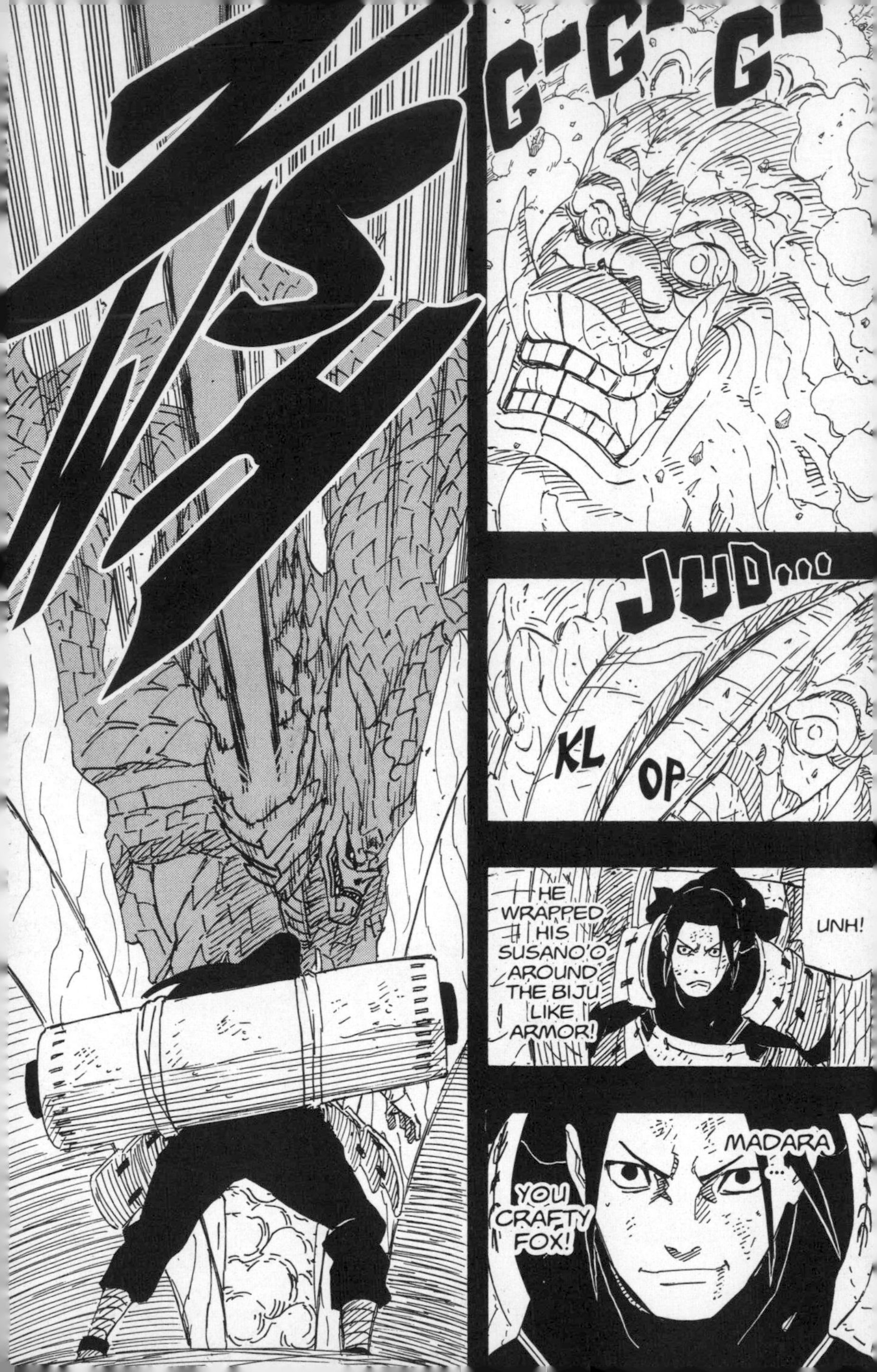
G-G-G
JUD...
KLOP
UNH!
HE WRAPPED HIS SUSANO'O AROUND THE BIJU LIKE ARMOR!
MADARA...
YOU CRAFTY FOX!

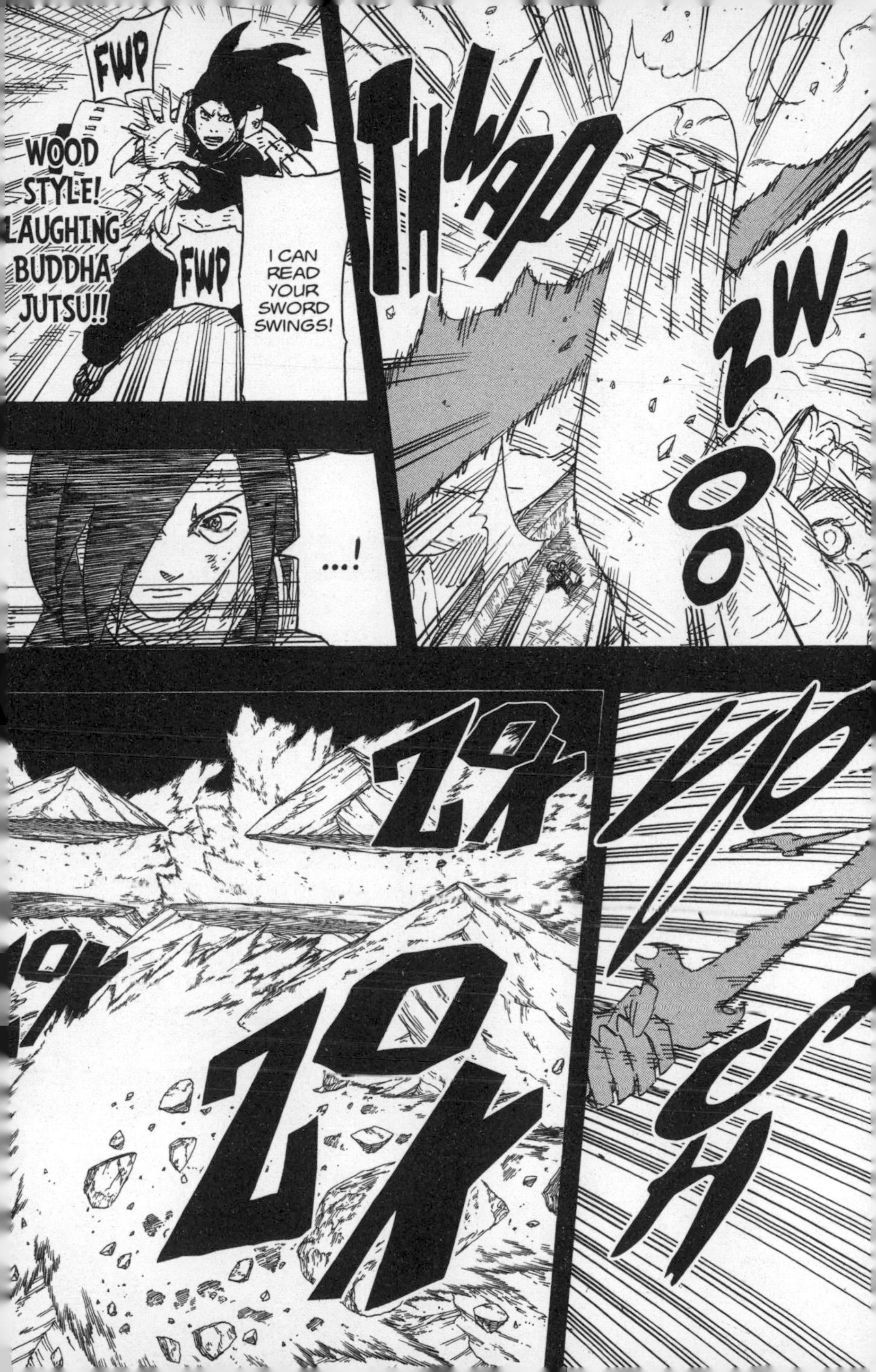
THWAP
ZWOO
FWP
WOOD STYLE! LAUGHING BUDDHA JUTSU!!
FWP
I CAN READ YOUR SWORD SWINGS!
...!

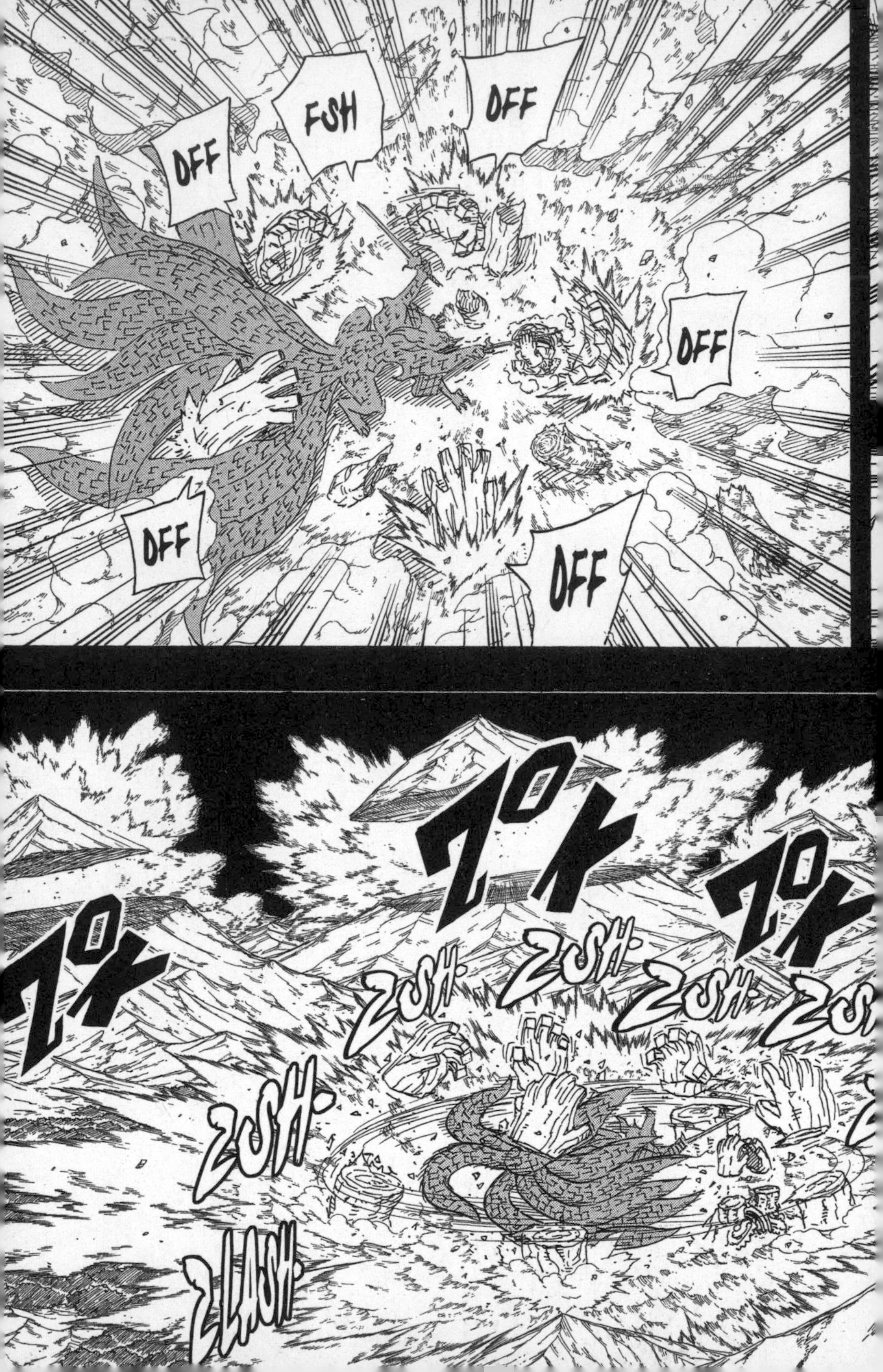

OFF
FSH
OFF
OFF
OFF
OFF
ZSH
ZSH
ZSH
ZSH
ZLASH

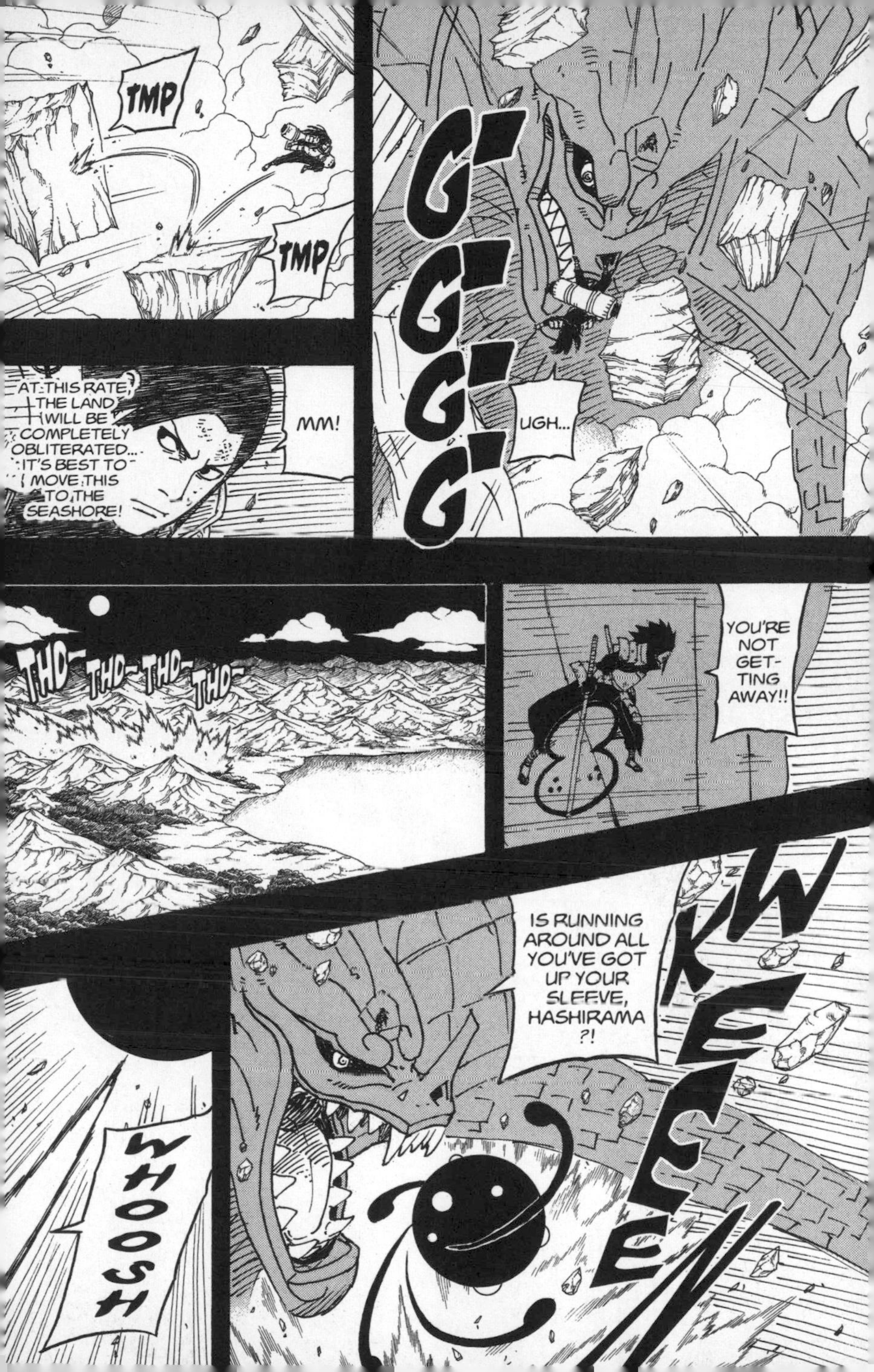
GIGIGIGIG
UGH...
TMP
TMP
MM!
AT THIS RATE, THE LAND WILL BE COMPLETELY OBLITERATED... IT'S BEST TO MOVE THIS TO THE SEASHORE!
YOU'RE NOT GET-TING AWAY!!
THD-THD-THD-THD-
IS RUNNING AROUND ALL YOU'VE GOT UP YOUR SLEEVE, HASHIRAMA?!
KWEEEEN
WHOOSH

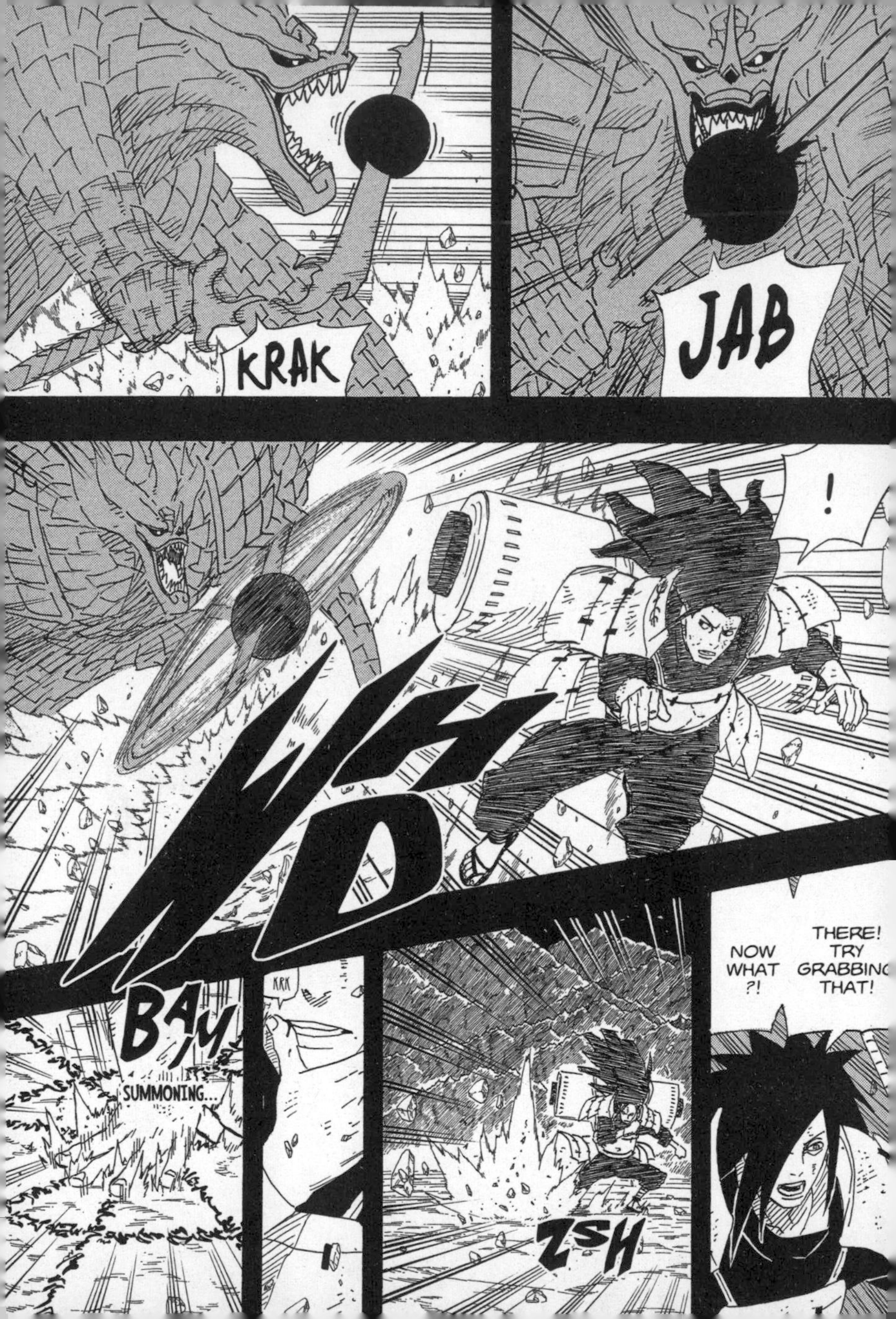
JAB
KRAK
!
THERE! TRY GRABBING THAT!
NOW WHAT ?!
ZSH
KRK
BAM
SUMMONING...

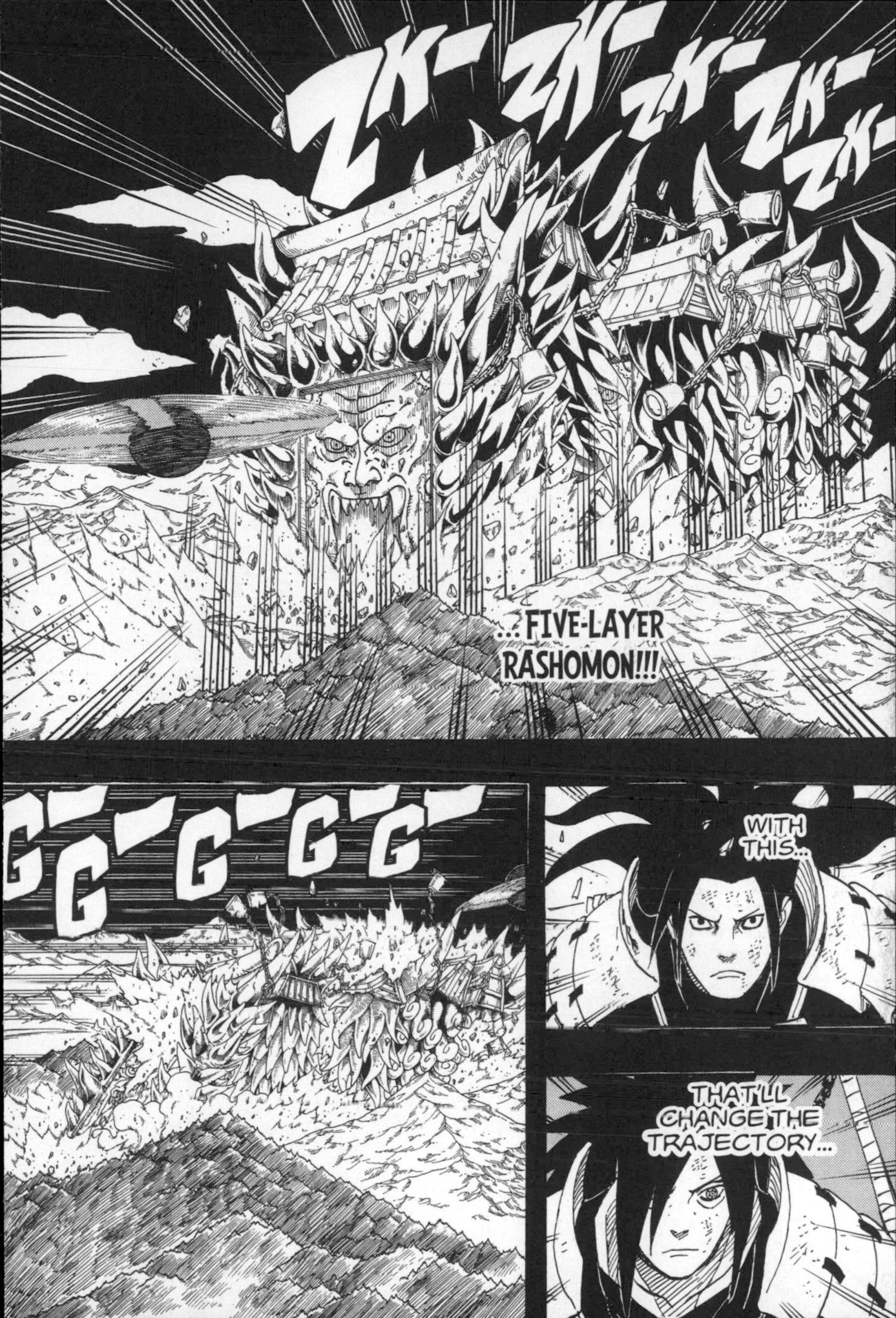
ZK- ZK- ZK- ZK- ZK- ZK-
...FIVE-LAYER RASHOMON!!!
WITH THIS...
THAT'LL CHANGE THE TRAJECTORY...
G- G- G- G- G-

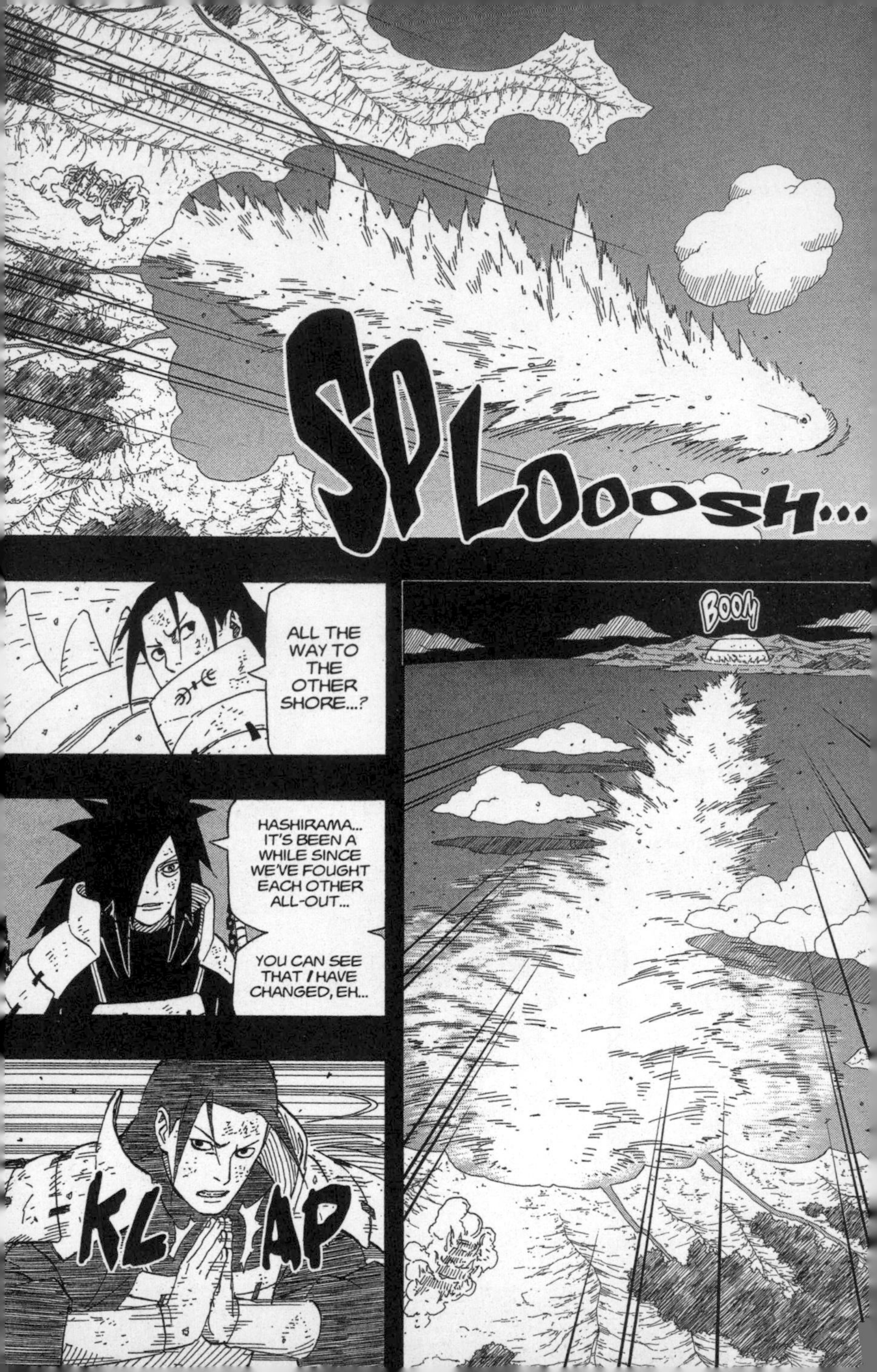
SPLOOOSH...
BOOM
ALL THE WAY TO THE OTHER SHORE...?
HASHIRAMA... IT'S BEEN A WHILE SINCE WE'VE FOUGHT EACH OTHER ALL-OUT...
YOU CAN SEE THAT I HAVE CHANGED, EH...
KLAP

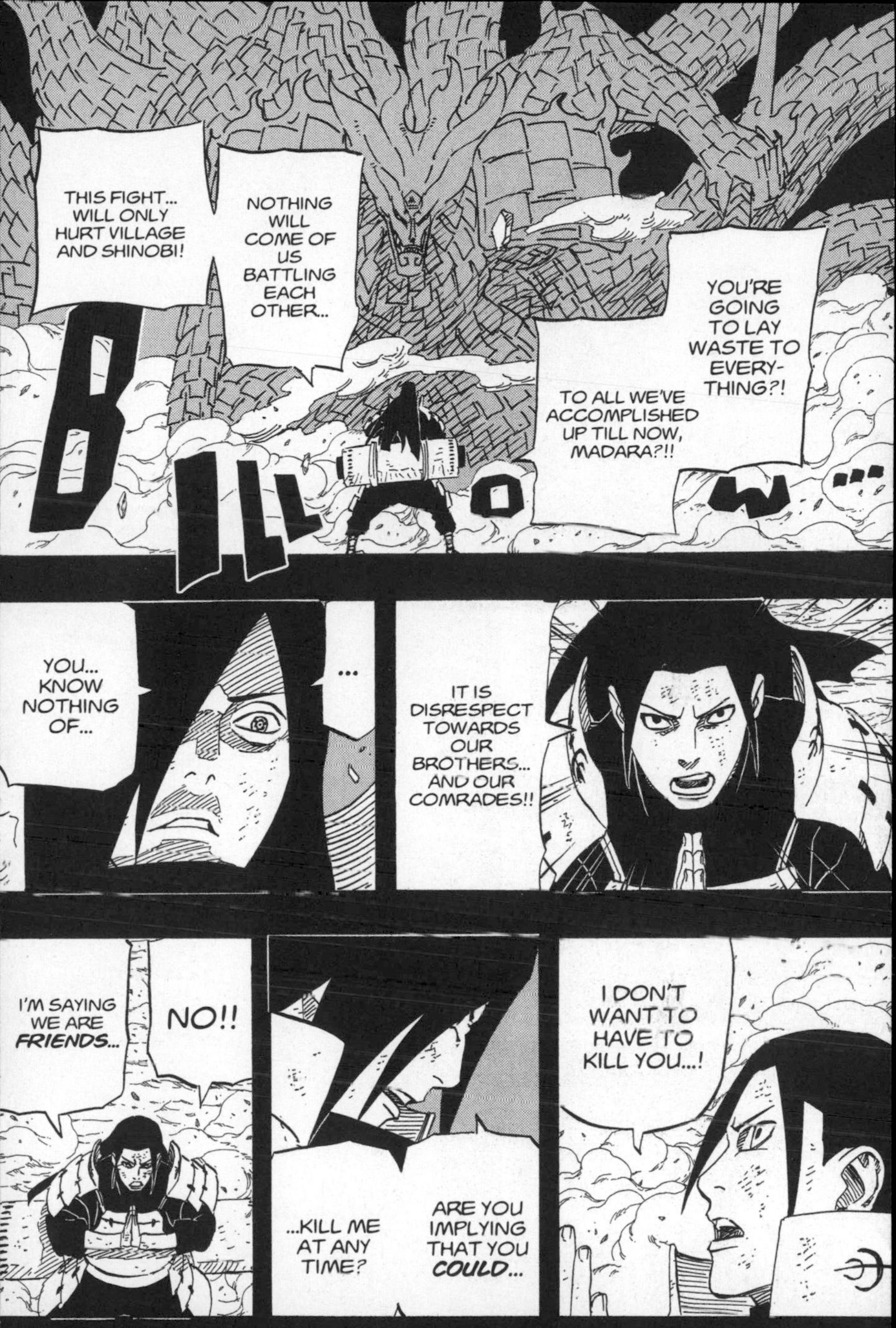
YOU'RE GOING TO LAY WASTE TO EVERYTHING?!
TO ALL WE'VE ACCOMPLISHED UP TILL NOW, MADARA?!!
NOTHING WILL COME OF US BATTLING EACH OTHER...
THIS FIGHT... WILL ONLY HURT VILLAGE AND SHINOBI!
BILLOW...
IT IS DISRESPECT TOWARDS OUR BROTHERS... AND OUR COMRADES!!
...
YOU... KNOW NOTHING OF...
I DON'T WANT TO HAVE TO KILL YOU...!
ARE YOU IMPLYING THAT YOU ***COULD***...
...KILL ME AT ANY TIME?
NO!!
I'M SAYING WE ARE ***FRIENDS***...

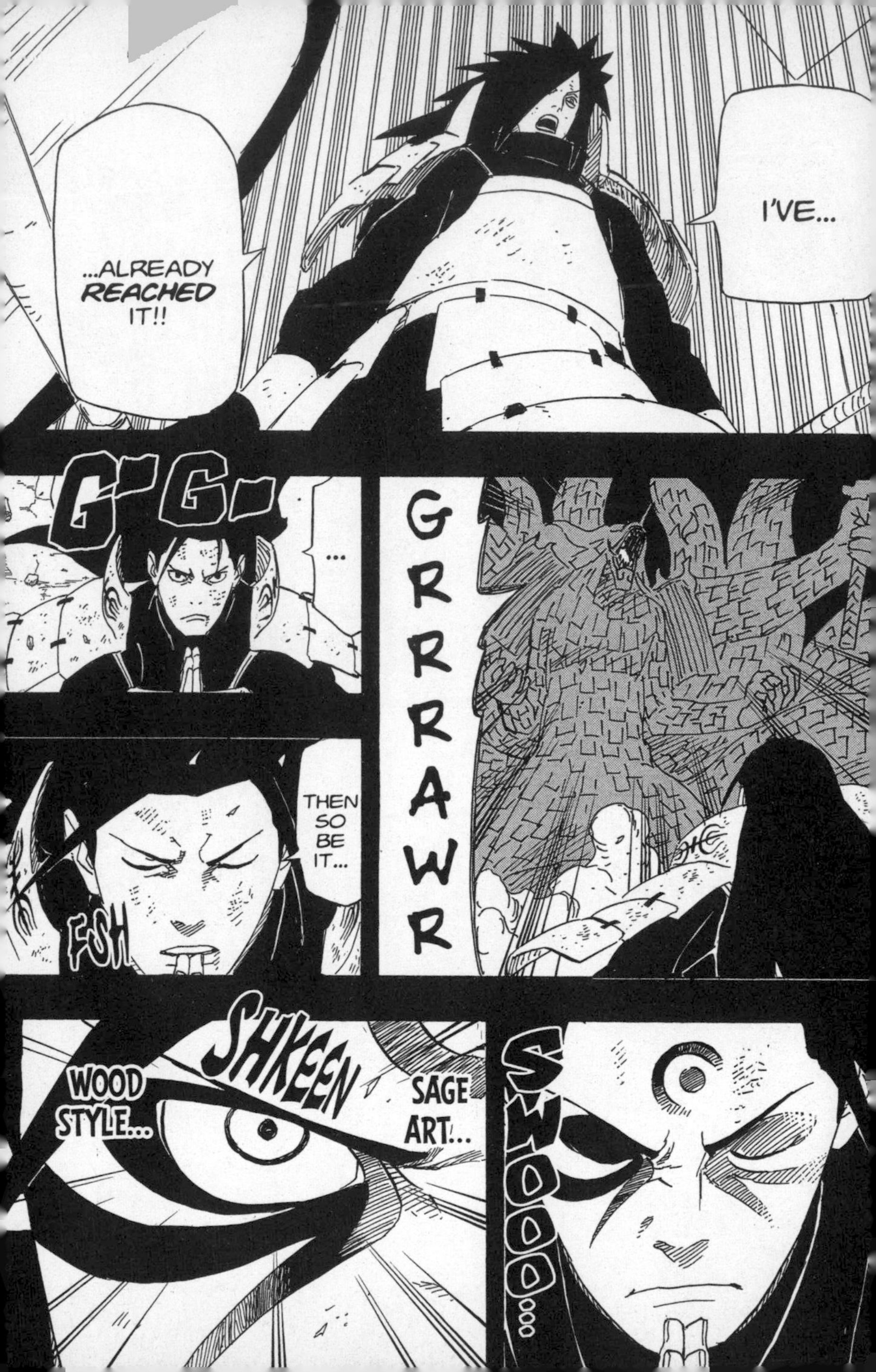
I'VE...
...ALREADY REACHED IT!!
GRRRAWR
G'G-
...
THEN SO BE IT...
FSH
SWOOO...
SHKEEN
SAGE ART...
WOOD STYLE...

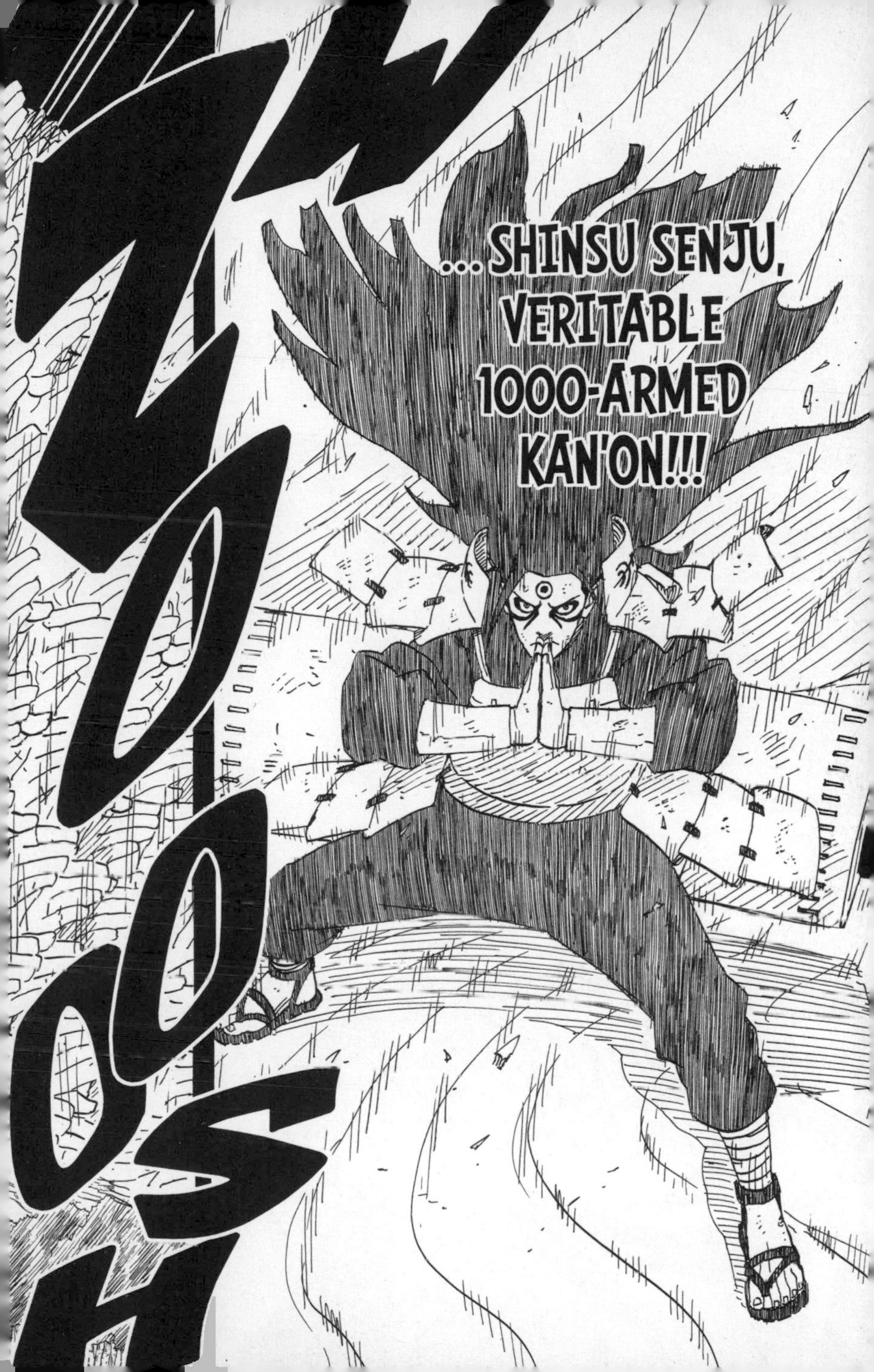
...SHINSU SENJU, VERITABLE 1000-ARMED KAN'ON!!!
WHOOOSH

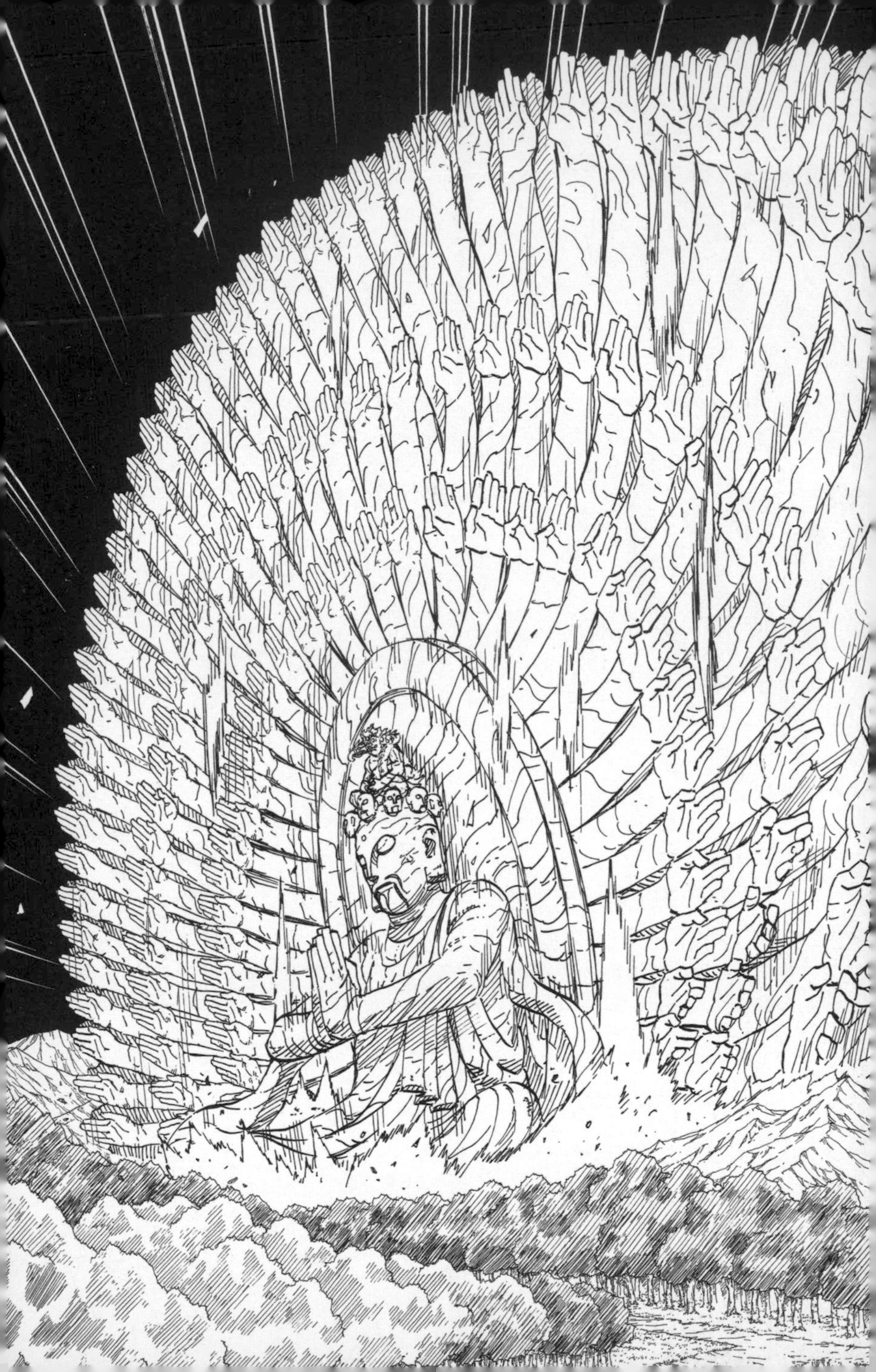

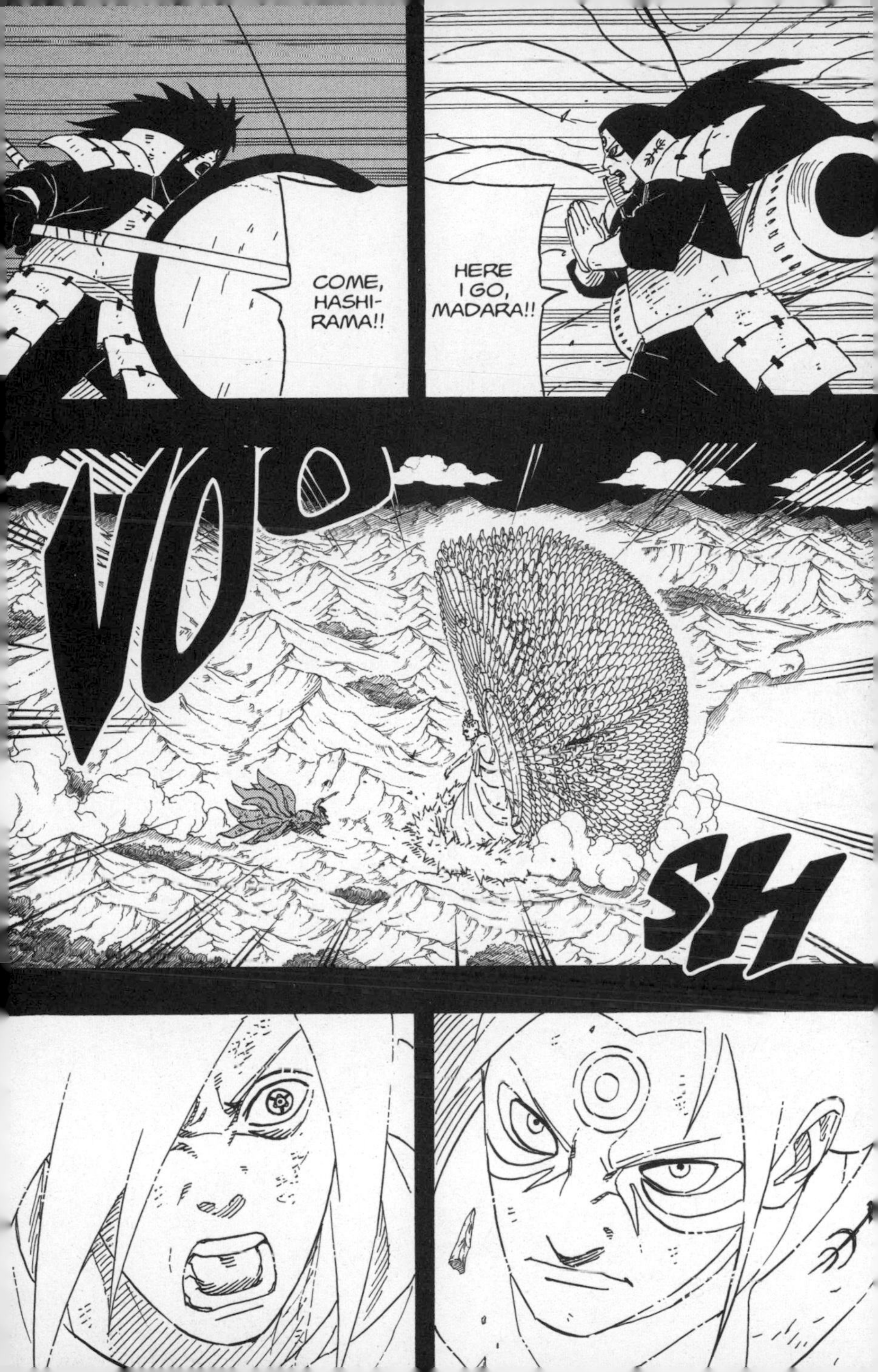
HERE I GO, MADARA!!
COME, HASHI-RAMA!!
VOO
SH

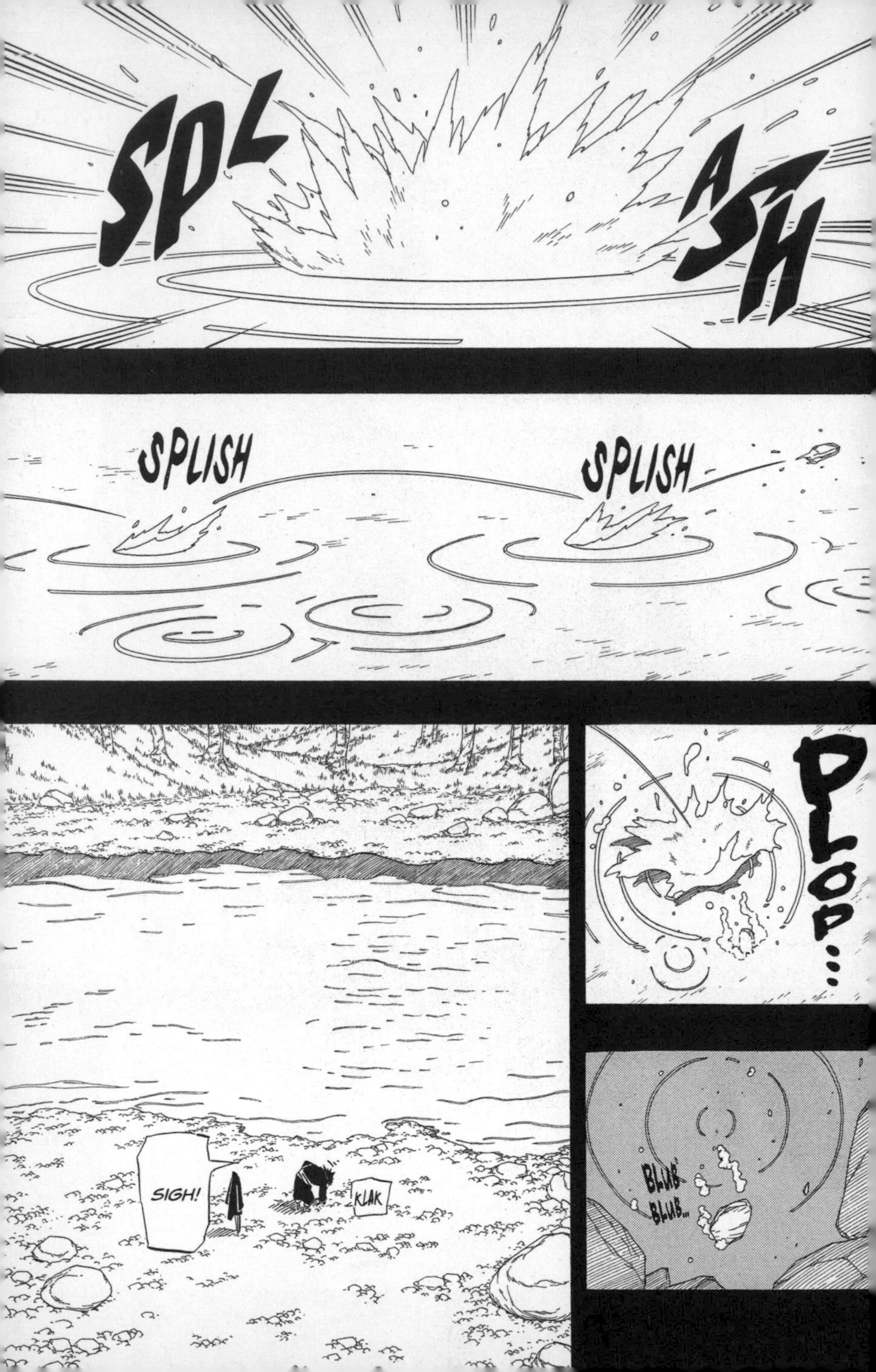
SPLASH
SPLISH
SPLISH
PLOP...
BLUB BLUB...
KLAK
SIGH!

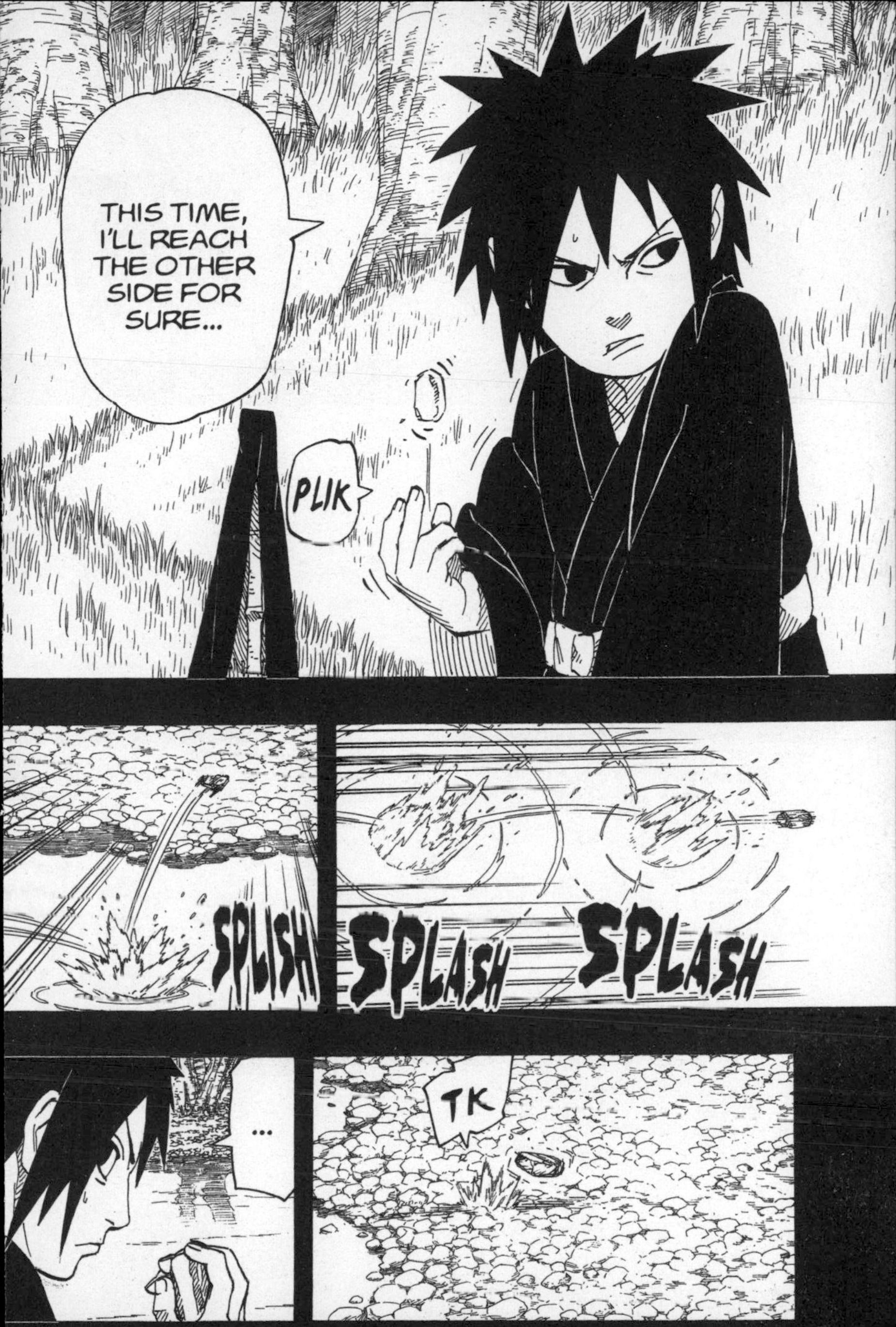
THIS TIME, I'LL REACH THE OTHER SIDE FOR SURE...
PLIK
SPLASH
SPLASH
SPLISH
TK
...

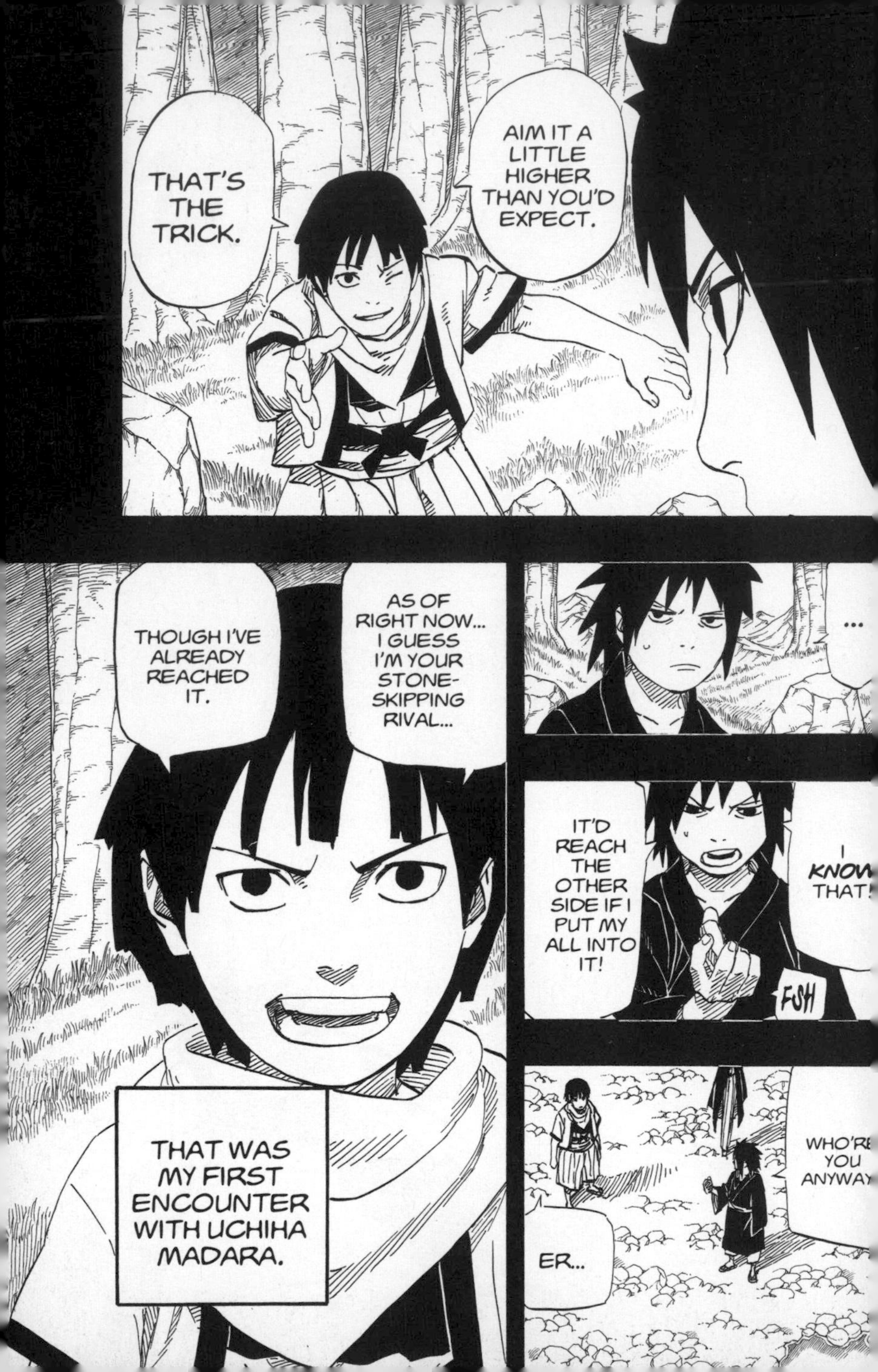
AIM IT A LITTLE HIGHER THAN YOU'D EXPECT.
THAT'S THE TRICK.
...
I KNOW THAT!
IT'D REACH THE OTHER SIDE IF I PUT MY ALL INTO IT!
FSH
WHO'RE YOU ANYWAY
ER...
AS OF RIGHT NOW... I GUESS I'M YOUR STONE-SKIPPING RIVAL...
THOUGH I'VE ALREADY REACHED IT.
THAT WAS MY FIRST ENCOUNTER WITH UCHIHA MADARA.

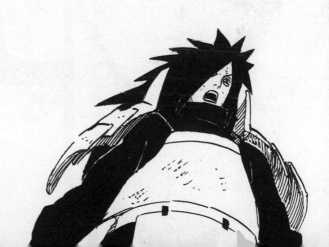

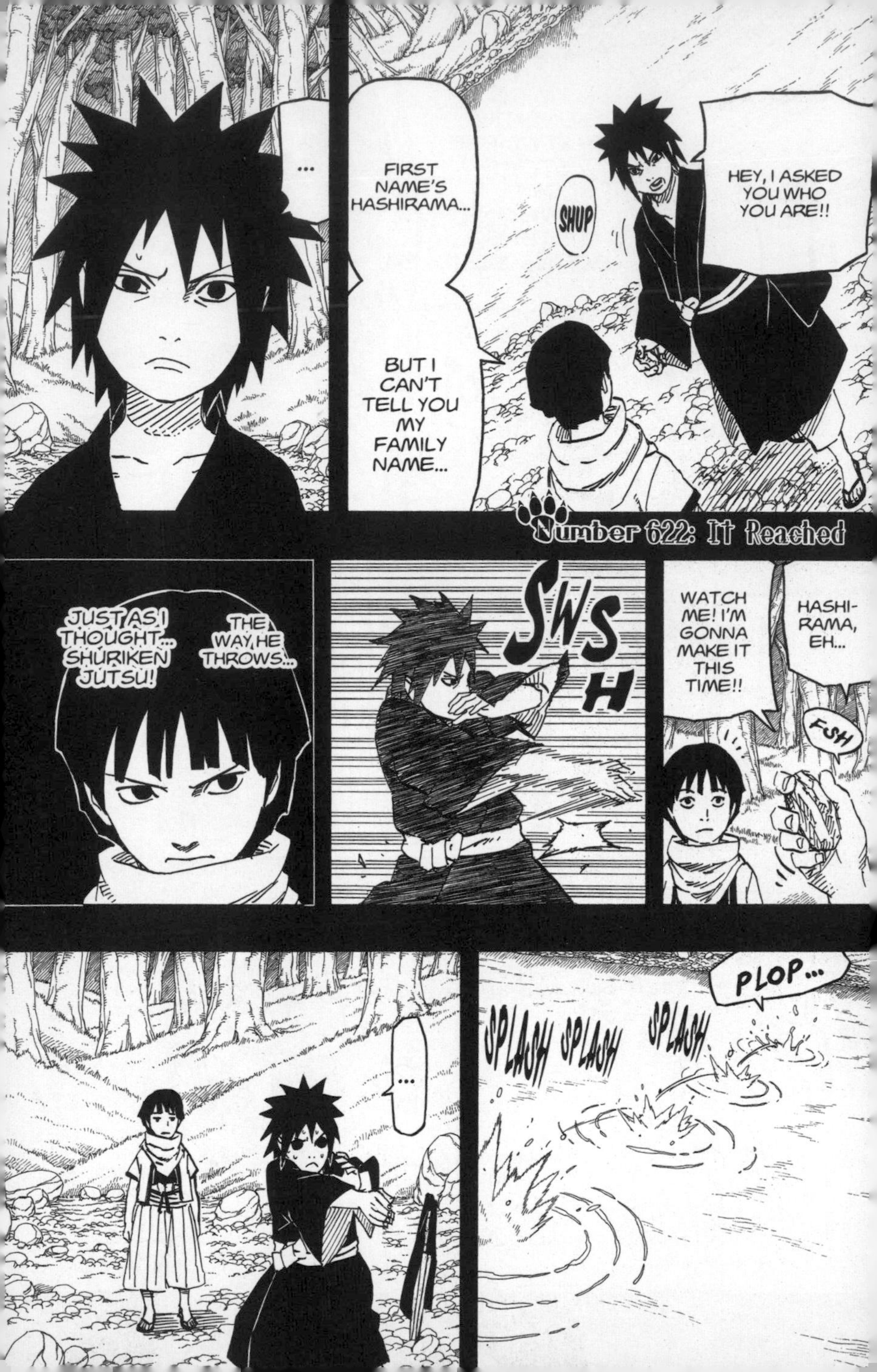
HEY, I ASKED YOU WHO YOU ARE!!
SHUP
FIRST NAME'S HASHIRAMA...
BUT I CAN'T TELL YOU MY FAMILY NAME...
...
Number 622: It Reached
HASHI-RAMA, EH...
WATCH ME! I'M GONNA MAKE IT THIS TIME!!
FSH
SWSH
THE WAY HE THROWS...
JUST AS I THOUGHT... SHURIKEN JUTSU!
PLOP...
SPLASH
SPLASH
SPLASH
...

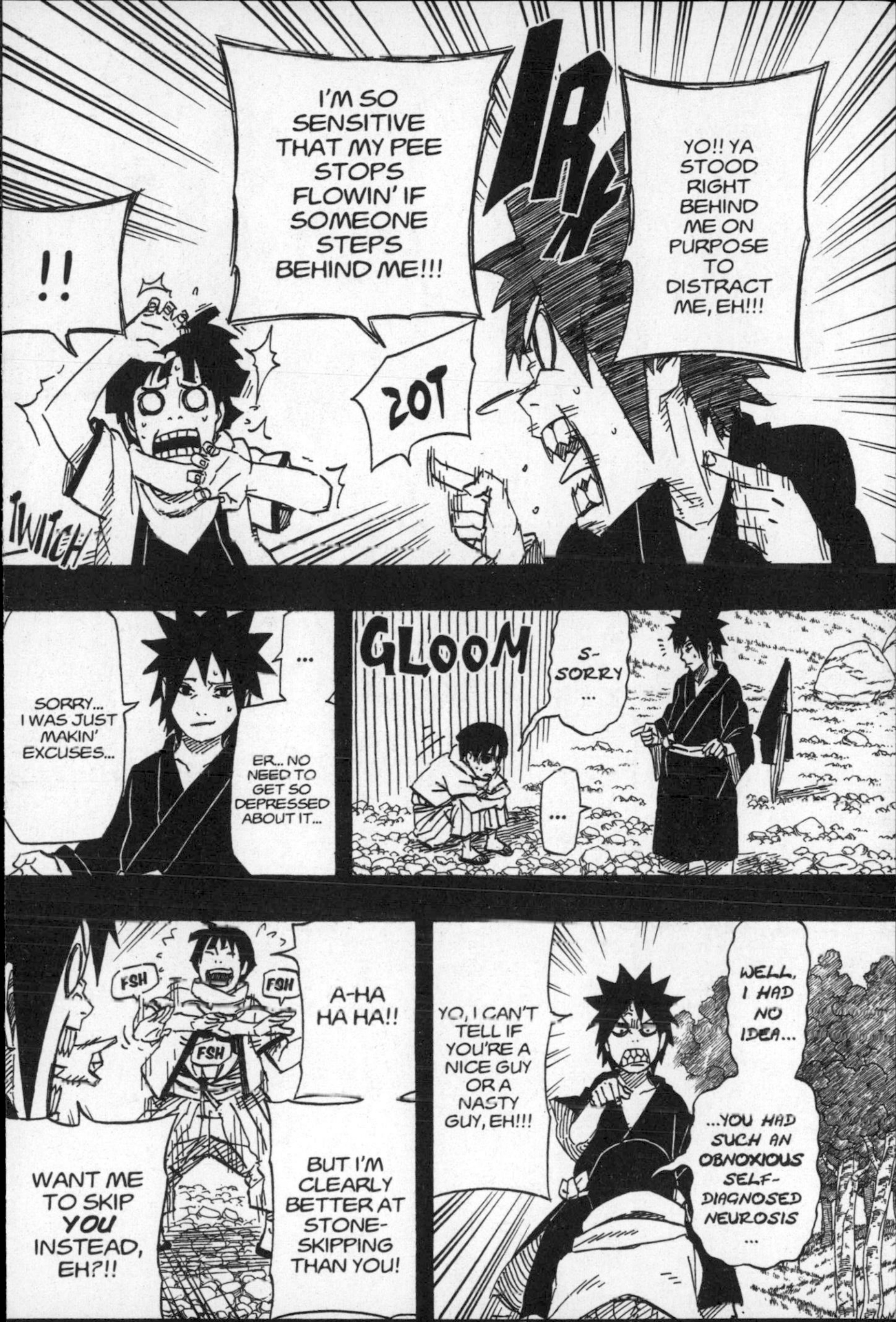
IRK
YO!! YA STOOD RIGHT BEHIND ME ON PURPOSE TO DISTRACT ME, EH!!!
I'M SO SENSITIVE THAT MY PEE STOPS FLOWIN' IF SOMEONE STEPS BEHIND ME!!!
ZOT
!!
TWITCH
GLOOM
S-SORRY...
...
...
SORRY... I WAS JUST MAKIN' EXCUSES...
ER... NO NEED TO GET SO DEPRESSED ABOUT IT...
WELL, I HAD NO IDEA...
...YOU HAD SUCH AN OBNOXIOUS SELF-DIAGNOSED NEUROSIS...
YO, I CAN'T TELL IF YOU'RE A NICE GUY OR A NASTY GUY, EH!!!
A-HA HA HA!!
FSH
FSH
FSH
BUT I'M CLEARLY BETTER AT STONE-SKIPPING THAN YOU!
WANT ME TO SKIP YOU INSTEAD, EH?!!

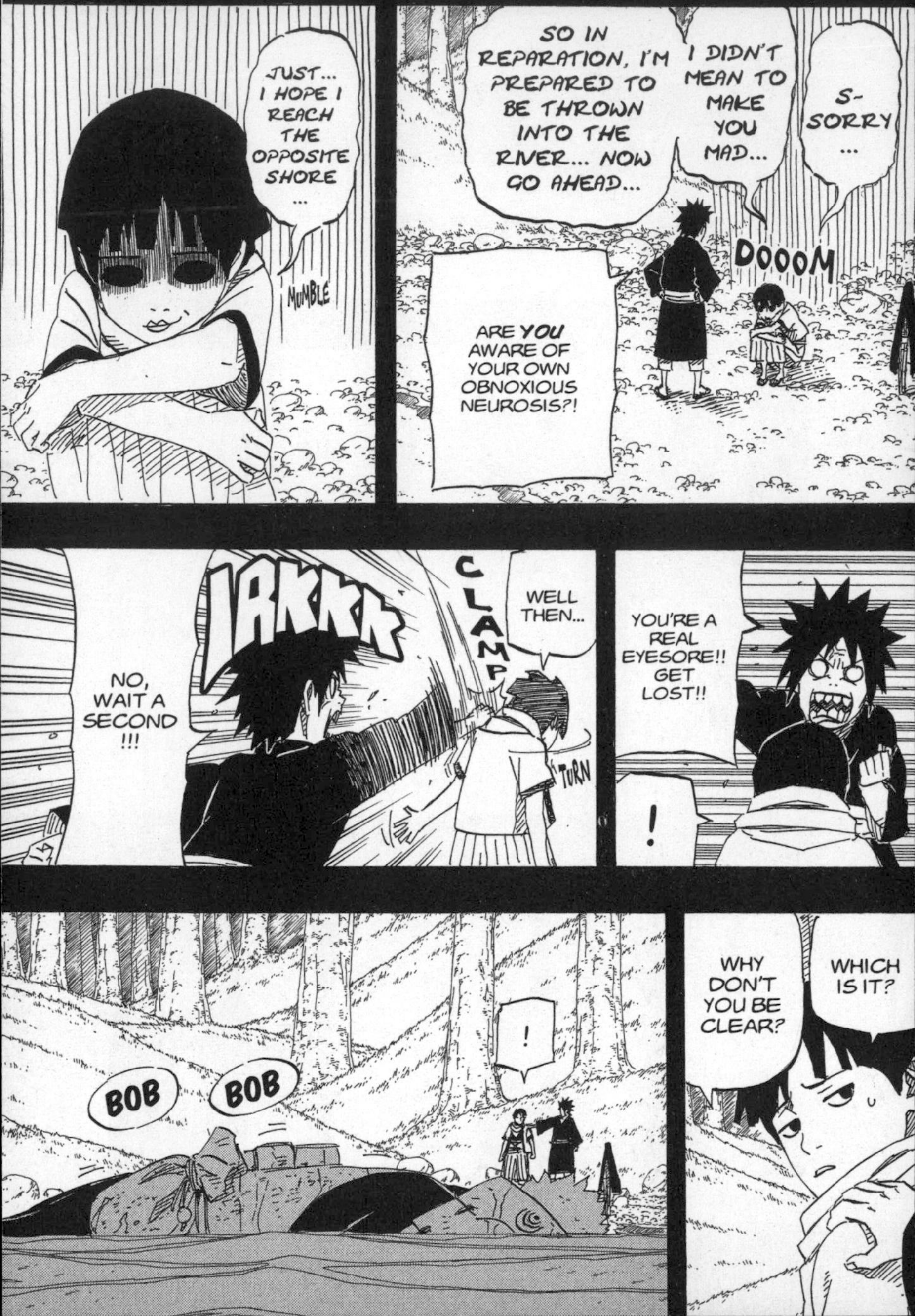
S-SORRY ...
I DIDN'T MEAN TO MAKE YOU MAD...
SO IN REPARATION, I'M PREPARED TO BE THROWN INTO THE RIVER... NOW GO AHEAD...
DOOOM
ARE YOU AWARE OF YOUR OWN OBNOXIOUS NEUROSIS?!
JUST... I HOPE I REACH THE OPPOSITE SHORE ...
MUMBLE
YOU'RE A REAL EYESORE!! GET LOST!!
!
WELL THEN...
CLAMP
TURN
NO, WAIT A SECOND !!!
WHICH IS IT?
WHY DON'T YOU BE CLEAR?
!
BOB
BOB

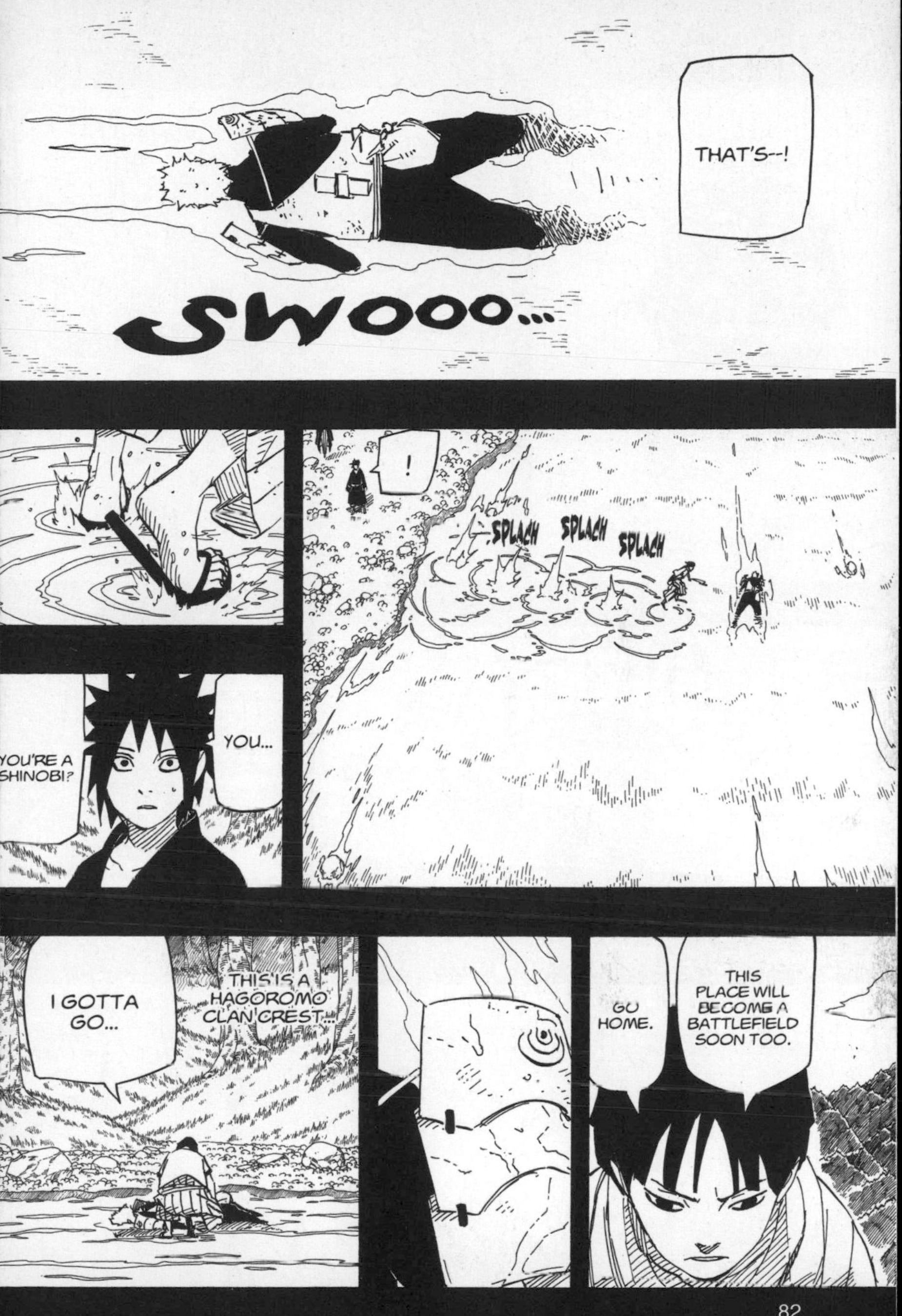
THAT'S--!
SWOOO...
!
SPLACH
SPLACH
SPLACH
YOU...
YOU'RE A SHINOBI?
THIS PLACE WILL BECOME A BATTLEFIELD SOON TOO.
GO HOME.
THIS IS A HAGOROMO CLAN CREST...
I GOTTA GO...

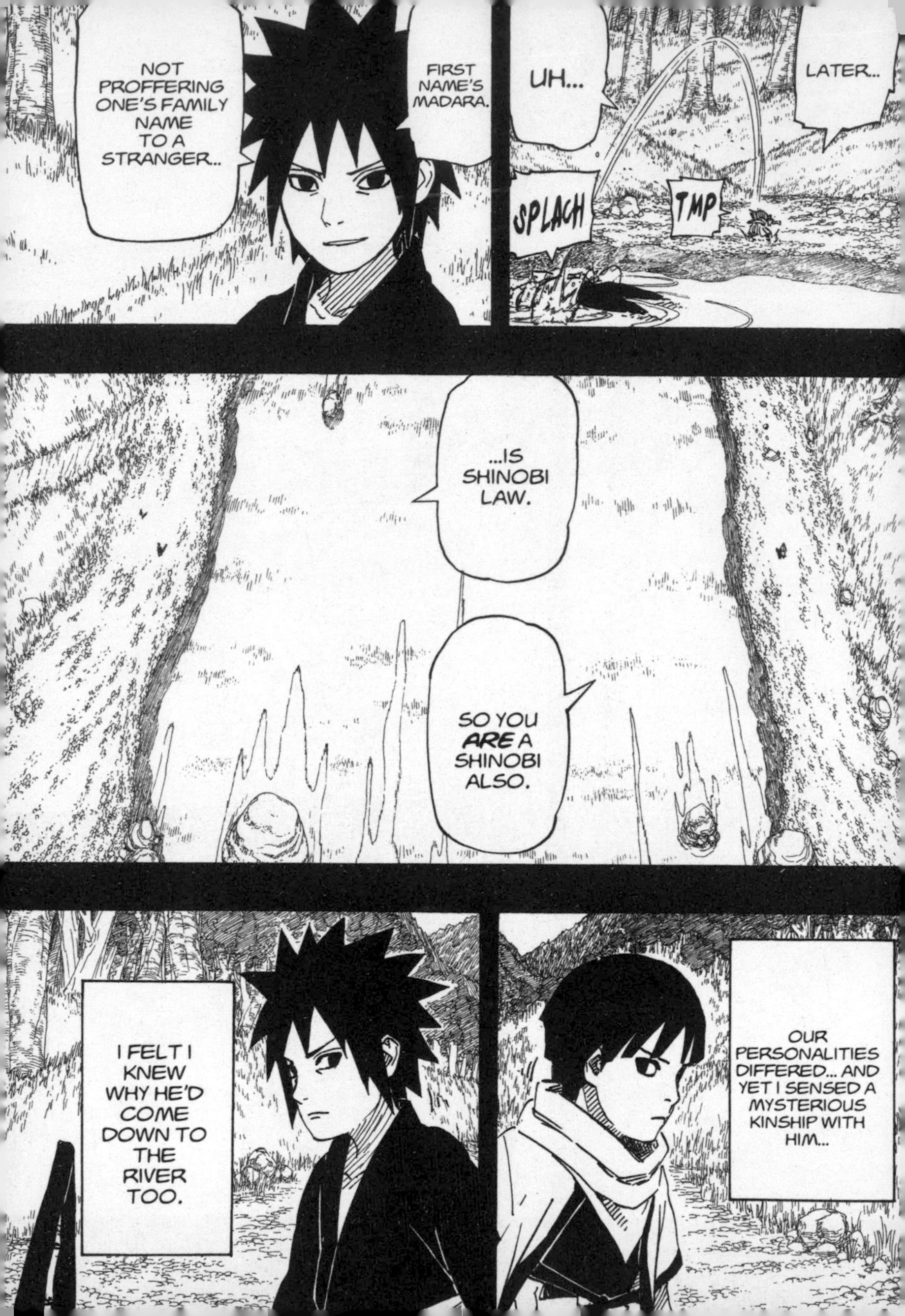
LATER...
UH...
TMP
SPLACH
FIRST NAME'S MADARA.
NOT PROFFERING ONE'S FAMILY NAME TO A STRANGER...
...IS SHINOBI LAW.
SO YOU ARE A SHINOBI ALSO.
OUR PERSONALITIES DIFFERED... AND YET I SENSED A MYSTERIOUS KINSHIP WITH HIM...
I FELT I KNEW WHY HE'D COME DOWN TO THE RIVER TOO.

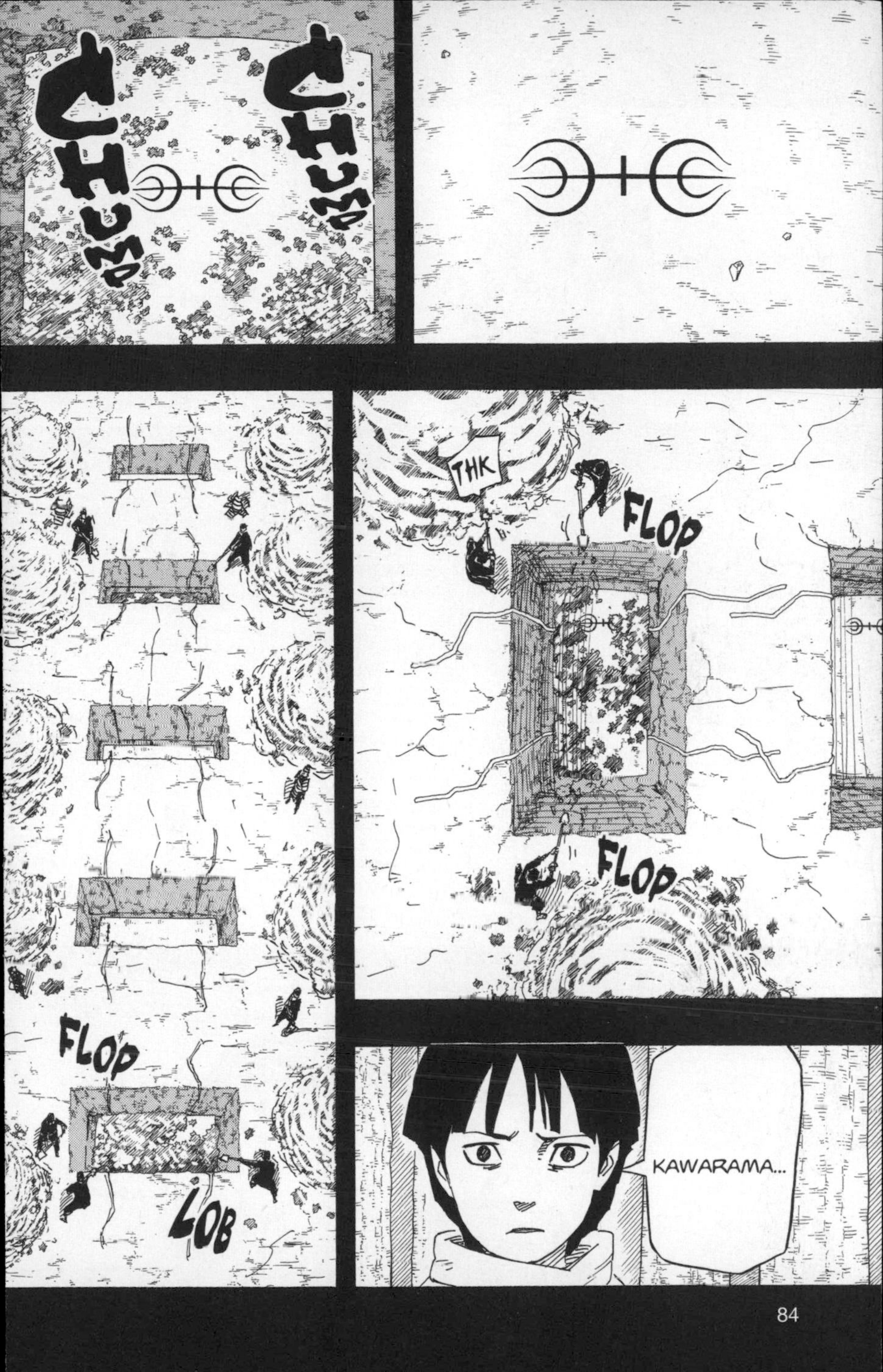
CHUMP
CHUMP
THK
FLOP
FLOP
KAWARAMA...
FLOP
LOB

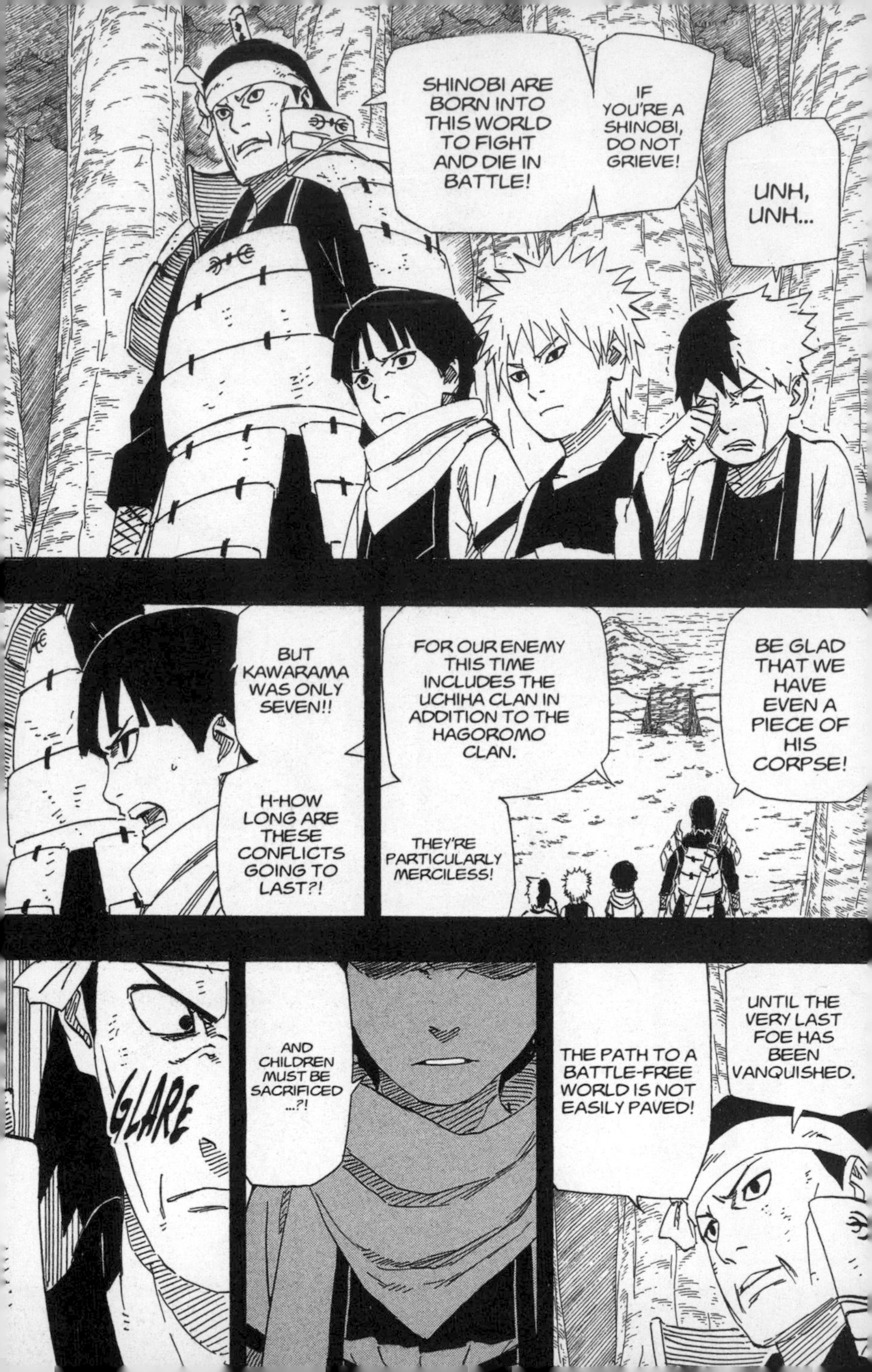
UNH, UNH...
IF YOU'RE A SHINOBI, DO NOT GRIEVE!
SHINOBI ARE BORN INTO THIS WORLD TO FIGHT AND DIE IN BATTLE!
BE GLAD THAT WE HAVE EVEN A PIECE OF HIS CORPSE!
FOR OUR ENEMY THIS TIME INCLUDES THE UCHIHA CLAN IN ADDITION TO THE HAGOROMO CLAN.
THEY'RE PARTICULARLY MERCILESS!
BUT KAWARAMA WAS ONLY SEVEN!!
H-HOW LONG ARE THESE CONFLICTS GOING TO LAST?!
UNTIL THE VERY LAST FOE HAS BEEN VANQUISHED.
THE PATH TO A BATTLE-FREE WORLD IS NOT EASILY PAVED!
AND CHILDREN MUST BE SACRIFICED ...?!
GLARE

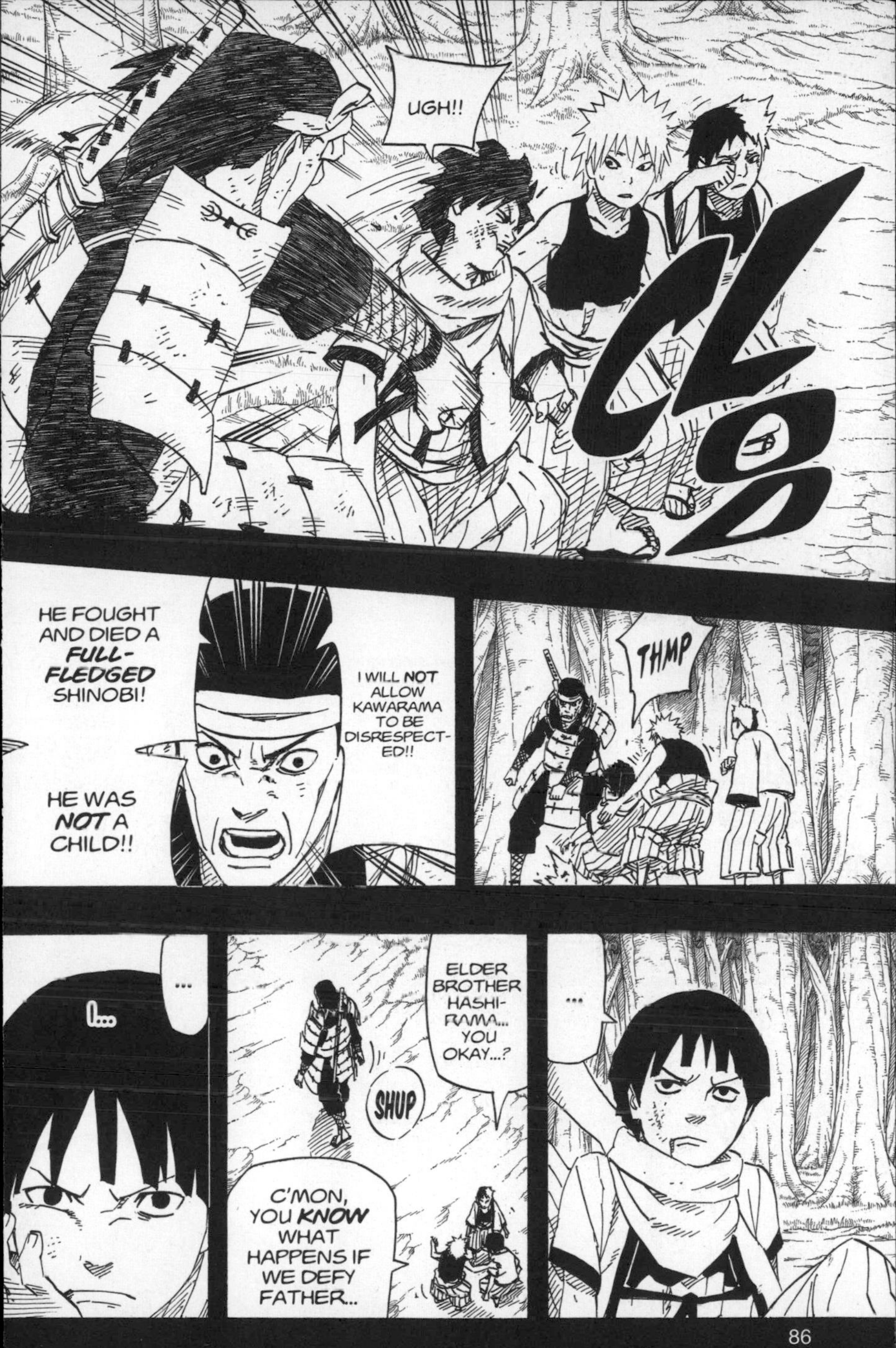
UGH!!
THMP
I WILL NOT ALLOW KAWARAMA TO BE DISRESPECTED!!
HE FOUGHT AND DIED A FULL-FLEDGED SHINOBI!
HE WAS NOT A CHILD!!
...
ELDER BROTHER HASHIRAMA... YOU OKAY...?
SHUP
C'MON, YOU KNOW WHAT HAPPENS IF WE DEFY FATHER...
...
I...

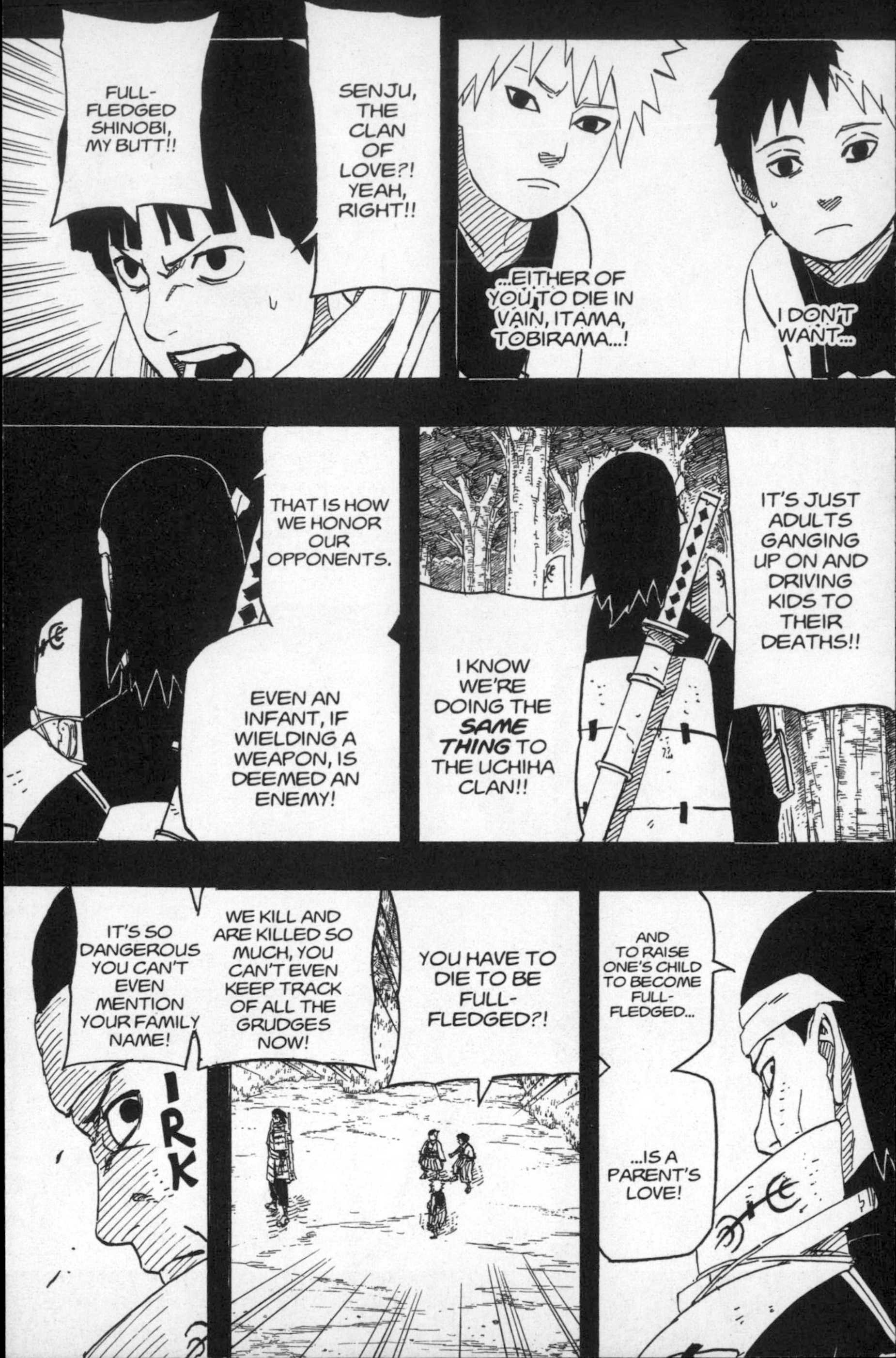
I DON'T WANT...
...EITHER OF YOU TO DIE IN VAIN, ITAMA, TOBIRAMA...!
SENJU, THE CLAN OF LOVE?! YEAH, RIGHT!!
FULL-FLEDGED SHINOBI, MY BUTT!!
IT'S JUST ADULTS GANGING UP ON AND DRIVING KIDS TO THEIR DEATHS!!
I KNOW WE'RE DOING THE ***SAME THING*** TO THE UCHIHA CLAN!!
THAT IS HOW WE HONOR OUR OPPONENTS.
EVEN AN INFANT, IF WIELDING A WEAPON, IS DEEMED AN ENEMY!
AND TO RAISE ONE'S CHILD TO BECOME FULL-FLEDGED...
...IS A PARENT'S LOVE!
YOU HAVE TO DIE TO BE FULL-FLEDGED?!
WE KILL AND ARE KILLED SO MUCH, YOU CAN'T EVEN KEEP TRACK OF ALL THE GRUDGES NOW!
IT'S SO DANGEROUS YOU CAN'T EVEN MENTION YOUR FAMILY NAME!
IRK

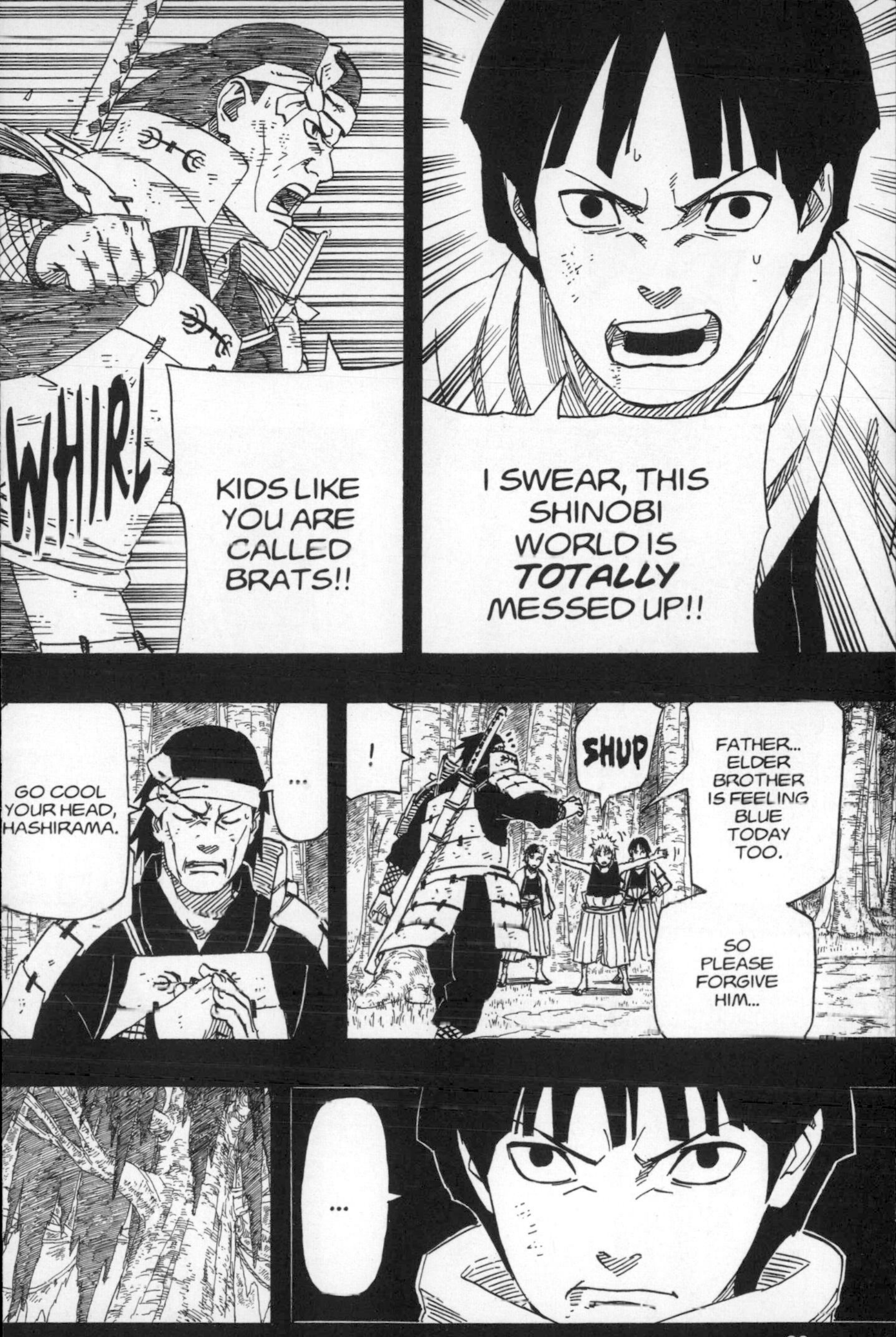
I SWEAR, THIS SHINOBI WORLD IS *TOTALLY* MESSED UP!!
WHIRL
KIDS LIKE YOU ARE CALLED BRATS!!
FATHER... ELDER BROTHER IS FEELING BLUE TODAY TOO.
SHUP
SO PLEASE FORGIVE HIM...
!
...
GO COOL YOUR HEAD, HASHIRAMA.
...

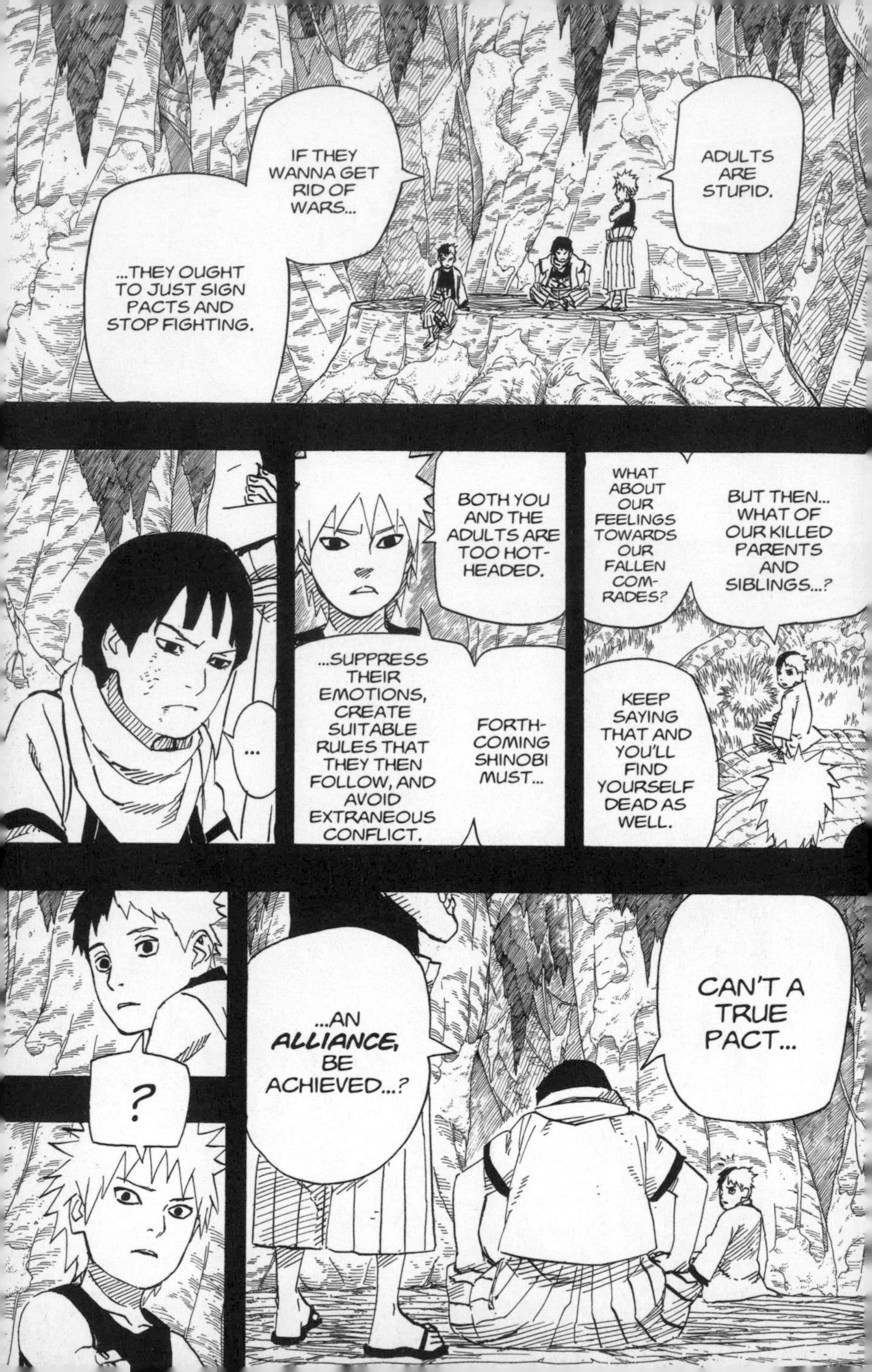
ADULTS ARE STUPID.
IF THEY WANNA GET RID OF WARS...
...THEY OUGHT TO JUST SIGN PACTS AND STOP FIGHTING.
BUT THEN... WHAT OF OUR KILLED PARENTS AND SIBLINGS...?
WHAT ABOUT OUR FEELINGS TOWARDS OUR FALLEN COM-RADES?
KEEP SAYING THAT AND YOU'LL FIND YOURSELF DEAD AS WELL.
BOTH YOU AND THE ADULTS ARE TOO HOT-HEADED.
FORTH-COMING SHINOBI MUST...
...SUPPRESS THEIR EMOTIONS, CREATE SUITABLE RULES THAT THEY THEN FOLLOW, AND AVOID EXTRANEOUS CONFLICT.
...
CAN'T A TRUE PACT...
...AN *ALLIANCE,* BE ACHIEVED...?
?

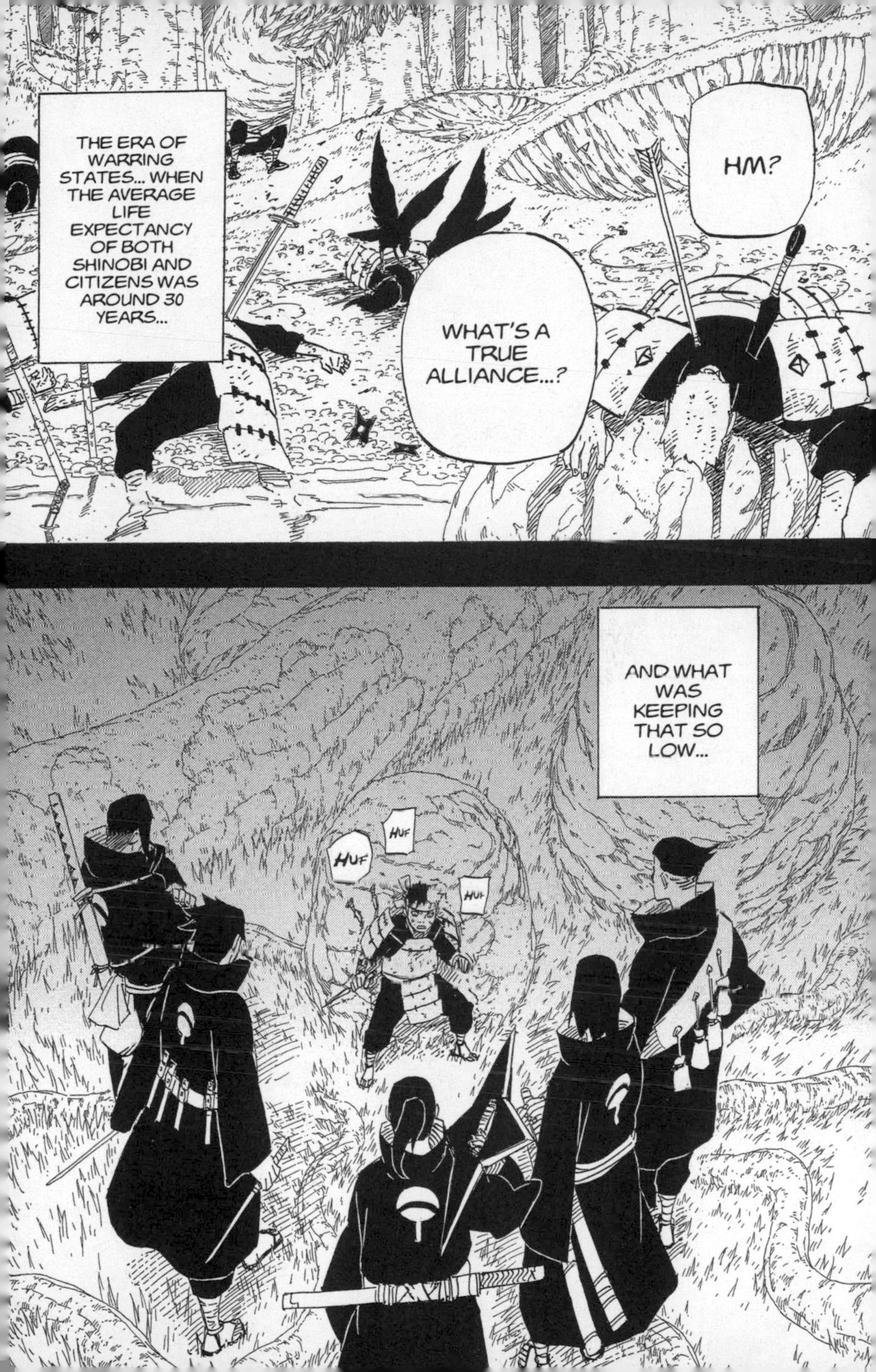
HM?
WHAT'S A TRUE ALLIANCE...?
THE ERA OF WARRING STATES... WHEN THE AVERAGE LIFE EXPECTANCY OF BOTH SHINOBI AND CITIZENS WAS AROUND 30 YEARS...
AND WHAT WAS KEEPING THAT SO LOW...
HUF
HUF
HUF

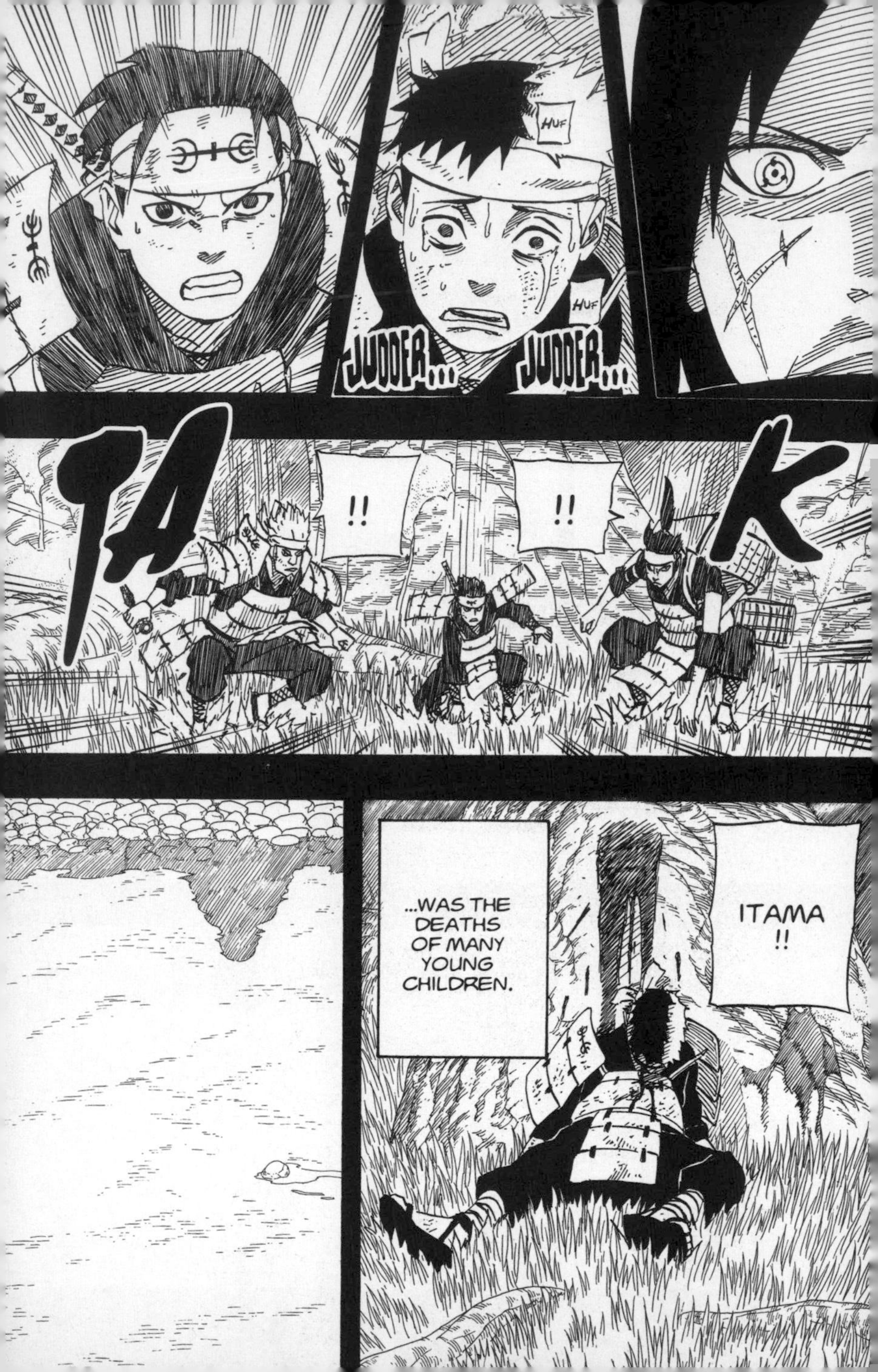
HUF
HUF
JUDDER... JUDDER...
TA K
!!
!!
ITAMA !!
...WAS THE DEATHS OF MANY YOUNG CHILDREN.

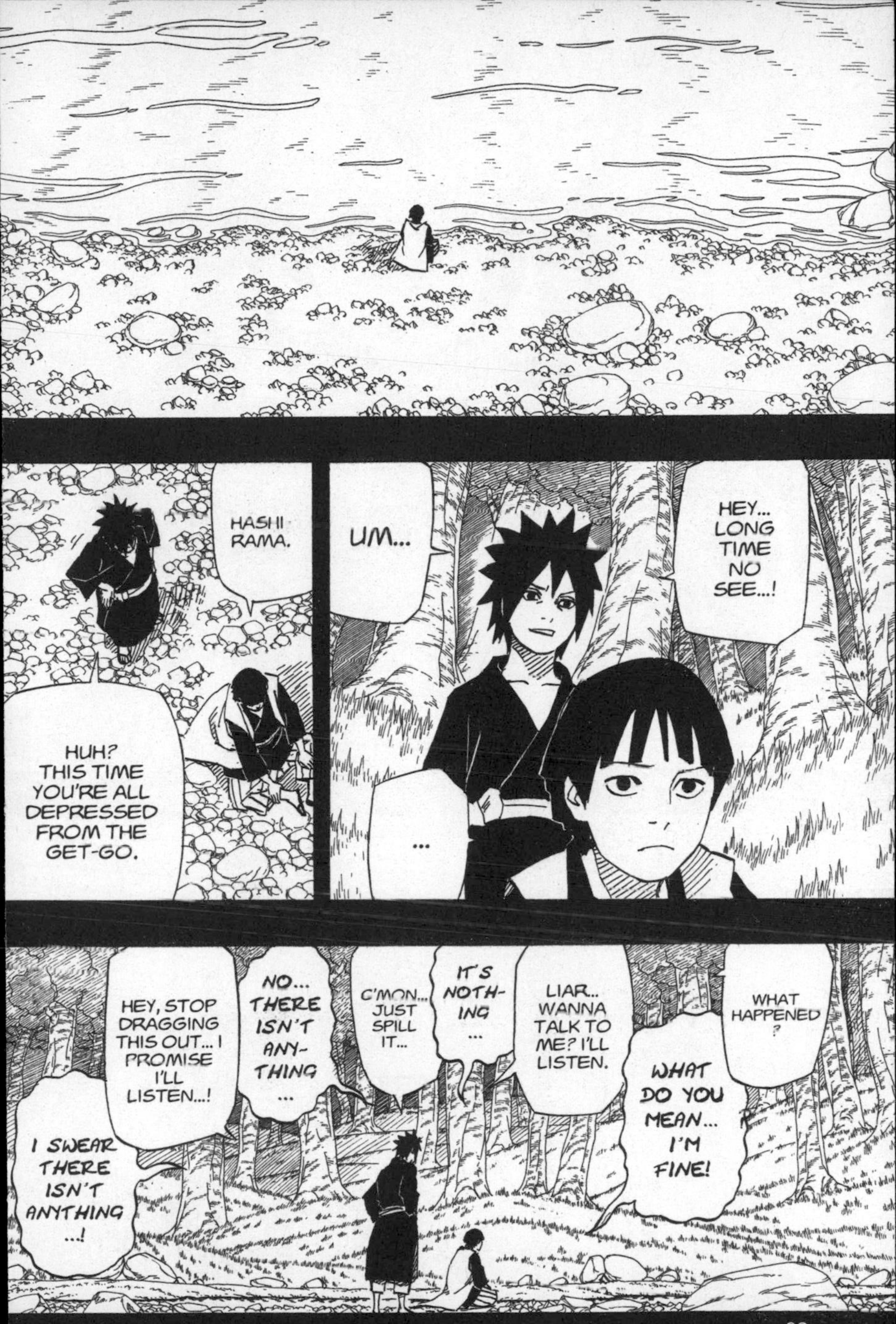
HEY... LONG TIME NO SEE...!
UM...
...
HASHI RAMA.
HUH? THIS TIME YOU'RE ALL DEPRESSED FROM THE GET-GO.
WHAT HAPPENED?
WHAT DO YOU MEAN... I'M FINE!
LIAR... WANNA TALK TO ME? I'LL LISTEN.
IT'S NOTHING...
C'MON... JUST SPILL IT...
NO... THERE ISN'T ANYTHING...
HEY, STOP DRAGGING THIS OUT... I PROMISE I'LL LISTEN...!
I SWEAR THERE ISN'T ANYTHING...!

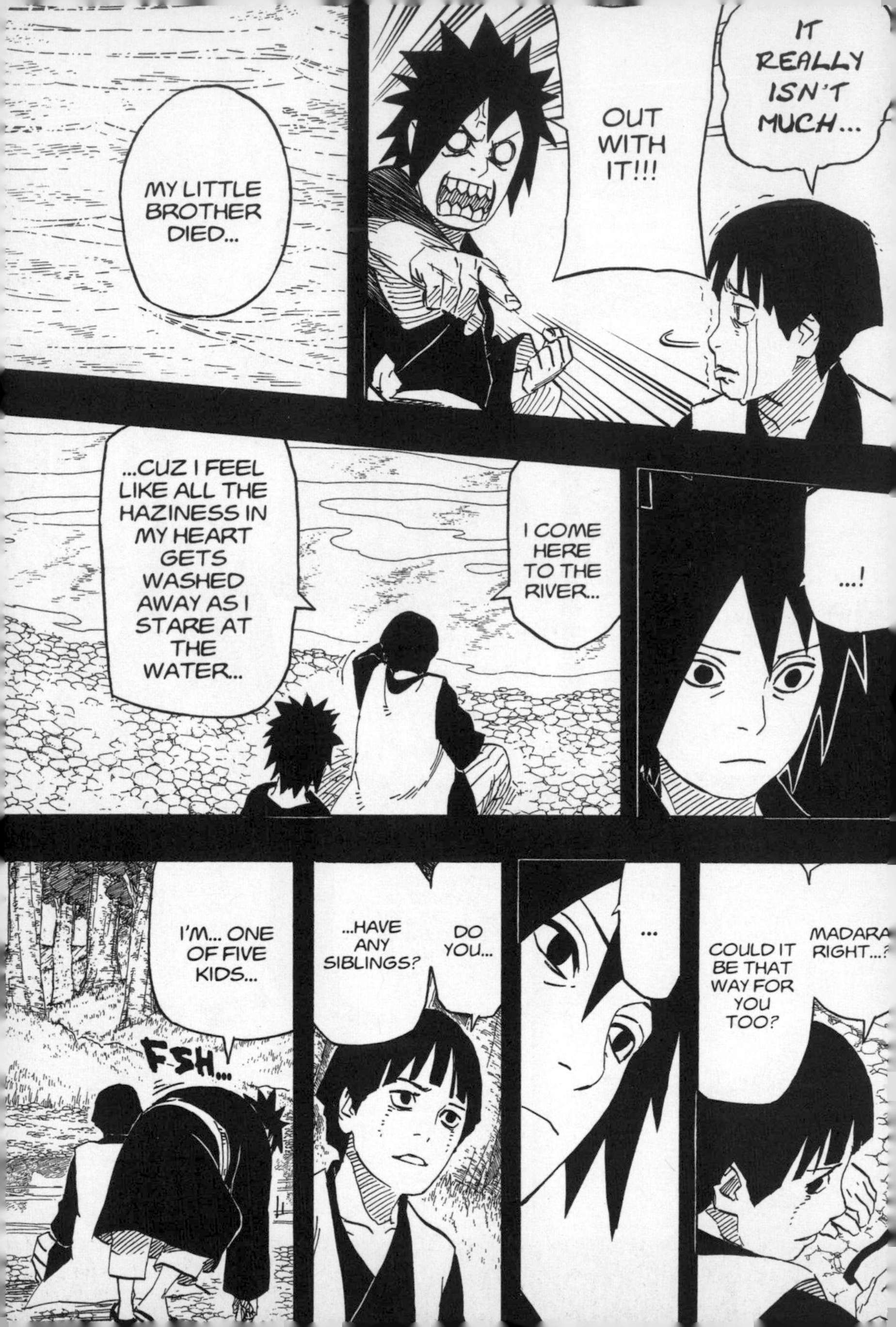
IT REALLY ISN'T MUCH...
OUT WITH IT!!!
MY LITTLE BROTHER DIED...
...!
I COME HERE TO THE RIVER...
...CUZ I FEEL LIKE ALL THE HAZINESS IN MY HEART GETS WASHED AWAY AS I STARE AT THE WATER...
MADARA RIGHT...?
COULD IT BE THAT WAY FOR YOU TOO?
...
DO YOU...
...HAVE ANY SIBLINGS?
I'M... ONE OF FIVE KIDS...
FSH...

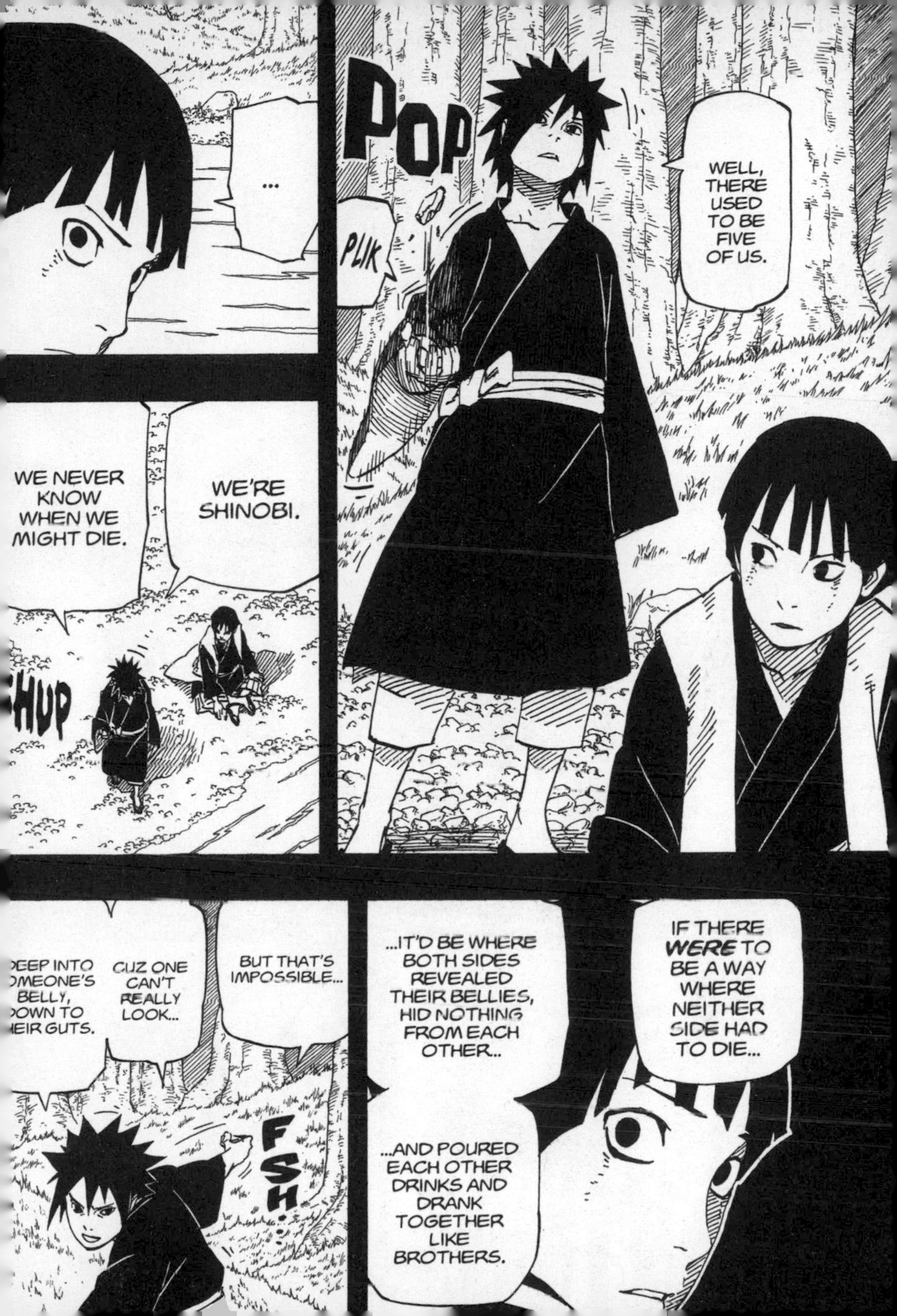
WELL, THERE USED TO BE FIVE OF US.
POP
PLIK
...
WE'RE SHINOBI.
WE NEVER KNOW WHEN WE MIGHT DIE.
SHUP
IF THERE *WERE* TO BE A WAY WHERE NEITHER SIDE HAD TO DIE...
...IT'D BE WHERE BOTH SIDES REVEALED THEIR BELLIES, HID NOTHING FROM EACH OTHER...
...AND POURED EACH OTHER DRINKS AND DRANK TOGETHER LIKE BROTHERS.
BUT THAT'S IMPOSSIBLE...
CUZ ONE CAN'T REALLY LOOK...
DEEP INTO OMEONE'S BELLY, DOWN TO HEIR GUTS.
FSH

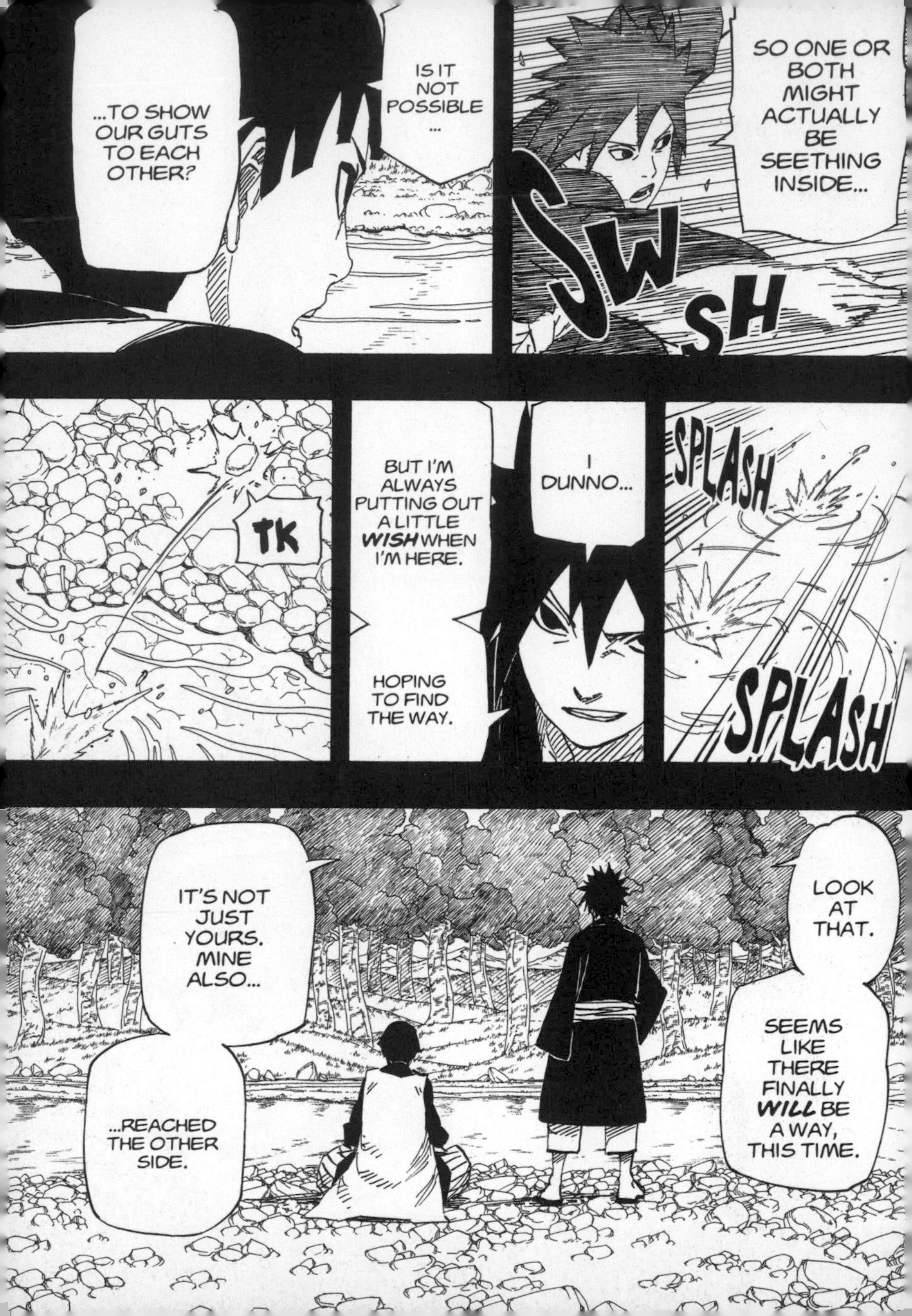
SO ONE OR BOTH MIGHT ACTUALLY BE SEETHING INSIDE...
SWSH
IS IT NOT POSSIBLE...
...TO SHOW OUR GUTS TO EACH OTHER?
SPLASH
SPLASH
I DUNNO...
BUT I'M ALWAYS PUTTING OUT A LITTLE WISH WHEN I'M HERE.
HOPING TO FIND THE WAY.
TK
LOOK AT THAT.
SEEMS LIKE THERE FINALLY WILL BE A WAY, THIS TIME.
IT'S NOT JUST YOURS. MINE ALSO...
...REACHED THE OTHER SIDE.

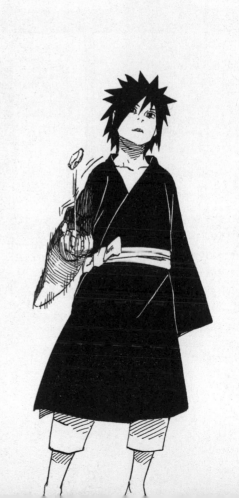

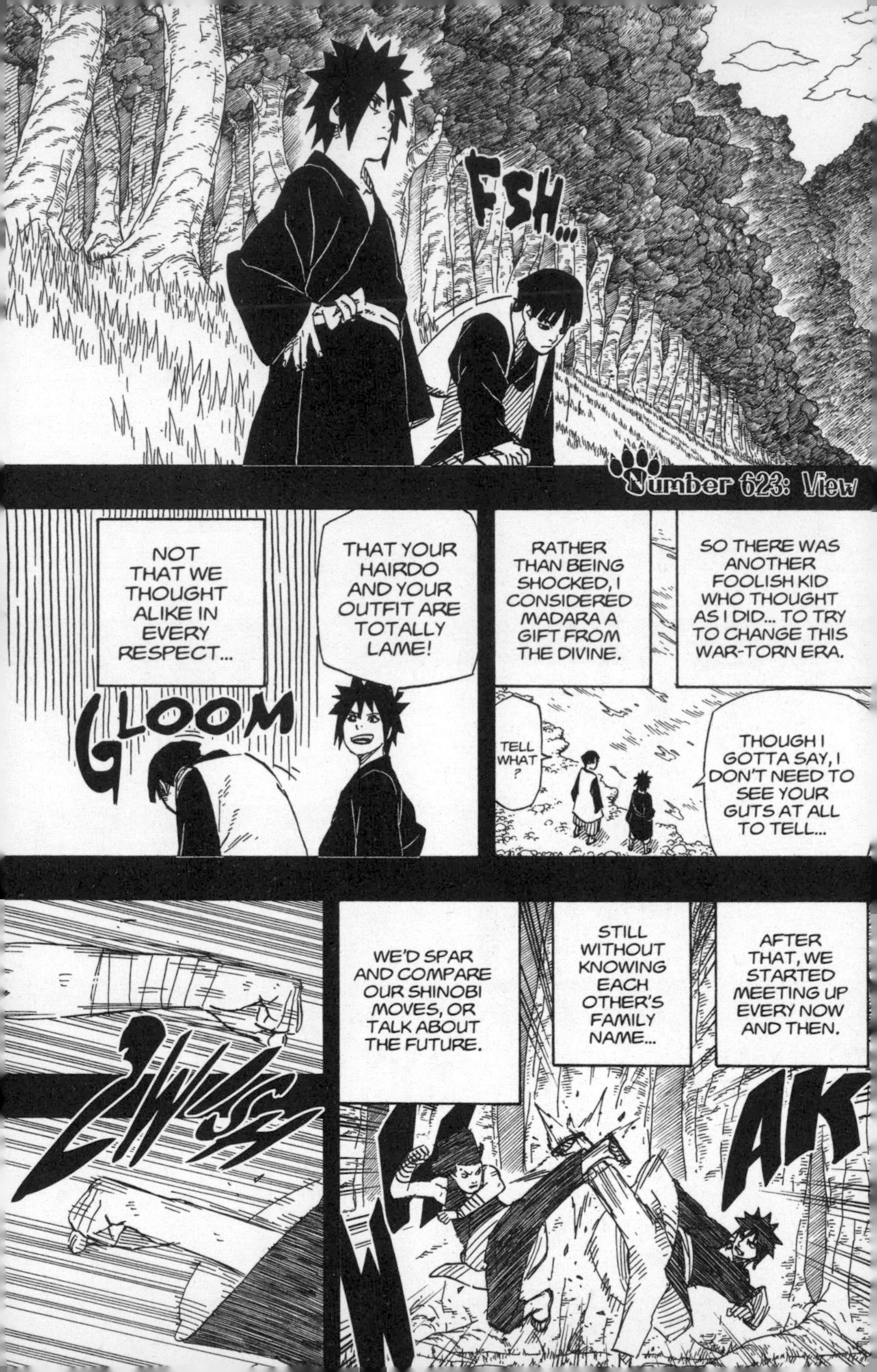
FSH...
Number 623: View
SO THERE WAS ANOTHER FOOLISH KID WHO THOUGHT AS I DID... TO TRY TO CHANGE THIS WAR-TORN ERA.
RATHER THAN BEING SHOCKED, I CONSIDERED MADARA A GIFT FROM THE DIVINE.
THOUGH I GOTTA SAY, I DON'T NEED TO SEE YOUR GUTS AT ALL TO TELL...
TELL WHAT?
THAT YOUR HAIRDO AND YOUR OUTFIT ARE TOTALLY LAME!
NOT THAT WE THOUGHT ALIKE IN EVERY RESPECT...
GLOOM
AFTER THAT, WE STARTED MEETING UP EVERY NOW AND THEN.
STILL WITHOUT KNOWING EACH OTHER'S FAMILY NAME...
WE'D SPAR AND COMPARE OUR SHINOBI MOVES, OR TALK ABOUT THE FUTURE.
AK
W
ZWISH

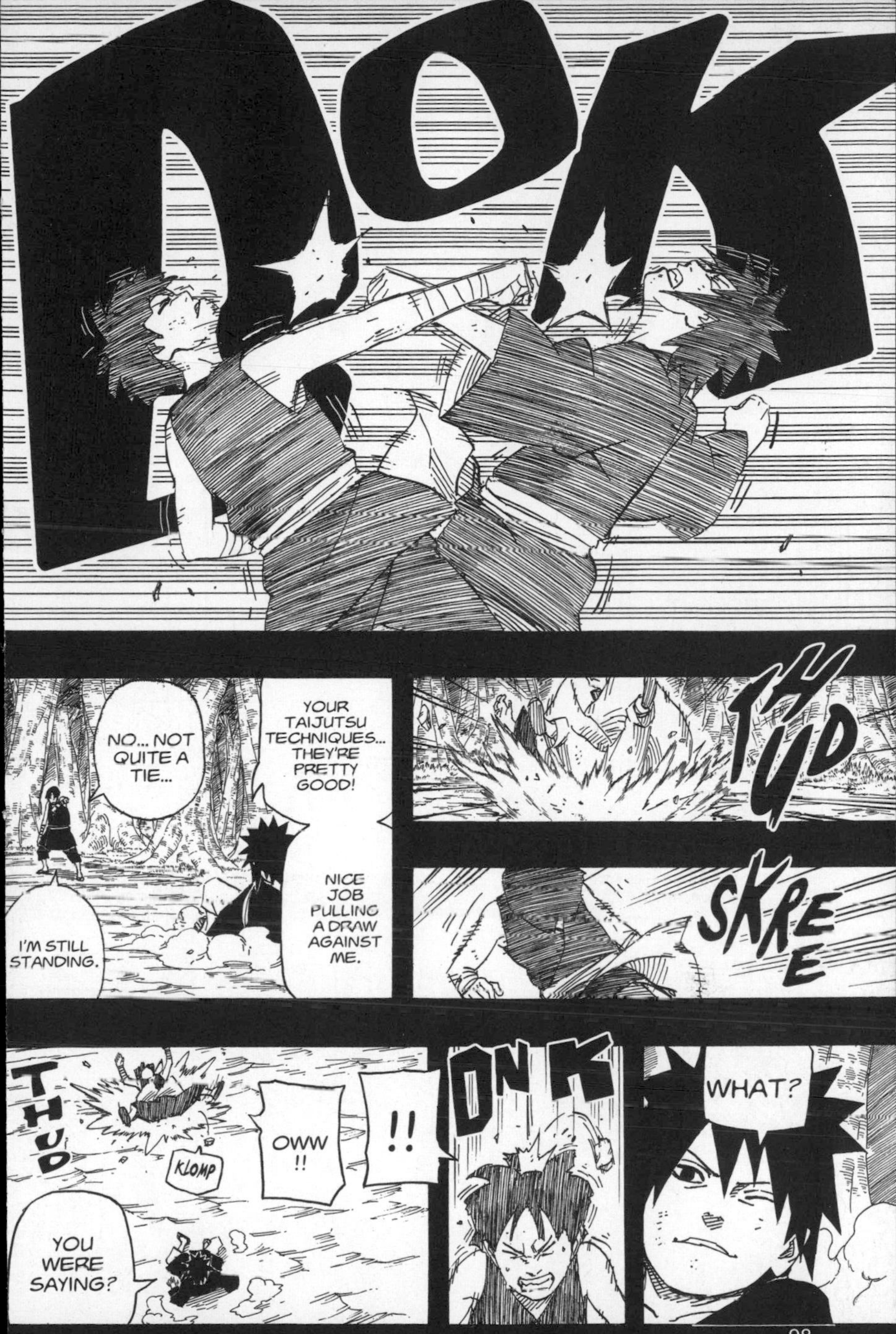
DOK
THUD
SKREE
YOUR TAIJUTSU TECHNIQUES... THEY'RE PRETTY GOOD!
NICE JOB PULLING A DRAW AGAINST ME.
NO... NOT QUITE A TIE...
I'M STILL STANDING.
WHAT?
DONK
!!
OWW !!
THUD
KLOMP
YOU WERE SAYING?

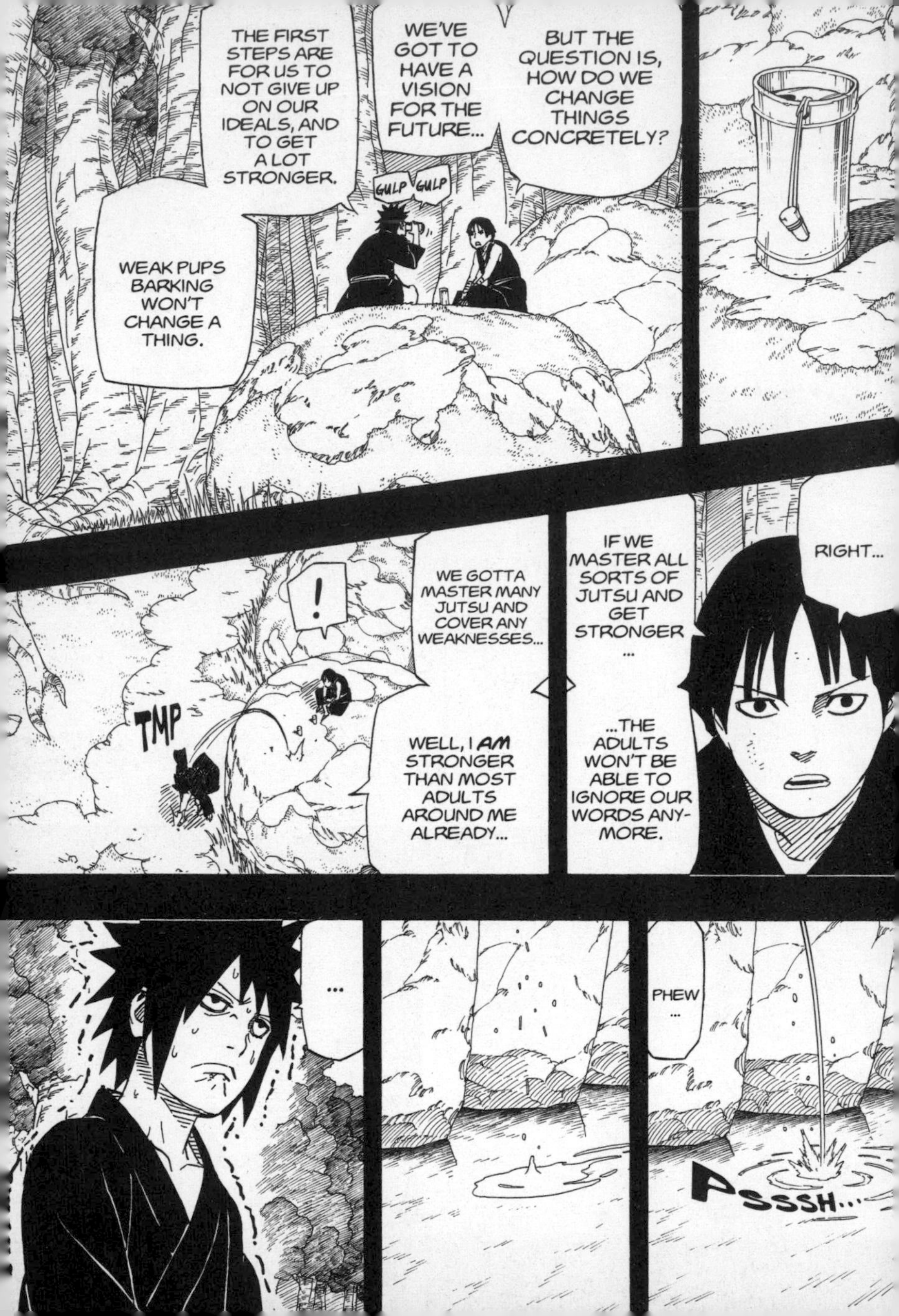

BUT THE QUESTION IS, HOW DO WE CHANGE THINGS CONCRETELY?
WE'VE GOT TO HAVE A VISION FOR THE FUTURE...
THE FIRST STEPS ARE FOR US TO NOT GIVE UP ON OUR IDEALS, AND TO GET A LOT STRONGER.
GULP GULP
WEAK PUPS BARKING WON'T CHANGE A THING.
RIGHT...
IF WE MASTER ALL SORTS OF JUTSU AND GET STRONGER...
...THE ADULTS WON'T BE ABLE TO IGNORE OUR WORDS ANY-MORE.
WE GOTTA MASTER MANY JUTSU AND COVER ANY WEAKNESSES...
WELL, I *AM* STRONGER THAN MOST ADULTS AROUND ME ALREADY...
!
TMP
PHEW...
PSSSH...
...

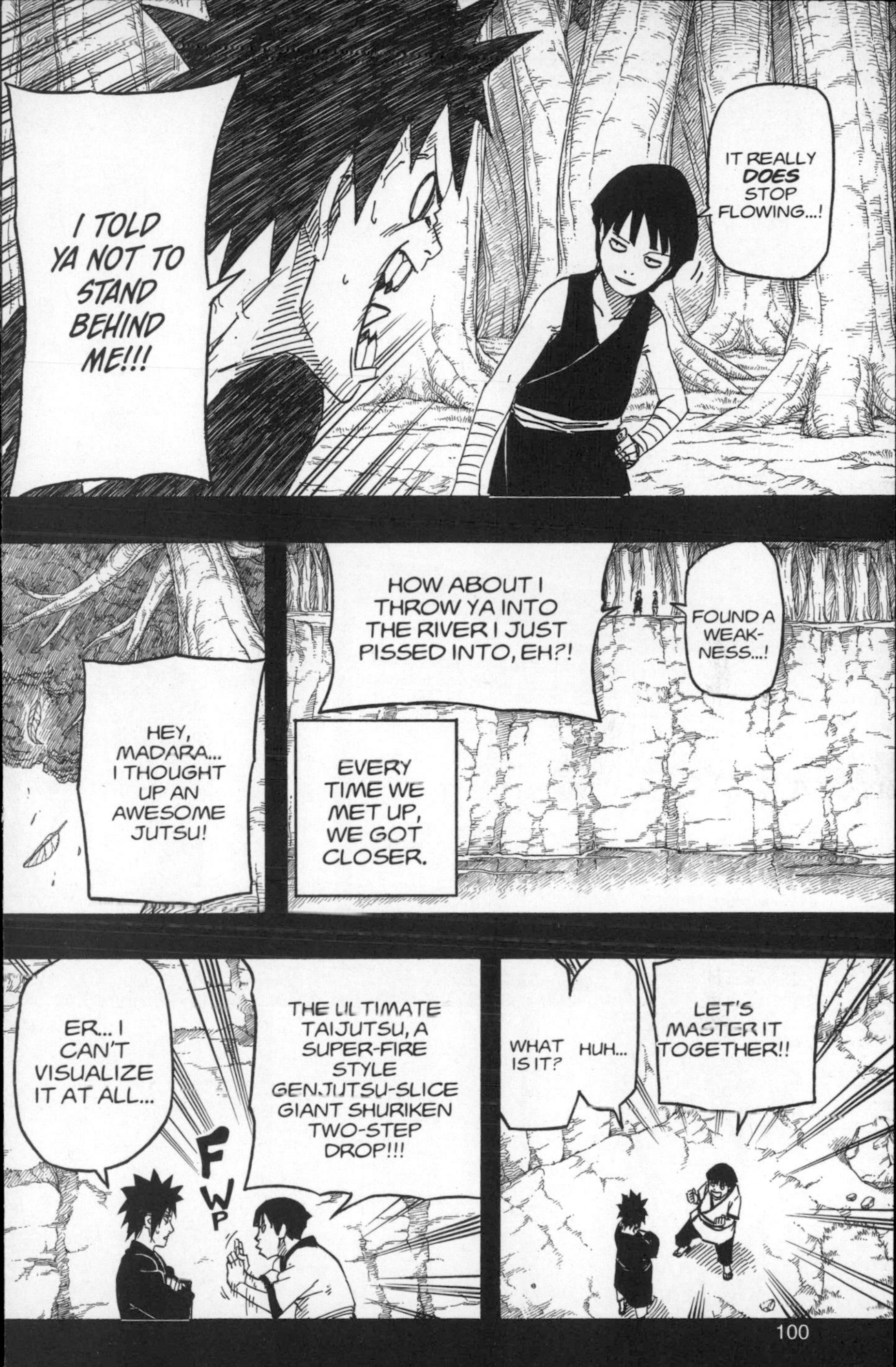
IT REALLY **DOES** STOP FLOWING...!
I TOLD YA NOT TO STAND BEHIND ME!!!
FOUND A WEAK-NESS...!
HOW ABOUT I THROW YA INTO THE RIVER I JUST PISSED INTO, EH?!
EVERY TIME WE MET UP, WE GOT CLOSER.
HEY, MADARA... I THOUGHT UP AN AWESOME JUTSU!
LET'S MASTER IT TOGETHER!!
HUH...
WHAT IS IT?
THE ULTIMATE TAIJUTSU, A SUPER-FIRE STYLE GENJUTSU-SLICE GIANT SHURIKEN TWO-STEP DROP!!!
FWP
ER... I CAN'T VISUALIZE IT AT ALL...

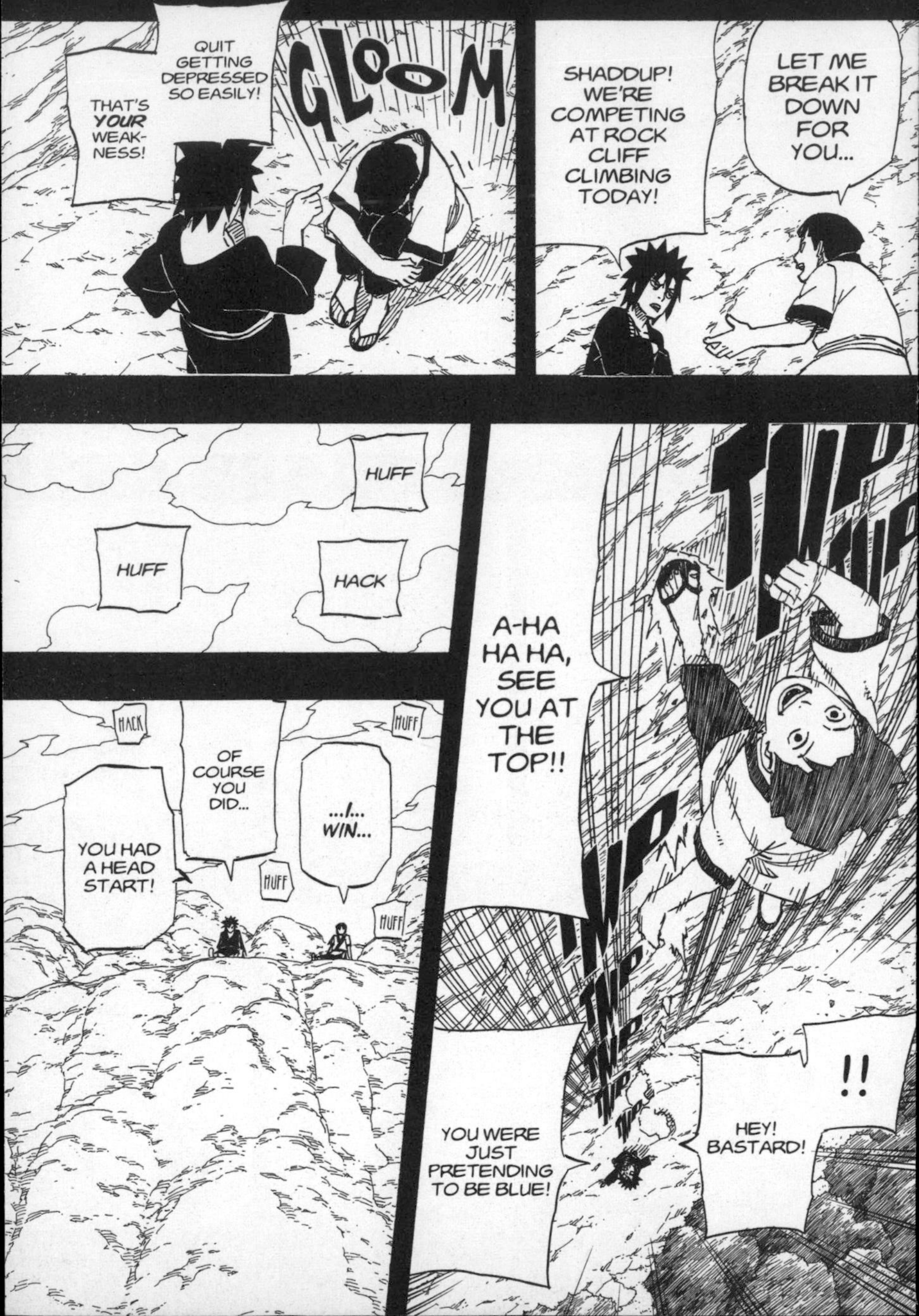
LET ME BREAK IT DOWN FOR YOU...
SHADDUP! WE'RE COMPETING AT ROCK CLIFF CLIMBING TODAY!
GLOOM
QUIT GETTING DEPRESSED SO EASILY!
THAT'S *YOUR* WEAKNESS!
TMP
TMP
A-HA HA HA, SEE YOU AT THE TOP!!
TMP
TMP
TMP
!!
HEY! BASTARD!
YOU WERE JUST PRETENDING TO BE BLUE!
HUFF
HACK
HUFF
HUFF
...I... WIN...
OF COURSE YOU DID...
YOU HAD A HEAD START!
HACK
HUFF
HUFF

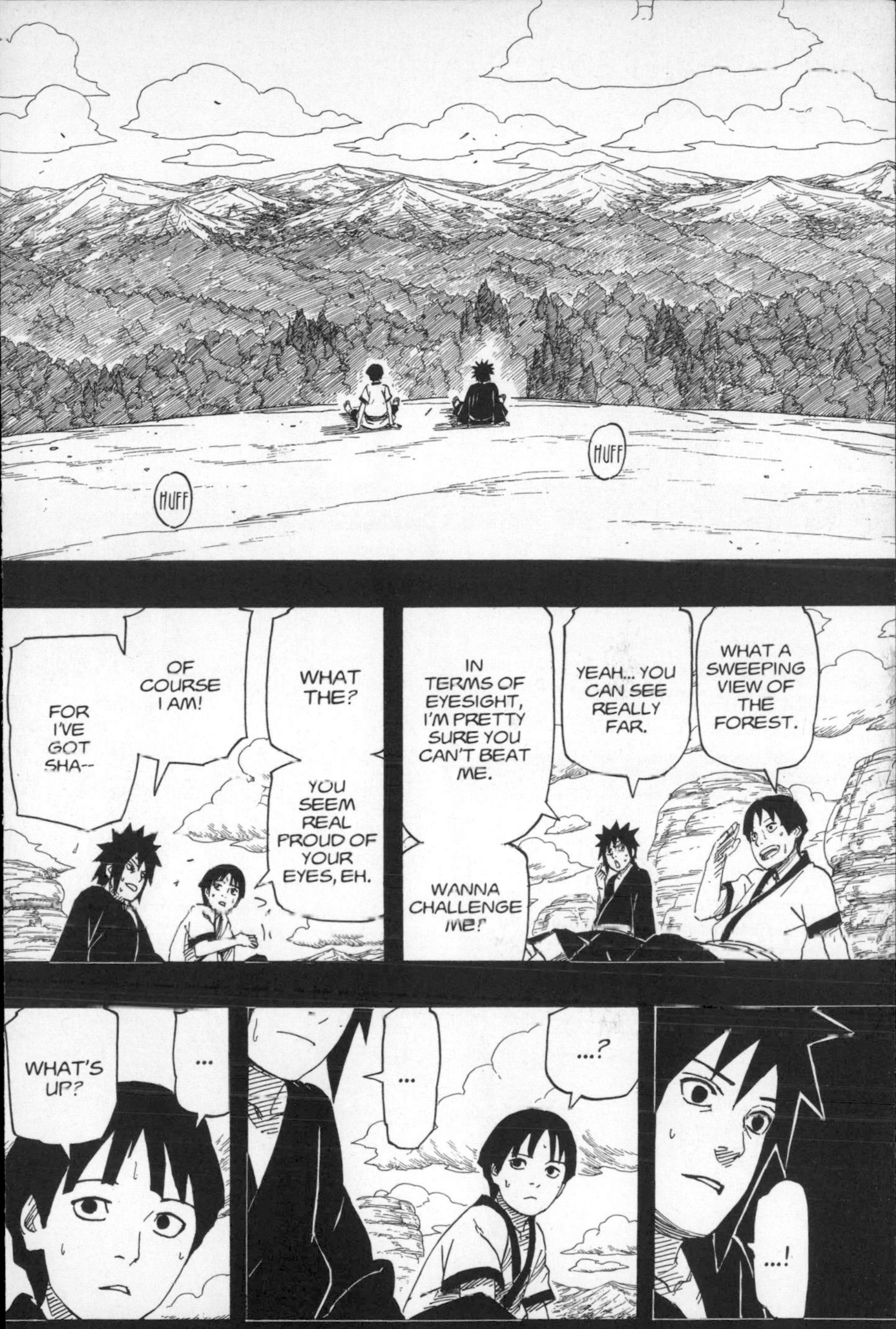
HUFF
HUFF
WHAT A SWEEPING VIEW OF THE FOREST.
YEAH... YOU CAN SEE REALLY FAR.
IN TERMS OF EYESIGHT, I'M PRETTY SURE YOU CAN'T BEAT ME.
WANNA CHALLENGE ME?
WHAT THE?
YOU SEEM REAL PROUD OF YOUR EYES, EH.
OF COURSE I AM!
FOR I'VE GOT SHA--
...!
...?
...
...
WHAT'S UP?

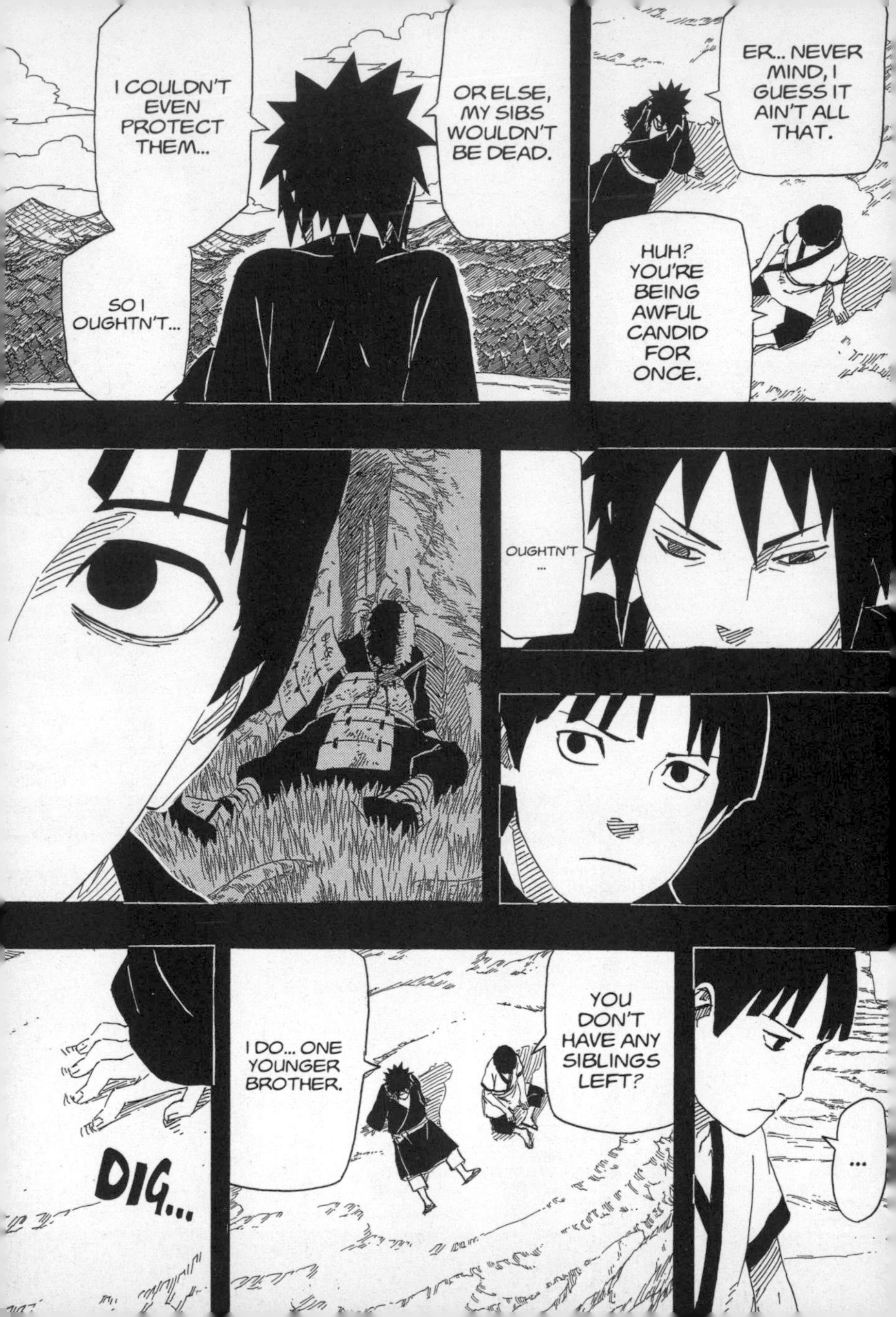
ER... NEVER MIND, I GUESS IT AIN'T ALL THAT.
HUH? YOU'RE BEING AWFUL CANDID FOR ONCE.
OR ELSE, MY SIBS WOULDN'T BE DEAD.
I COULDN'T EVEN PROTECT THEM...
SO I OUGHTN'T...
OUGHTN'T ...
...
YOU DON'T HAVE ANY SIBLINGS LEFT?
I DO... ONE YOUNGER BROTHER.
DIG...

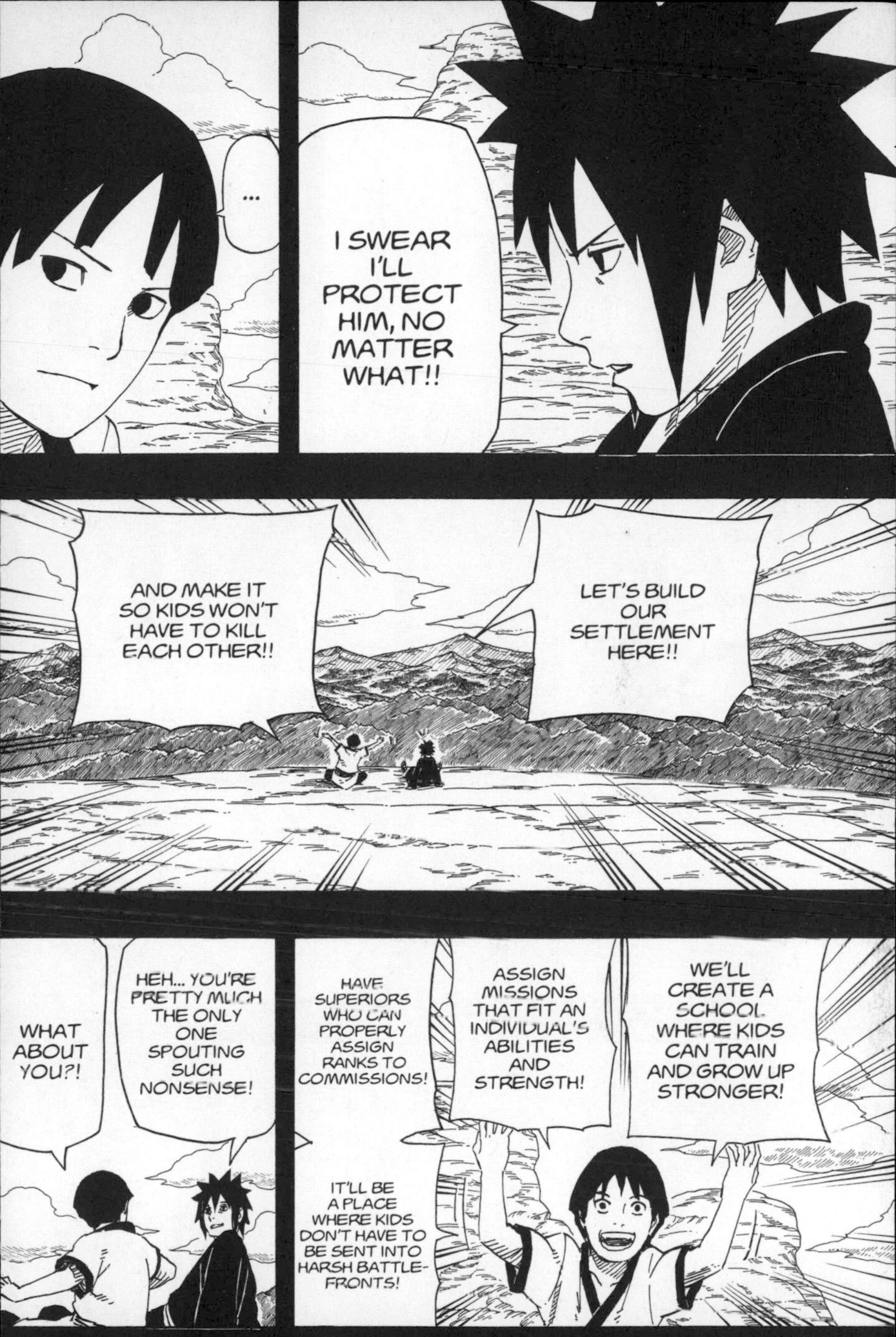
I SWEAR I'LL PROTECT HIM, NO MATTER WHAT!!
...
LET'S BUILD OUR SETTLEMENT HERE!!
AND MAKE IT SO KIDS WON'T HAVE TO KILL EACH OTHER!!
WE'LL CREATE A SCHOOL WHERE KIDS CAN TRAIN AND GROW UP STRONGER!
ASSIGN MISSIONS THAT FIT AN INDIVIDUAL'S ABILITIES AND STRENGTH!
HAVE SUPERIORS WHO CAN PROPERLY ASSIGN RANKS TO COMMISSIONS!
IT'LL BE A PLACE WHERE KIDS DON'T HAVE TO BE SENT INTO HARSH BATTLE-FRONTS!
HEH... YOU'RE PRETTY MUCH THE ONLY ONE SPOUTING SUCH NONSENSE!
WHAT ABOUT YOU?!

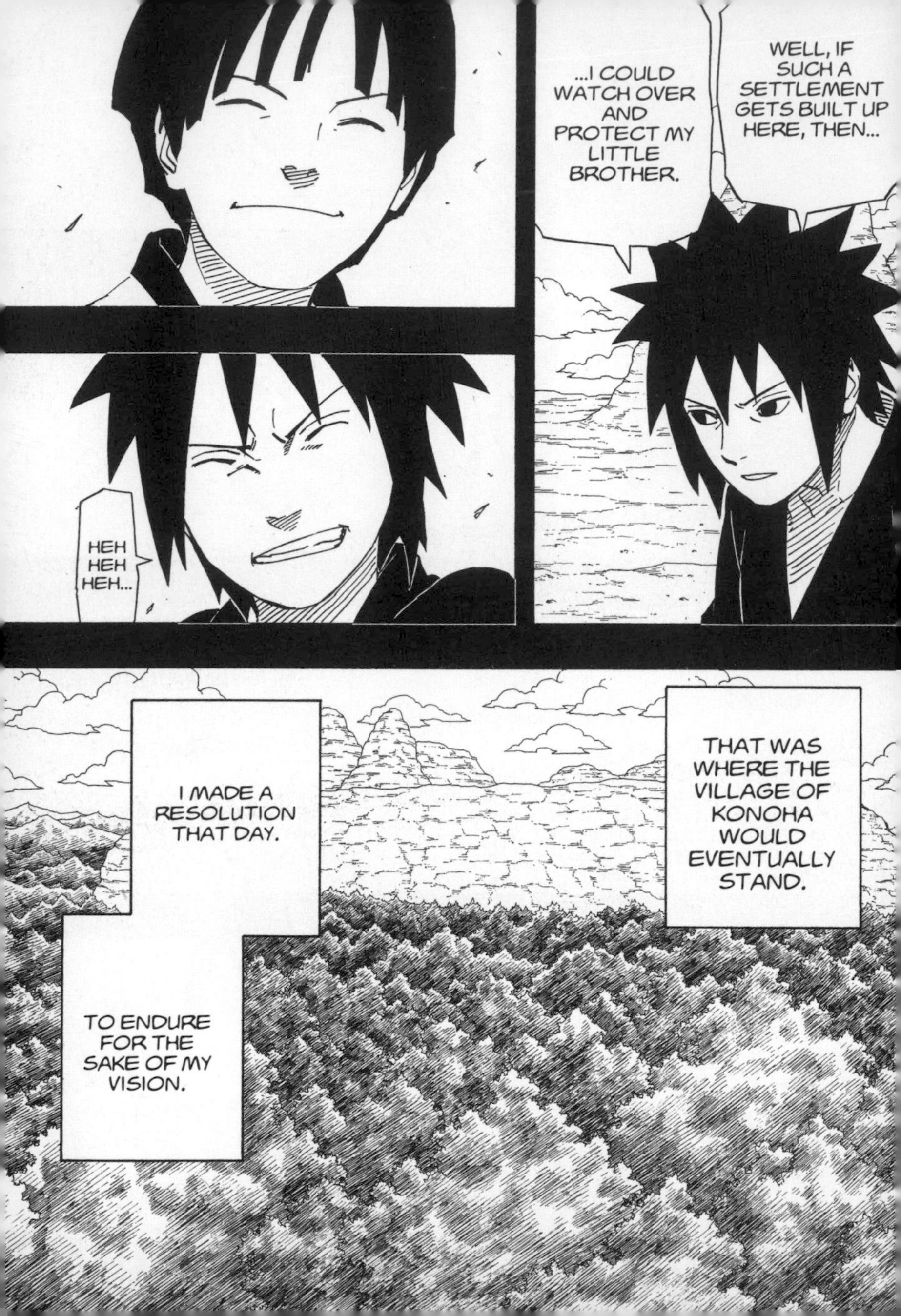
WELL, IF SUCH A SETTLEMENT GETS BUILT UP HERE, THEN...
...I COULD WATCH OVER AND PROTECT MY LITTLE BROTHER.
HEH HEH HEH...
THAT WAS WHERE THE VILLAGE OF KONOHA WOULD EVENTUALLY STAND.
I MADE A RESOLUTION THAT DAY.
TO ENDURE FOR THE SAKE OF MY VISION.

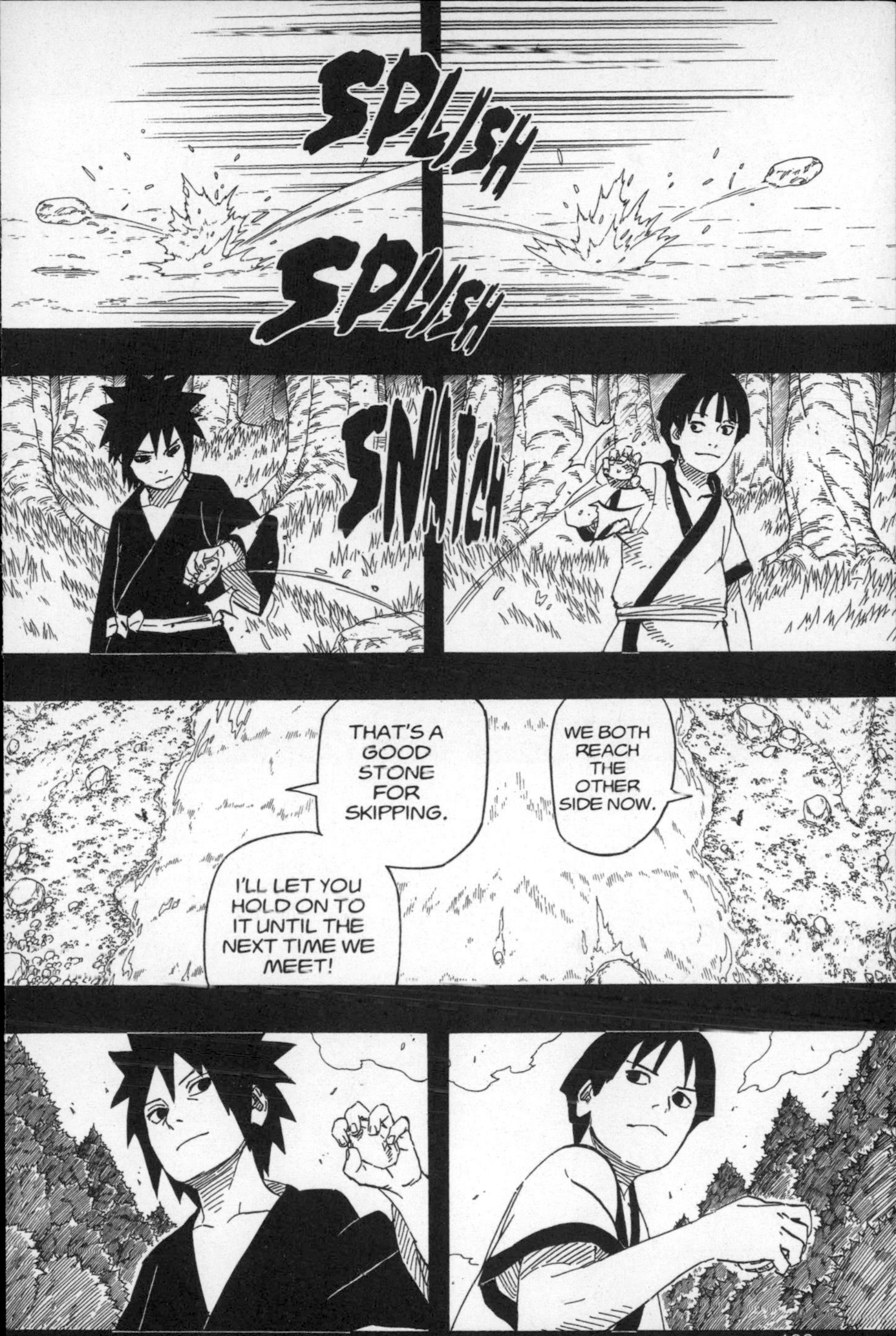
SPLISH
SPLISH
SNATCH
WE BOTH REACH THE OTHER SIDE NOW.
THAT'S A GOOD STONE FOR SKIPPING.
I'LL LET YOU HOLD ON TO IT UNTIL THE NEXT TIME WE MEET!

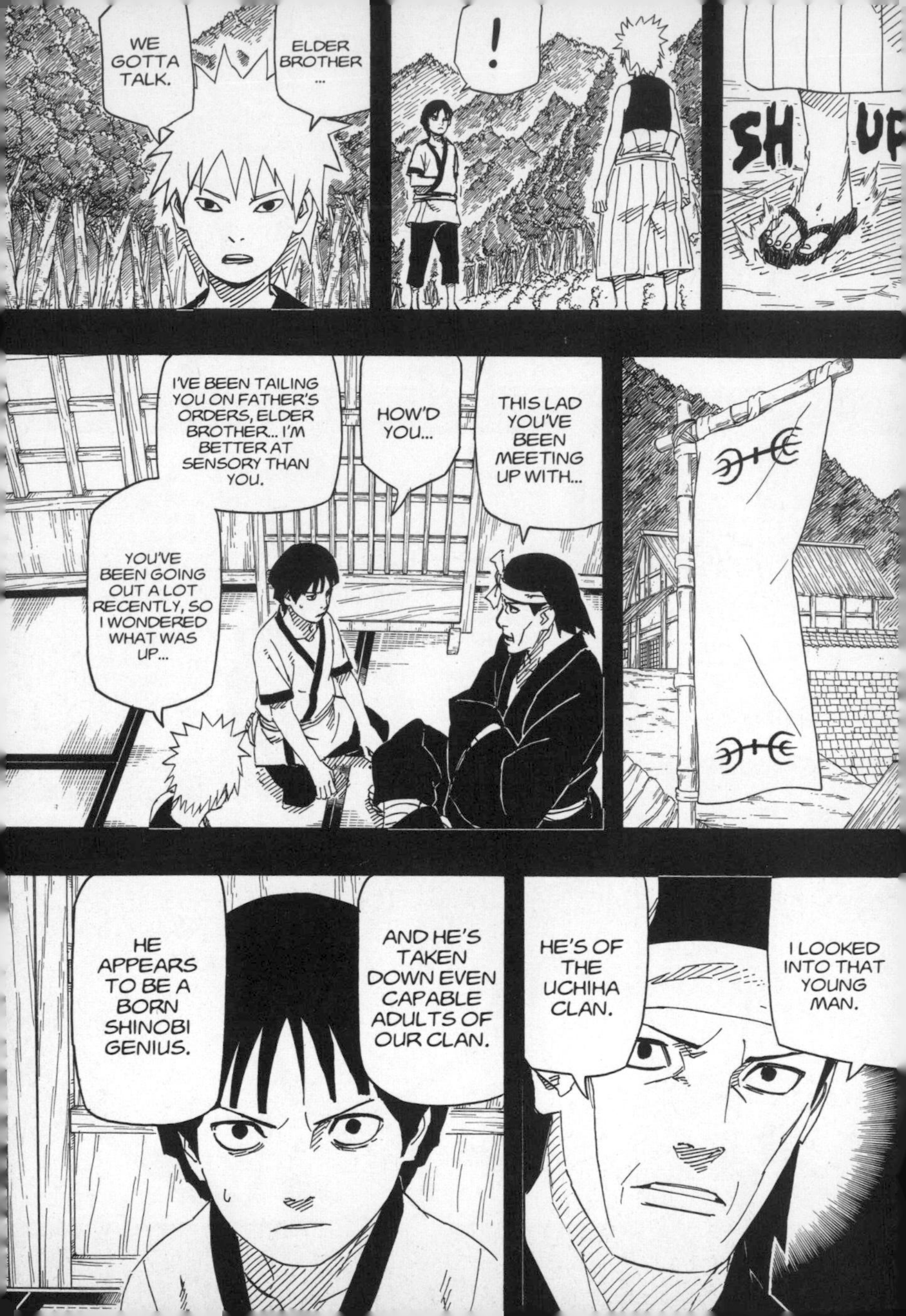
SH UP
!
ELDER BROTHER ...
WE GOTTA TALK.
THIS LAD YOU'VE BEEN MEETING UP WITH...
HOW'D YOU...
I'VE BEEN TAILING YOU ON FATHER'S ORDERS, ELDER BROTHER... I'M BETTER AT SENSORY THAN YOU.
YOU'VE BEEN GOING OUT A LOT RECENTLY, SO I WONDERED WHAT WAS UP...
I LOOKED INTO THAT YOUNG MAN.
HE'S OF THE UCHIHA CLAN.
AND HE'S TAKEN DOWN EVEN CAPABLE ADULTS OF OUR CLAN.
HE APPEARS TO BE A BORN SHINOBI GENIUS.

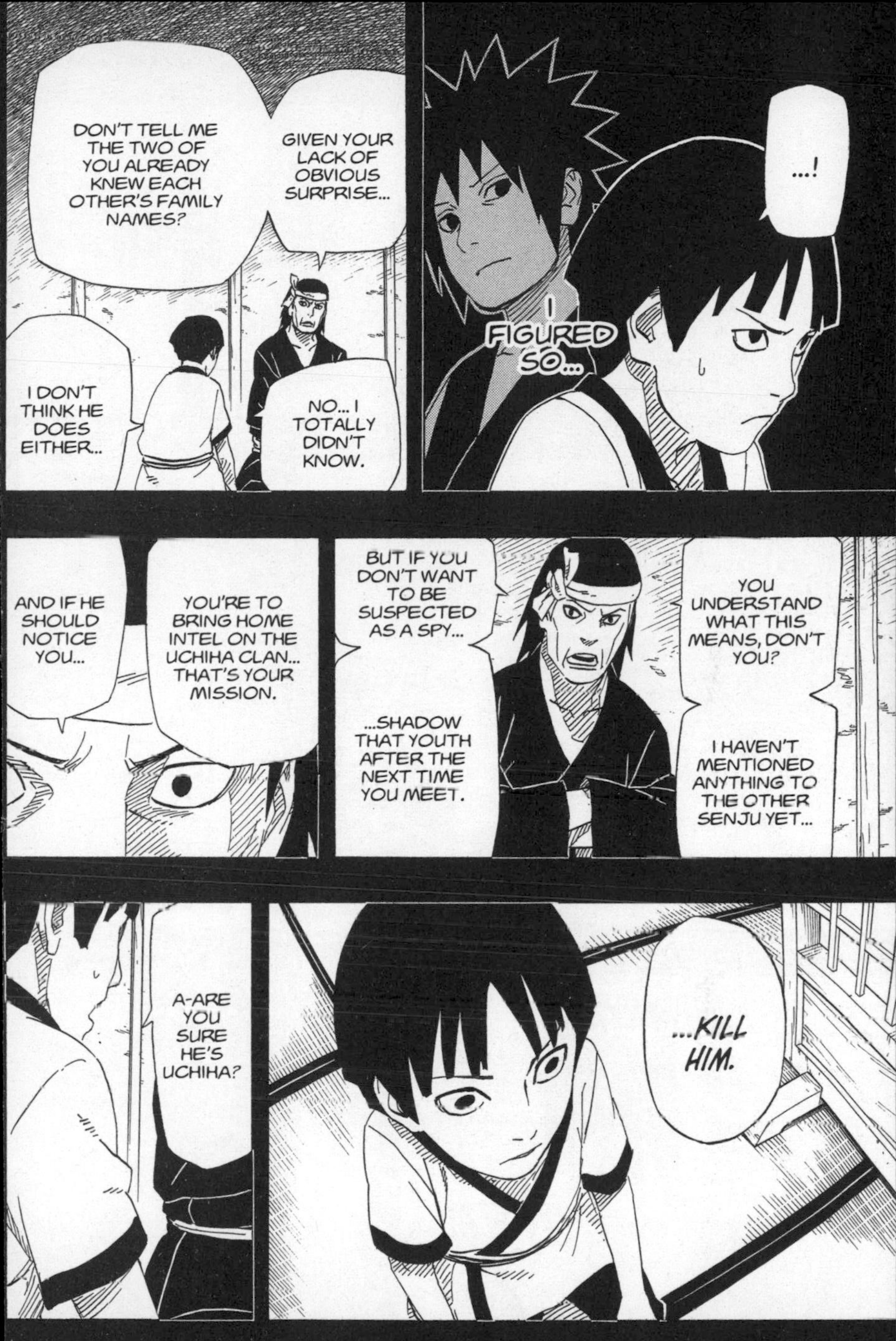
...!
I FIGURED SO...
GIVEN YOUR LACK OF OBVIOUS SURPRISE...
DON'T TELL ME THE TWO OF YOU ALREADY KNEW EACH OTHER'S FAMILY NAMES?
NO... I TOTALLY DIDN'T KNOW.
I DON'T THINK HE DOES EITHER...
YOU UNDERSTAND WHAT THIS MEANS, DON'T YOU?
I HAVEN'T MENTIONED ANYTHING TO THE OTHER SENJU YET...
BUT IF YOU DON'T WANT TO BE SUSPECTED AS A SPY...
...SHADOW THAT YOUTH AFTER THE NEXT TIME YOU MEET.
YOU'RE TO BRING HOME INTEL ON THE UCHIHA CLAN... THAT'S YOUR MISSION.
AND IF HE SHOULD NOTICE YOU...
...KILL HIM.
A-ARE YOU SURE HE'S UCHIHA?

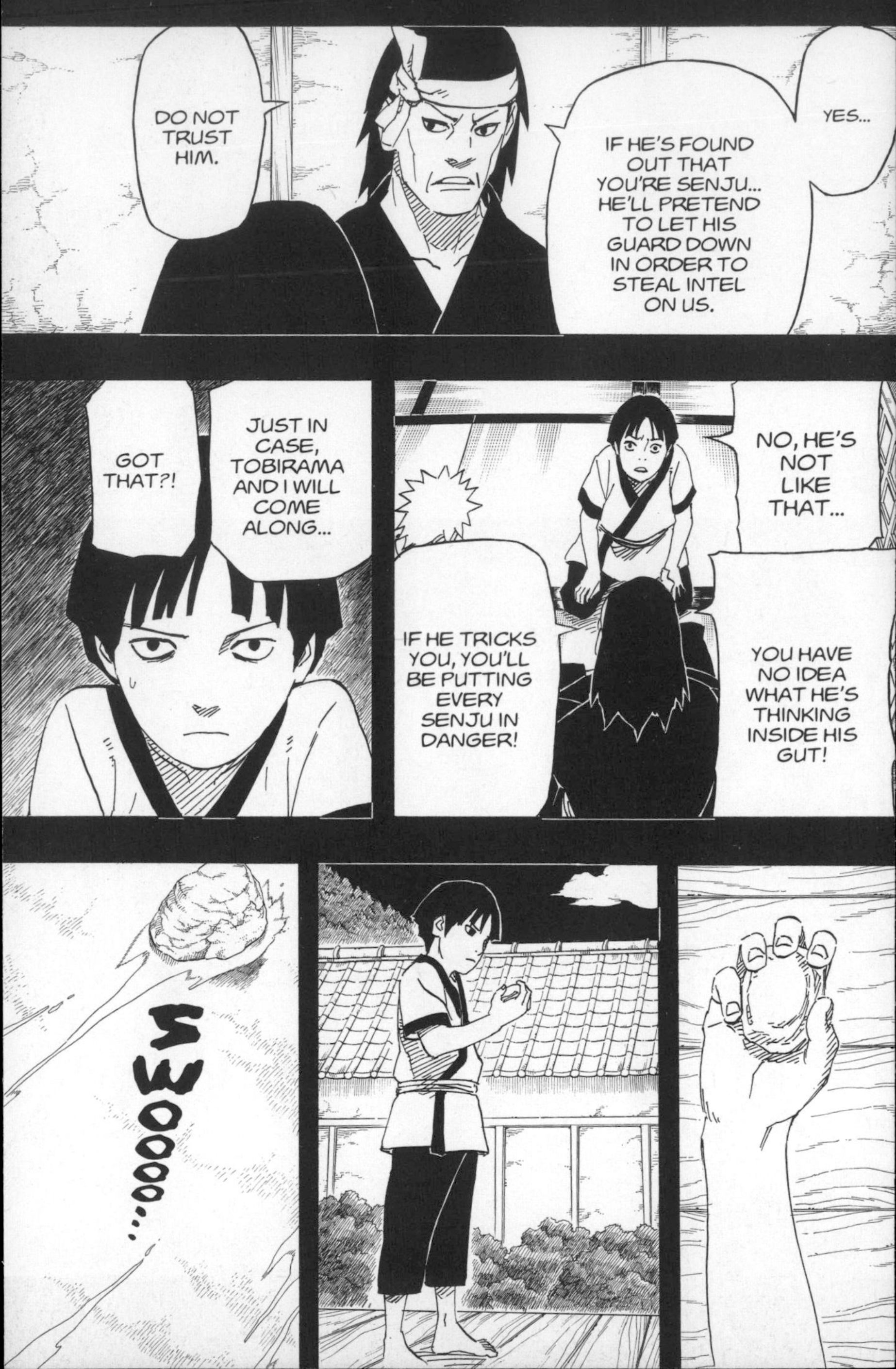
YES...
IF HE'S FOUND OUT THAT YOU'RE SENJU... HE'LL PRETEND TO LET HIS GUARD DOWN IN ORDER TO STEAL INTEL ON US.
DO NOT TRUST HIM.
NO, HE'S NOT LIKE THAT...
YOU HAVE NO IDEA WHAT HE'S THINKING INSIDE HIS GUT!
IF HE TRICKS YOU, YOU'LL BE PUTTING EVERY SENJU IN DANGER!
JUST IN CASE, TOBIRAMA AND I WILL COME ALONG...
GOT THAT?!
SWOOOOO...

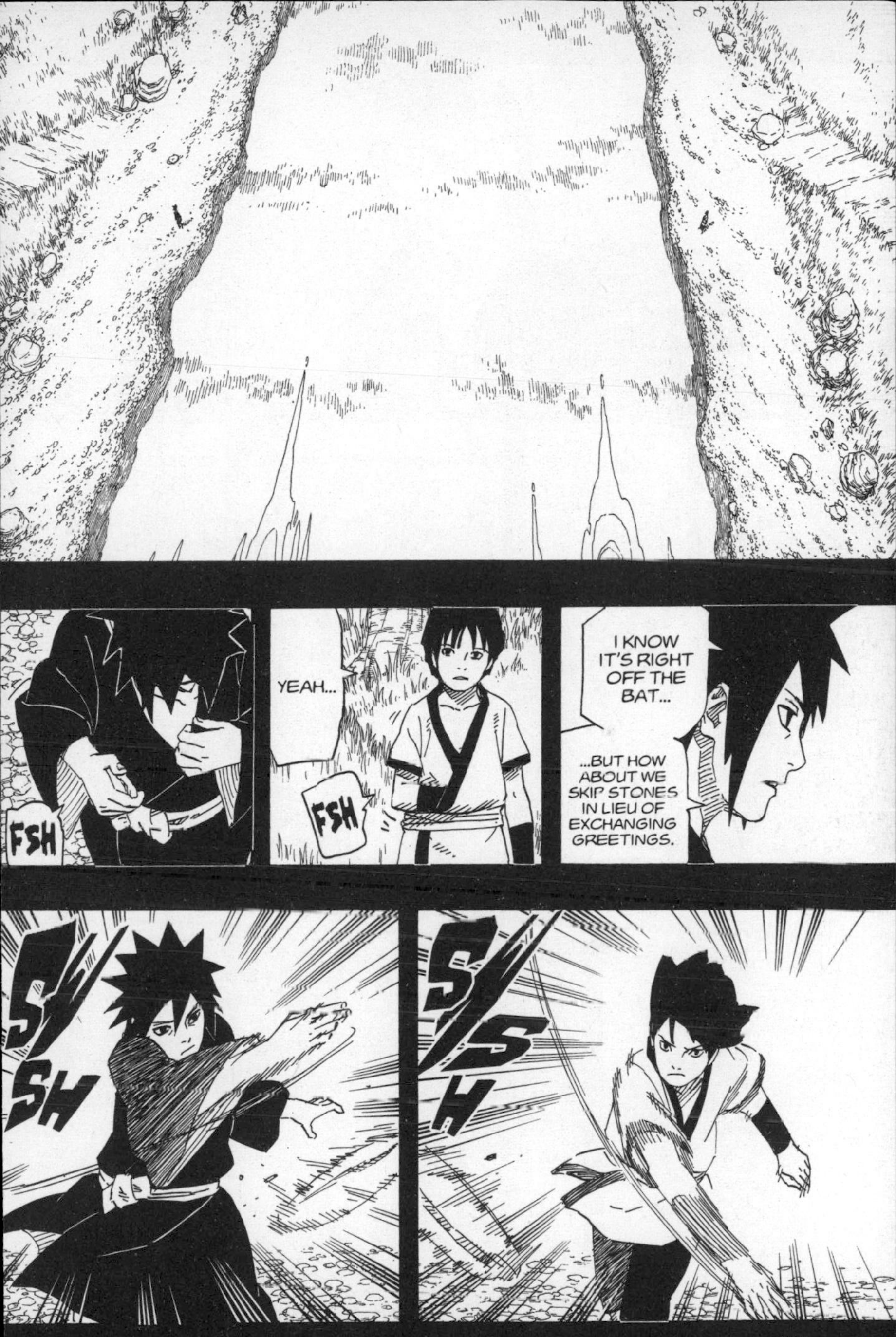
I KNOW IT'S RIGHT OFF THE BAT...
...BUT HOW ABOUT WE SKIP STONES IN LIEU OF EXCHANGING GREETINGS.
YEAH...
FSH
FSH

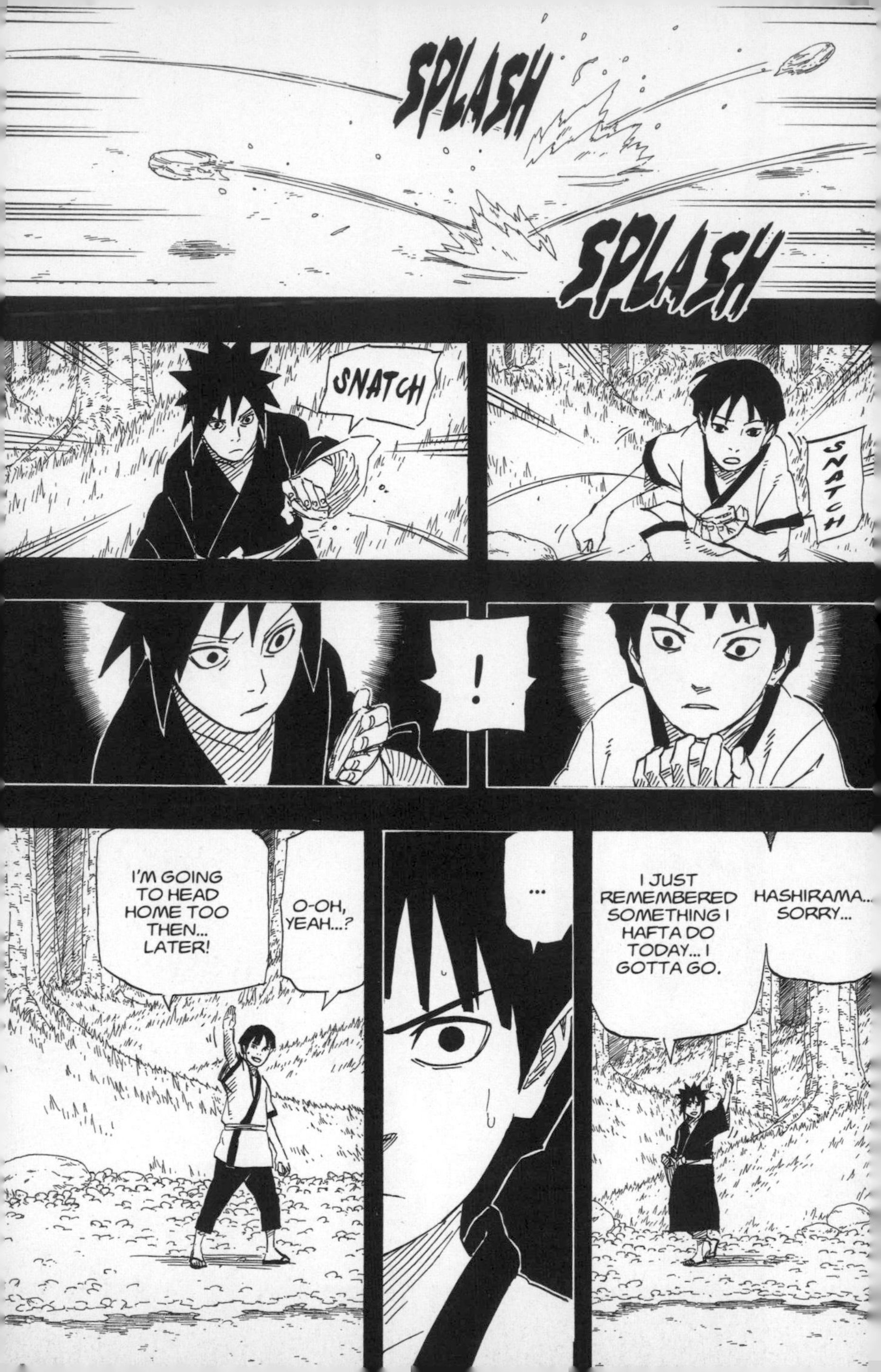
SPLASH
SPLASH
SNATCH
SNATCH
!
HASHIRAMA... SORRY...
I JUST REMEMBERED SOMETHING I HAFTA DO TODAY... I GOTTA GO.
...
O-OH, YEAH...?
I'M GOING TO HEAD HOME TOO THEN... LATER!

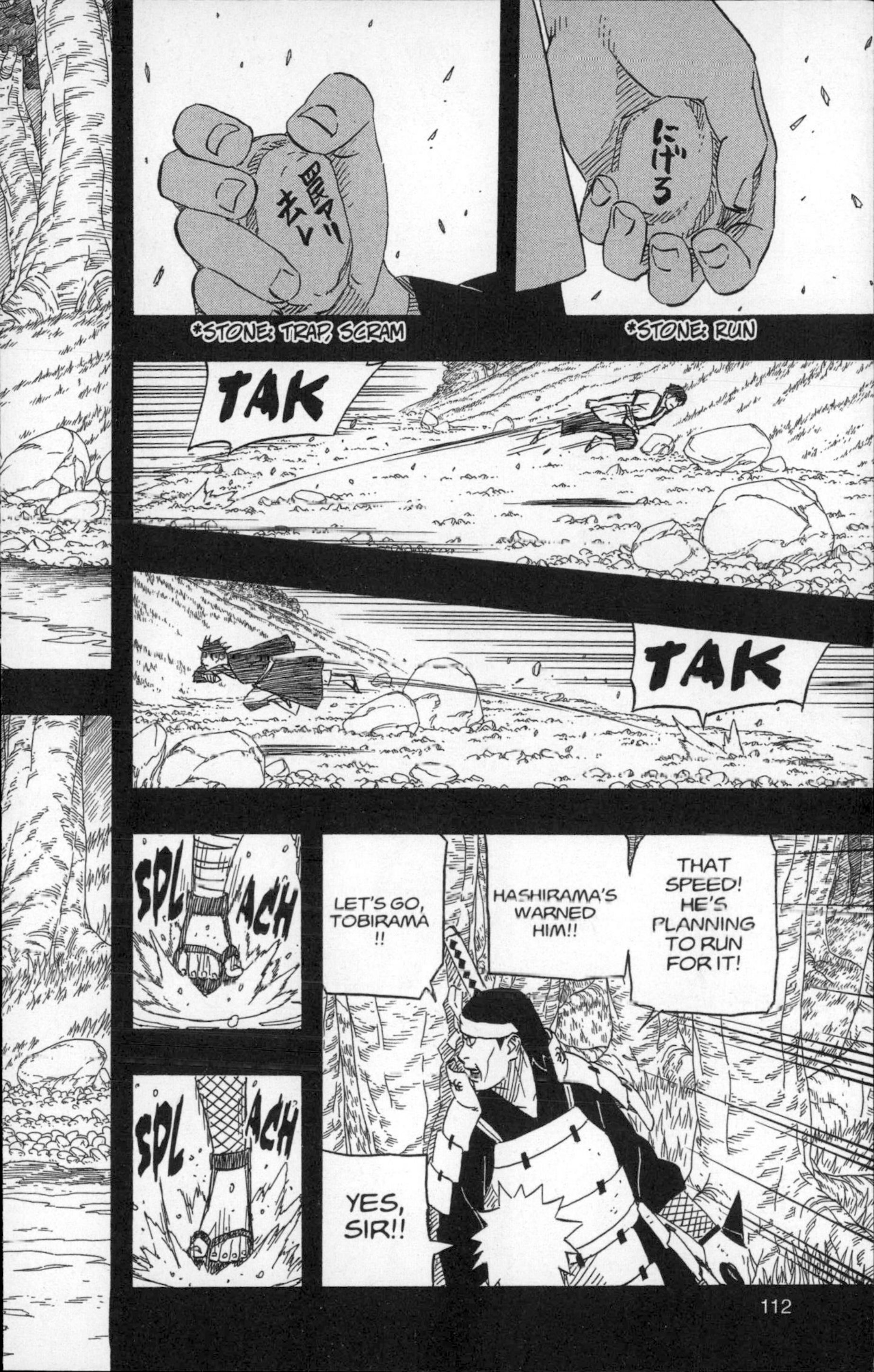
にげろ
*STONE: RUN
罠アリ去レ
*STONE: TRAP, SCRAM
TAK
TAK
THAT SPEED! HE'S PLANNING TO RUN FOR IT!
HASHIRAMA'S WARNED HIM!!
LET'S GO, TOBIRAMA!!
YES, SIR!!
SPLACH
SPLACH

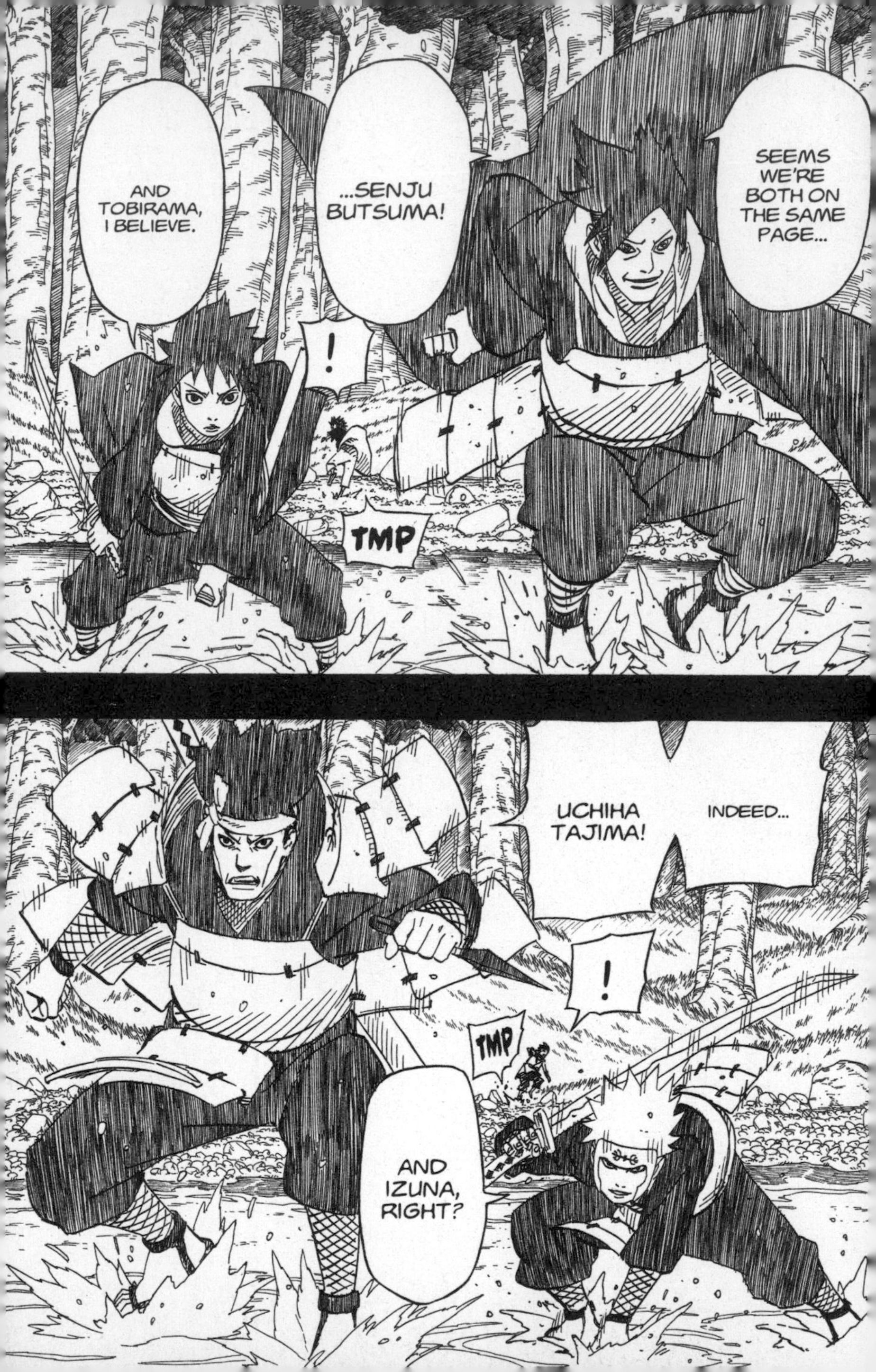
SEEMS WE'RE BOTH ON THE SAME PAGE...
...SENJU BUTSUMA!
!
AND TOBIRAMA, I BELIEVE.
TMP
INDEED...
UCHIHA TAJIMA!
!
TMP
AND IZUNA, RIGHT?

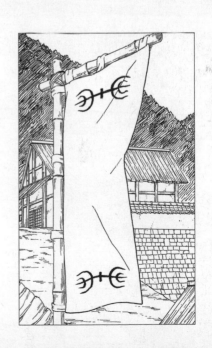

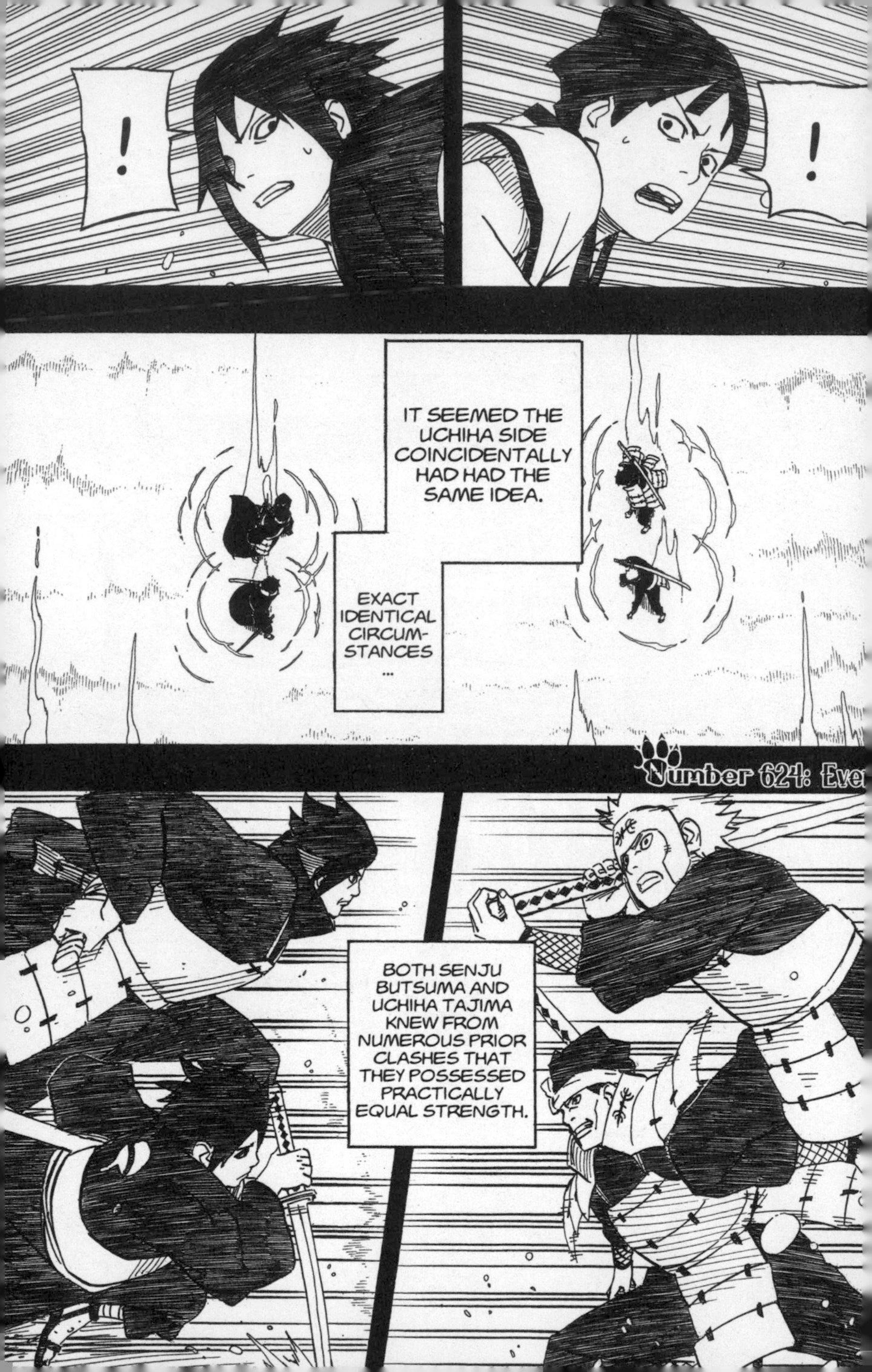
!
!
IT SEEMED THE UCHIHA SIDE COINCIDENTALLY HAD HAD THE SAME IDEA.
EXACT IDENTICAL CIRCUM-STANCES ...
Number 624: Eve
BOTH SENJU BUTSUMA AND UCHIHA TAJIMA KNEW FROM NUMEROUS PRIOR CLASHES THAT THEY POSSESSED PRACTICALLY EQUAL STRENGTH.

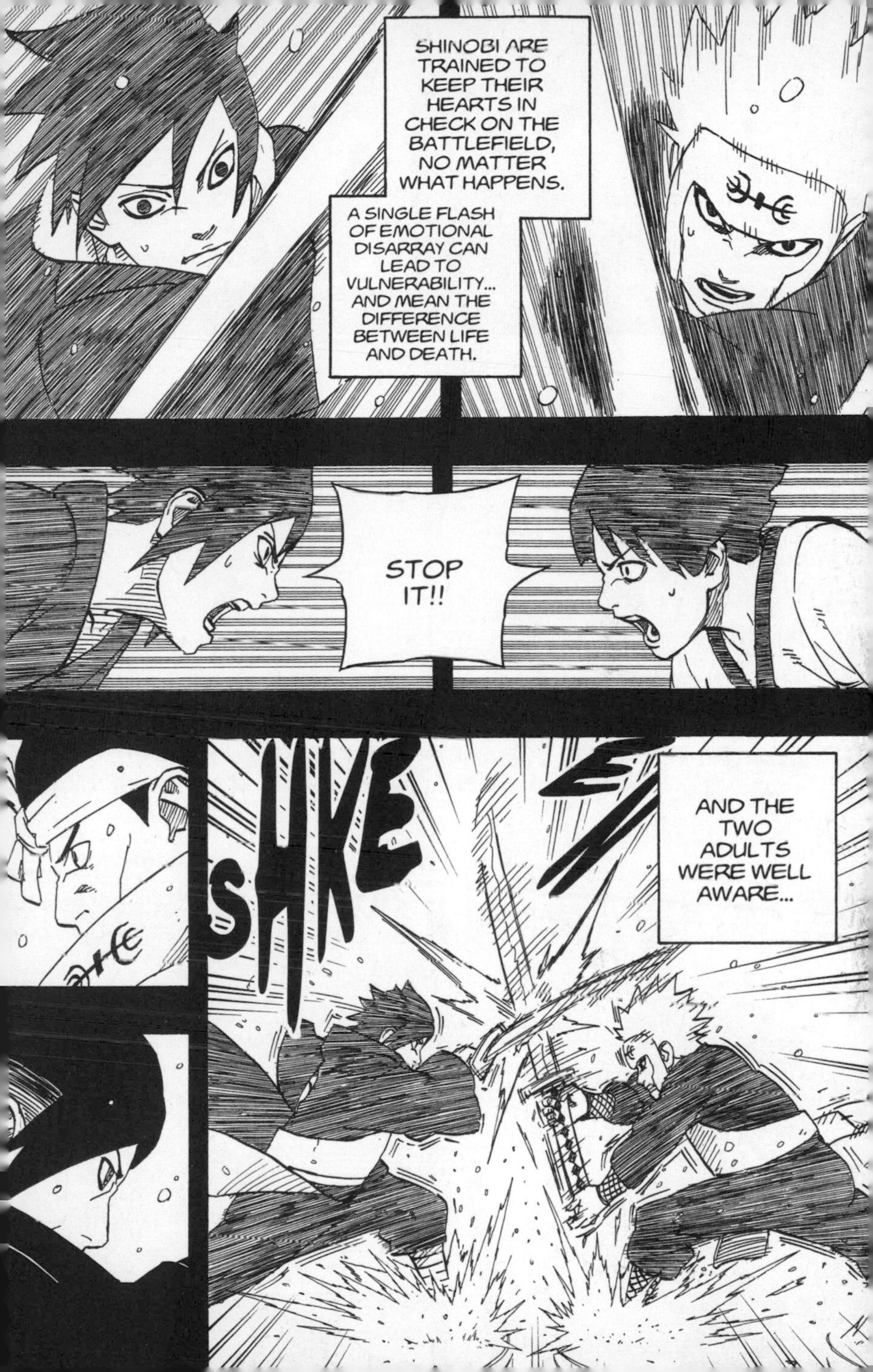
SHINOBI ARE TRAINED TO KEEP THEIR HEARTS IN CHECK ON THE BATTLEFIELD, NO MATTER WHAT HAPPENS.
A SINGLE FLASH OF EMOTIONAL DISARRAY CAN LEAD TO VULNERABILITY... AND MEAN THE DIFFERENCE BETWEEN LIFE AND DEATH.
STOP IT!!
AND THE TWO ADULTS WERE WELL AWARE...

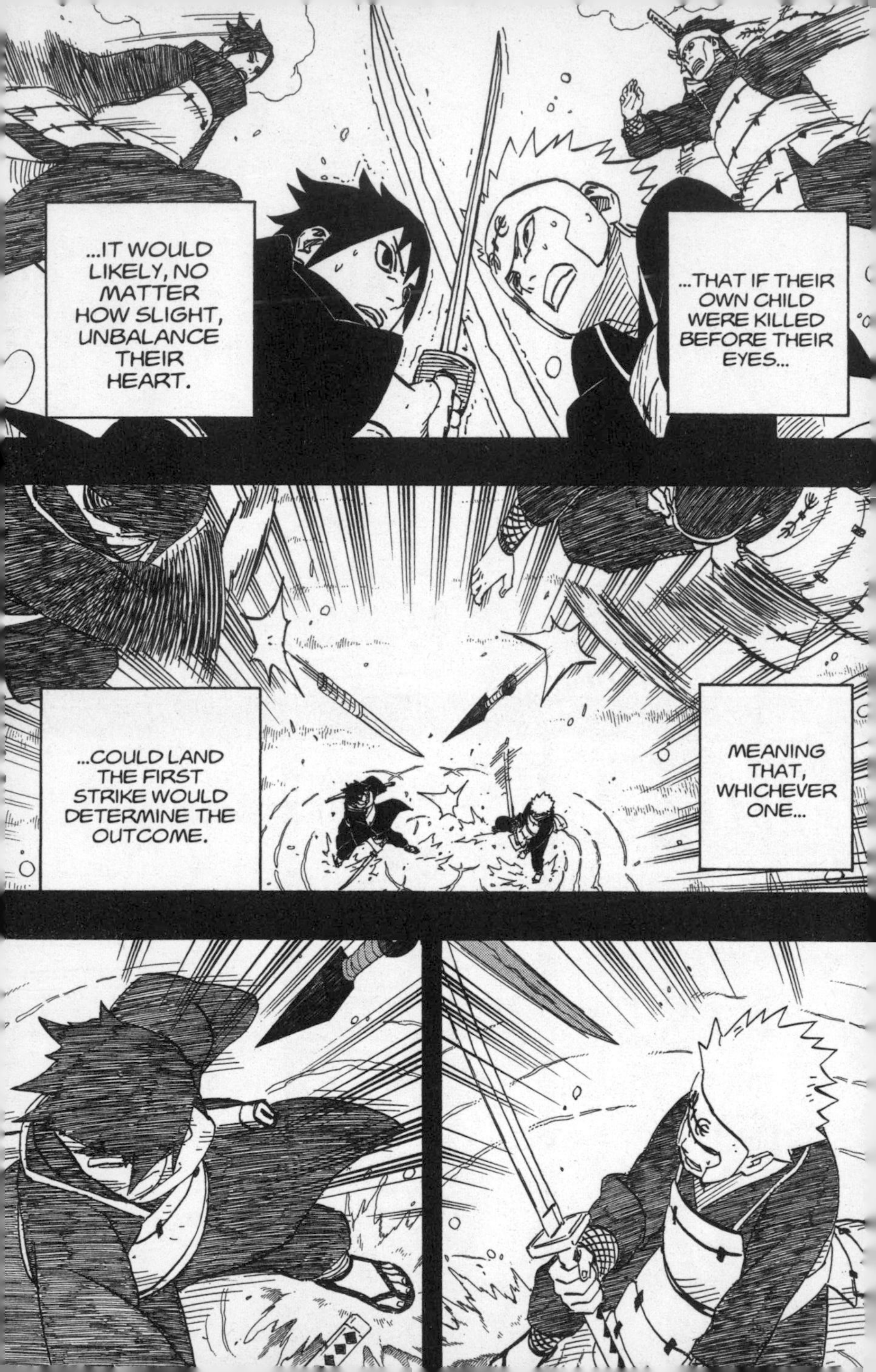
...THAT IF THEIR OWN CHILD WERE KILLED BEFORE THEIR EYES...
...IT WOULD LIKELY, NO MATTER HOW SLIGHT, UNBALANCE THEIR HEART.
MEANING THAT, WHICHEVER ONE...
...COULD LAND THE FIRST STRIKE WOULD DETERMINE THE OUTCOME.

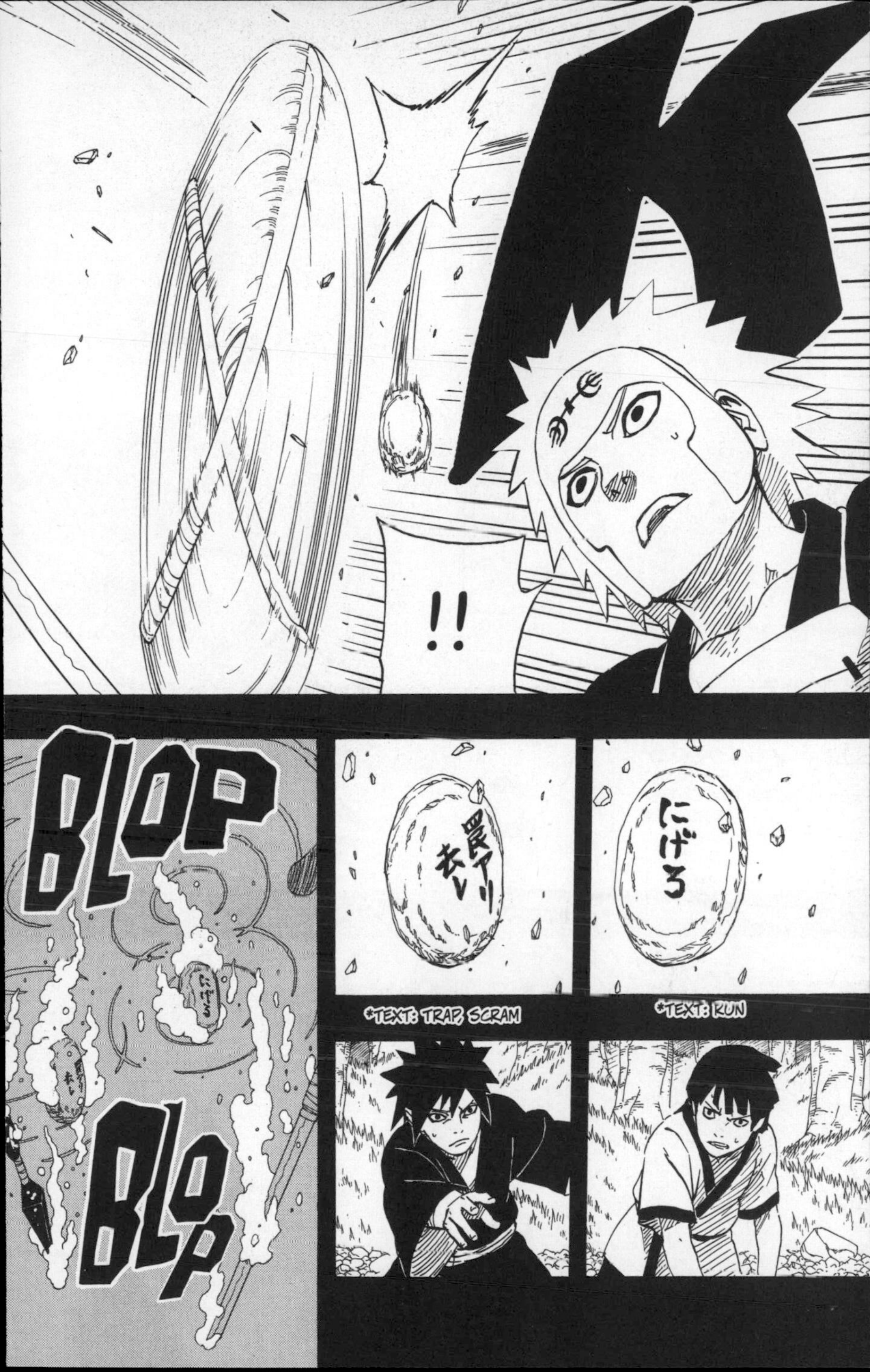
!!
にげろ
*TEXT: RUN
罠アリ去レ
*TEXT: TRAP, SCRAM
BLOP
BLOP

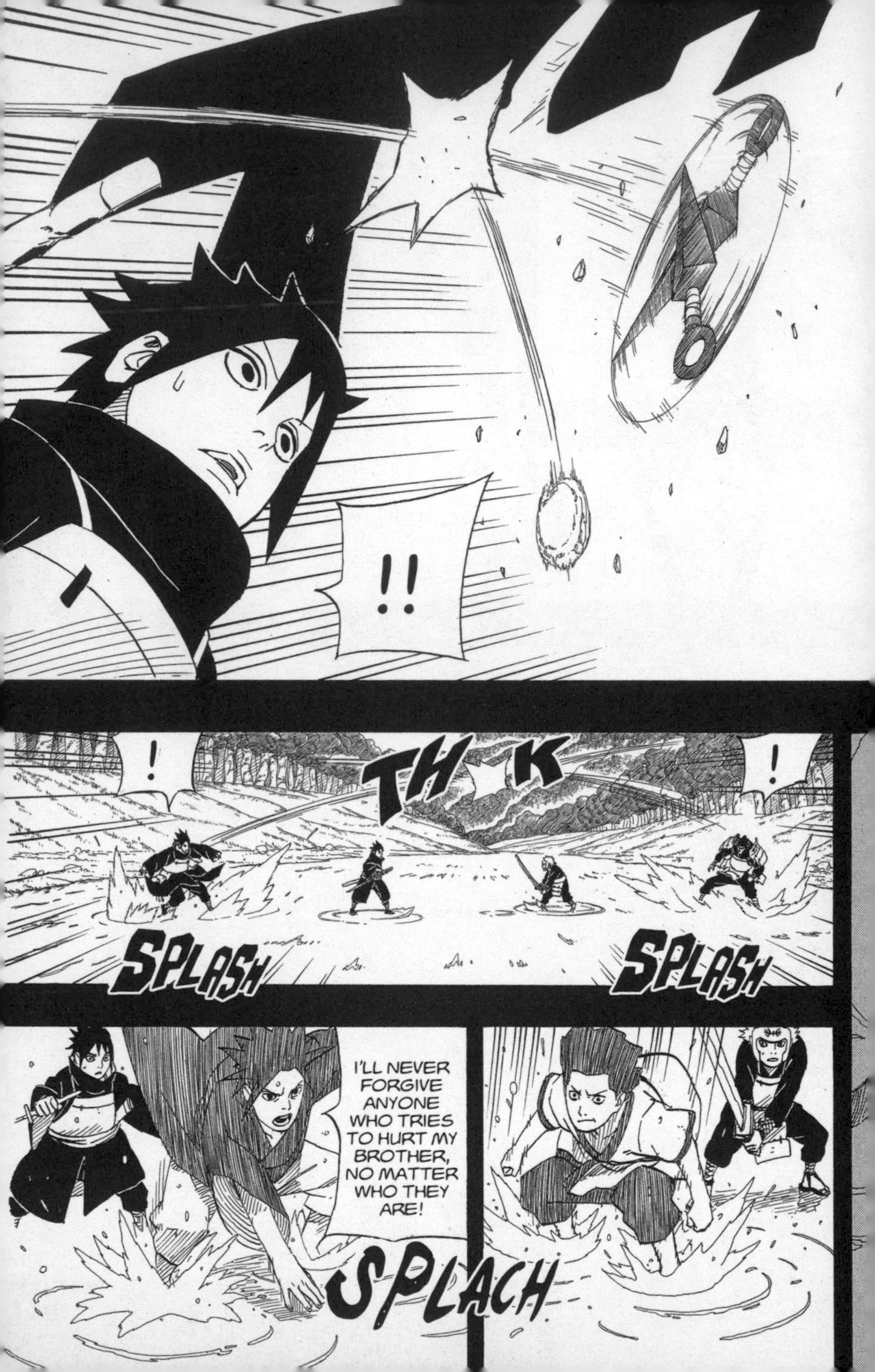
!!
!
TH K
!
SPLASH
SPLASH
I'LL NEVER FORGIVE ANYONE WHO TRIES TO HURT MY BROTHER, NO MATTER WHO THEY ARE!
SPLACH

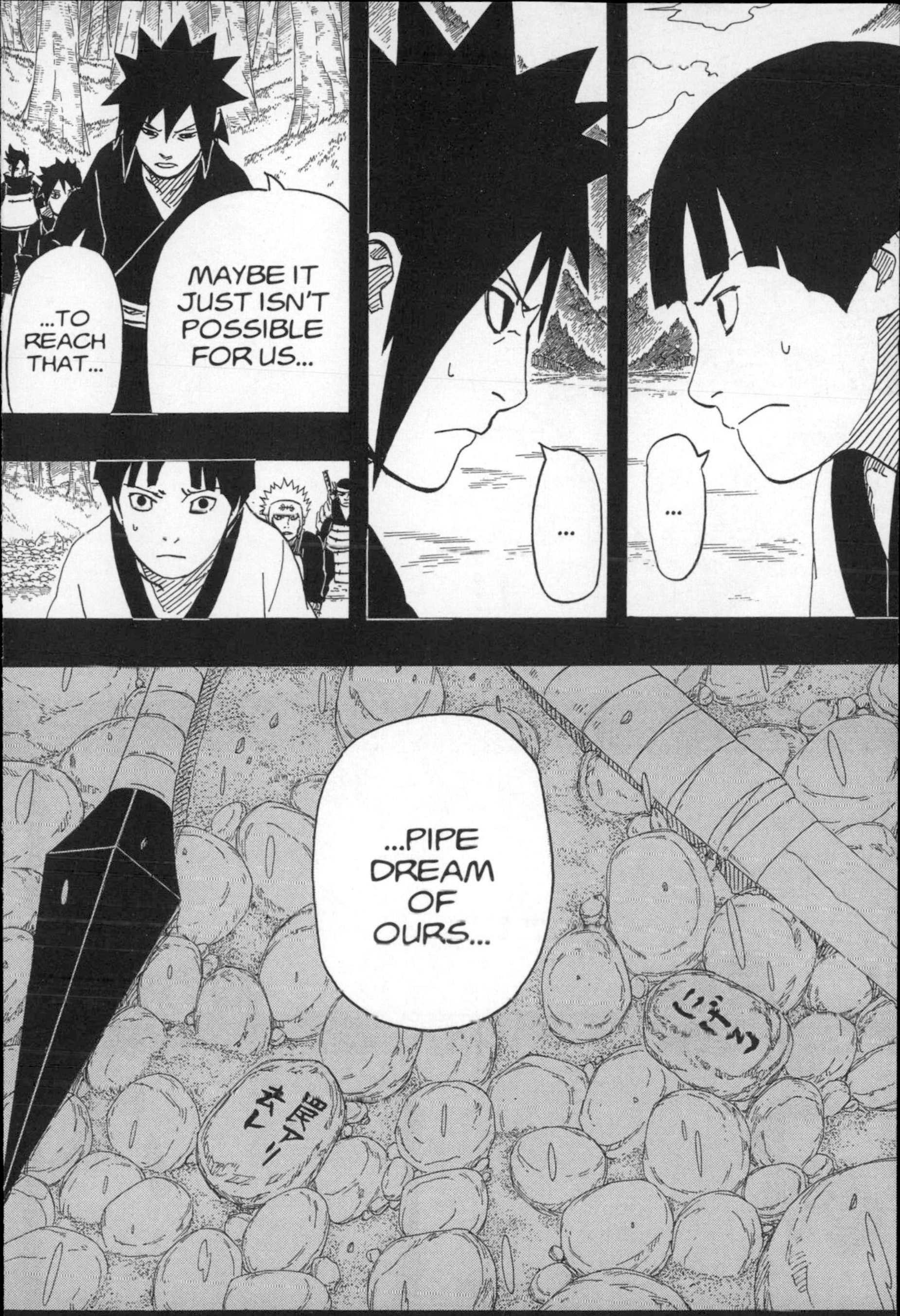
...
...
MAYBE IT JUST ISN'T POSSIBLE FOR US...
...TO REACH THAT...
...PIPE DREAM OF OURS...

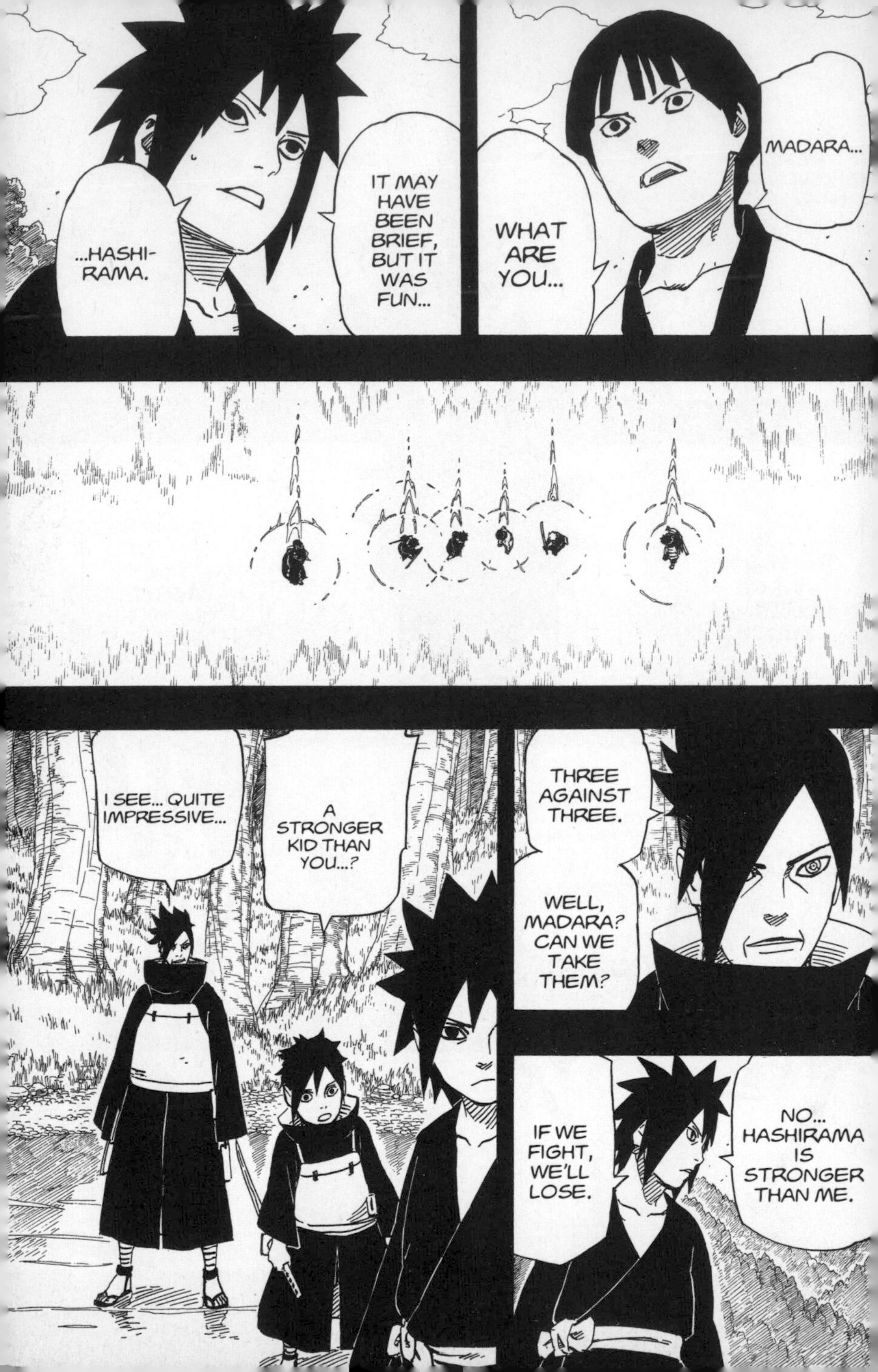
MADARA...
WHAT ARE YOU...
IT MAY HAVE BEEN BRIEF, BUT IT WAS FUN...
...HASHI-RAMA.
THREE AGAINST THREE.
WELL, MADARA? CAN WE TAKE THEM?
NO... HASHIRAMA IS STRONGER THAN ME.
IF WE FIGHT, WE'LL LOSE.
A STRONGER KID THAN YOU...?
I SEE... QUITE IMPRESSIVE...

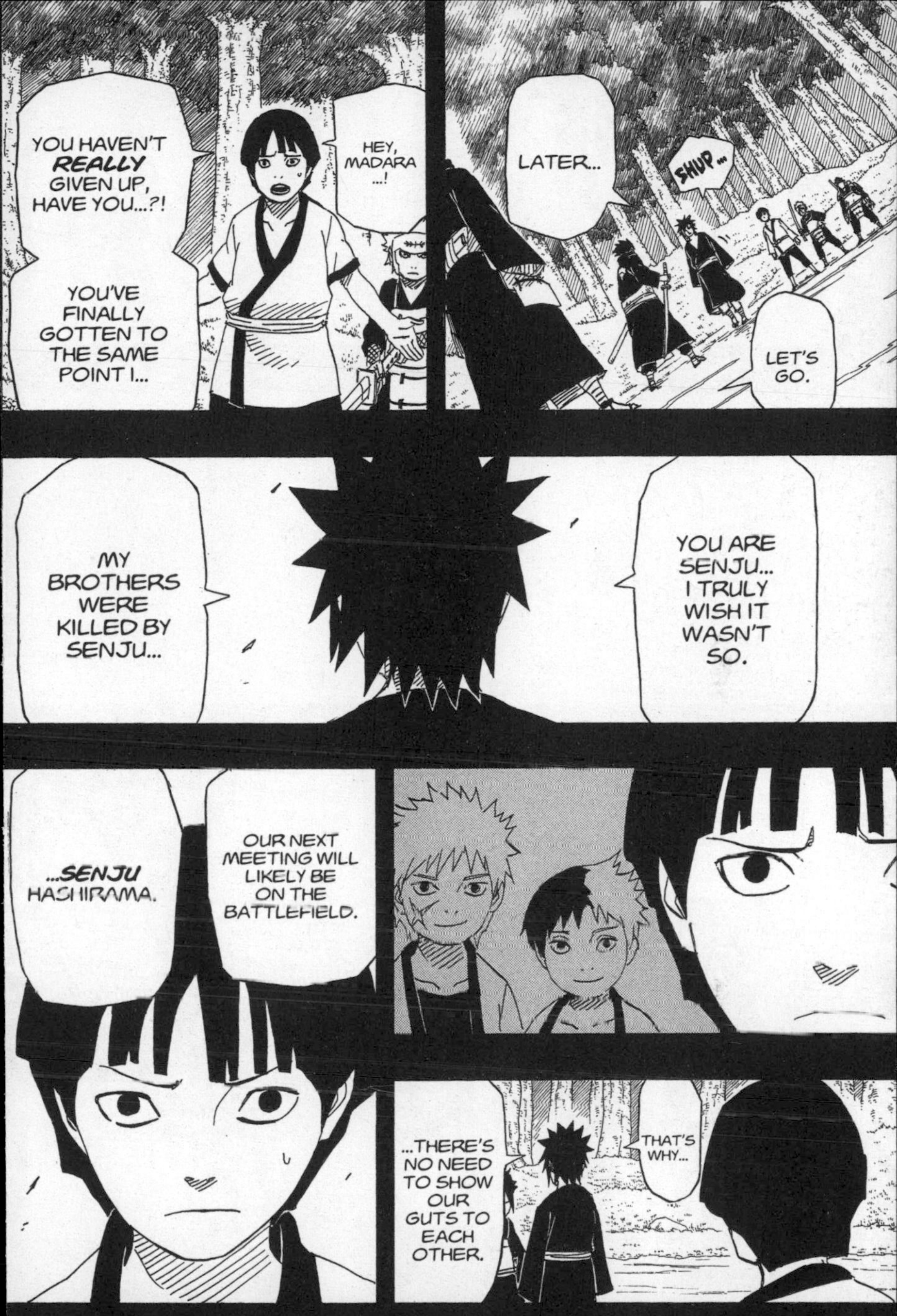
LATER...
SHUP...
LET'S GO.
HEY, MADARA ...!
YOU HAVEN'T **REALLY** GIVEN UP, HAVE YOU...?!
YOU'VE FINALLY GOTTEN TO THE SAME POINT I...
YOU ARE SENJU... I TRULY WISH IT WASN'T SO.
MY BROTHERS WERE KILLED BY SENJU...
THAT'S WHY...
...THERE'S NO NEED TO SHOW OUR GUTS TO EACH OTHER.
OUR NEXT MEETING WILL LIKELY BE ON THE BATTLEFIELD.
...**SENJU** HASHIRAMA.

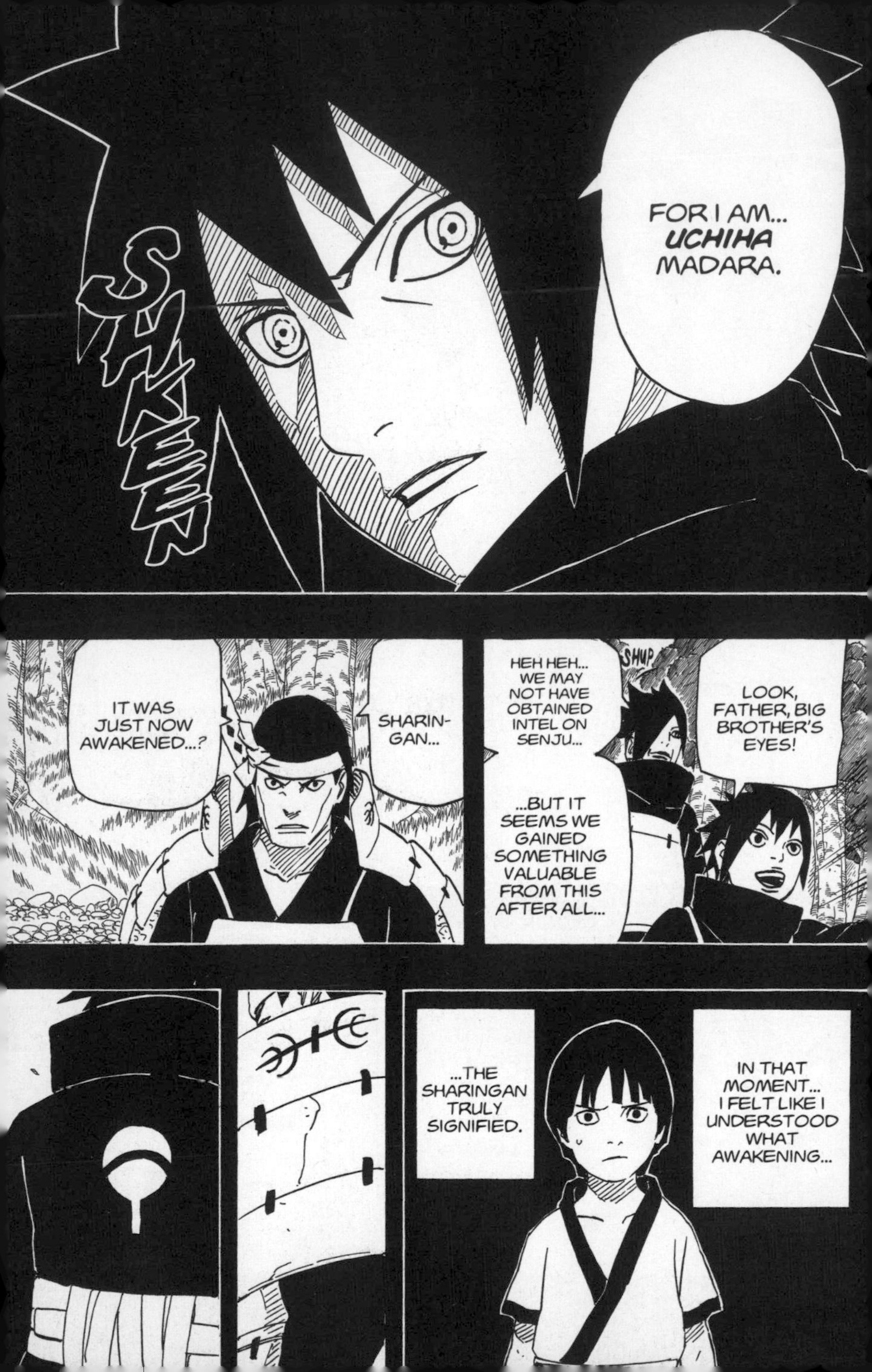
FOR I AM... UCHIHA MADARA.
SHKEEN
SHUP
LOOK, FATHER, BIG BROTHER'S EYES!
HEH HEH... WE MAY NOT HAVE OBTAINED INTEL ON SENJU...
...BUT IT SEEMS WE GAINED SOMETHING VALUABLE FROM THIS AFTER ALL...
SHARIN-GAN...
IT WAS JUST NOW AWAKENED...?
IN THAT MOMENT... I FELT LIKE I UNDERSTOOD WHAT AWAKENING...
...THE SHARINGAN TRULY SIGNIFIED.

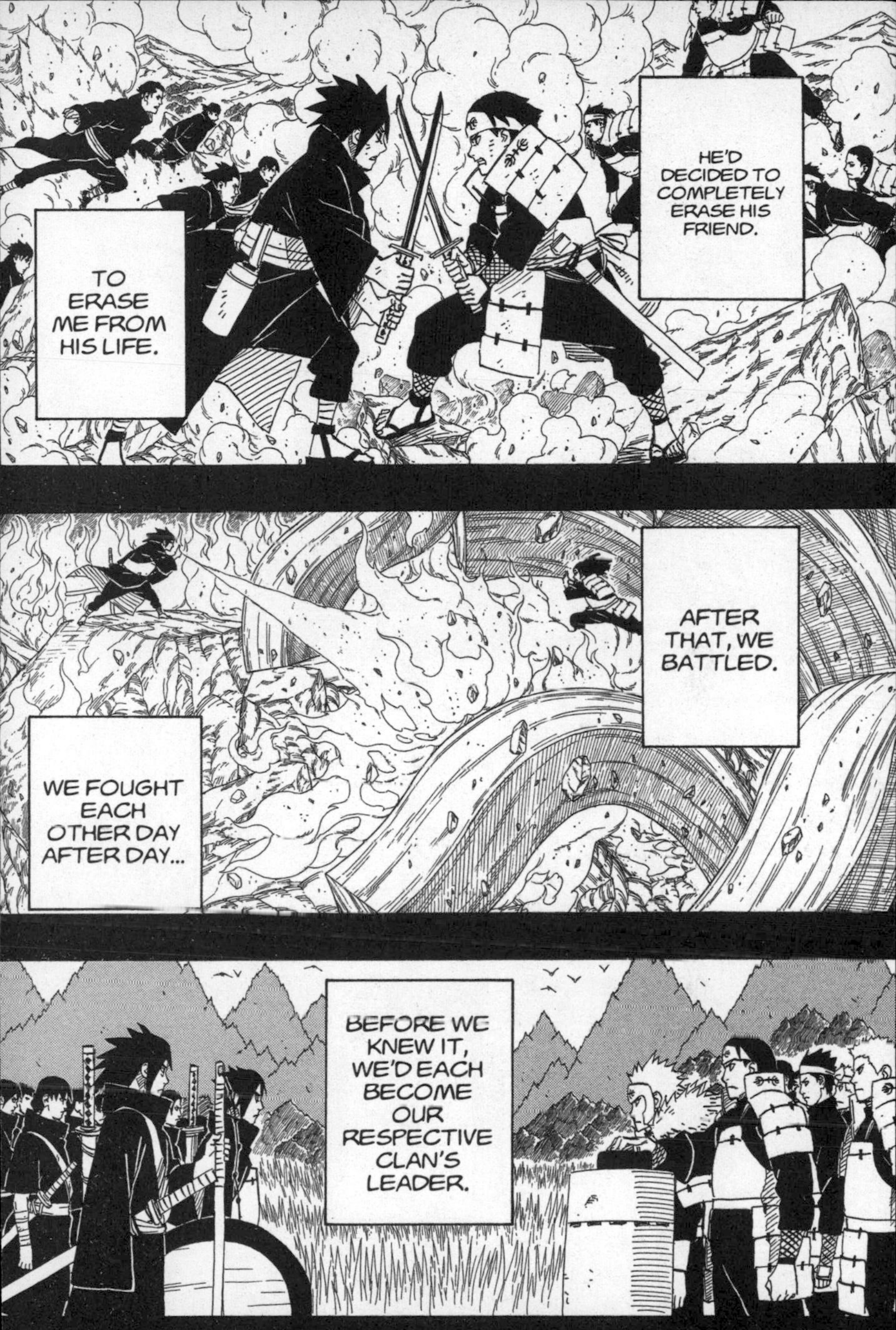
HE'D DECIDED TO COMPLETELY ERASE HIS FRIEND.
TO ERASE ME FROM HIS LIFE.
AFTER THAT, WE BATTLED.
WE FOUGHT EACH OTHER DAY AFTER DAY...
BEFORE WE KNEW IT, WE'D EACH BECOME OUR RESPECTIVE CLAN'S LEADER.

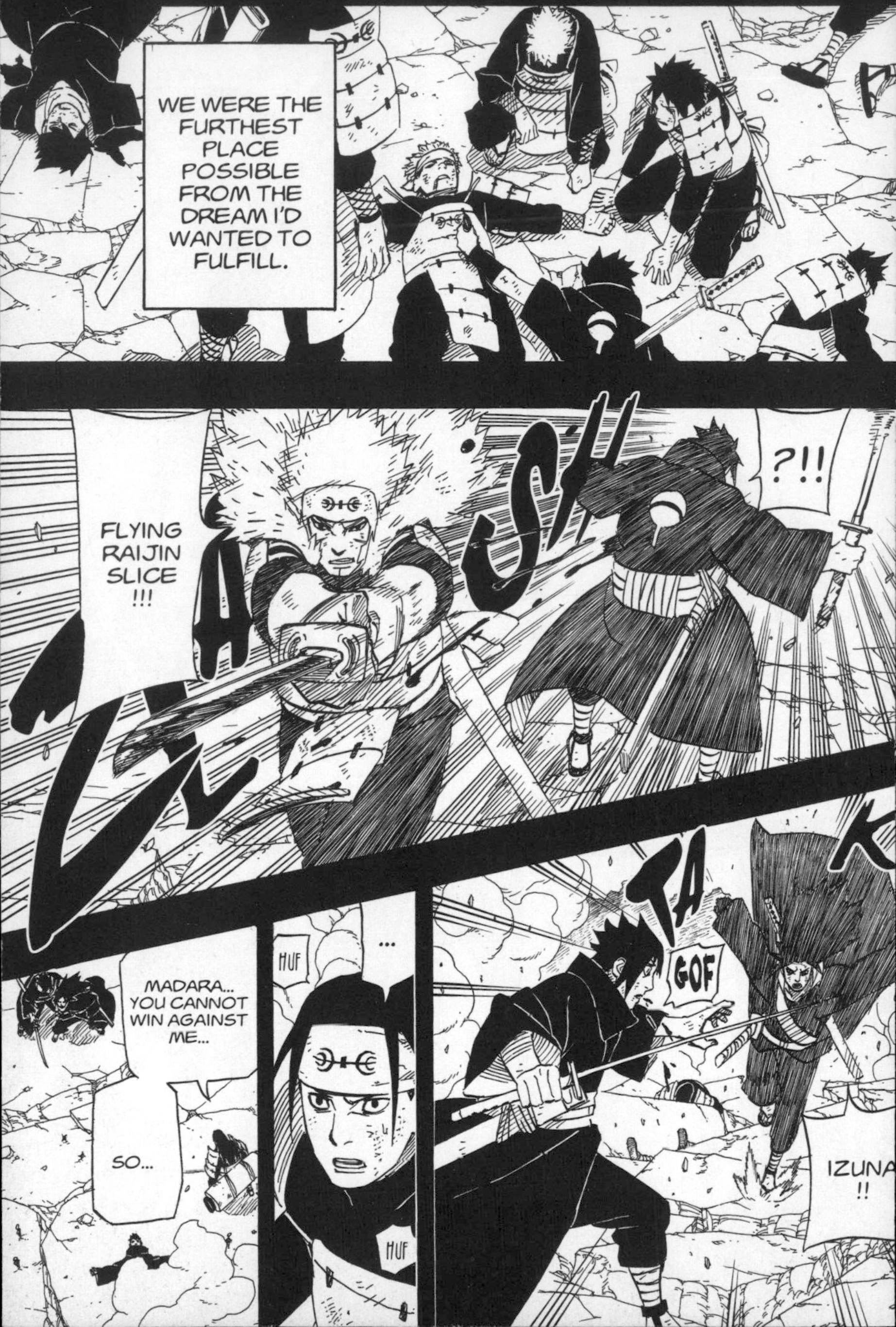
WE WERE THE FURTHEST PLACE POSSIBLE FROM THE DREAM I'D WANTED TO FULFILL.
?!!
FLYING RAIJIN SLICE !!!
ZASH
TAK
GOF
IZUNA !!
...
HUF
HUF
MADARA... YOU CANNOT WIN AGAINST ME...
SO...

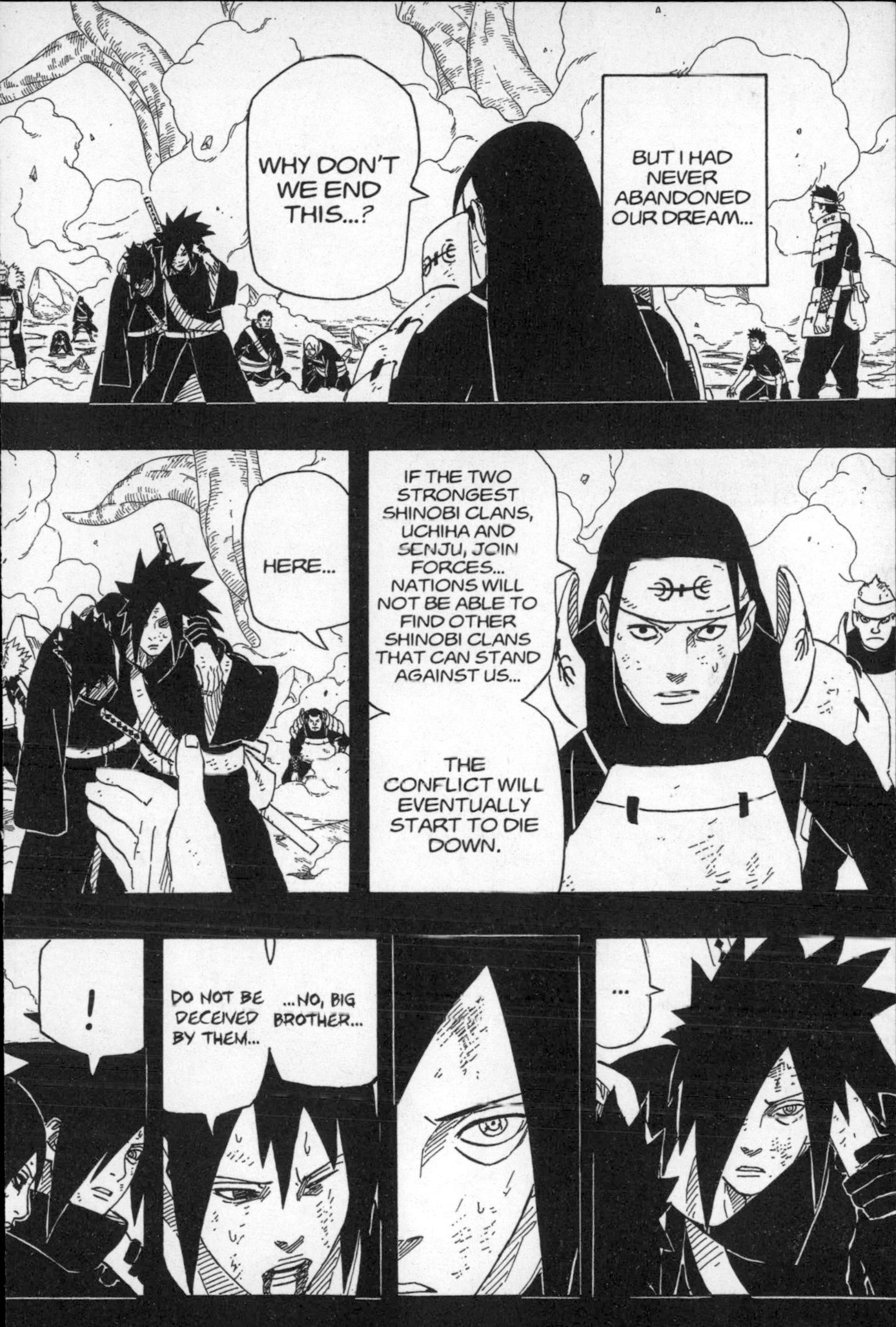
BUT I HAD NEVER ABANDONED OUR DREAM...
WHY DON'T WE END THIS...?
IF THE TWO STRONGEST SHINOBI CLANS, UCHIHA AND SENJU, JOIN FORCES... NATIONS WILL NOT BE ABLE TO FIND OTHER SHINOBI CLANS THAT CAN STAND AGAINST US...
THE CONFLICT WILL EVENTUALLY START TO DIE DOWN.
HERE...
...
...NO, BIG BROTHER...
DO NOT BE DECEIVED BY THEM...
!

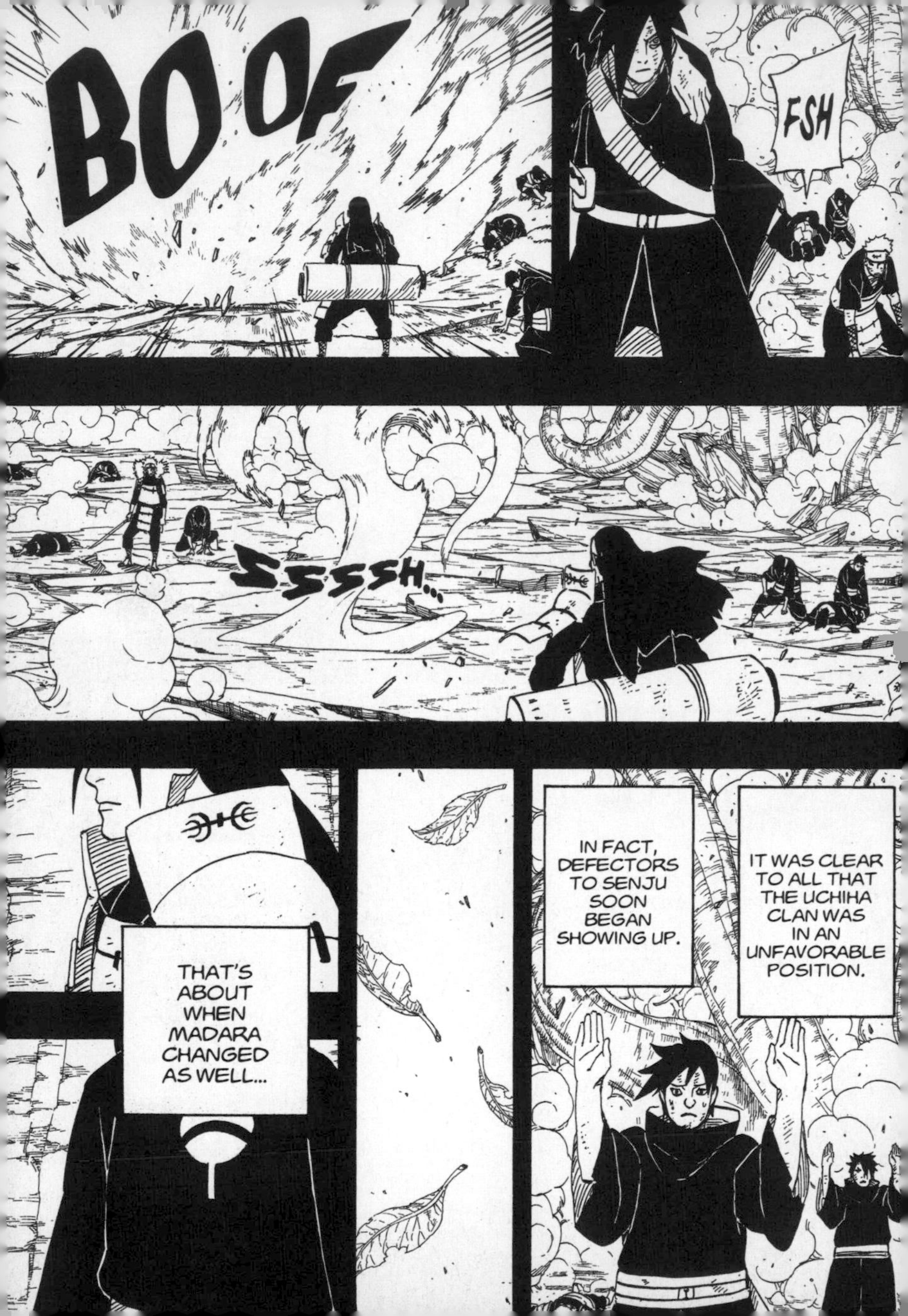
FSH
BOOF
SSSSH...
IT WAS CLEAR TO ALL THAT THE UCHIHA CLAN WAS IN AN UNFAVORABLE POSITION.
IN FACT, DEFECTORS TO SENJU SOON BEGAN SHOWING UP.
THAT'S ABOUT WHEN MADARA CHANGED AS WELL...

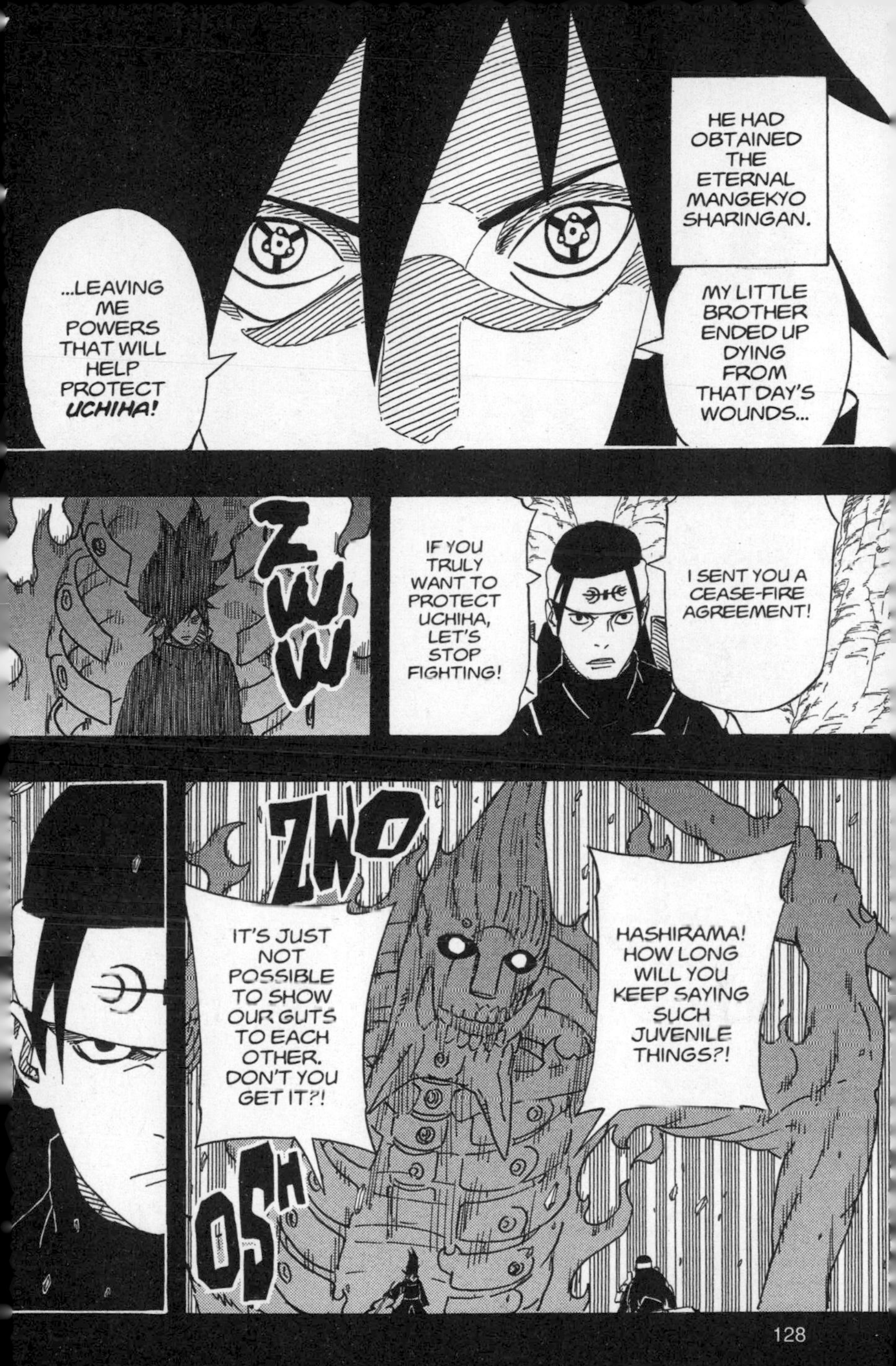
HE HAD OBTAINED THE ETERNAL MANGEKYO SHARINGAN.
MY LITTLE BROTHER ENDED UP DYING FROM THAT DAY'S WOUNDS...
...LEAVING ME POWERS THAT WILL HELP PROTECT *UCHIHA!*
I SENT YOU A CEASE-FIRE AGREEMENT!
IF YOU TRULY WANT TO PROTECT UCHIHA, LET'S STOP FIGHTING!
ZWW
ZWO
HASHIRAMA! HOW LONG WILL YOU KEEP SAYING SUCH JUVENILE THINGS?!
IT'S JUST NOT POSSIBLE TO SHOW OUR GUTS TO EACH OTHER. DON'T YOU GET IT?!
OSH

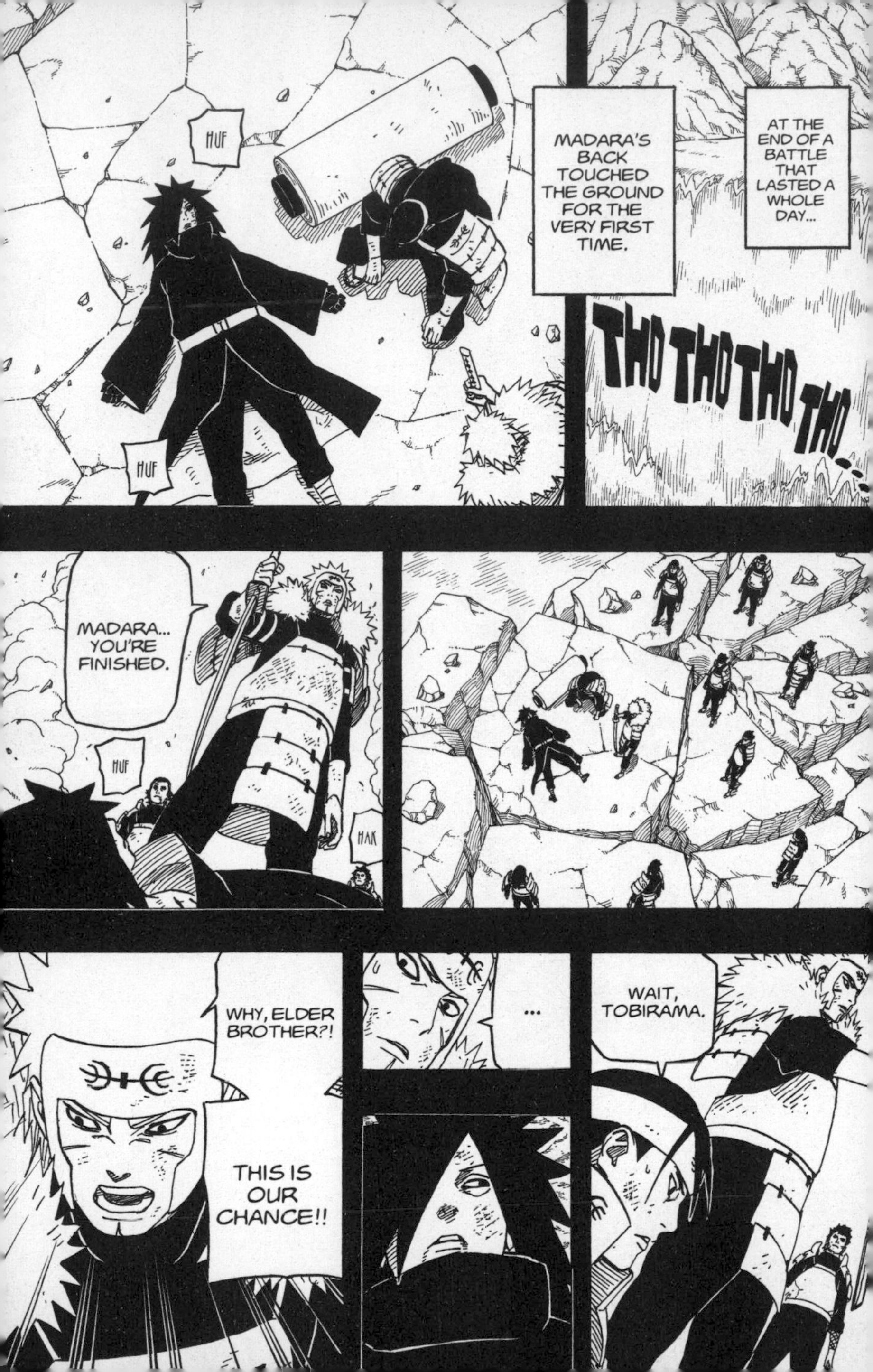
AT THE END OF A BATTLE THAT LASTED A WHOLE DAY...
MADARA'S BACK TOUCHED THE GROUND FOR THE VERY FIRST TIME.
THO THO THO THO...
HUF
HUF
MADARA... YOU'RE FINISHED.
HUF
HAK
WAIT, TOBIRAMA.
...
WHY, ELDER BROTHER?!
THIS IS OUR CHANCE!!

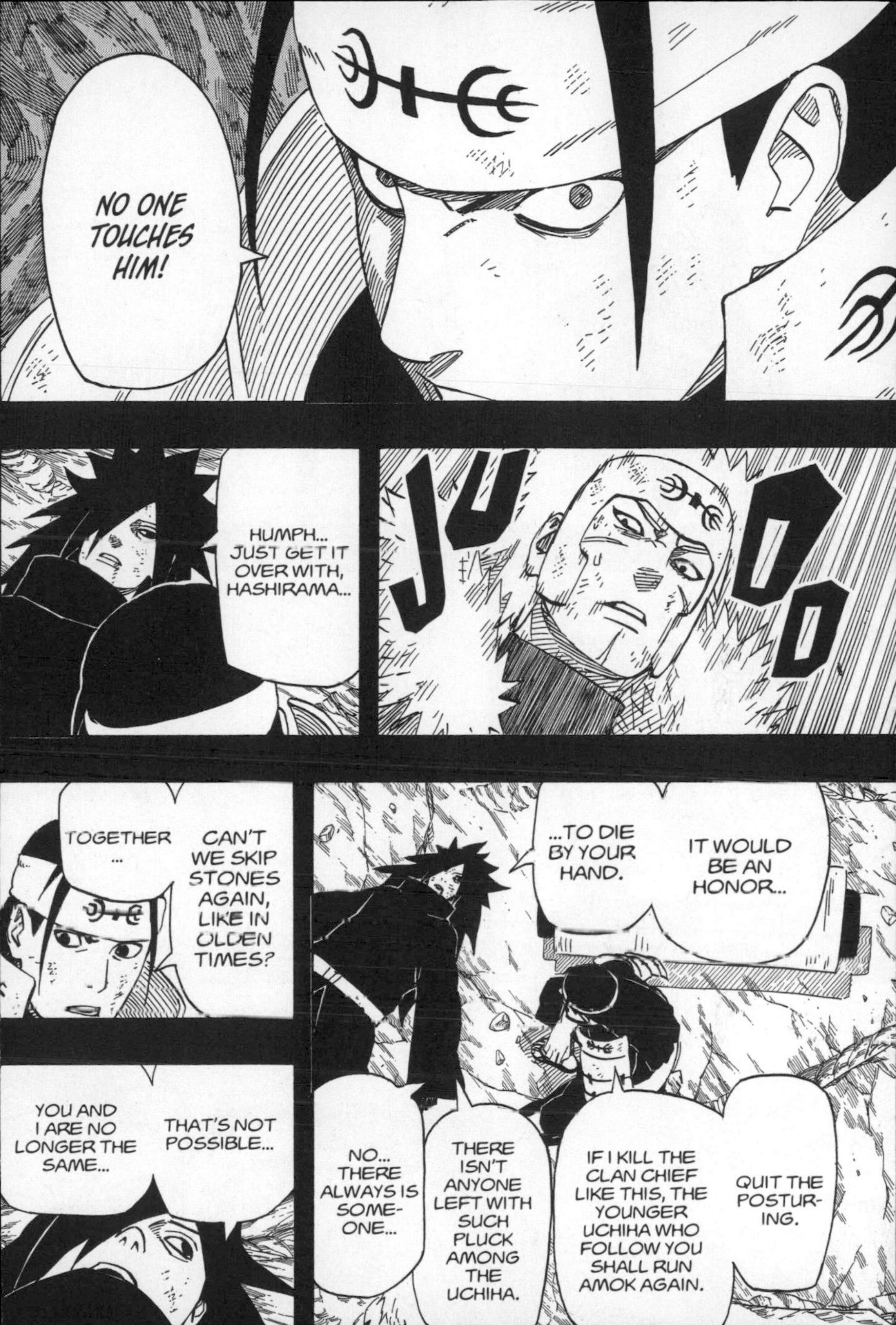
NO ONE TOUCHES HIM!
HUMPH... JUST GET IT OVER WITH, HASHIRAMA...
IT WOULD BE AN HONOR...
...TO DIE BY YOUR HAND.
QUIT THE POSTUR-ING.
IF I KILL THE CLAN CHIEF LIKE THIS, THE YOUNGER UCHIHA WHO FOLLOW YOU SHALL RUN AMOK AGAIN.
THERE ISN'T ANYONE LEFT WITH SUCH PLUCK AMONG THE UCHIHA.
NO... THERE ALWAYS IS SOME-ONE...
CAN'T WE SKIP STONES AGAIN, LIKE IN OLDEN TIMES?
TOGETHER ...
THAT'S NOT POSSIBLE...
YOU AND I ARE NO LONGER THE SAME...

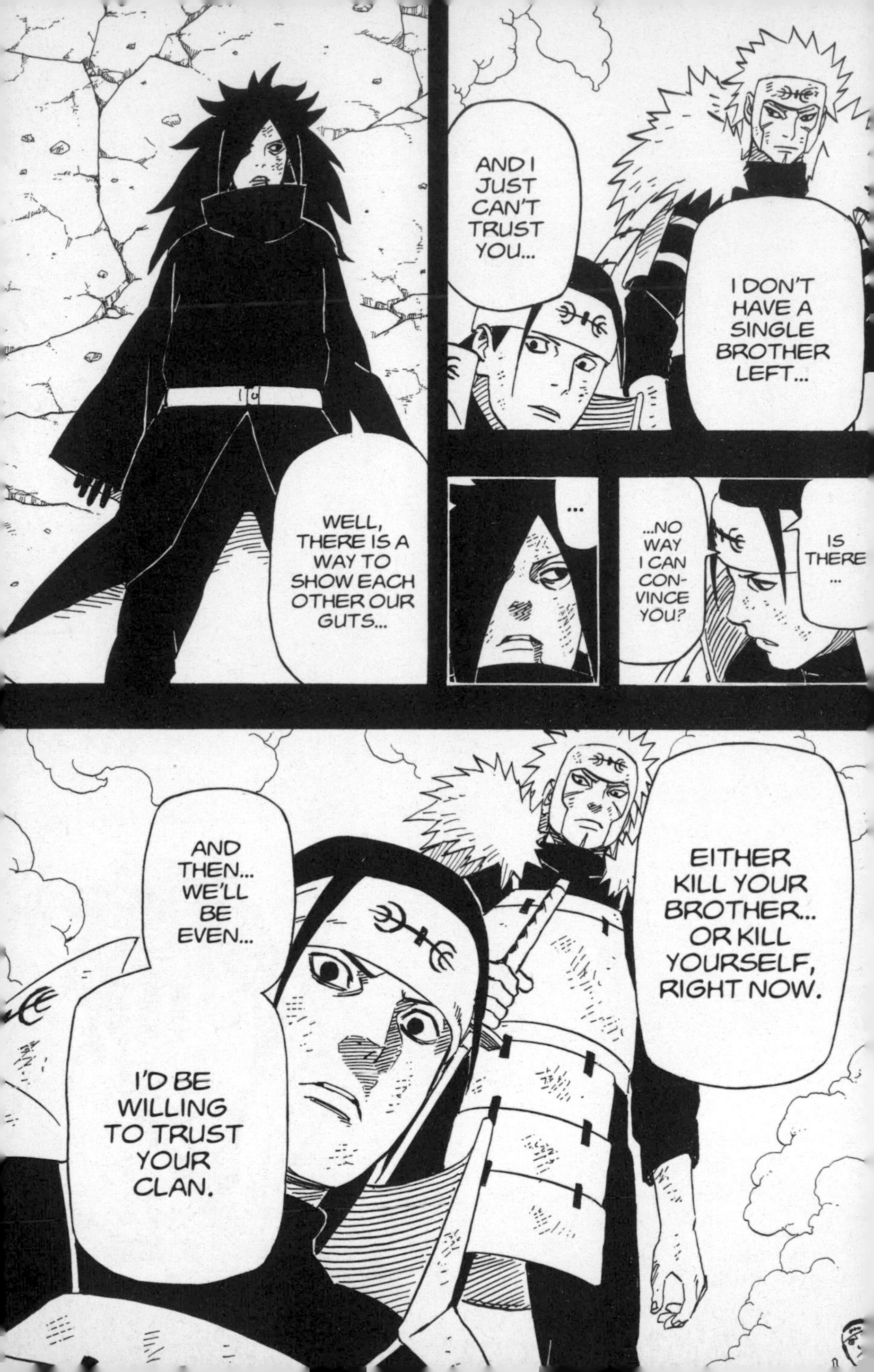
I DON'T HAVE A SINGLE BROTHER LEFT...
AND I JUST CAN'T TRUST YOU...
IS THERE ...
...NO WAY I CAN CON-VINCE YOU?
...
WELL, THERE IS A WAY TO SHOW EACH OTHER OUR GUTS...
EITHER KILL YOUR BROTHER... OR KILL YOURSELF, RIGHT NOW.
AND THEN... WE'LL BE EVEN...
I'D BE WILLING TO TRUST YOUR CLAN.

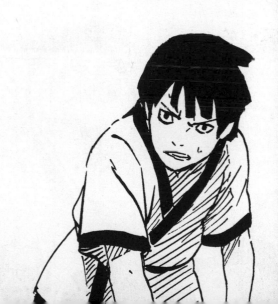

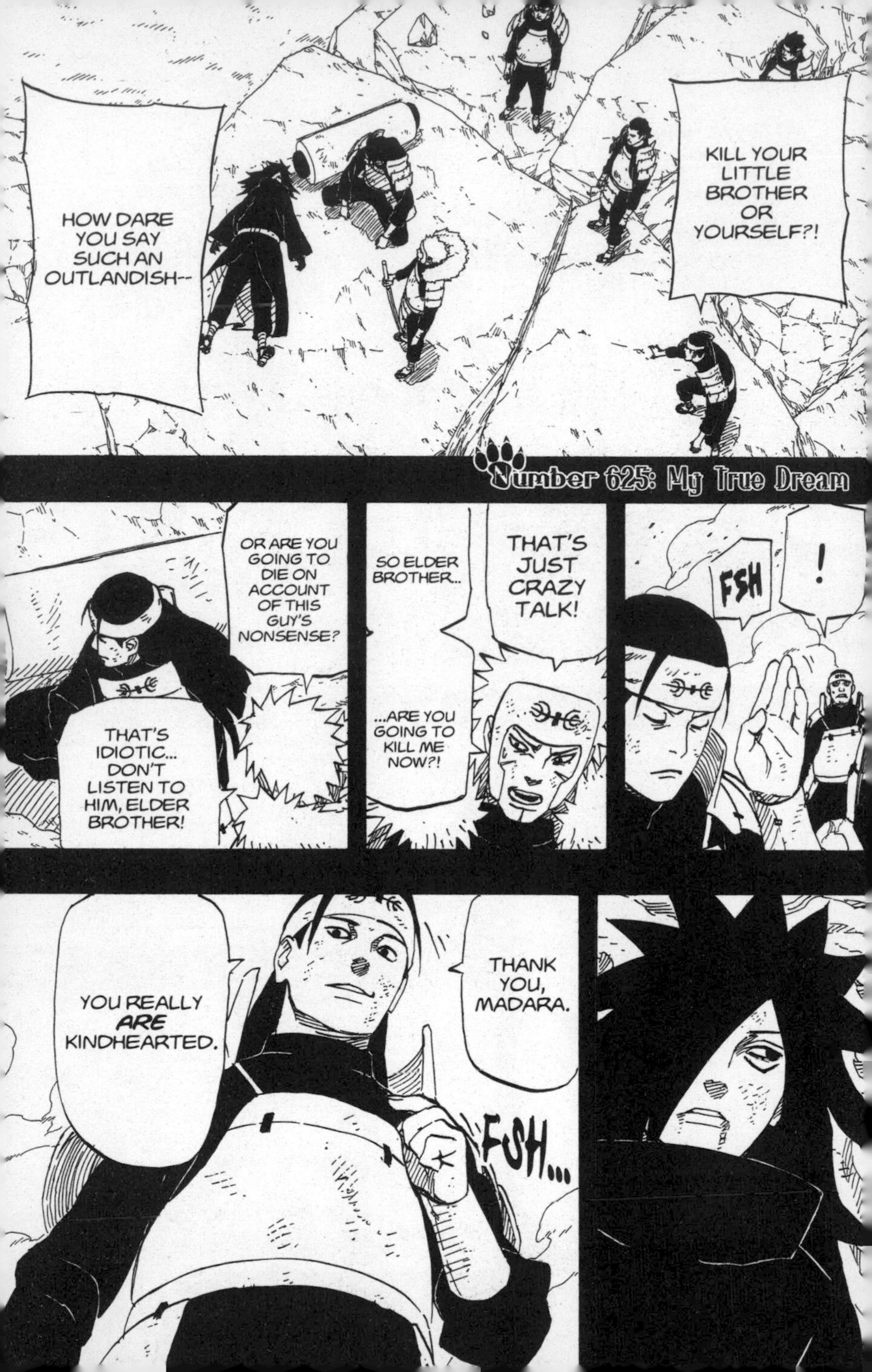
KILL YOUR LITTLE BROTHER OR YOURSELF?!
HOW DARE YOU SAY SUCH AN OUTLANDISH--
Number 625: My True Dream
!
FSH
THAT'S JUST CRAZY TALK!
SO ELDER BROTHER...
...ARE YOU GOING TO KILL ME NOW?!
OR ARE YOU GOING TO DIE ON ACCOUNT OF THIS GUY'S NONSENSE?
THAT'S IDIOTIC... DON'T LISTEN TO HIM, ELDER BROTHER!
THANK YOU, MADARA.
YOU REALLY **ARE** KINDHEARTED.
FSH...

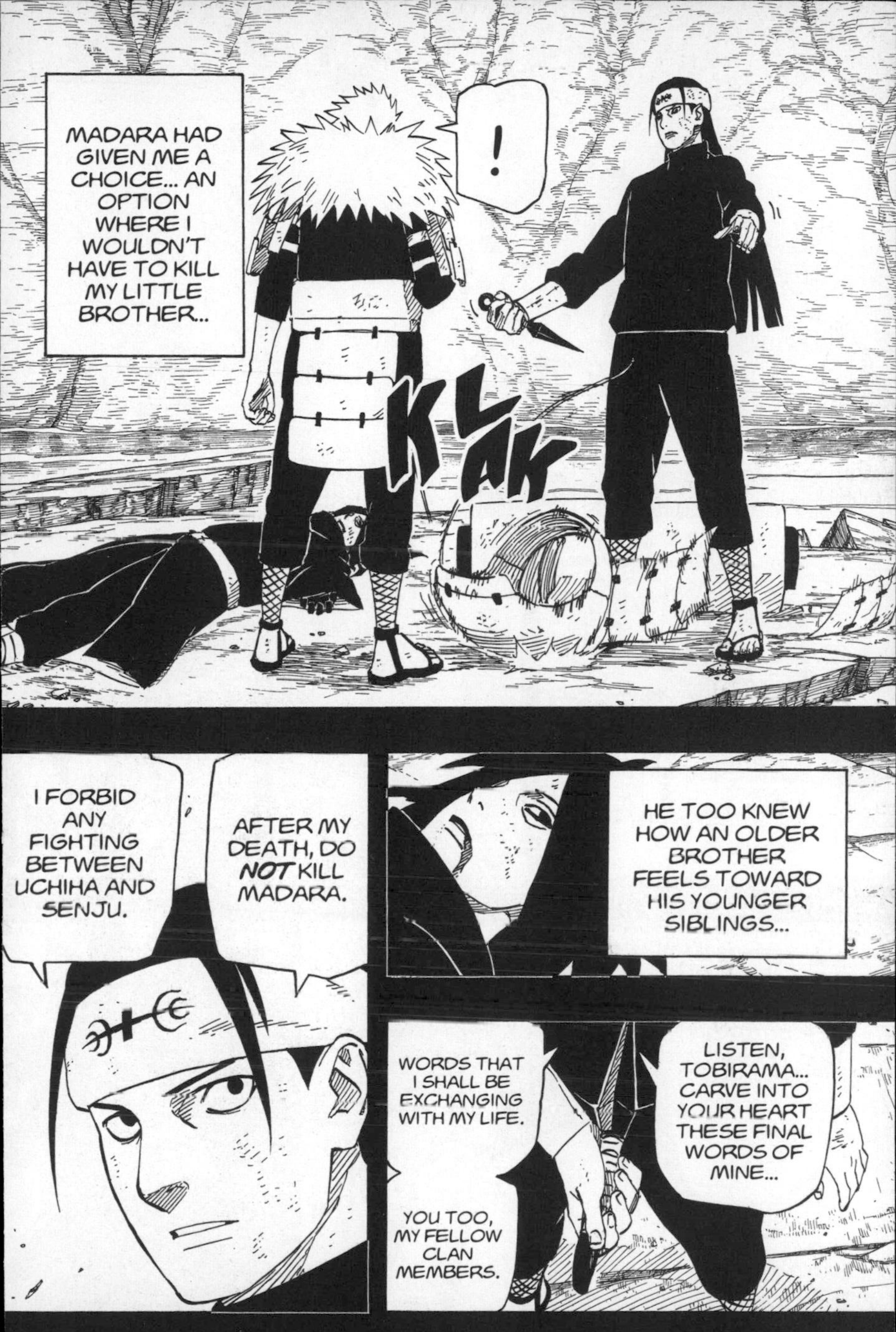

!
MADARA HAD GIVEN ME A CHOICE... AN OPTION WHERE I WOULDN'T HAVE TO KILL MY LITTLE BROTHER...
KLAK
HE TOO KNEW HOW AN OLDER BROTHER FEELS TOWARD HIS YOUNGER SIBLINGS...
LISTEN, TOBIRAMA... CARVE INTO YOUR HEART THESE FINAL WORDS OF MINE...
WORDS THAT I SHALL BE EXCHANGING WITH MY LIFE.
YOU TOO, MY FELLOW CLAN MEMBERS.
AFTER MY DEATH, DO *NOT* KILL MADARA.
I FORBID ANY FIGHTING BETWEEN UCHIHA AND SENJU.

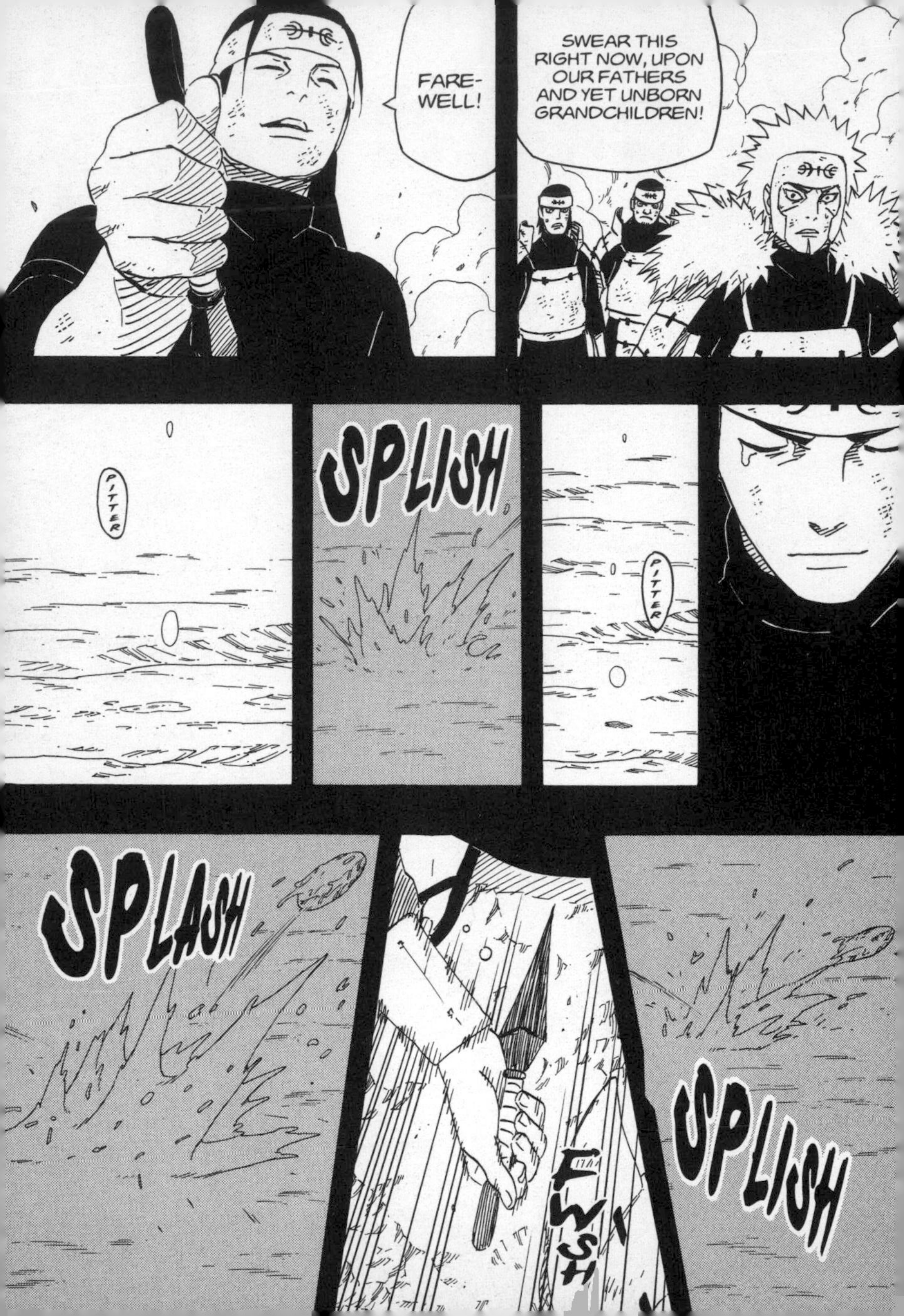
SWEAR THIS RIGHT NOW, UPON OUR FATHERS AND YET UNBORN GRANDCHILDREN!
FARE-WELL!
PITTER
SPLISH
PITTER
SPLISH
FWSH
SPLASH

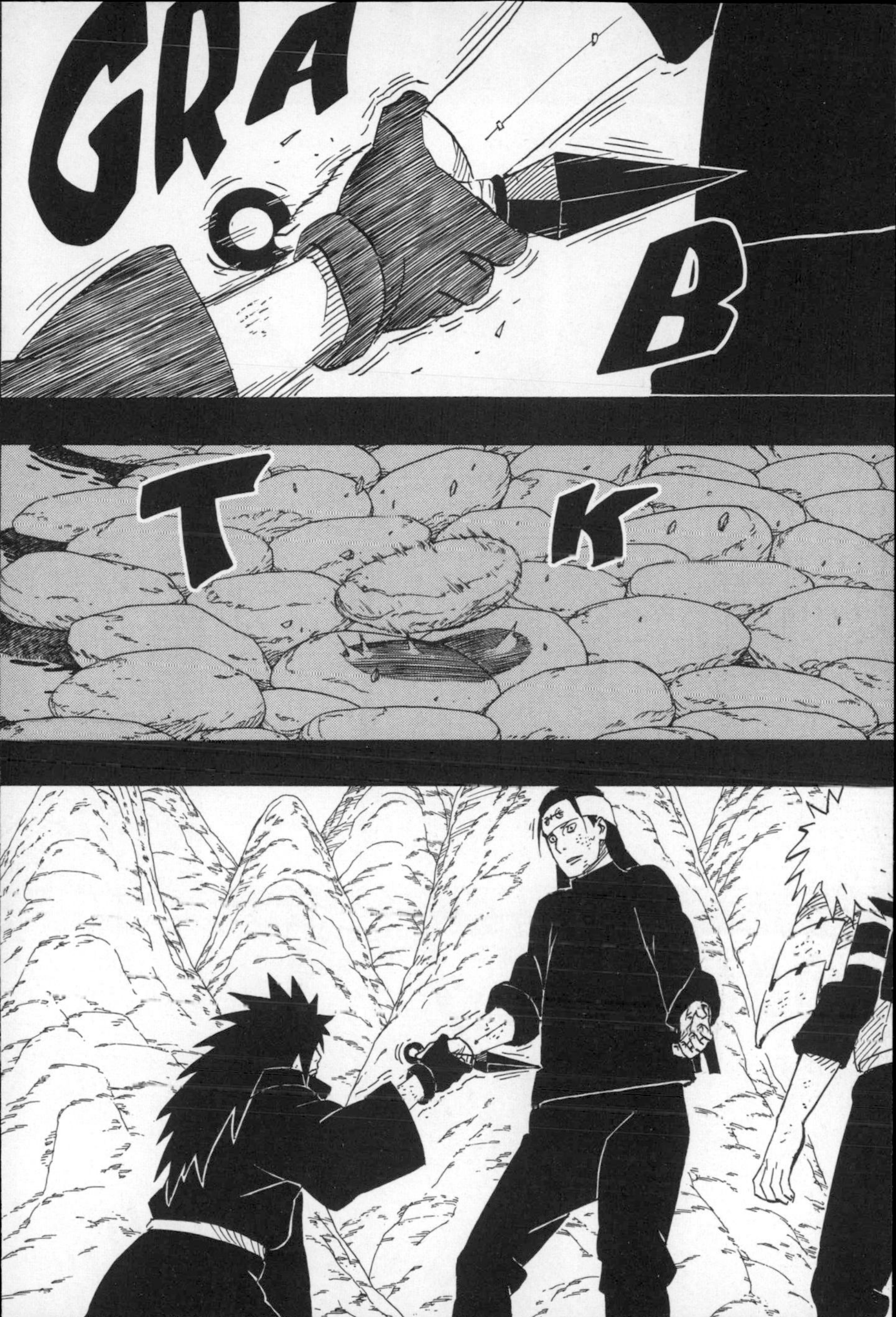
GRAB
TK

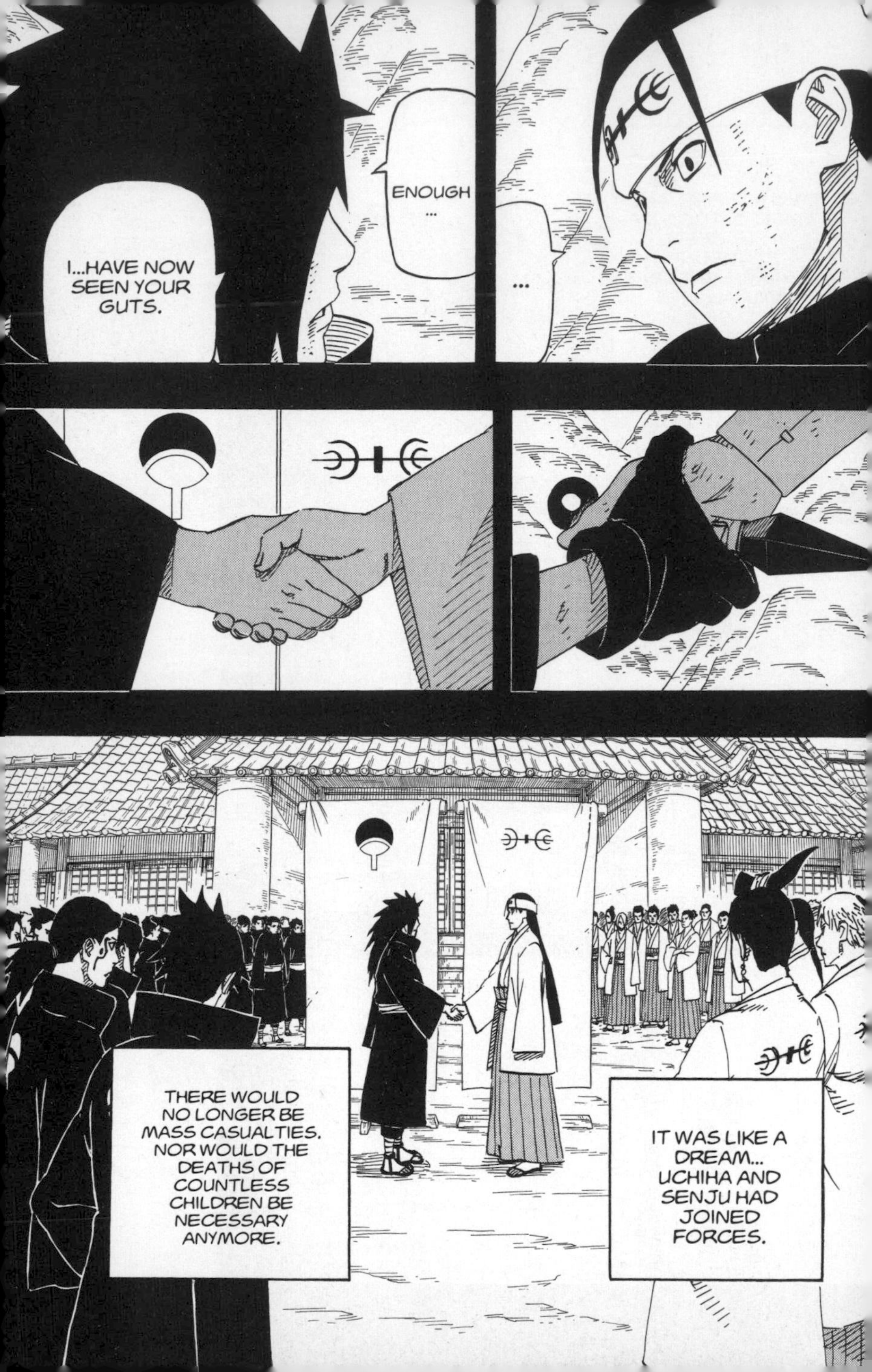
...
ENOUGH ...
I...HAVE NOW SEEN YOUR GUTS.
IT WAS LIKE A DREAM... UCHIHA AND SENJU HAD JOINED FORCES.
THERE WOULD NO LONGER BE MASS CASUALTIES. NOR WOULD THE DEATHS OF COUNTLESS CHILDREN BE NECESSARY ANYMORE.

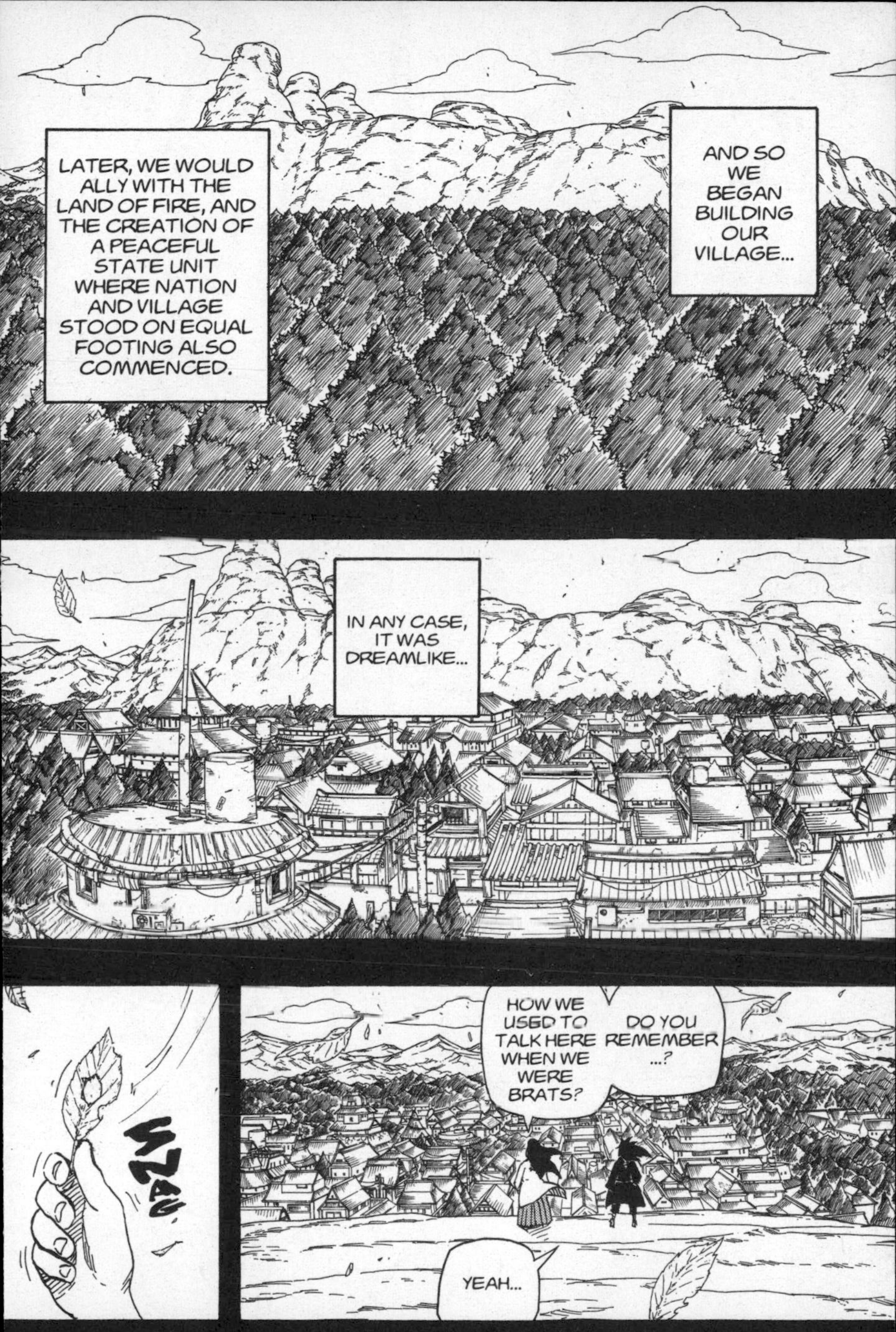
AND SO WE BEGAN BUILDING OUR VILLAGE...
LATER, WE WOULD ALLY WITH THE LAND OF FIRE, AND THE CREATION OF A PEACEFUL STATE UNIT WHERE NATION AND VILLAGE STOOD ON EQUAL FOOTING ALSO COMMENCED.
IN ANY CASE, IT WAS DREAMLIKE...
DO YOU REMEMBER...?
HOW WE USED TO TALK HERE WHEN WE WERE BRATS?
YEAH...
SNAG

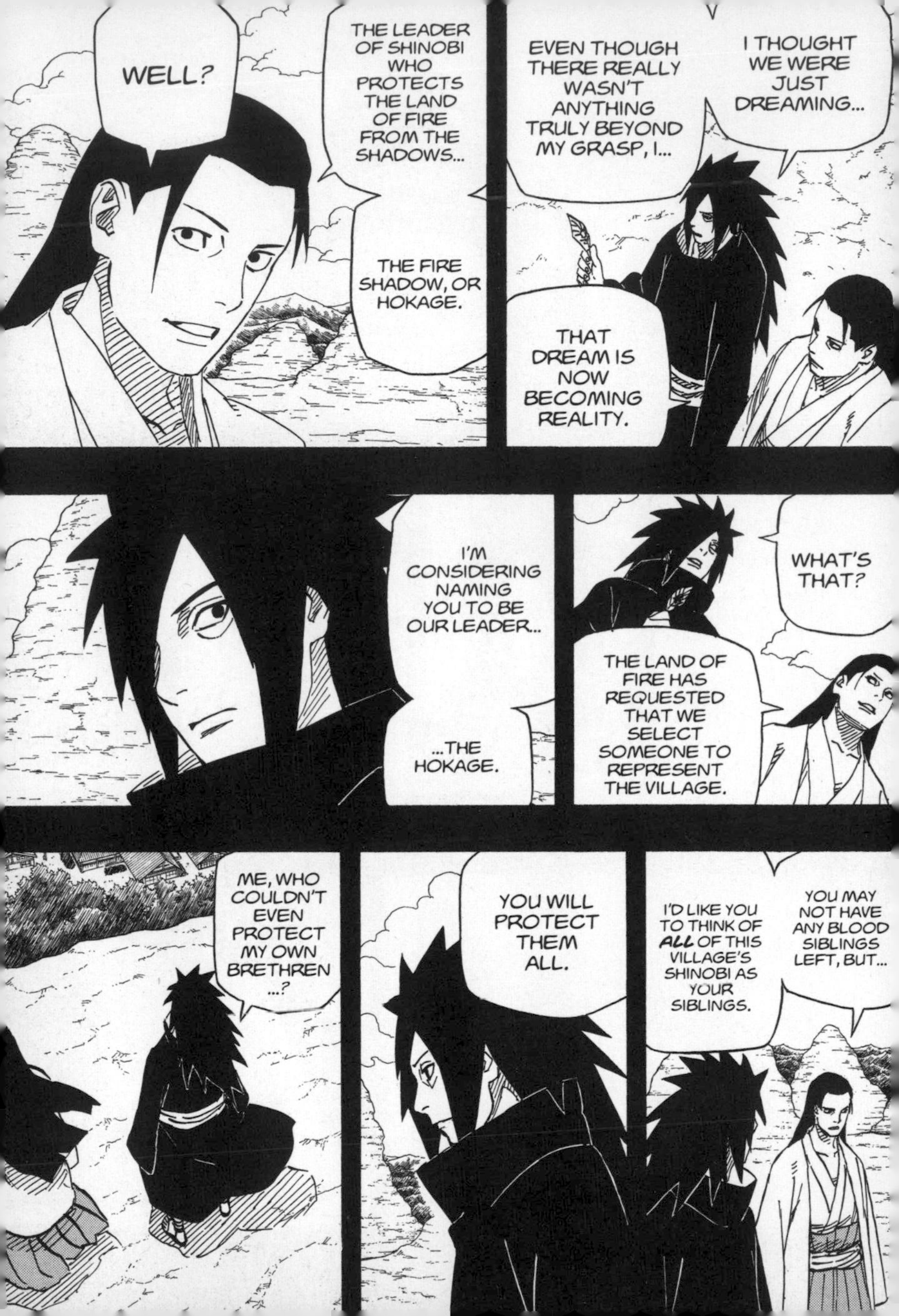
I THOUGHT WE WERE JUST DREAMING...
EVEN THOUGH THERE REALLY WASN'T ANYTHING TRULY BEYOND MY GRASP, I...
THAT DREAM IS NOW BECOMING REALITY.
THE LEADER OF SHINOBI WHO PROTECTS THE LAND OF FIRE FROM THE SHADOWS...
WELL?
THE FIRE SHADOW, OR HOKAGE.
WHAT'S THAT?
THE LAND OF FIRE HAS REQUESTED THAT WE SELECT SOMEONE TO REPRESENT THE VILLAGE.
I'M CONSIDERING NAMING YOU TO BE OUR LEADER...
...THE HOKAGE.
YOU MAY NOT HAVE ANY BLOOD SIBLINGS LEFT, BUT...
I'D LIKE YOU TO THINK OF *ALL* OF THIS VILLAGE'S SHINOBI AS YOUR SIBLINGS.
YOU WILL PROTECT THEM ALL.
ME, WHO COULDN'T EVEN PROTECT MY OWN BRETHREN ...?

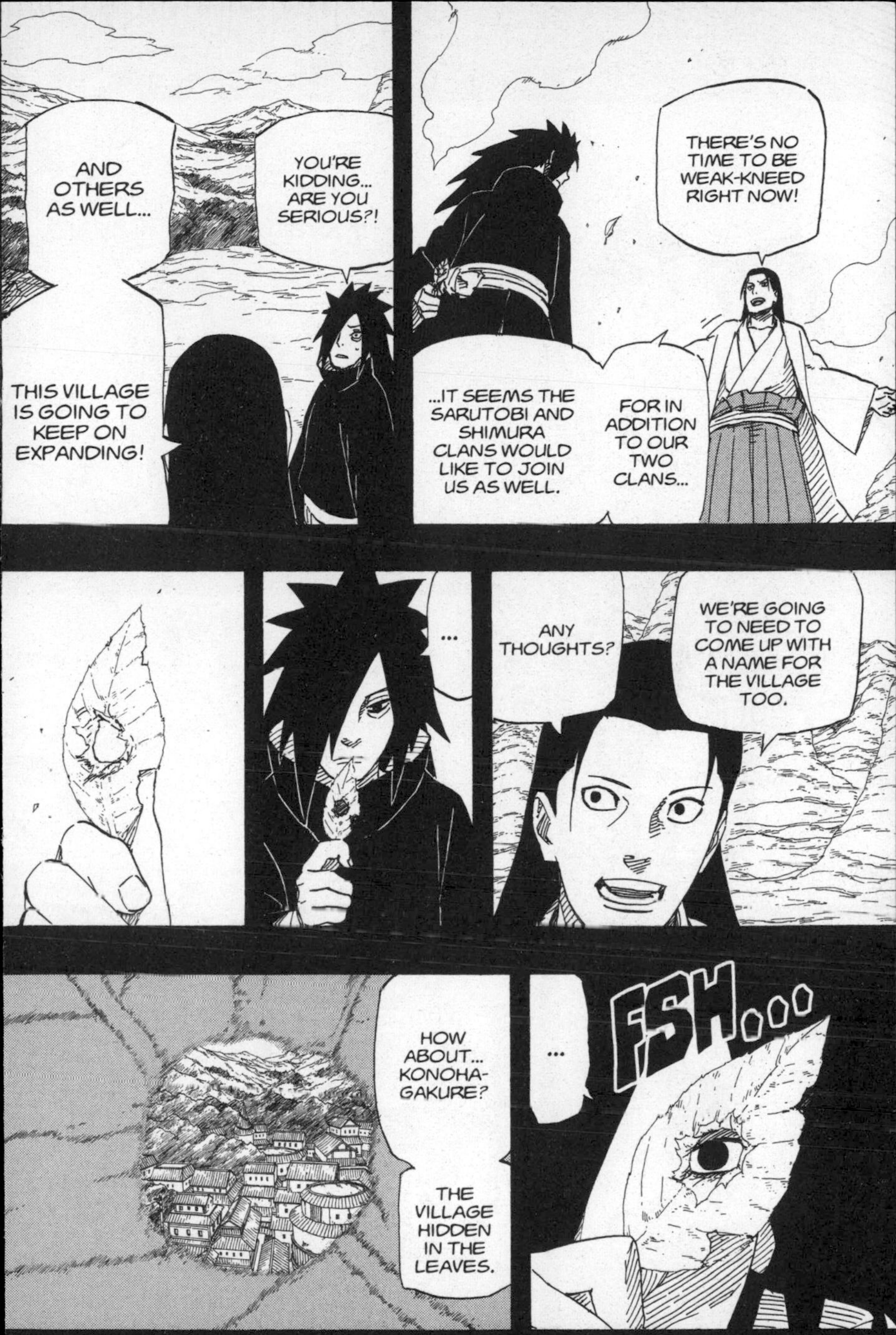
THERE'S NO TIME TO BE WEAK-KNEED RIGHT NOW!
FOR IN ADDITION TO OUR TWO CLANS...
...IT SEEMS THE SARUTOBI AND SHIMURA CLANS WOULD LIKE TO JOIN US AS WELL.
YOU'RE KIDDING... ARE YOU SERIOUS?!
AND OTHERS AS WELL...
THIS VILLAGE IS GOING TO KEEP ON EXPANDING!
WE'RE GOING TO NEED TO COME UP WITH A NAME FOR THE VILLAGE TOO.
ANY THOUGHTS?
...
FSH...
...
HOW ABOUT... KONOHA-GAKURE?
THE VILLAGE HIDDEN IN THE LEAVES.

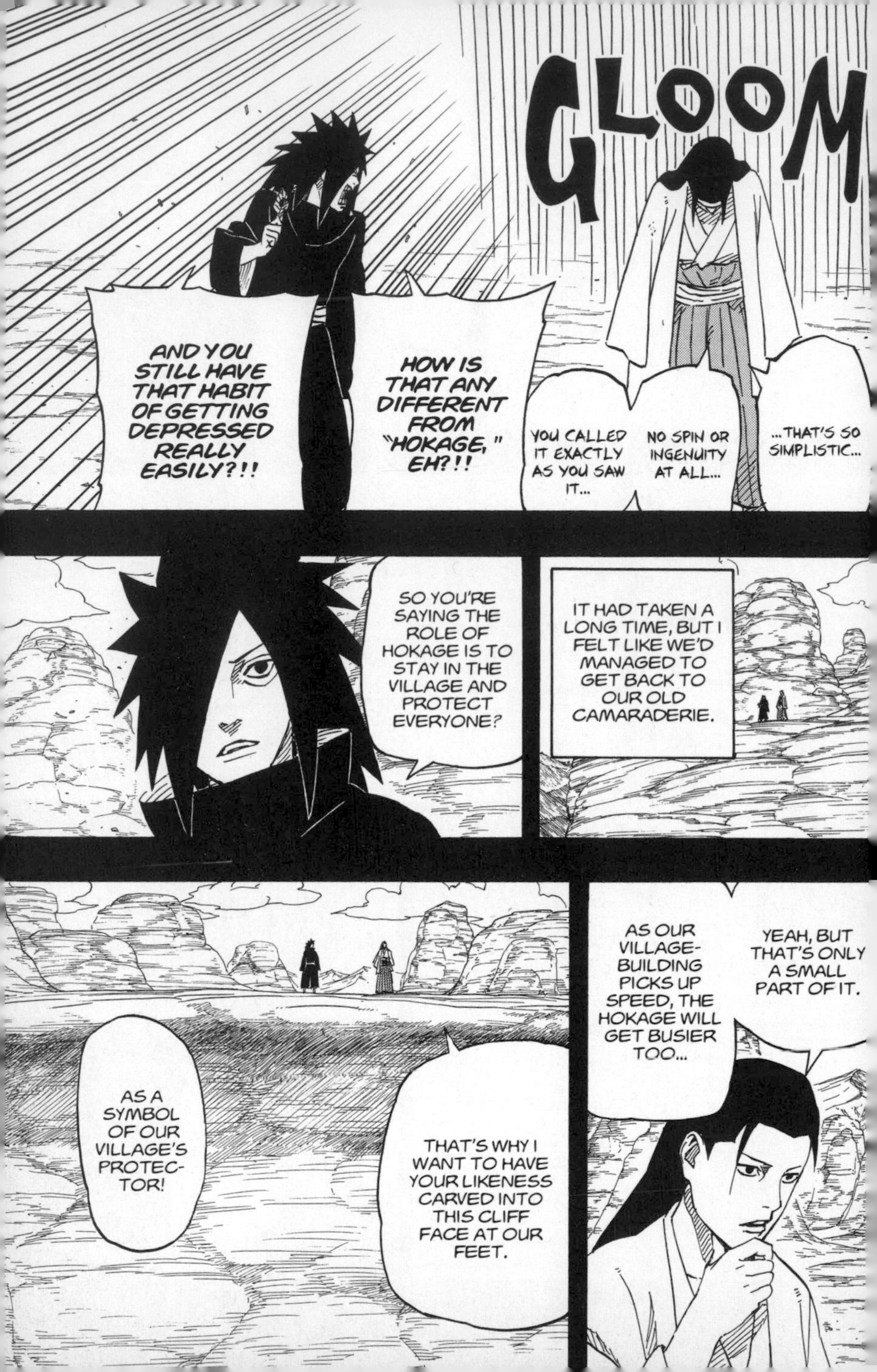
GLOOM
...THAT'S SO SIMPLISTIC...
NO SPIN OR INGENUITY AT ALL...
YOU CALLED IT EXACTLY AS YOU SAW IT...
HOW IS THAT ANY DIFFERENT FROM "HOKAGE," EH?!!
AND YOU STILL HAVE THAT HABIT OF GETTING DEPRESSED REALLY EASILY?!!
IT HAD TAKEN A LONG TIME, BUT I FELT LIKE WE'D MANAGED TO GET BACK TO OUR OLD CAMARADERIE.
SO YOU'RE SAYING THE ROLE OF HOKAGE IS TO STAY IN THE VILLAGE AND PROTECT EVERYONE?
YEAH, BUT THAT'S ONLY A SMALL PART OF IT.
AS OUR VILLAGE-BUILDING PICKS UP SPEED, THE HOKAGE WILL GET BUSIER TOO...
THAT'S WHY I WANT TO HAVE YOUR LIKENESS CARVED INTO THIS CLIFF FACE AT OUR FEET.
AS A SYMBOL OF OUR VILLAGE'S PROTECTOR!

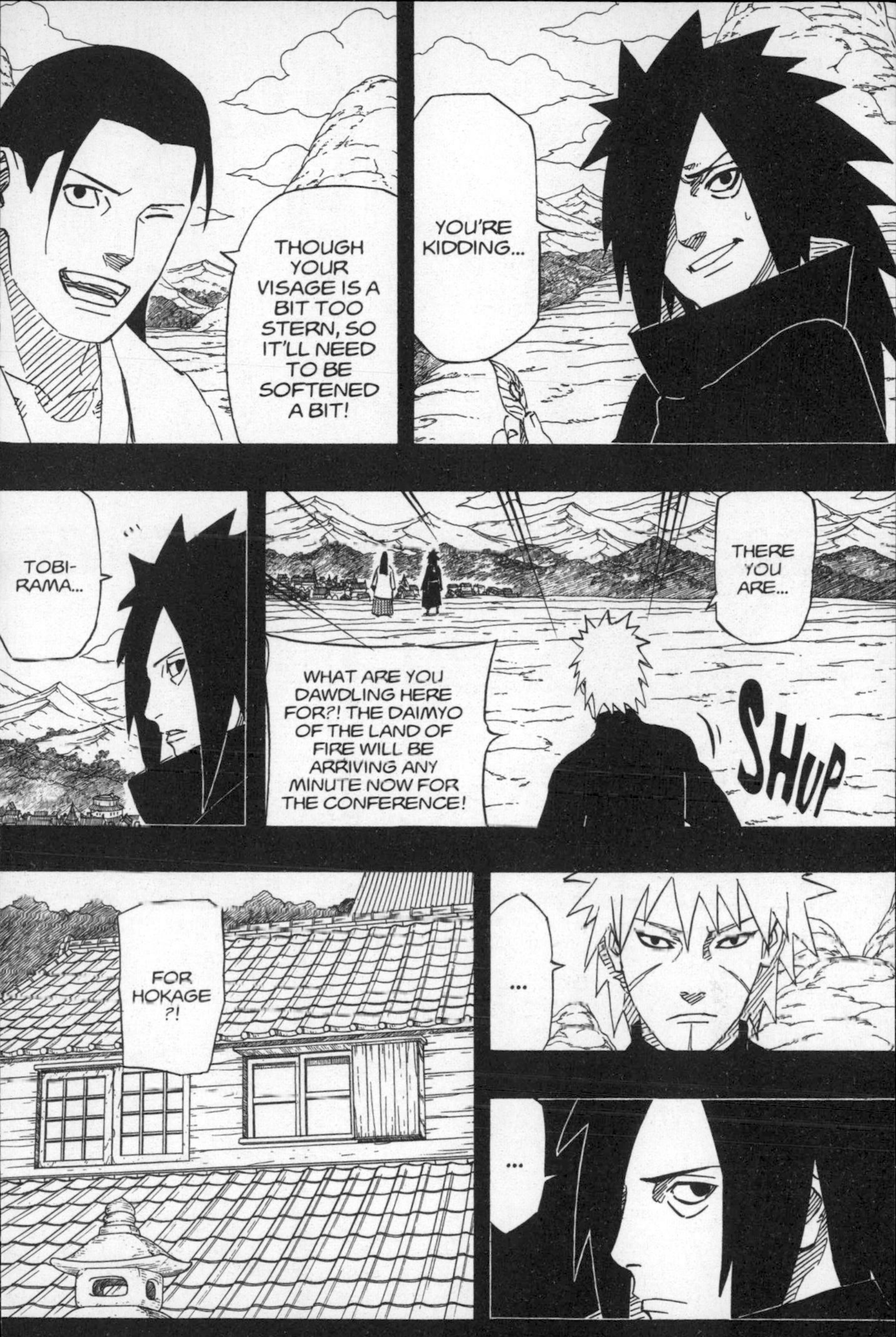
YOU'RE KIDDING...
THOUGH YOUR VISAGE IS A BIT TOO STERN, SO IT'LL NEED TO BE SOFTENED A BIT!
THERE YOU ARE...
WHAT ARE YOU DAWDLING HERE FOR?! THE DAIMYO OF THE LAND OF FIRE WILL BE ARRIVING ANY MINUTE NOW FOR THE CONFERENCE!
SHUP
TOBI-RAMA...
...
...
FOR HOKAGE ?!

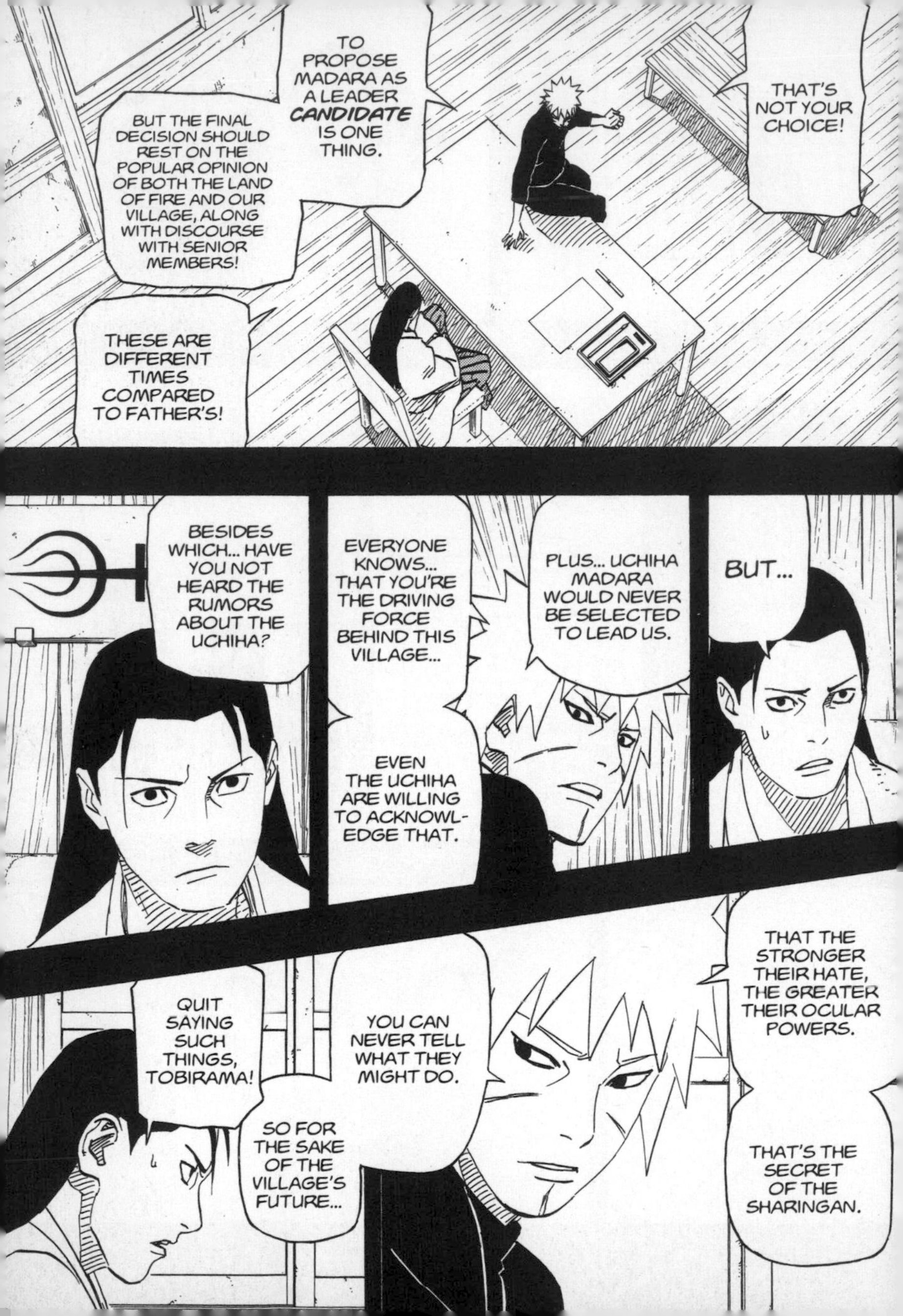
THAT'S NOT YOUR CHOICE!
TO PROPOSE MADARA AS A LEADER **CANDIDATE** IS ONE THING.
BUT THE FINAL DECISION SHOULD REST ON THE POPULAR OPINION OF BOTH THE LAND OF FIRE AND OUR VILLAGE, ALONG WITH DISCOURSE WITH SENIOR MEMBERS!
THESE ARE DIFFERENT TIMES COMPARED TO FATHER'S!
BUT...
PLUS... UCHIHA MADARA WOULD NEVER BE SELECTED TO LEAD US.
EVERYONE KNOWS... THAT YOU'RE THE DRIVING FORCE BEHIND THIS VILLAGE...
EVEN THE UCHIHA ARE WILLING TO ACKNOWL-EDGE THAT.
BESIDES WHICH... HAVE YOU NOT HEARD THE RUMORS ABOUT THE UCHIHA?
THAT THE STRONGER THEIR HATE, THE GREATER THEIR OCULAR POWERS.
THAT'S THE SECRET OF THE SHARINGAN.
YOU CAN NEVER TELL WHAT THEY MIGHT DO.
SO FOR THE SAKE OF THE VILLAGE'S FUTURE...
QUIT SAYING SUCH THINGS, TOBIRAMA!

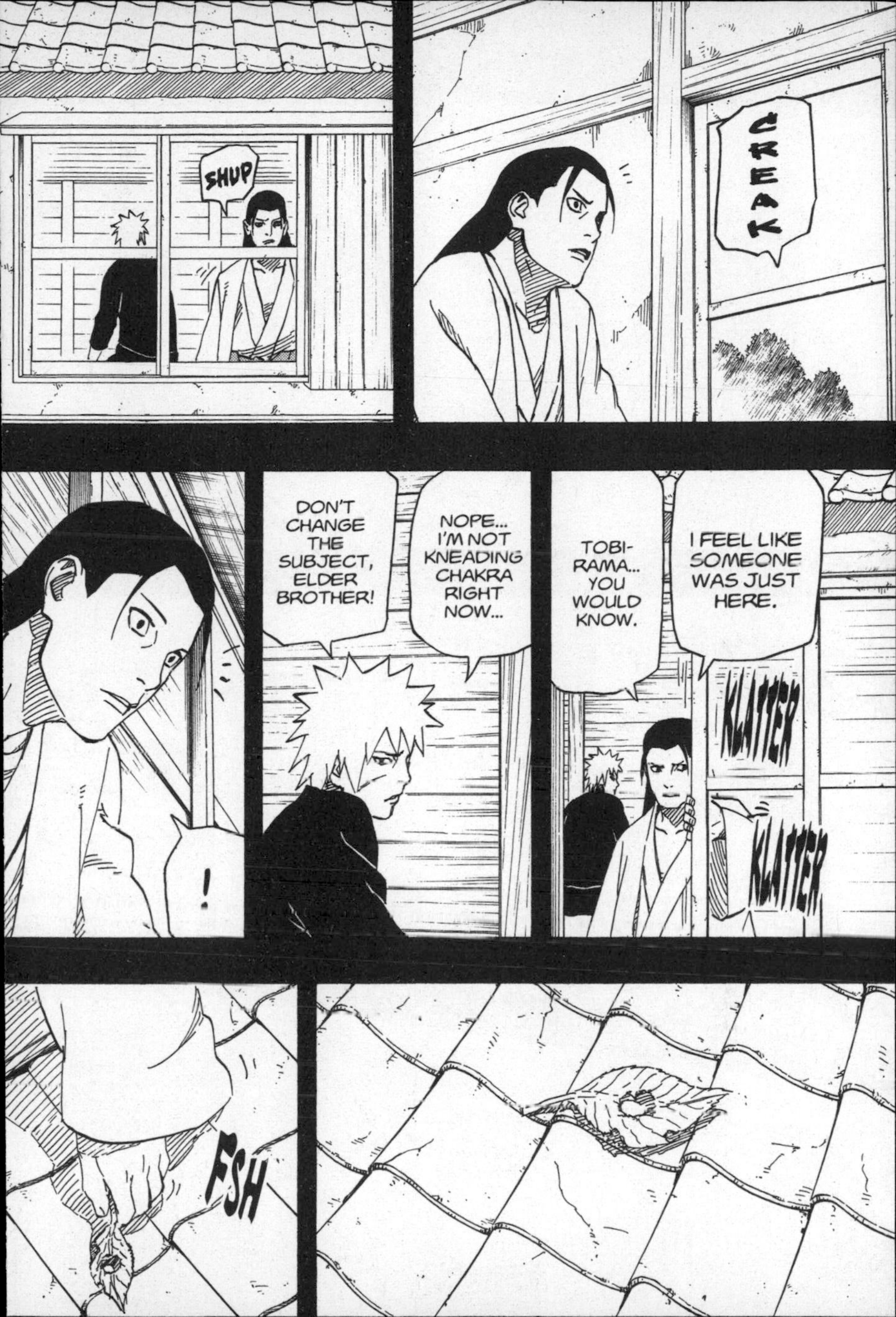
CREAK
SHUP
I FEEL LIKE SOMEONE WAS JUST HERE.
TOBI-RAMA... YOU WOULD KNOW.
KLATTER
KLATTER
NOPE... I'M NOT KNEADING CHAKRA RIGHT NOW...
DON'T CHANGE THE SUBJECT, ELDER BROTHER!
!
FSH

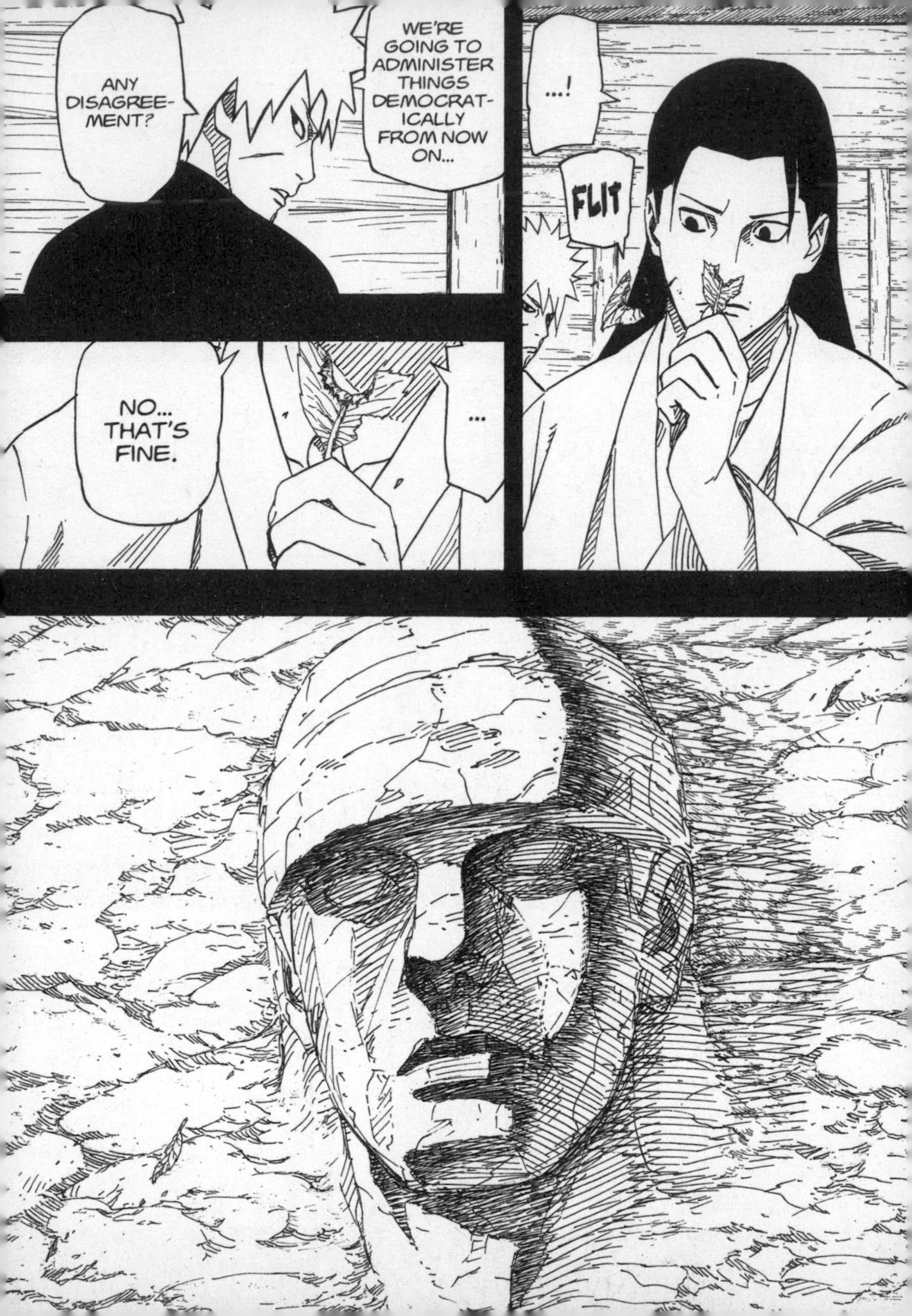
...!
FLIT
WE'RE GOING TO ADMINISTER THINGS DEMOCRATICALLY FROM NOW ON...
ANY DISAGREEMENT?
...
NO... THAT'S FINE.

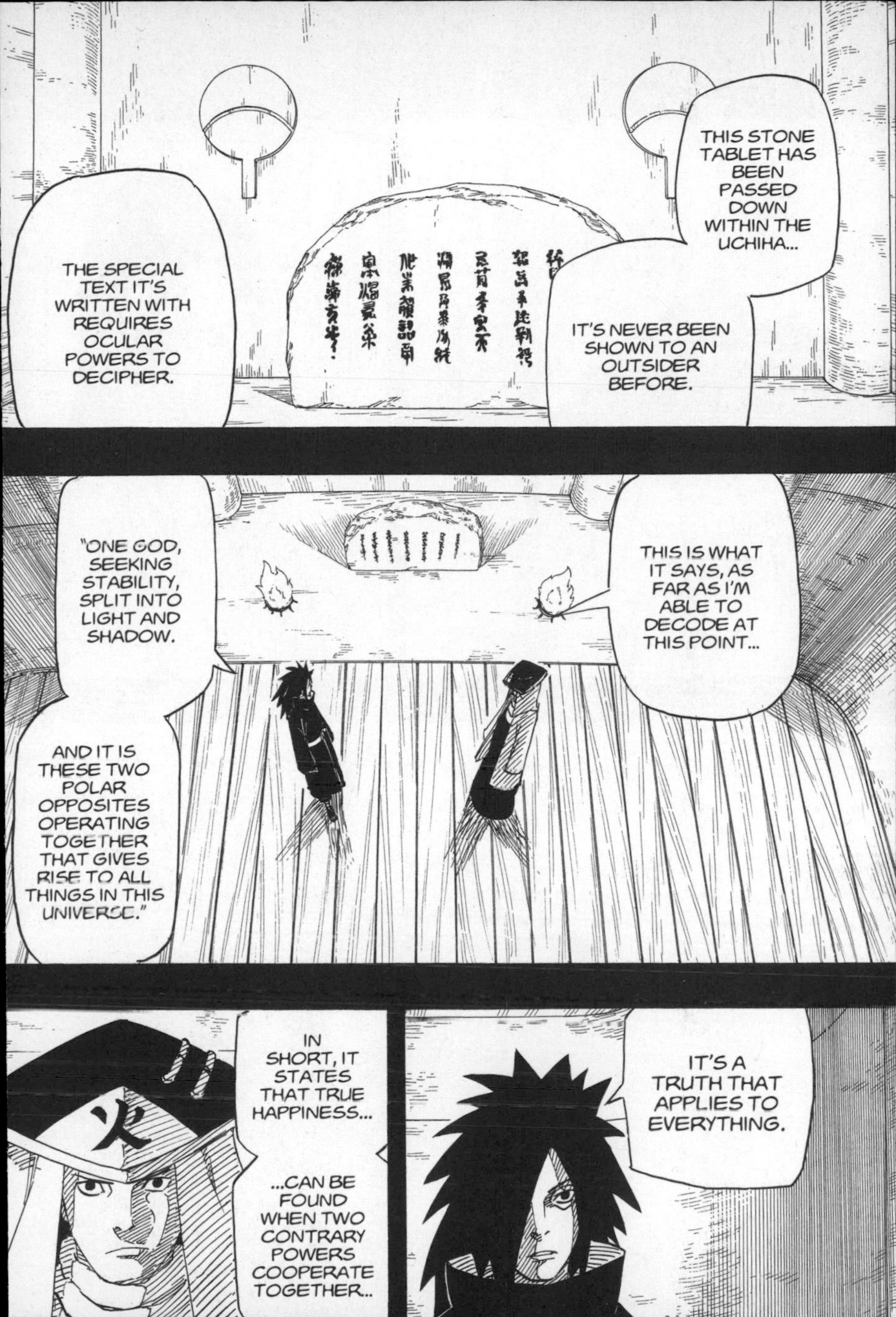
THIS STONE TABLET HAS BEEN PASSED DOWN WITHIN THE UCHIHA...
IT'S NEVER BEEN SHOWN TO AN OUTSIDER BEFORE.
THE SPECIAL TEXT IT'S WRITTEN WITH REQUIRES OCULAR POWERS TO DECIPHER.
THIS IS WHAT IT SAYS, AS FAR AS I'M ABLE TO DECODE AT THIS POINT...
"ONE GOD, SEEKING STABILITY, SPLIT INTO LIGHT AND SHADOW.
AND IT IS THESE TWO POLAR OPPOSITES OPERATING TOGETHER THAT GIVES RISE TO ALL THINGS IN THIS UNIVERSE."
IT'S A TRUTH THAT APPLIES TO EVERYTHING.
IN SHORT, IT STATES THAT TRUE HAPPINESS...
...CAN BE FOUND WHEN TWO CONTRARY POWERS COOPERATE TOGETHER...

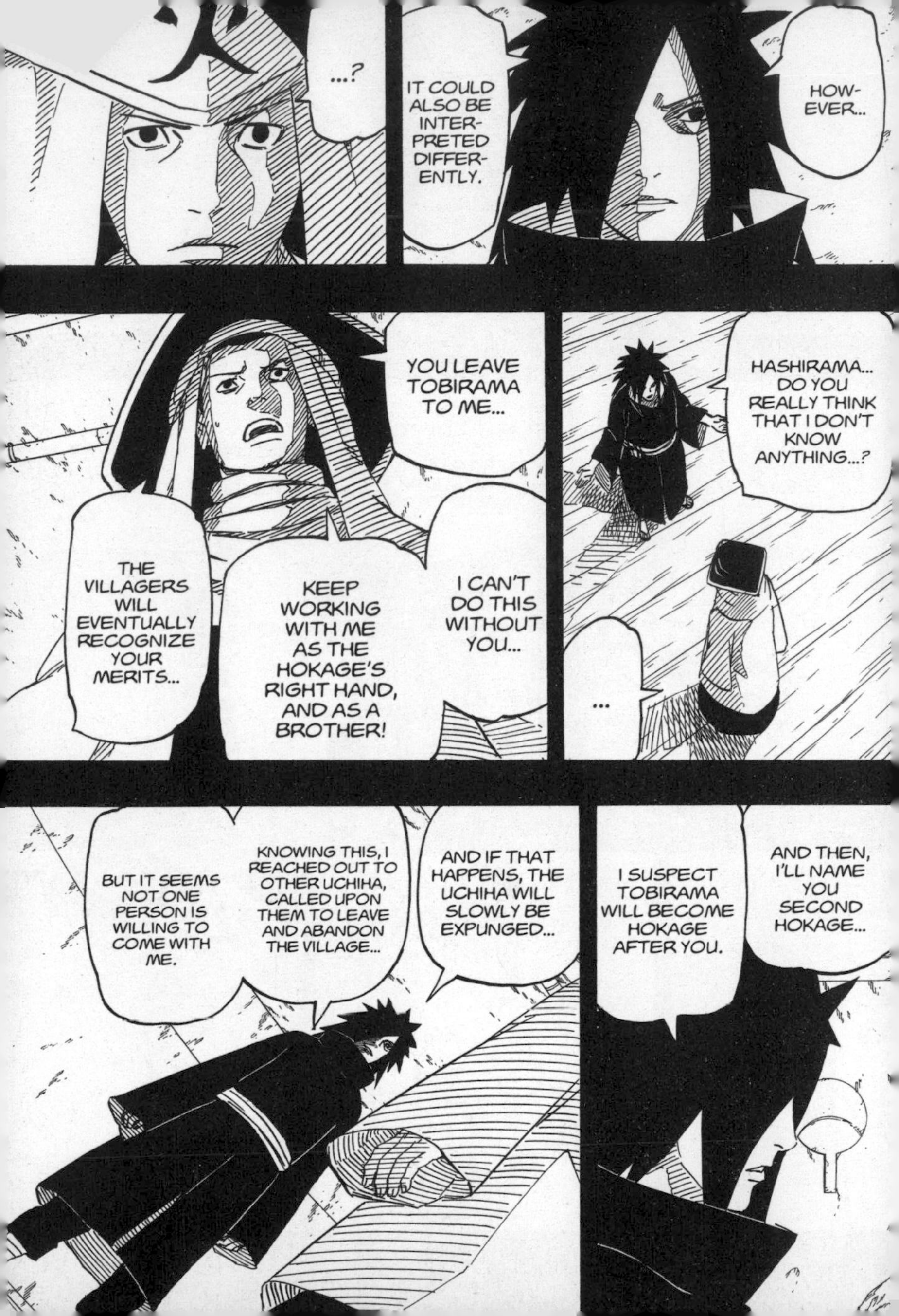
HOWEVER...
IT COULD ALSO BE INTERPRETED DIFFERENTLY.
...?
HASHIRAMA... DO YOU REALLY THINK THAT I DON'T KNOW ANYTHING...?
...
YOU LEAVE TOBIRAMA TO ME...
I CAN'T DO THIS WITHOUT YOU...
KEEP WORKING WITH ME AS THE HOKAGE'S RIGHT HAND, AND AS A BROTHER!
THE VILLAGERS WILL EVENTUALLY RECOGNIZE YOUR MERITS...
AND THEN, I'LL NAME YOU SECOND HOKAGE...
I SUSPECT TOBIRAMA WILL BECOME HOKAGE AFTER YOU.
AND IF THAT HAPPENS, THE UCHIHA WILL SLOWLY BE EXPUNGED...
KNOWING THIS, I REACHED OUT TO OTHER UCHIHA, CALLED UPON THEM TO LEAVE AND ABANDON THE VILLAGE...
BUT IT SEEMS NOT ONE PERSON IS WILLING TO COME WITH ME.

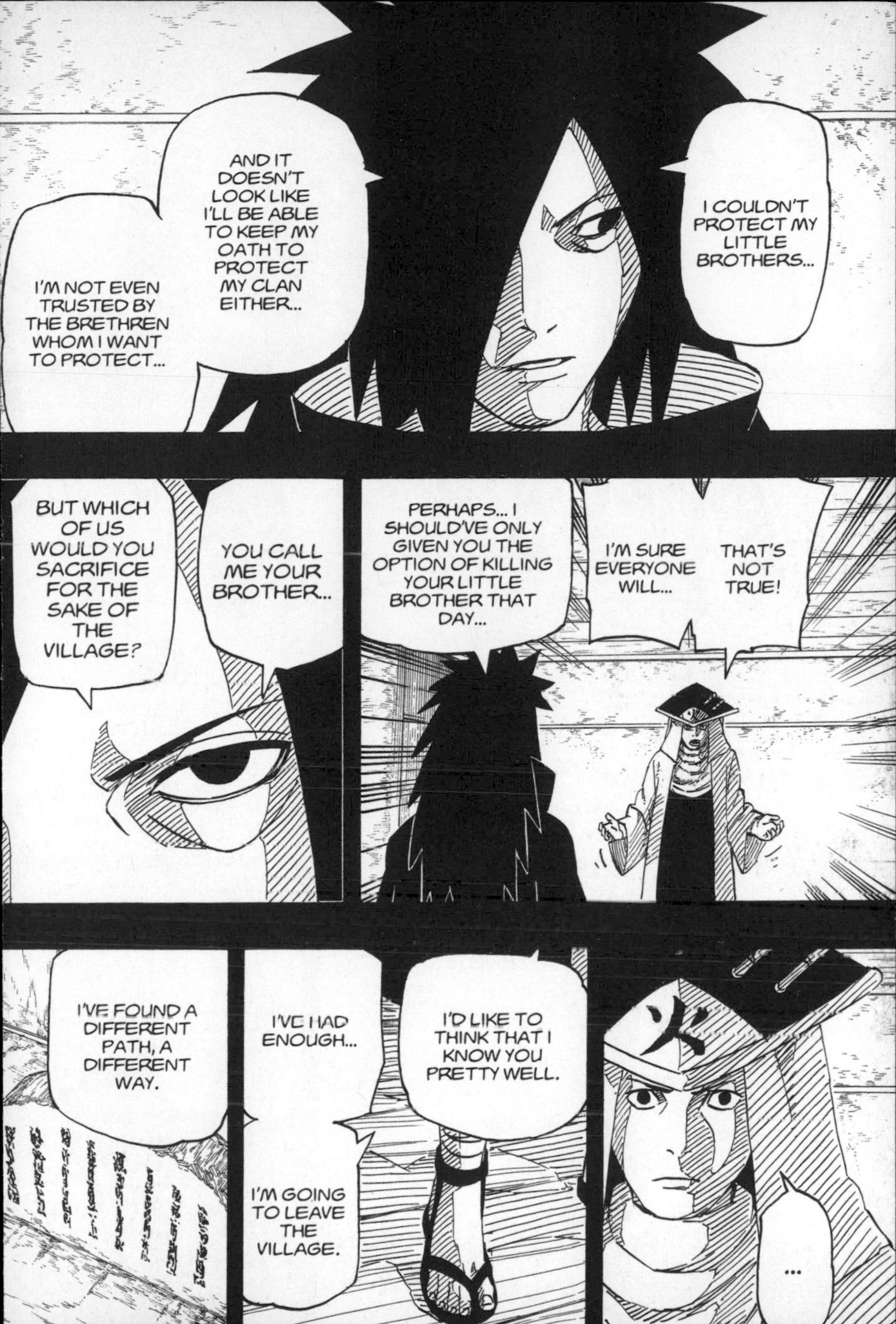
I COULDN'T PROTECT MY LITTLE BROTHERS...
AND IT DOESN'T LOOK LIKE I'LL BE ABLE TO KEEP MY OATH TO PROTECT MY CLAN EITHER...
I'M NOT EVEN TRUSTED BY THE BRETHREN WHOM I WANT TO PROTECT...
THAT'S NOT TRUE!
I'M SURE EVERYONE WILL...
PERHAPS... I SHOULD'VE ONLY GIVEN YOU THE OPTION OF KILLING YOUR LITTLE BROTHER THAT DAY...
YOU CALL ME YOUR BROTHER...
BUT WHICH OF US WOULD YOU SACRIFICE FOR THE SAKE OF THE VILLAGE?
...
I'D LIKE TO THINK THAT I KNOW YOU PRETTY WELL.
I'VE HAD ENOUGH...
I'M GOING TO LEAVE THE VILLAGE.
I'VE FOUND A DIFFERENT PATH, A DIFFERENT WAY.

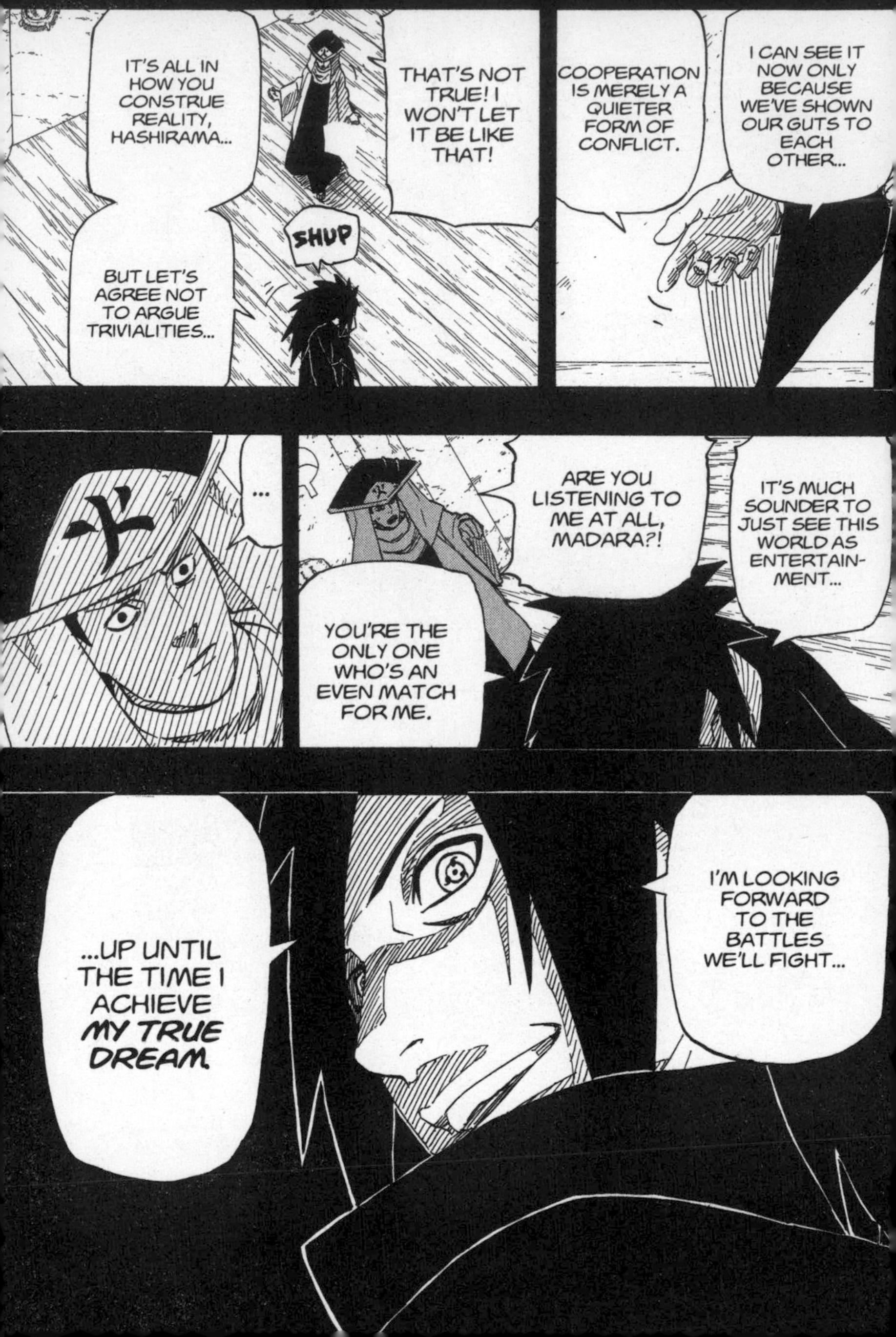
I CAN SEE IT NOW ONLY BECAUSE WE'VE SHOWN OUR GUTS TO EACH OTHER...
COOPERATION IS MERELY A QUIETER FORM OF CONFLICT.
THAT'S NOT TRUE! I WON'T LET IT BE LIKE THAT!
IT'S ALL IN HOW YOU CONSTRUE REALITY, HASHIRAMA...
SHUP
BUT LET'S AGREE NOT TO ARGUE TRIVIALITIES...
IT'S MUCH SOUNDER TO JUST SEE THIS WORLD AS ENTERTAIN-MENT...
ARE YOU LISTENING TO ME AT ALL, MADARA?!
YOU'RE THE ONLY ONE WHO'S AN EVEN MATCH FOR ME.
...
I'M LOOKING FORWARD TO THE BATTLES WE'LL FIGHT...
...UP UNTIL THE TIME I ACHIEVE *MY TRUE DREAM.*

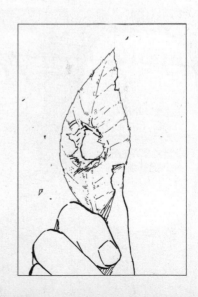

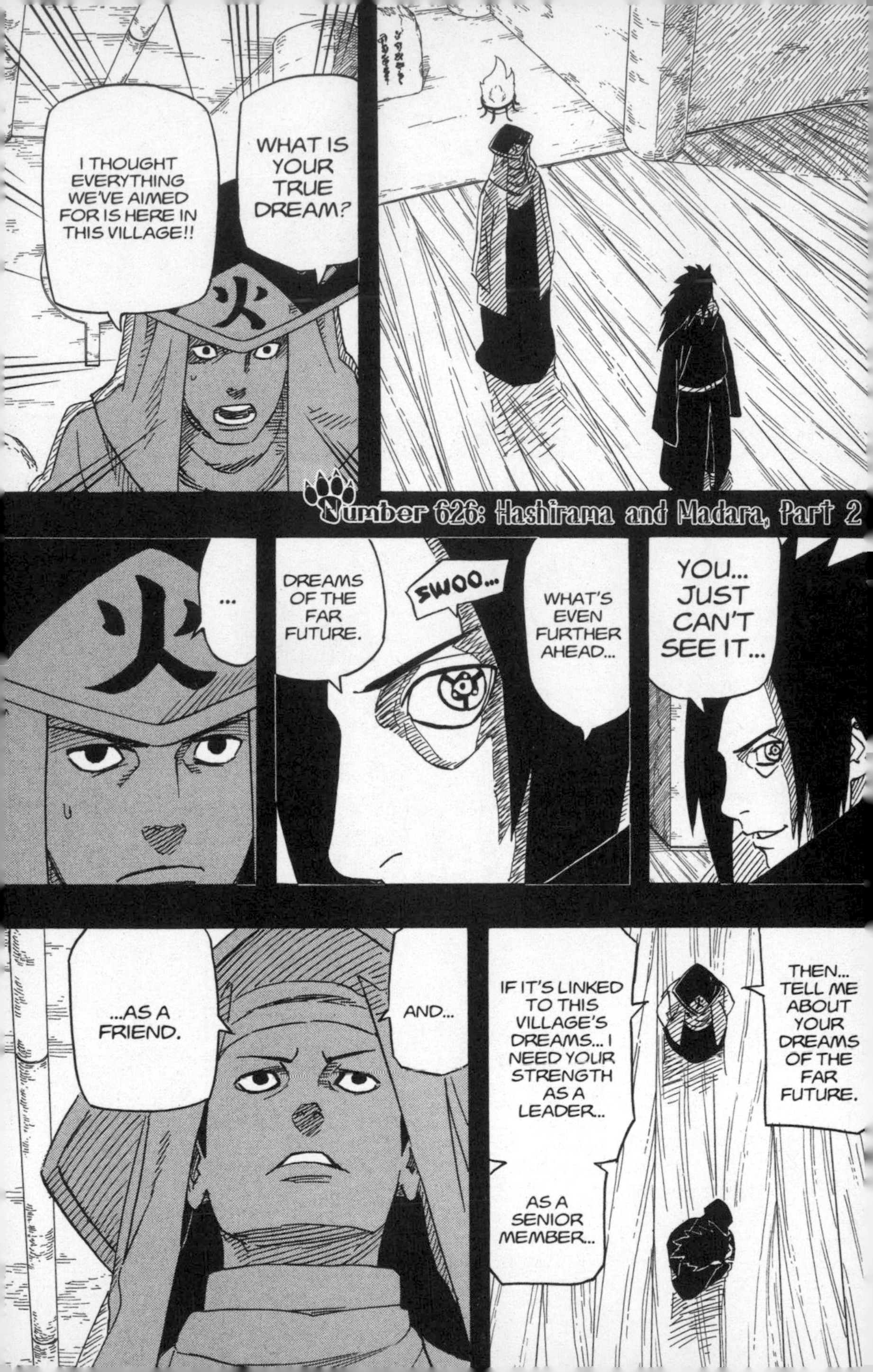
WHAT IS YOUR TRUE DREAM?
I THOUGHT EVERYTHING WE'VE AIMED FOR IS HERE IN THIS VILLAGE!!
Number 626: Hashirama and Madara, Part 2
YOU... JUST CAN'T SEE IT...
WHAT'S EVEN FURTHER AHEAD...
SWOO...
DREAMS OF THE FAR FUTURE.
...
THEN... TELL ME ABOUT YOUR DREAMS OF THE FAR FUTURE.
IF IT'S LINKED TO THIS VILLAGE'S DREAMS... I NEED YOUR STRENGTH AS A LEADER...
AS A SENIOR MEMBER...
AND...
...AS A FRIEND.

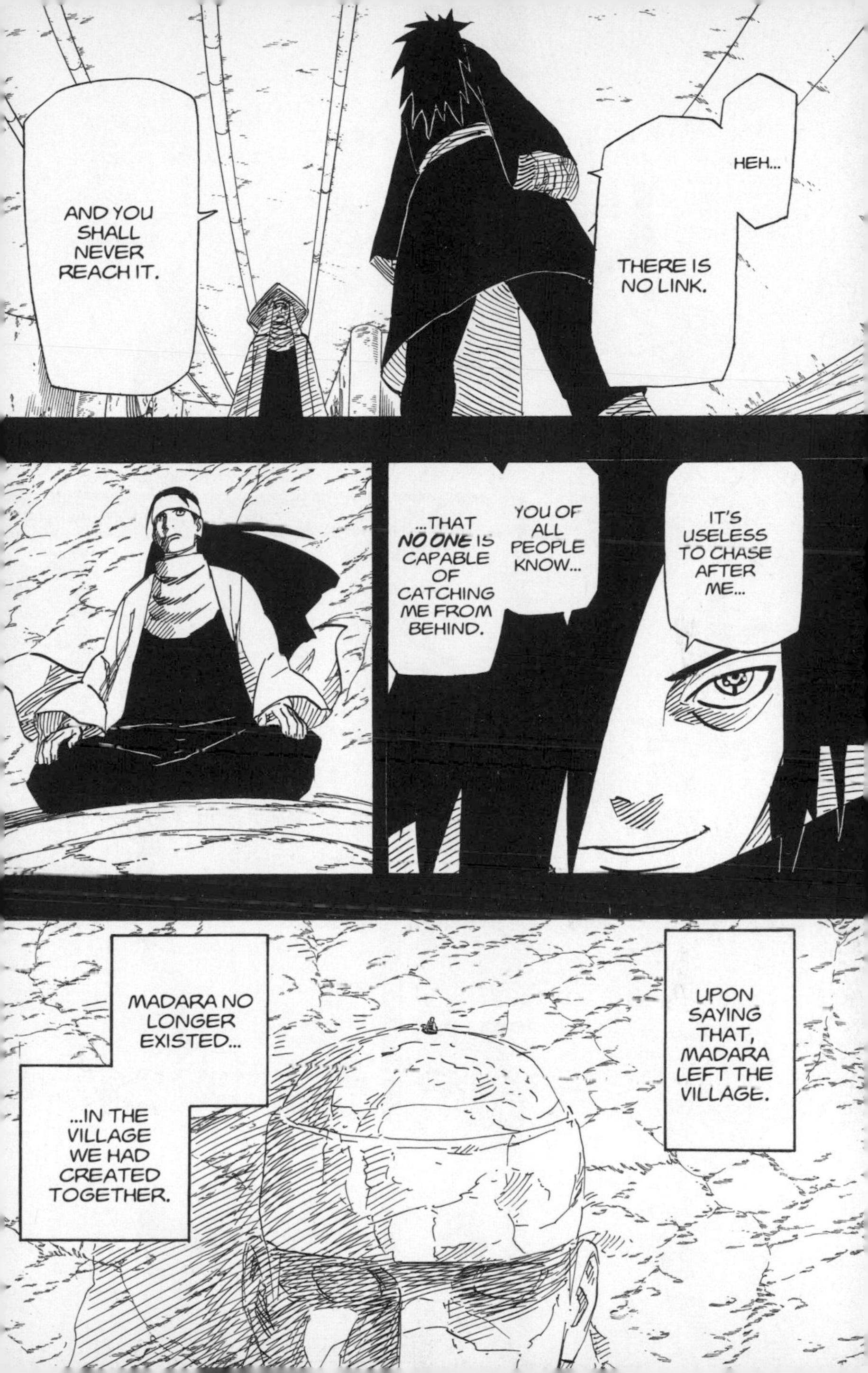
HEH...
THERE IS NO LINK.
AND YOU SHALL NEVER REACH IT.
IT'S USELESS TO CHASE AFTER ME...
YOU OF ALL PEOPLE KNOW...
...THAT *NO ONE* IS CAPABLE OF CATCHING ME FROM BEHIND.
UPON SAYING THAT, MADARA LEFT THE VILLAGE.
MADARA NO LONGER EXISTED...
...IN THE VILLAGE WE HAD CREATED TOGETHER.

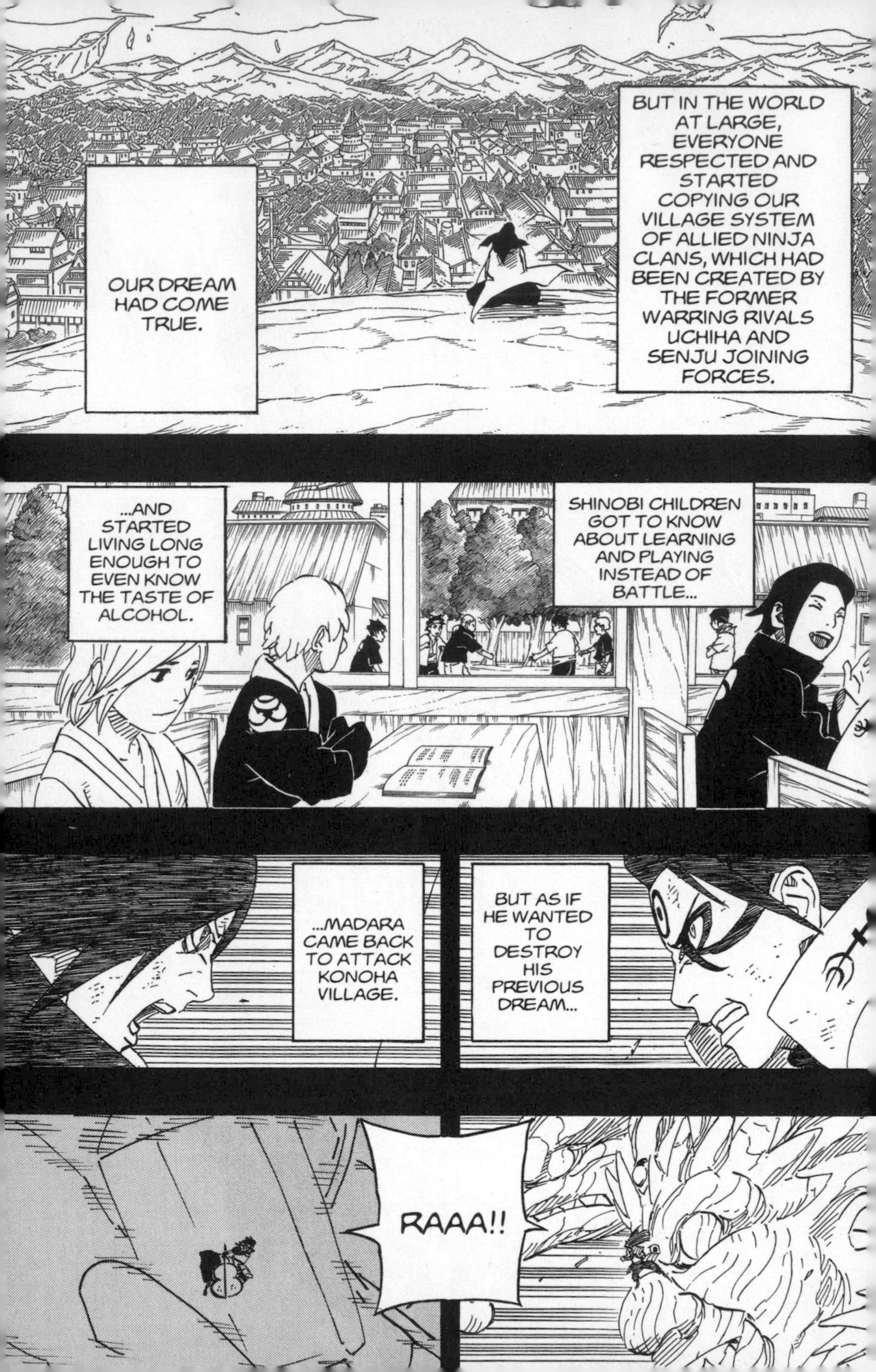
BUT IN THE WORLD AT LARGE, EVERYONE RESPECTED AND STARTED COPYING OUR VILLAGE SYSTEM OF ALLIED NINJA CLANS, WHICH HAD BEEN CREATED BY THE FORMER WARRING RIVALS UCHIHA AND SENJU JOINING FORCES.
OUR DREAM HAD COME TRUE.
SHINOBI CHILDREN GOT TO KNOW ABOUT LEARNING AND PLAYING INSTEAD OF BATTLE...
...AND STARTED LIVING LONG ENOUGH TO EVEN KNOW THE TASTE OF ALCOHOL.
BUT AS IF HE WANTED TO DESTROY HIS PREVIOUS DREAM...
...MADARA CAME BACK TO ATTACK KONOHA VILLAGE.
RAAA!!

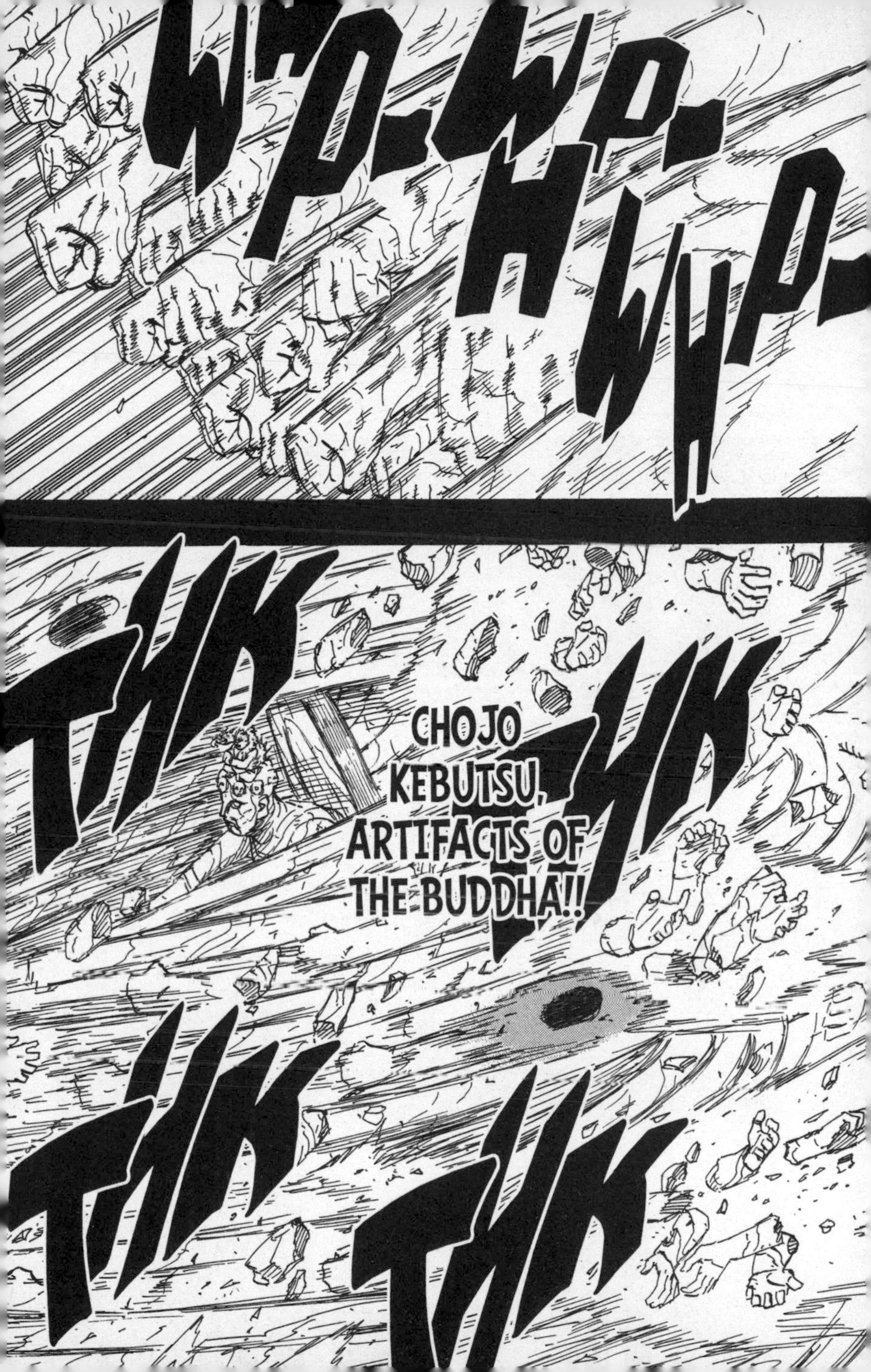
THK THK
CHOJO KEBUTSU, ARTIFACTS OF THE BUDDHA!!
THK THK

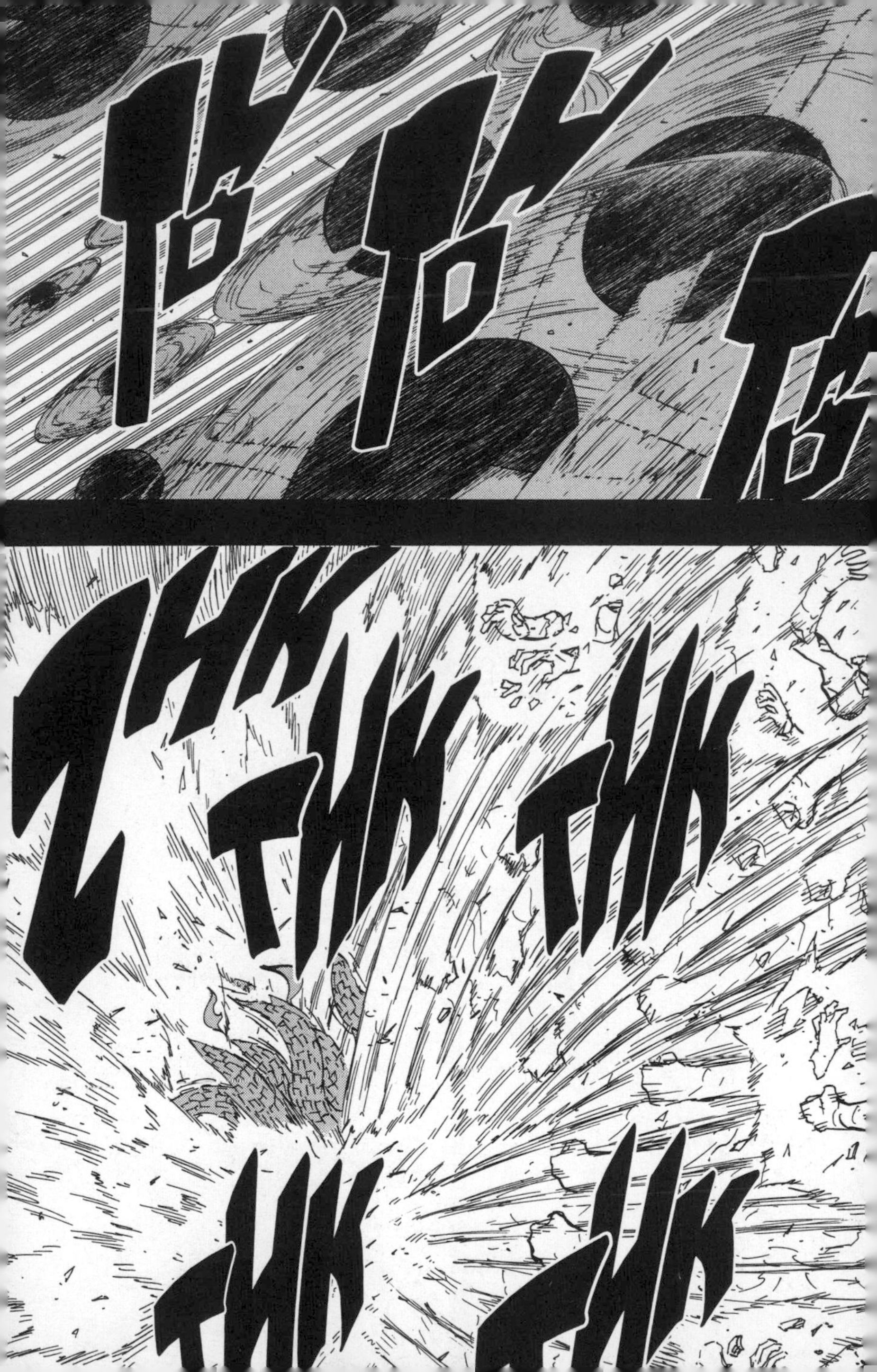
TOK TOK
THK THK THK THK

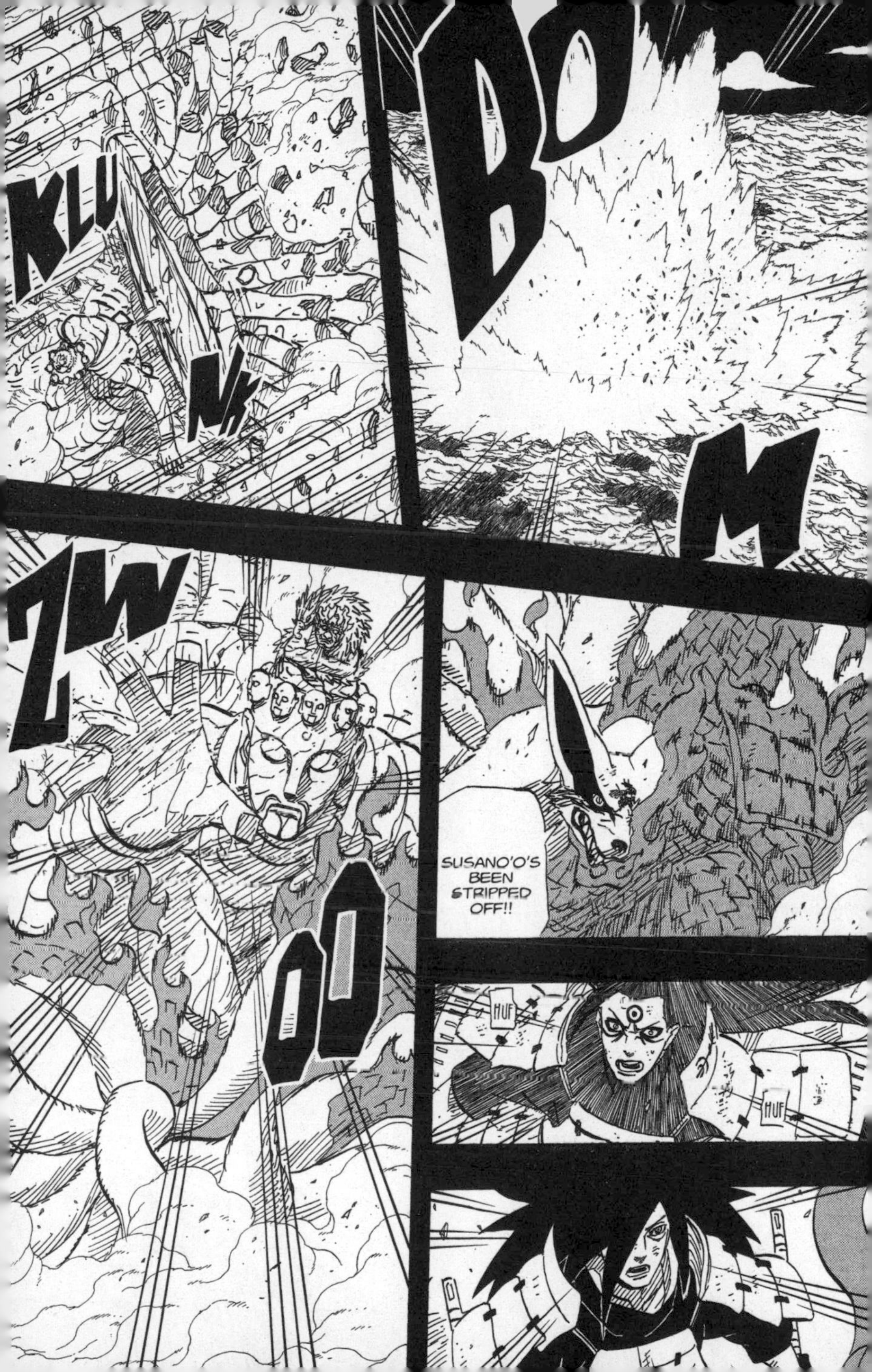
BOM
KLUNK
SUSANO'O'S BEEN STRIPPED OFF!!
HUF
HUF
ZWOO

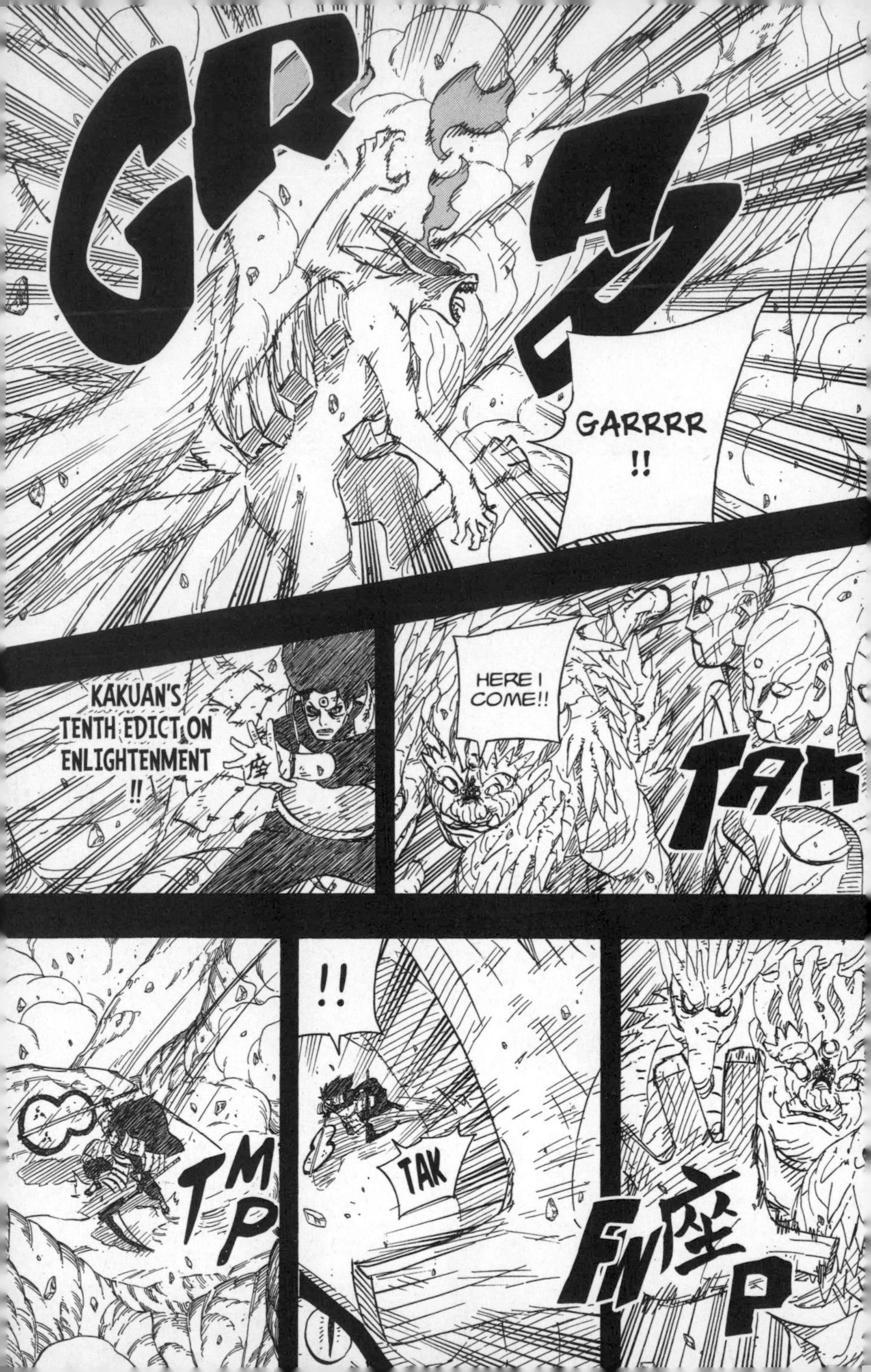
GARRRR !!
HERE I COME!!
TAK
KAKUAN'S TENTH EDICT ON ENLIGHTENMENT !!
!!
TAK
TMP

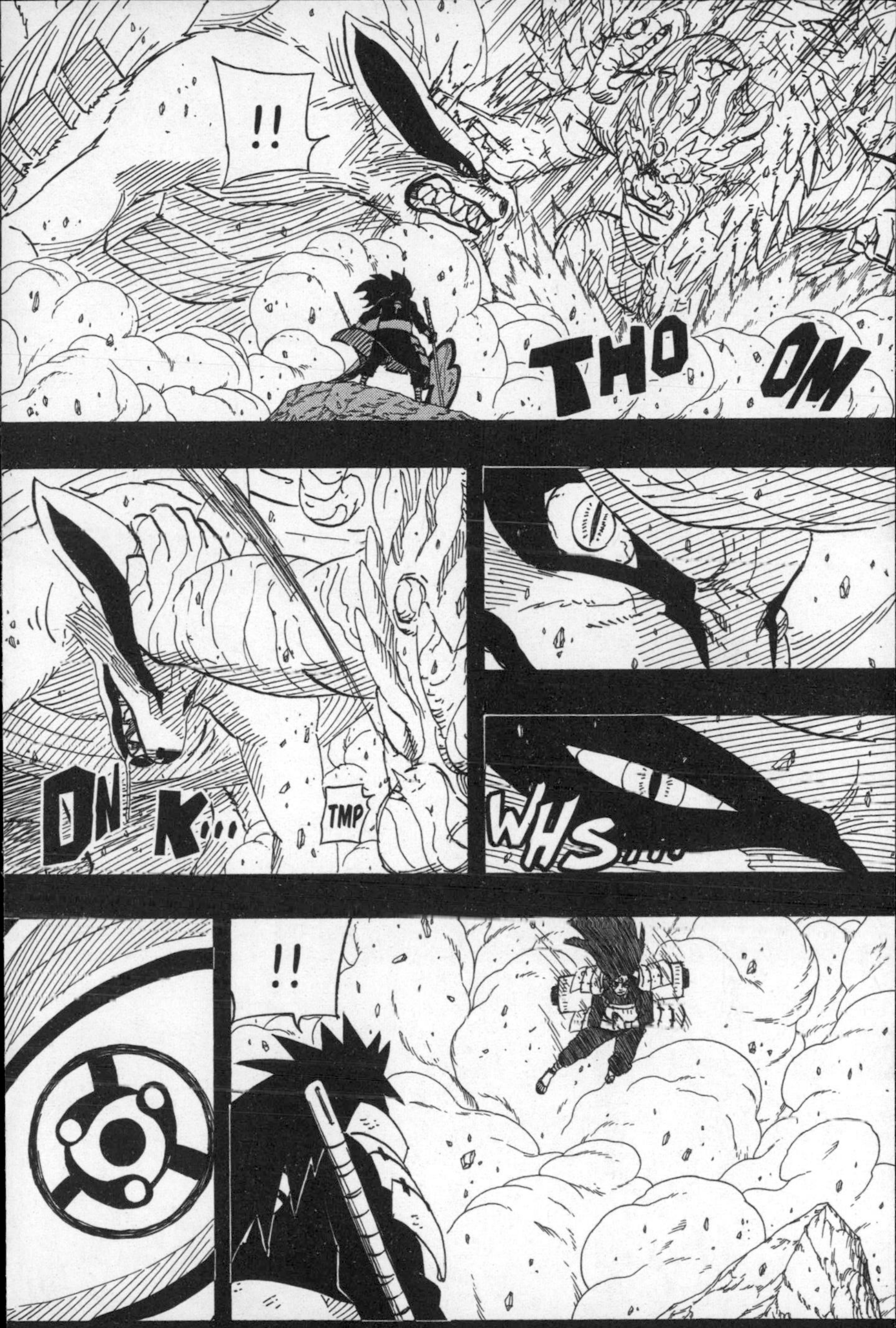

!!
THO OM
WHS...
DN K...
TMP
!!

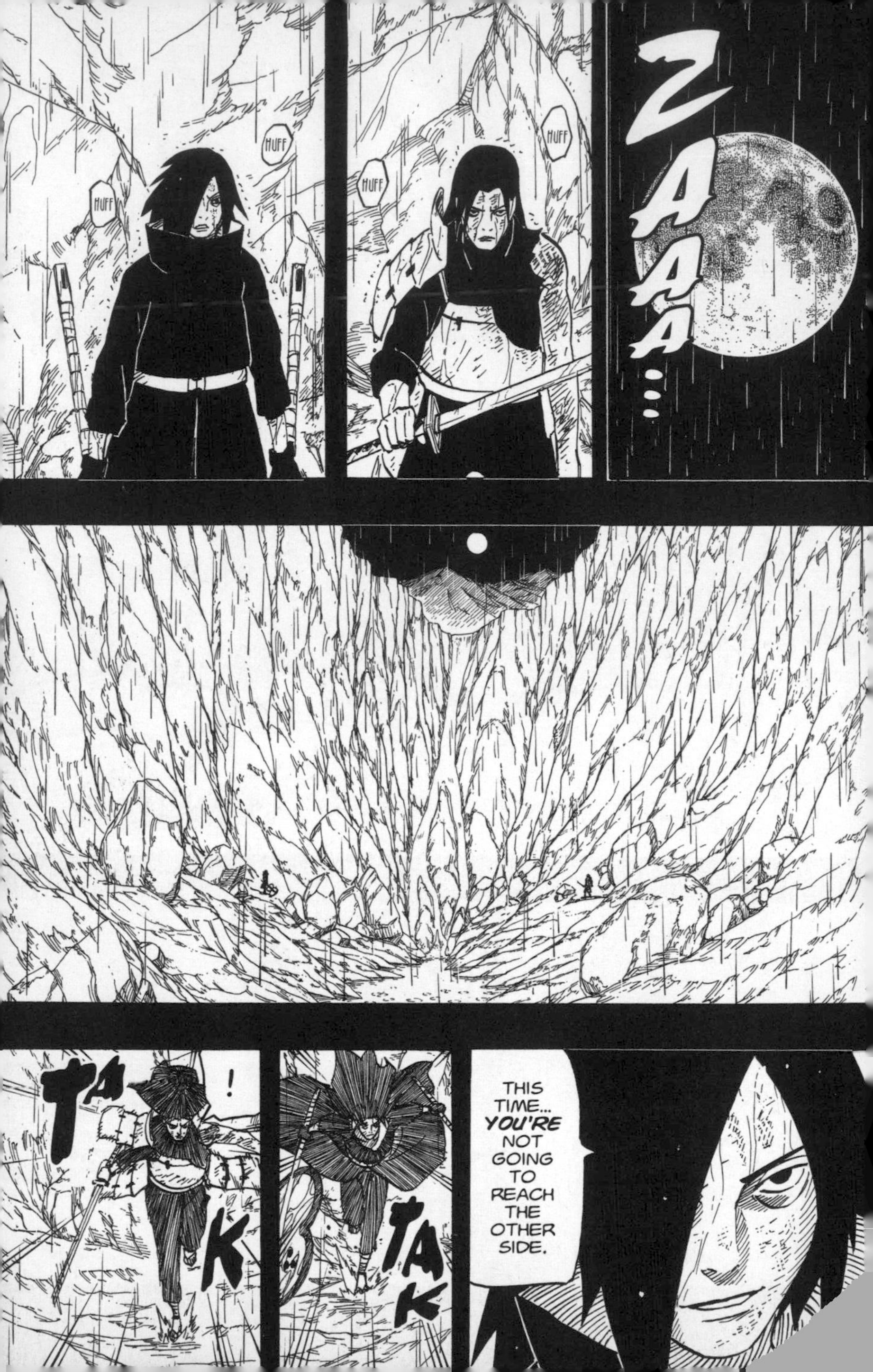
ZAAAA...
HUFF
HUFF
HUFF
HUFF
THIS TIME... ***YOU'RE*** NOT GOING TO REACH THE OTHER SIDE.
TAK
TAK
TAK
!

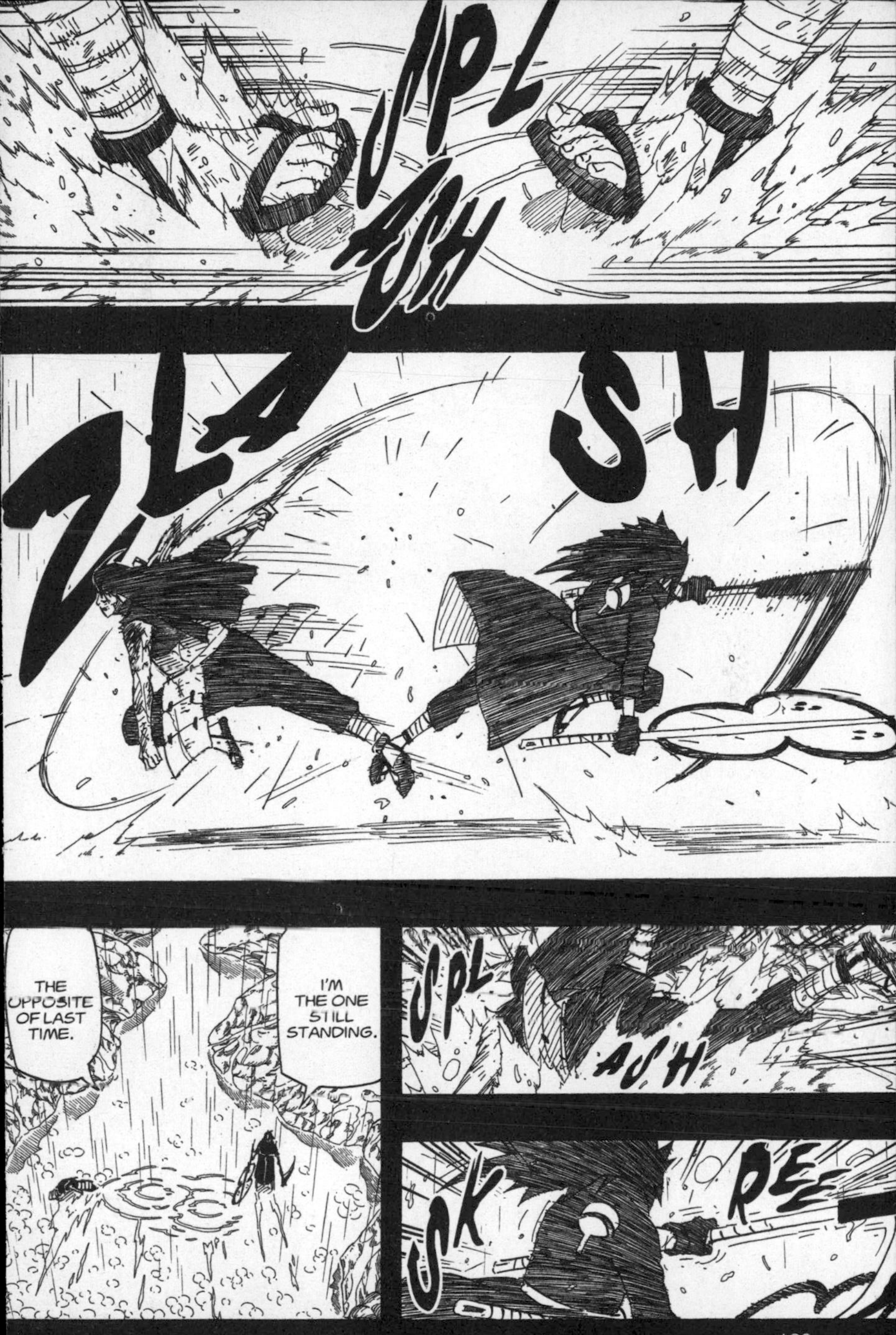
SPLASH
ZLASH
SPLASH
SKREE
I'M THE ONE STILL STANDING.
THE OPPOSITE OF LAST TIME.

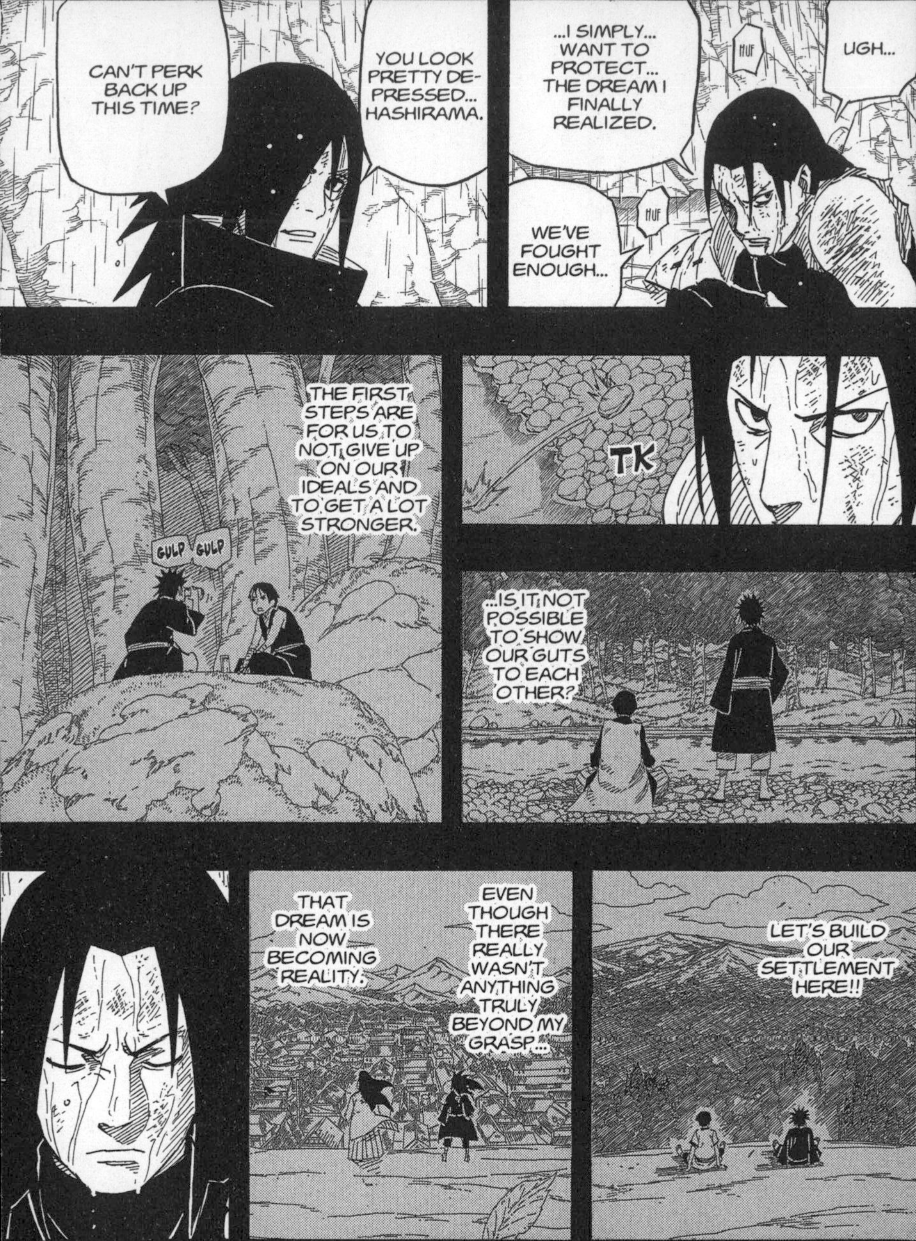
UGH...
HUF
...I SIMPLY... WANT TO PROTECT... THE DREAM I FINALLY REALIZED.
HUF
WE'VE FOUGHT ENOUGH...
YOU LOOK PRETTY DE-PRESSED... HASHIRAMA.
CAN'T PERK BACK UP THIS TIME?
TK
...IS IT NOT POSSIBLE TO SHOW OUR GUTS TO EACH OTHER?
THE FIRST STEPS ARE FOR US TO NOT GIVE UP ON OUR IDEALS AND TO GET A LOT STRONGER.
GULP
GULP
LET'S BUILD OUR SETTLEMENT HERE!!
EVEN THOUGH THERE REALLY WASN'T ANYTHING TRULY BEYOND MY GRASP...
THAT DREAM IS NOW BECOMING REALITY.

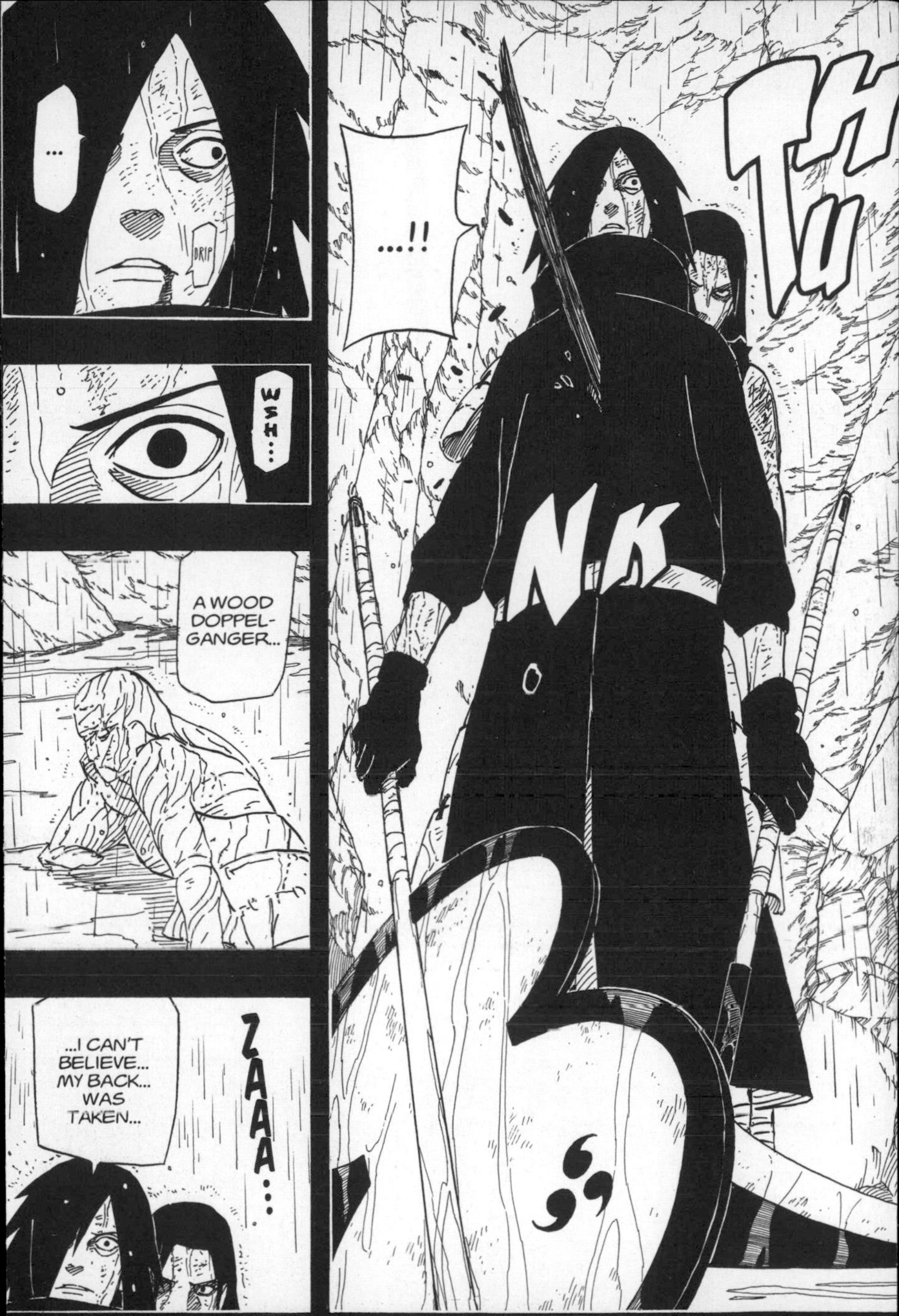
THU
...!!
NK
...
DRIP
WSH...
A WOOD DOPPEL-GANGER...
...I CAN'T BELIEVE... MY BACK... WAS TAKEN...
ZAAAA...

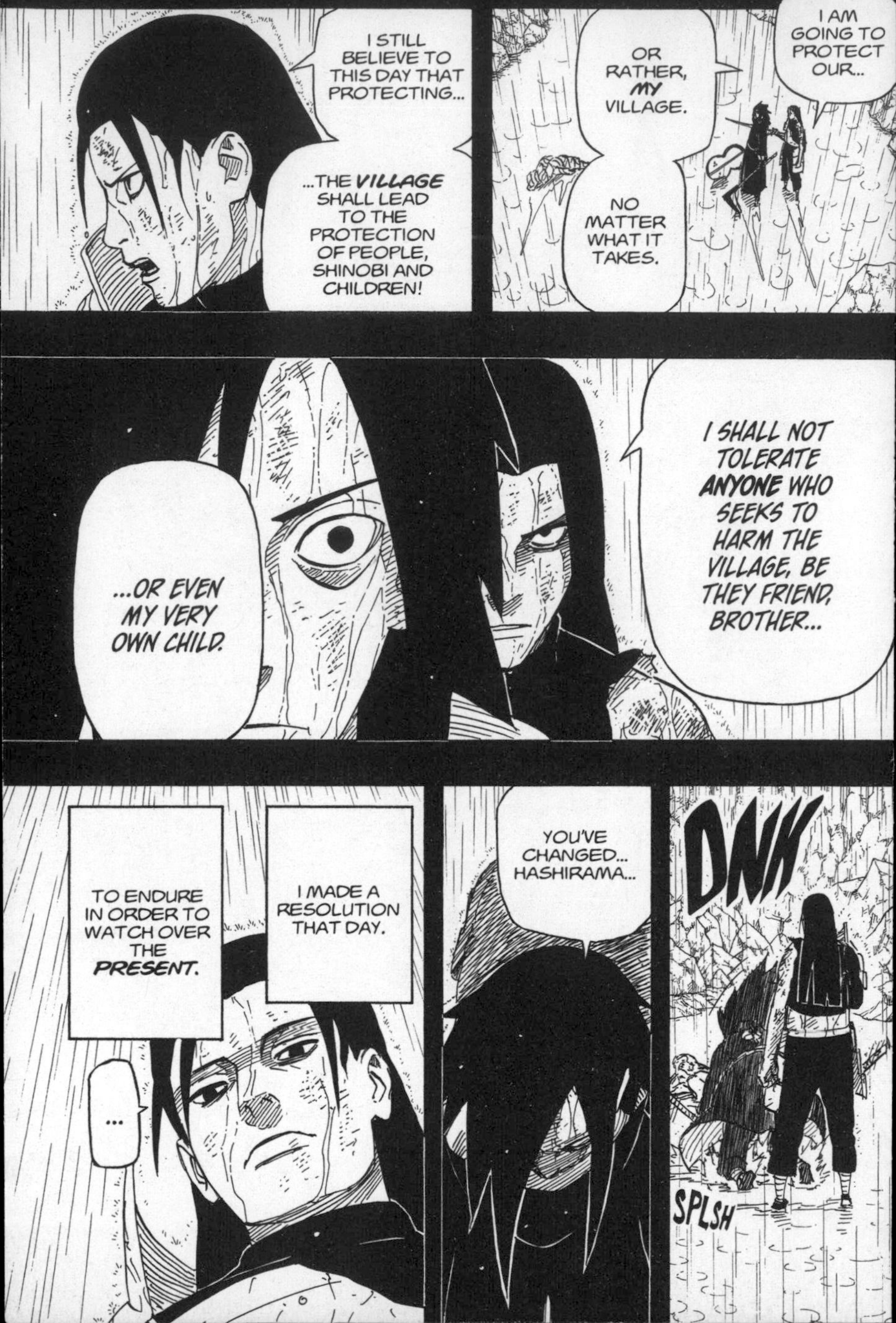
I AM GOING TO PROTECT OUR...
OR RATHER, MY VILLAGE.
NO MATTER WHAT IT TAKES.
I STILL BELIEVE TO THIS DAY THAT PROTECTING...
...THE VILLAGE SHALL LEAD TO THE PROTECTION OF PEOPLE, SHINOBI AND CHILDREN!
I SHALL NOT TOLERATE ANYONE WHO SEEKS TO HARM THE VILLAGE, BE THEY FRIEND, BROTHER...
...OR EVEN MY VERY OWN CHILD.
DNK
SPLSH
YOU'VE CHANGED... HASHIRAMA...
I MADE A RESOLUTION THAT DAY.
TO ENDURE IN ORDER TO WATCH OVER THE PRESENT.
...

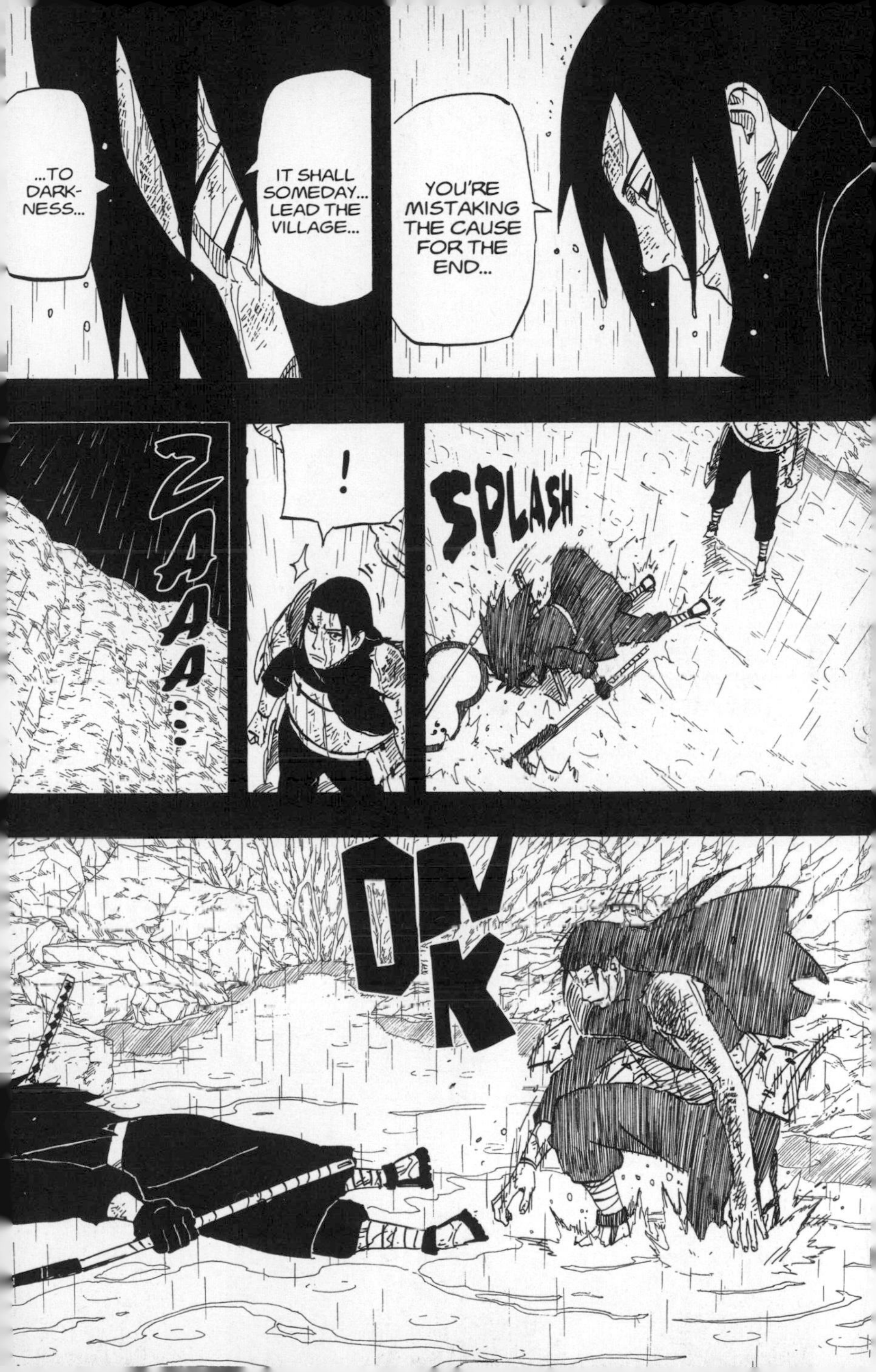
YOU'RE MISTAKING THE CAUSE FOR THE END...
IT SHALL SOMEDAY... LEAD THE VILLAGE...
...TO DARK-NESS...
SPLASH
!
ZAAAA...
DONK

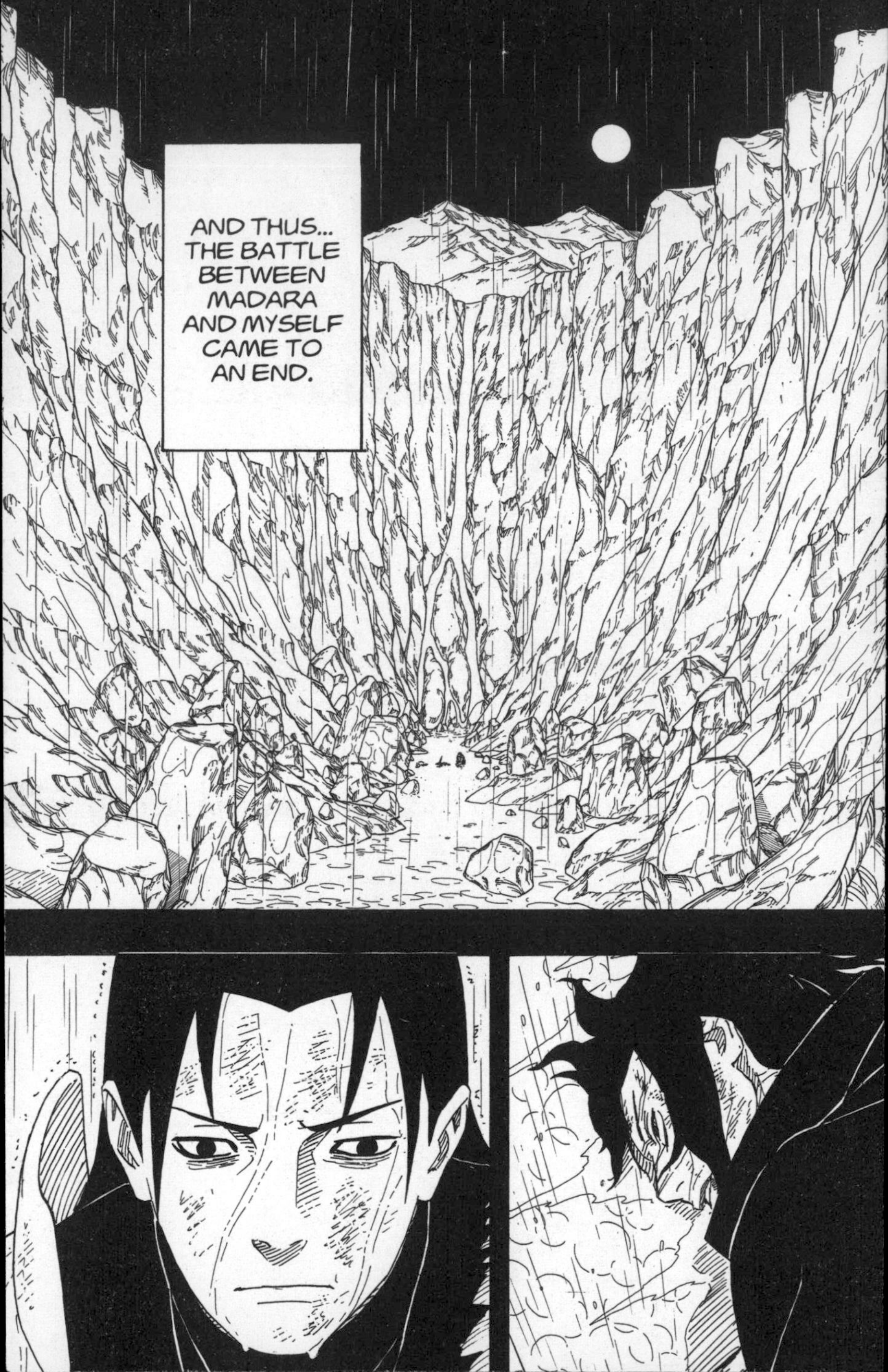
AND THUS... THE BATTLE BETWEEN MADARA AND MYSELF CAME TO AN END.

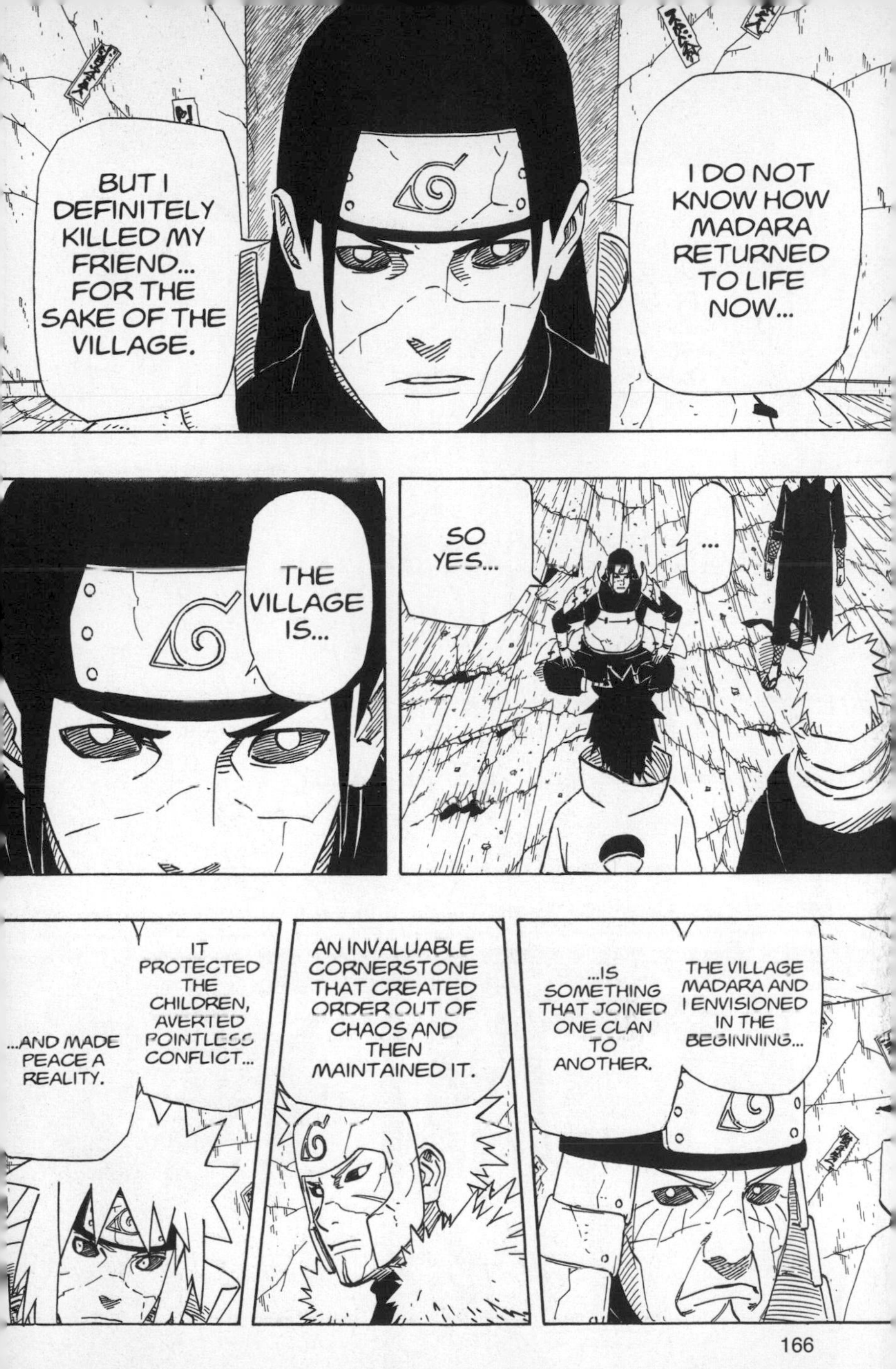
I DO NOT KNOW HOW MADARA RETURNED TO LIFE NOW...
BUT I DEFINITELY KILLED MY FRIEND... FOR THE SAKE OF THE VILLAGE.
...
SO YES...
THE VILLAGE IS...
THE VILLAGE MADARA AND I ENVISIONED IN THE BEGINNING...
...IS SOMETHING THAT JOINED ONE CLAN TO ANOTHER.
AN INVALUABLE CORNERSTONE THAT CREATED ORDER OUT OF CHAOS AND THEN MAINTAINED IT.
IT PROTECTED THE CHILDREN, AVERTED POINTLESS CONFLICT...
...AND MADE PEACE A REALITY.

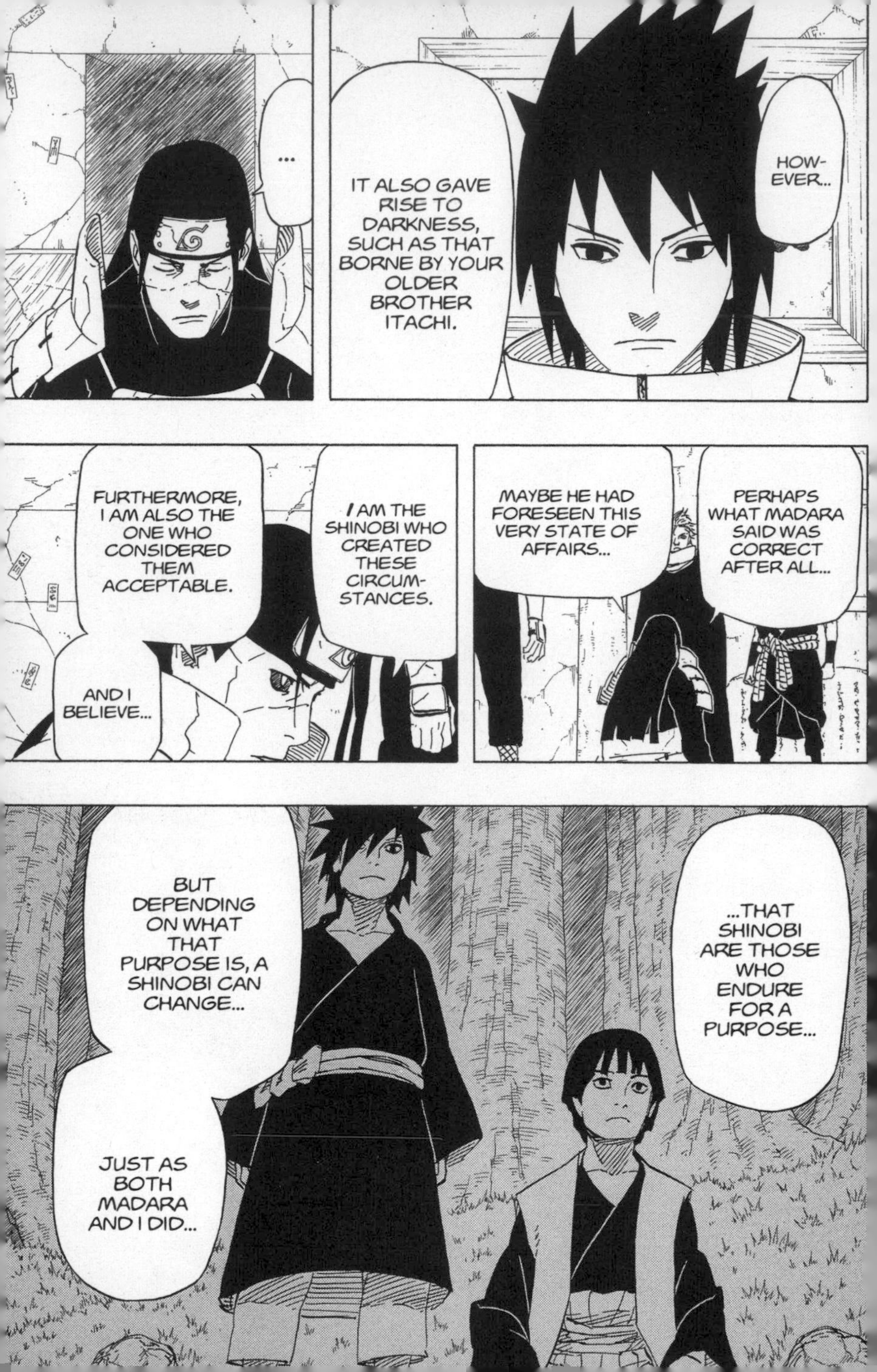
HOW-EVER...
IT ALSO GAVE RISE TO DARKNESS, SUCH AS THAT BORNE BY YOUR OLDER BROTHER ITACHI.
...
PERHAPS WHAT MADARA SAID WAS CORRECT AFTER ALL...
MAYBE HE HAD FORESEEN THIS VERY STATE OF AFFAIRS...
I AM THE SHINOBI WHO CREATED THESE CIRCUM-STANCES.
FURTHERMORE, I AM ALSO THE ONE WHO CONSIDERED THEM ACCEPTABLE.
AND I BELIEVE...
...THAT SHINOBI ARE THOSE WHO ENDURE FOR A PURPOSE...
BUT DEPENDING ON WHAT THAT PURPOSE IS, A SHINOBI CAN CHANGE...
JUST AS BOTH MADARA AND I DID...

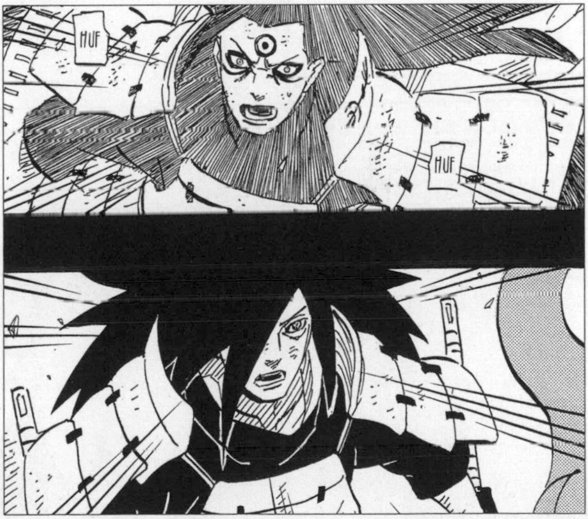
HUF
HUF

Number 627: Sasuke's Answer

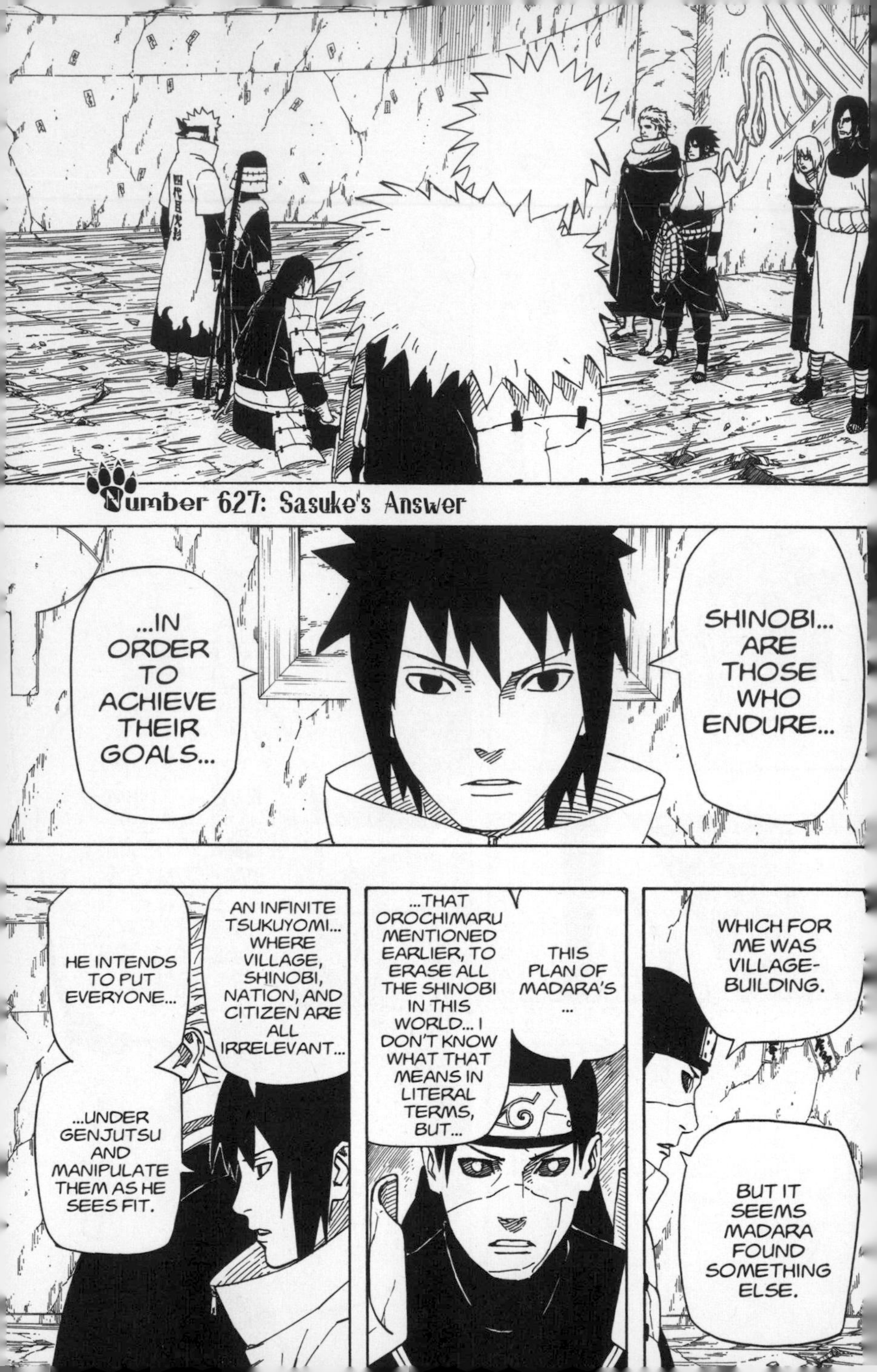
SHINOBI... ARE THOSE WHO ENDURE...
...IN ORDER TO ACHIEVE THEIR GOALS...
WHICH FOR ME WAS VILLAGE-BUILDING.
BUT IT SEEMS MADARA FOUND SOMETHING ELSE.
THIS PLAN OF MADARA'S...
...THAT OROCHIMARU MENTIONED EARLIER, TO ERASE ALL THE SHINOBI IN THIS WORLD... I DON'T KNOW WHAT THAT MEANS IN LITERAL TERMS, BUT...
AN INFINITE TSUKUYOMI... WHERE VILLAGE, SHINOBI, NATION, AND CITIZEN ARE ALL IRRELEVANT...
HE INTENDS TO PUT EVERYONE...
...UNDER GENJUTSU AND MANIPULATE THEM AS HE SEES FIT.

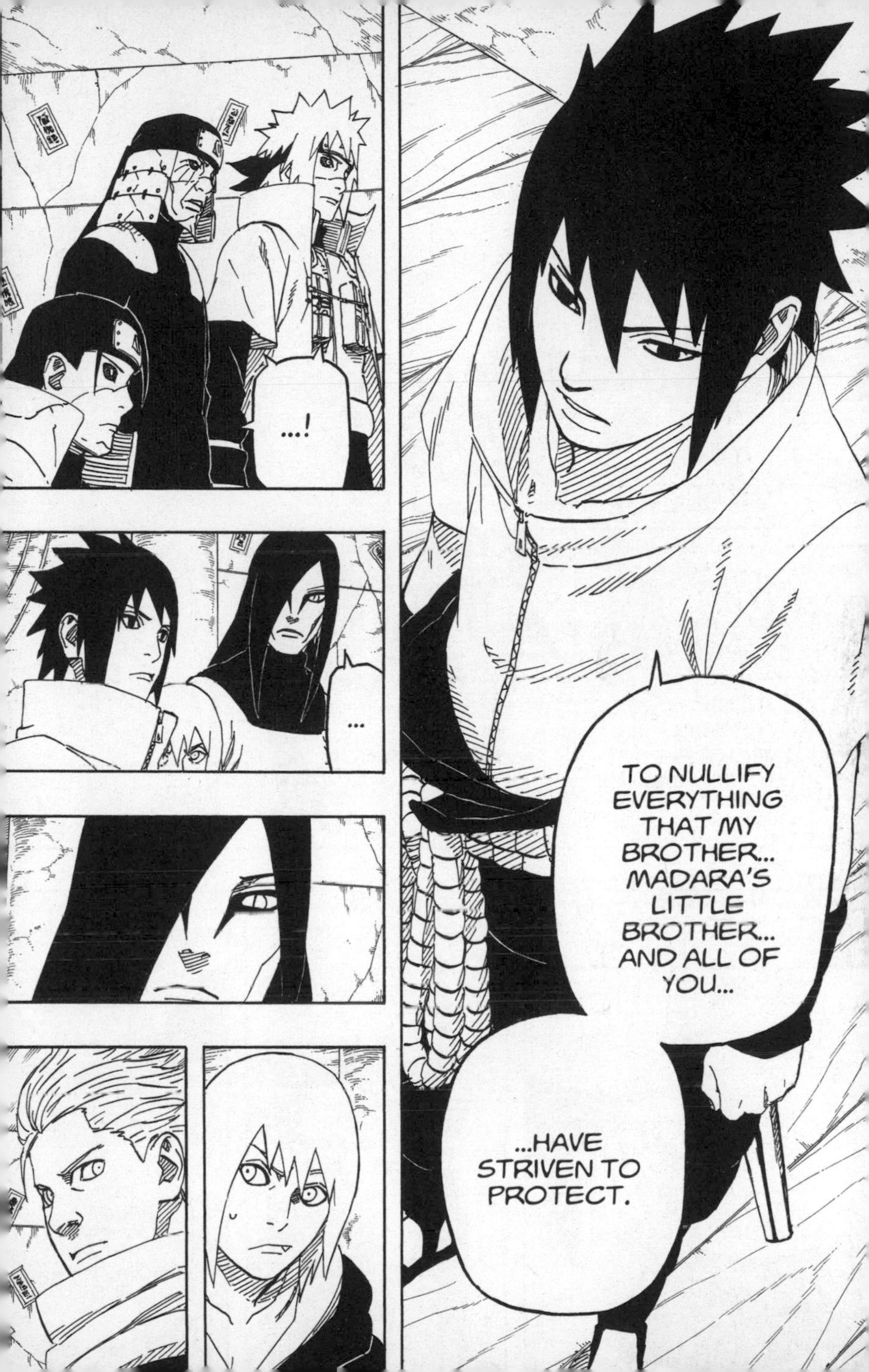
TO NULLIFY EVERYTHING THAT MY BROTHER... MADARA'S LITTLE BROTHER... AND ALL OF YOU...
...HAVE STRIVEN TO PROTECT.
...!
...

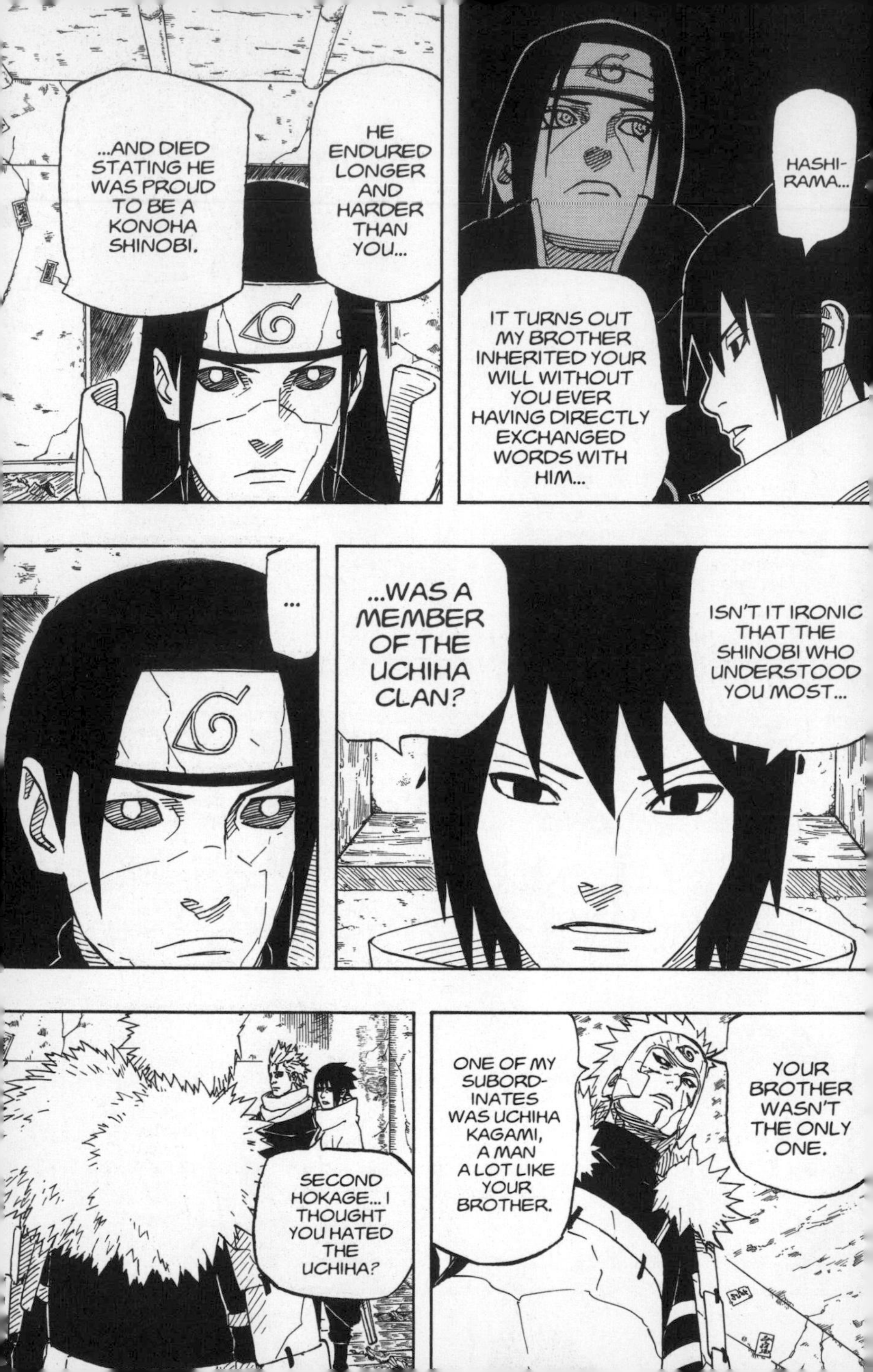
HASHIRAMA...
IT TURNS OUT MY BROTHER INHERITED YOUR WILL WITHOUT YOU EVER HAVING DIRECTLY EXCHANGED WORDS WITH HIM...
HE ENDURED LONGER AND HARDER THAN YOU...
...AND DIED STATING HE WAS PROUD TO BE A KONOHA SHINOBI.
ISN'T IT IRONIC THAT THE SHINOBI WHO UNDERSTOOD YOU MOST...
...WAS A MEMBER OF THE UCHIHA CLAN?
...
YOUR BROTHER WASN'T THE ONLY ONE.
ONE OF MY SUBORDINATES WAS UCHIHA KAGAMI, A MAN A LOT LIKE YOUR BROTHER.
SECOND HOKAGE... I THOUGHT YOU HATED THE UCHIHA?

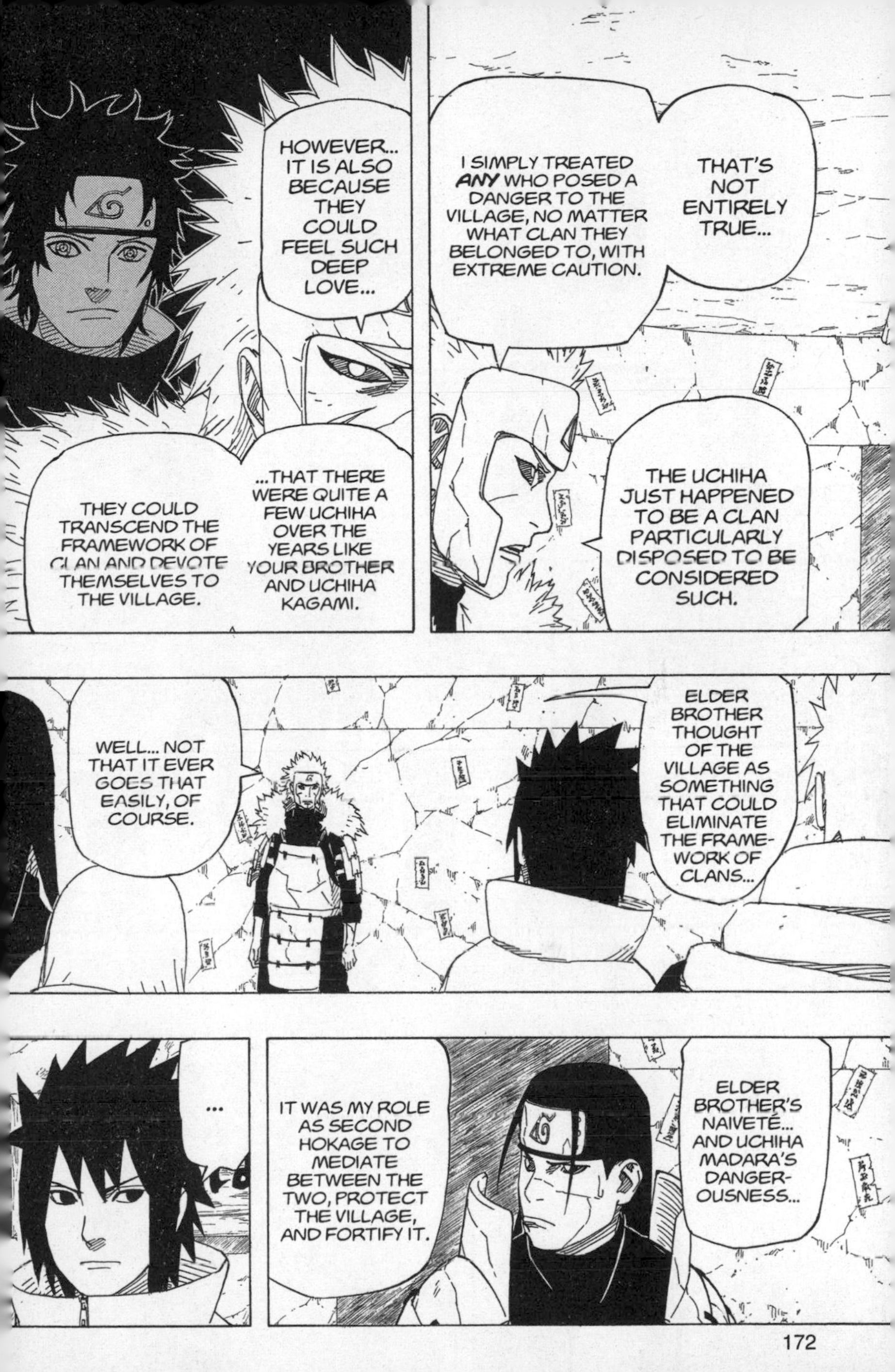
THAT'S NOT ENTIRELY TRUE...
I SIMPLY TREATED ANY WHO POSED A DANGER TO THE VILLAGE, NO MATTER WHAT CLAN THEY BELONGED TO, WITH EXTREME CAUTION.
THE UCHIHA JUST HAPPENED TO BE A CLAN PARTICULARLY DISPOSED TO BE CONSIDERED SUCH.
HOWEVER... IT IS ALSO BECAUSE THEY COULD FEEL SUCH DEEP LOVE...
...THAT THERE WERE QUITE A FEW UCHIHA OVER THE YEARS LIKE YOUR BROTHER AND UCHIHA KAGAMI.
THEY COULD TRANSCEND THE FRAMEWORK OF CLAN AND DEVOTE THEMSELVES TO THE VILLAGE.
ELDER BROTHER THOUGHT OF THE VILLAGE AS SOMETHING THAT COULD ELIMINATE THE FRAME-WORK OF CLANS...
WELL... NOT THAT IT EVER GOES THAT EASILY, OF COURSE.
ELDER BROTHER'S NAIVETÉ... AND UCHIHA MADARA'S DANGER-OUSNESS...
IT WAS MY ROLE AS SECOND HOKAGE TO MEDIATE BETWEEN THE TWO, PROTECT THE VILLAGE, AND FORTIFY IT.
...

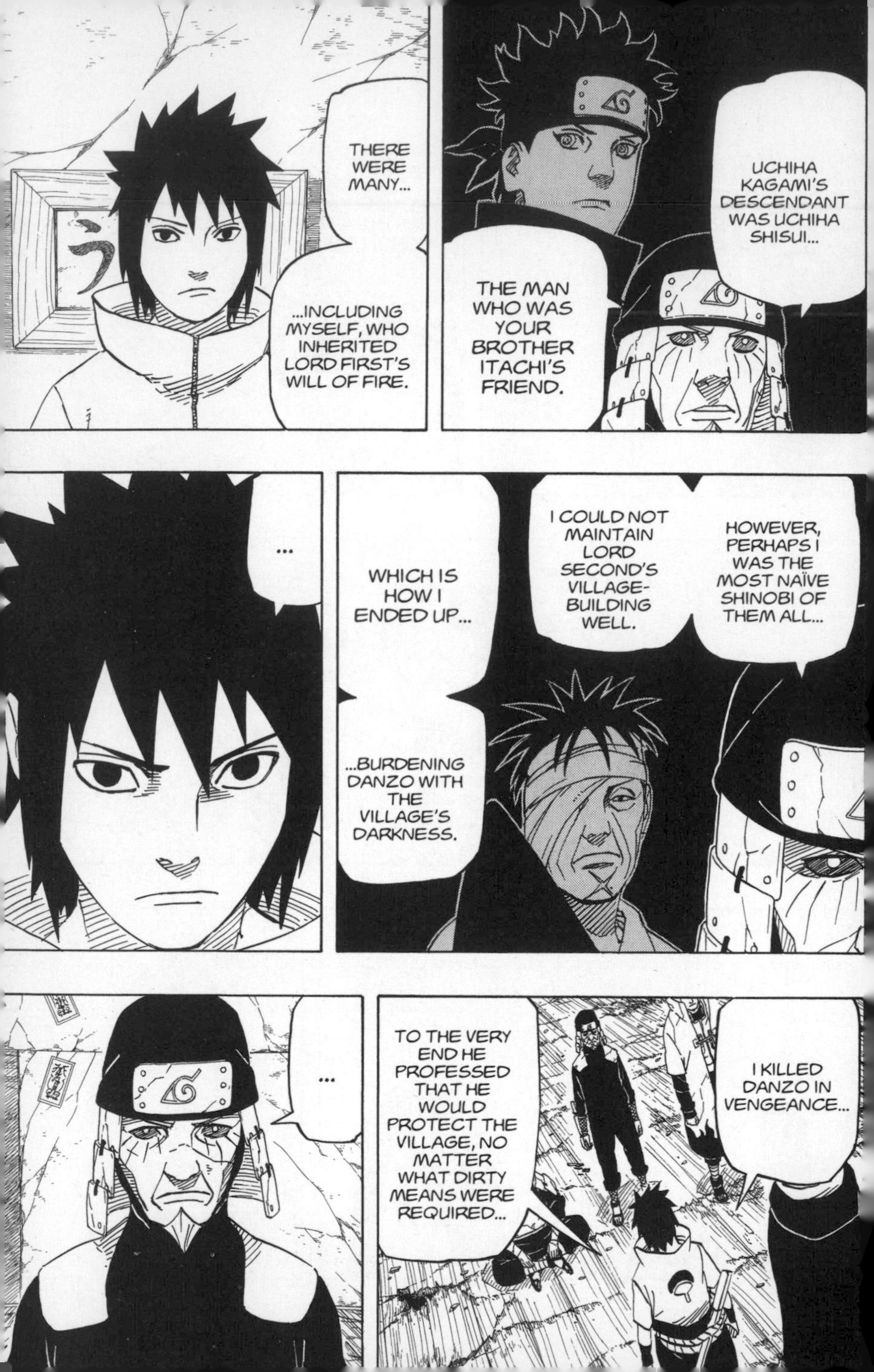
UCHIHA KAGAMI'S DESCENDANT WAS UCHIHA SHISUI...
THE MAN WHO WAS YOUR BROTHER ITACHI'S FRIEND.
THERE WERE MANY...
...INCLUDING MYSELF, WHO INHERITED LORD FIRST'S WILL OF FIRE.
HOWEVER, PERHAPS I WAS THE MOST NAÏVE SHINOBI OF THEM ALL...
I COULD NOT MAINTAIN LORD SECOND'S VILLAGE-BUILDING WELL.
WHICH IS HOW I ENDED UP...
...BURDENING DANZO WITH THE VILLAGE'S DARKNESS.
...
I KILLED DANZO IN VENGEANCE...
TO THE VERY END HE PROFESSED THAT HE WOULD PROTECT THE VILLAGE, NO MATTER WHAT DIRTY MEANS WERE REQUIRED...
...

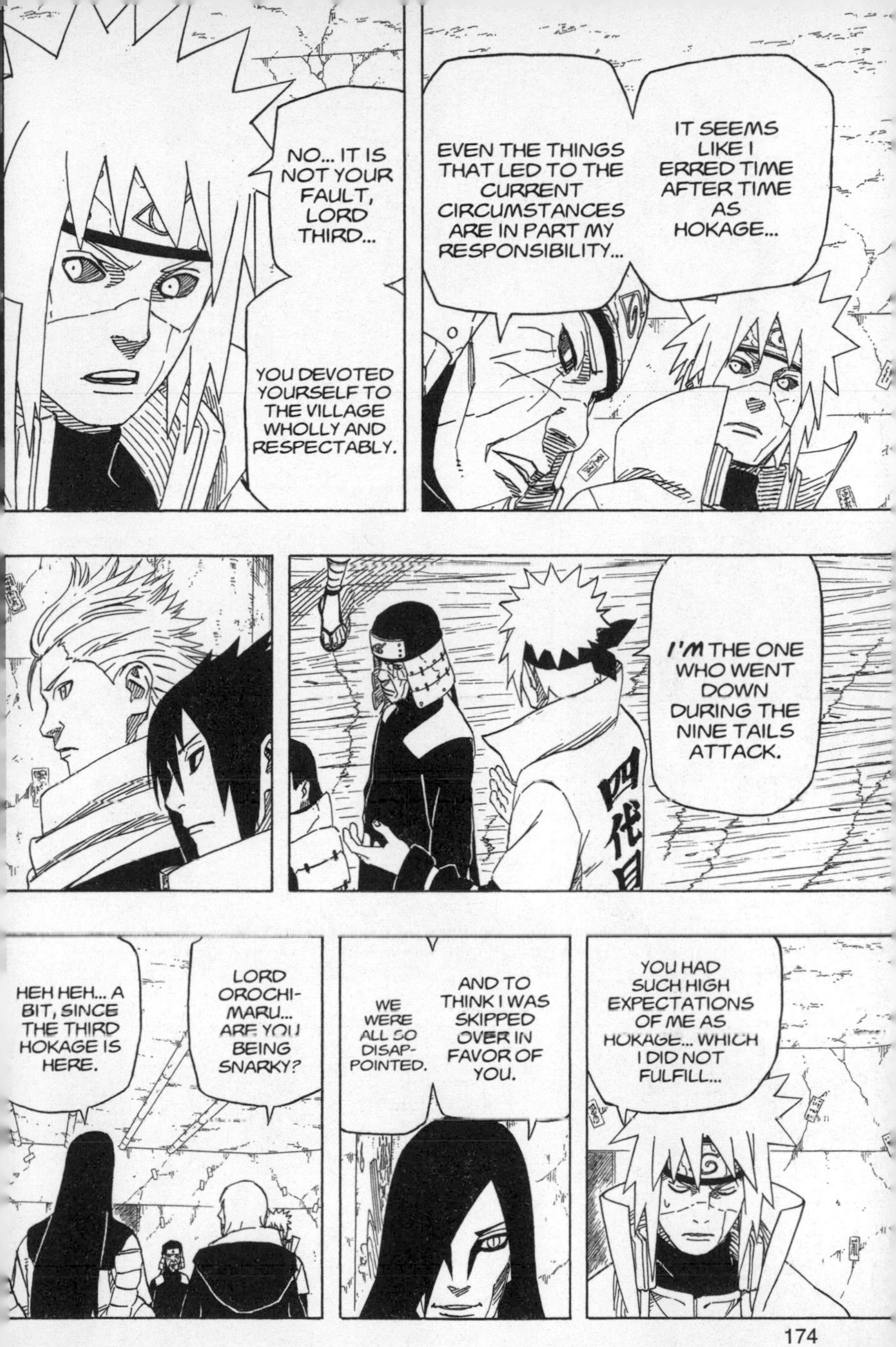
IT SEEMS LIKE I ERRED TIME AFTER TIME AS HOKAGE...
EVEN THE THINGS THAT LED TO THE CURRENT CIRCUMSTANCES ARE IN PART MY RESPONSIBILITY...
NO... IT IS NOT YOUR FAULT, LORD THIRD...
YOU DEVOTED YOURSELF TO THE VILLAGE WHOLLY AND RESPECTABLY.
I'M THE ONE WHO WENT DOWN DURING THE NINE TAILS ATTACK.
四代目
YOU HAD SUCH HIGH EXPECTATIONS OF ME AS HOKAGE... WHICH I DID NOT FULFILL...
AND TO THINK I WAS SKIPPED OVER IN FAVOR OF YOU.
WE WERE ALL SO DISAPPOINTED.
LORD OROCHIMARU... ARE YOU BEING SNARKY?
HEH HEH... A BIT, SINCE THE THIRD HOKAGE IS HERE.

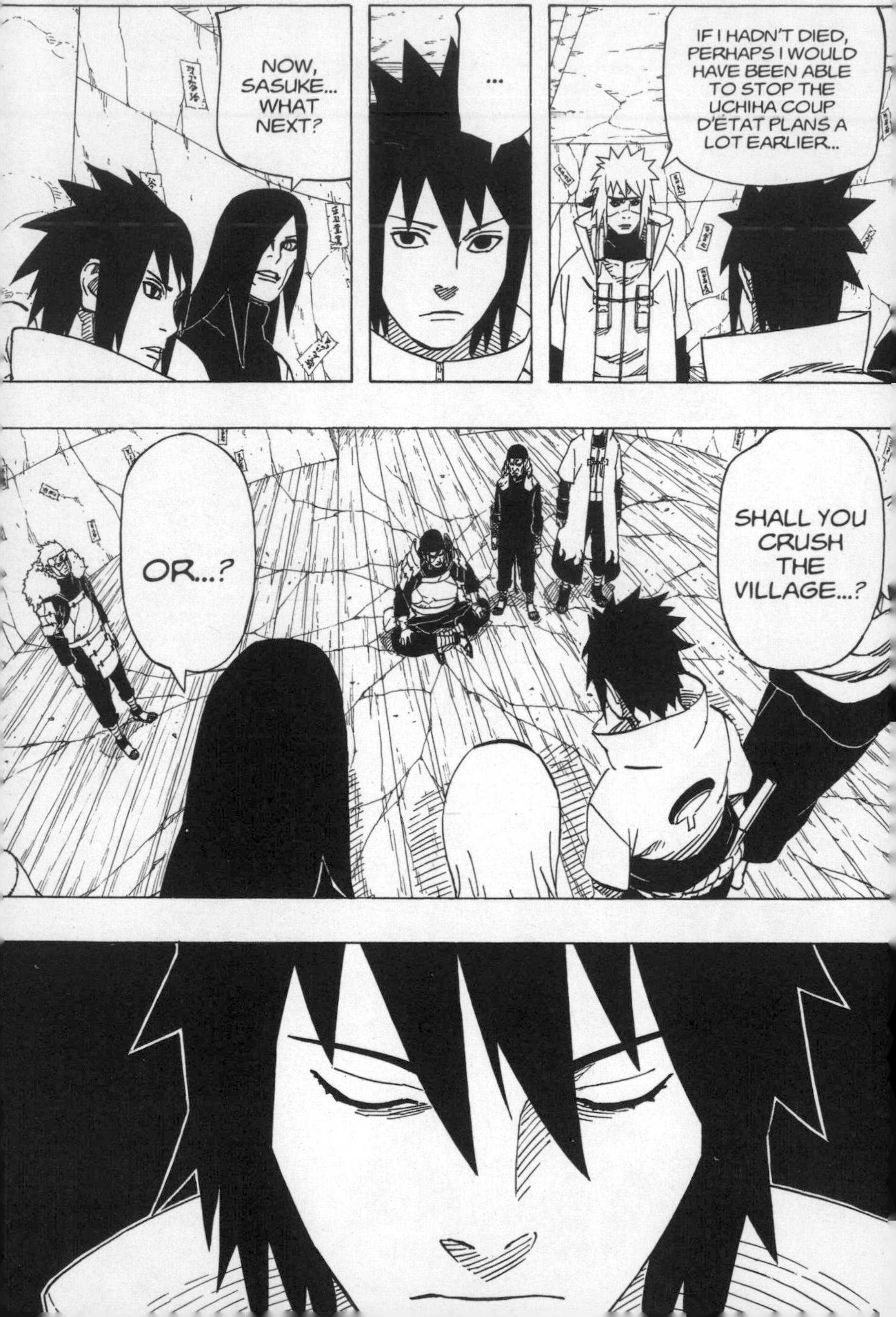
IF I HADN'T DIED, PERHAPS I WOULD HAVE BEEN ABLE TO STOP THE UCHIHA COUP D'ETAT PLANS A LOT EARLIER...
...
NOW, SASUKE... WHAT NEXT?
SHALL YOU CRUSH THE VILLAGE...?
OR...?

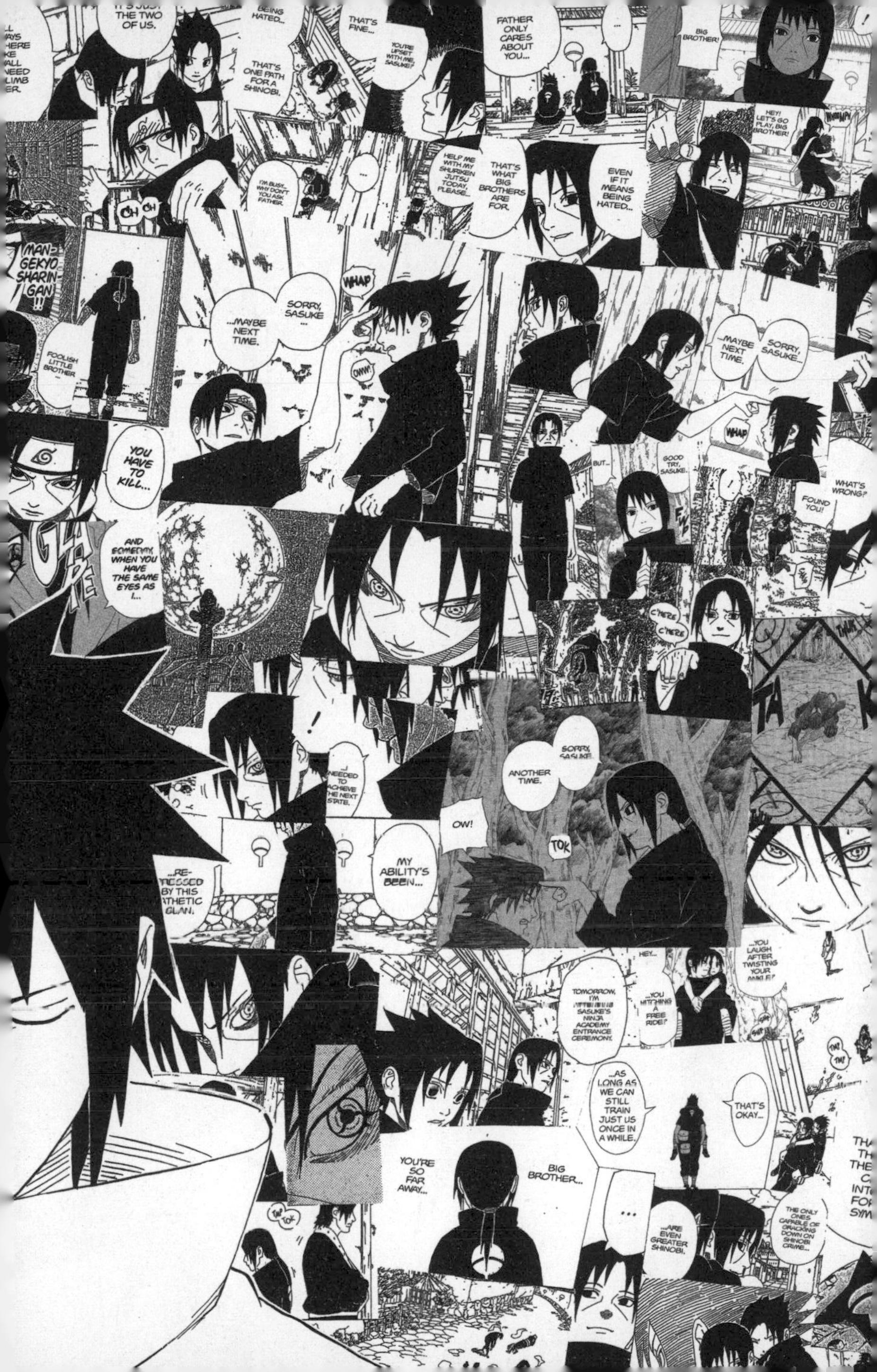
BIG BROTHER!
...
FATHER ONLY CARES ABOUT YOU...
THAT'S FINE...
YOU'RE UPSET WITH ME, SASUKE?
BEING HATED...
THAT'S ONE PATH FOR A SHINOBI.
IT'S JUST THE TWO OF US.
HEY! LET'S GO PLAY, BIG BROTHER!
EVEN IF IT MEANS BEING HATED...
THAT'S WHAT BIG BROTHERS ARE FOR.
HELP ME WITH MY SHURIKEN JUTSU TODAY, PLEASE...
...
I'M BUSY... WHY DON'T YOU ASK FATHER.
OH OH
SORRY, SASUKE...
...MAYBE NEXT TIME.
WHAP
WHAP
SORRY, SASUKE...
...MAYBE NEXT TIME.
OWW!
MANGEKYO SHARINGAN!!
FOOLISH LITTLE BROTHER...
WHAT'S WRONG?
FOUND YOU!
GOOD TRY, SASUKE.
BUT...
YOU HAVE TO KILL...
AND SOMEDAY, WHEN YOU HAVE THE SAME EYES AS I...
C'HERE C'HERE
SORRY, SASUKE.
ANOTHER TIME.
OW!
TOK
!
...I NEEDED TO ACHIEVE THE NEXT STATE.
MY ABILITY'S BEEN...
...YOU LAUGH AFTER TWISTING YOUR ANKLE?
HEY...
...YOU HITCHING A FREE RIDE?
TOMORROW, I'M SASUKE'S NINJA ACADEMY ENTRANCE CEREMONY.
...AS LONG AS WE CAN STILL TRAIN JUST US ONCE IN A WHILE.
THAT'S OKAY...
BIG BROTHER...
YOU'RE SO FAR AWAY...
...
...ARE EVEN GREATER SHINOBI.
THE ONLY ONES CAPABLE OF CRACKING DOWN ON SHINOBI CRIME...

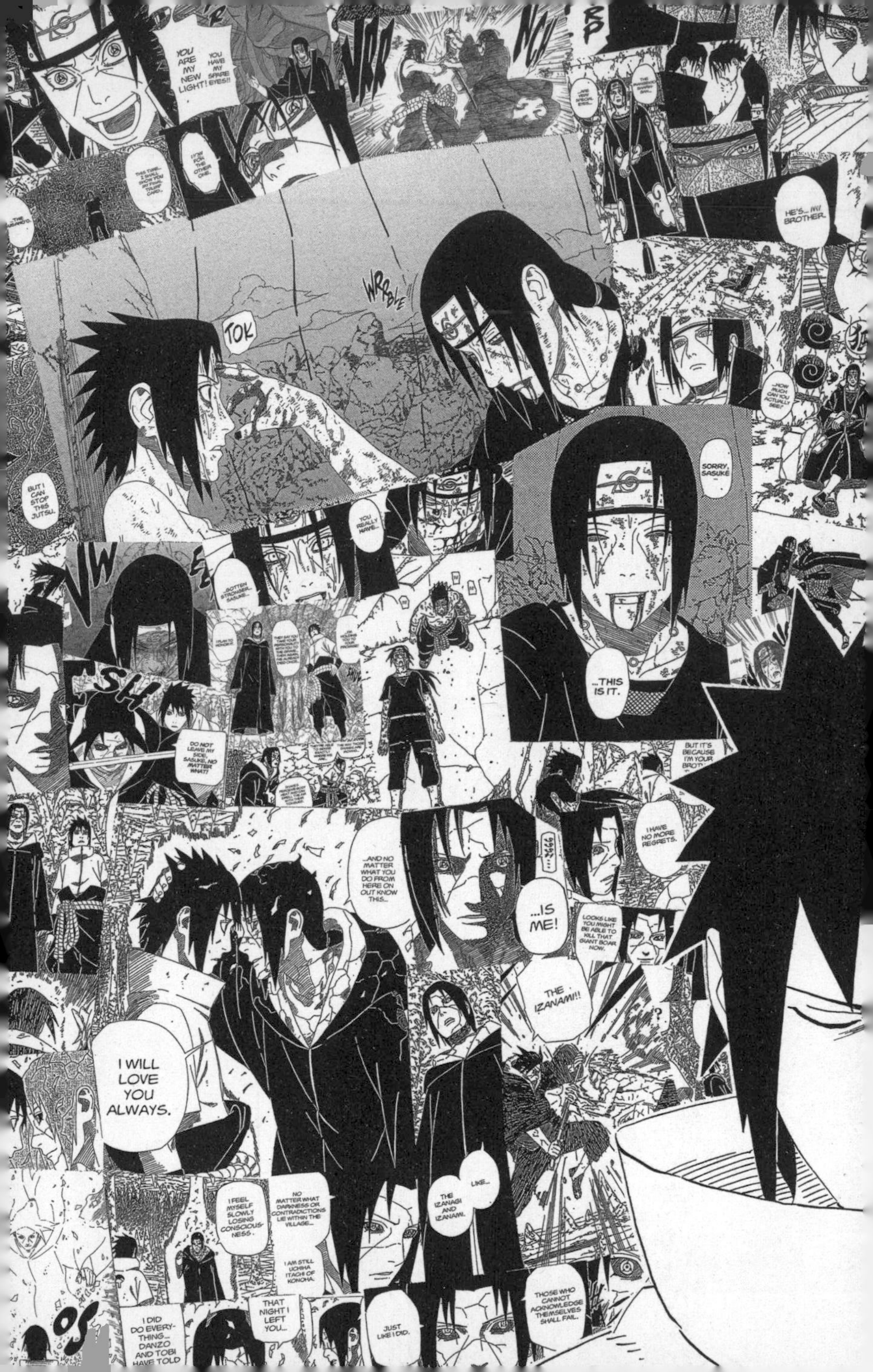
YOU HAVE MY SPARE EYES!!
YOU ARE MY NEW LIGHT!
HE'S... MY BROTHER.
I'M FOR THE OTHER ONE.
THIS TIME, I SHALL SHOW YOU MY FINAL TRUMP CARD.
...HOW MUCH CAN YOU ACTUALLY SEE?
TOK
SORRY, SASUKE...
BUT I CAN STOP THIS JUTSU.
YOU REALLY HAVE...
...GOTTEN STRONGER, SASUKE...
...THIS IS IT.
DO NOT LEAVE MY SIDE, SASUKE, NO MATTER WHAT!
BUT IT'S BECAUSE I'M YOUR BROT...
I HAVE NO MORE REGRETS.
...IS ME!
...AND NO MATTER WHAT YOU DO FROM HERE ON OUT KNOW THIS...
LOOKS LIKE YOU MIGHT BE ABLE TO KILL THAT GIANT BOAR NOW.
THE IZANAMI!!
I WILL LOVE YOU ALWAYS.
LIKE...
THE IZANAGI AND IZANAMI.
NO MATTER WHAT DARKNESS OR CONTRADICTIONS LIE WITHIN THE VILLAGE...
I AM STILL UCHIHA ITACHI OF KONOHA.
I FEEL MYSELF SLOWLY LOSING CONSCIOUS-NESS.
THOSE WHO CANNOT ACKNOWLEDGE THEMSELVES SHALL FAIL.
JUST LIKE I DID.
THAT NIGHT I LEFT YOU...
I DID DO EVERY-THING... DANZO AND TOBI HAVE TOLD

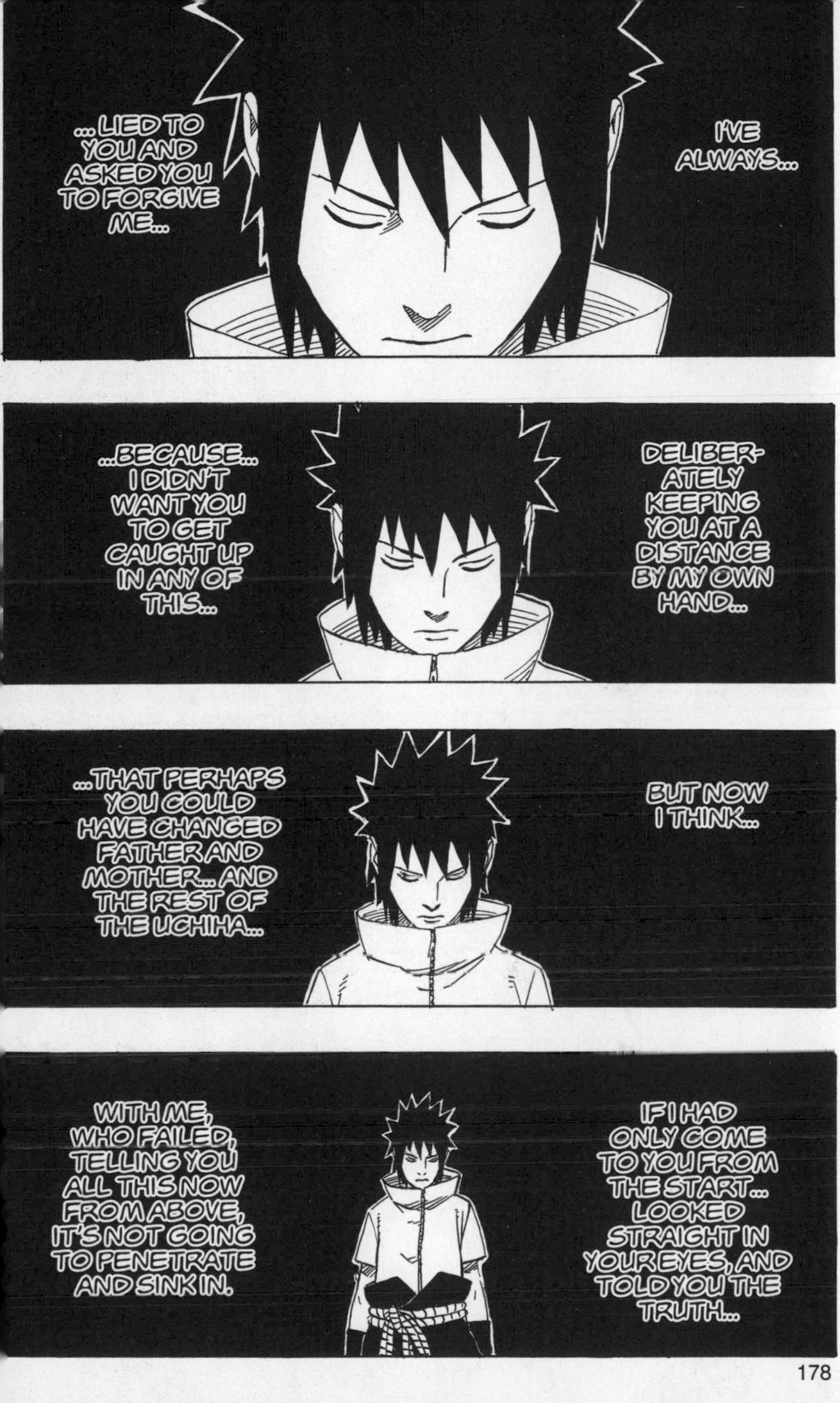
I'VE ALWAYS...
...LIED TO YOU AND ASKED YOU TO FORGIVE ME...
DELIBER-ATELY KEEPING YOU AT A DISTANCE BY MY OWN HAND...
...BECAUSE... I DIDN'T WANT YOU TO GET CAUGHT UP IN ANY OF THIS...
BUT NOW I THINK...
...THAT PERHAPS YOU COULD HAVE CHANGED FATHER AND MOTHER... AND THE REST OF THE UCHIHA...
IF I HAD ONLY COME TO YOU FROM THE START... LOOKED STRAIGHT IN YOUR EYES, AND TOLD YOU THE TRUTH...
WITH ME, WHO FAILED, TELLING YOU ALL THIS NOW FROM ABOVE, IT'S NOT GOING TO PENETRATE AND SINK IN.

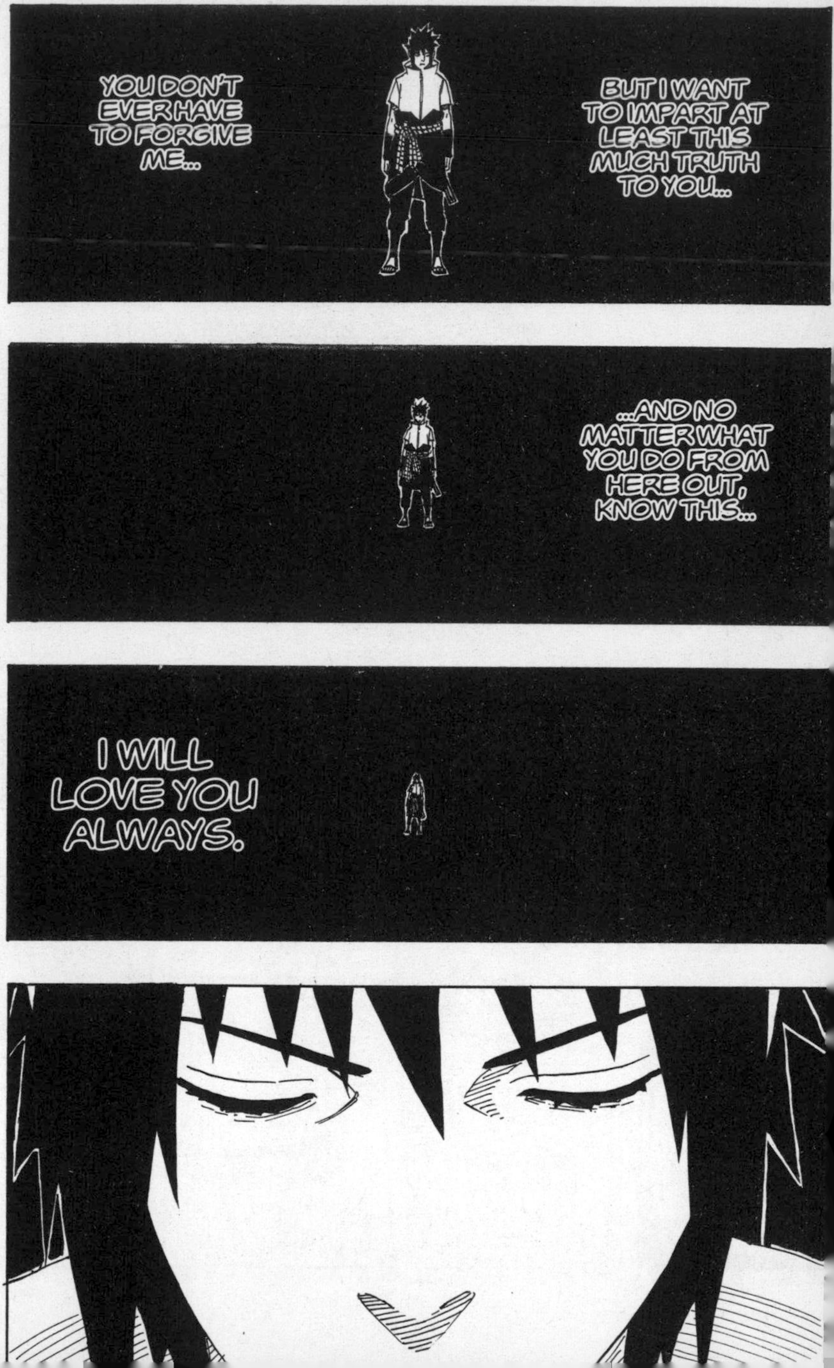
BUT I WANT TO IMPART AT LEAST THIS MUCH TRUTH TO YOU...
YOU DON'T EVER HAVE TO FORGIVE ME...
...AND NO MATTER WHAT YOU DO FROM HERE OUT, KNOW THIS...
I WILL LOVE YOU ALWAYS.

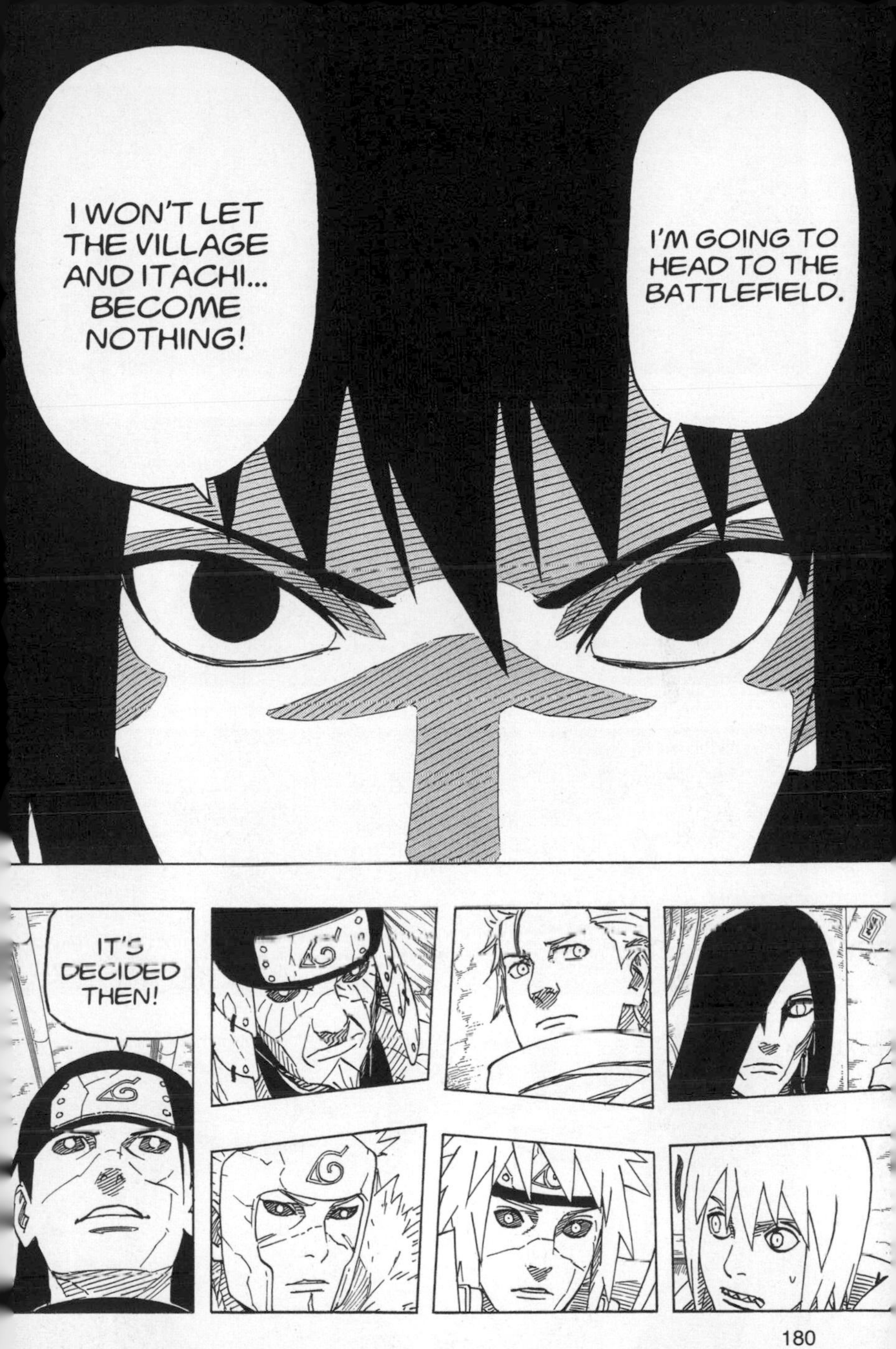
I'M GOING TO HEAD TO THE BATTLEFIELD.
I WON'T LET THE VILLAGE AND ITACHI... BECOME NOTHING!
IT'S DECIDED THEN!

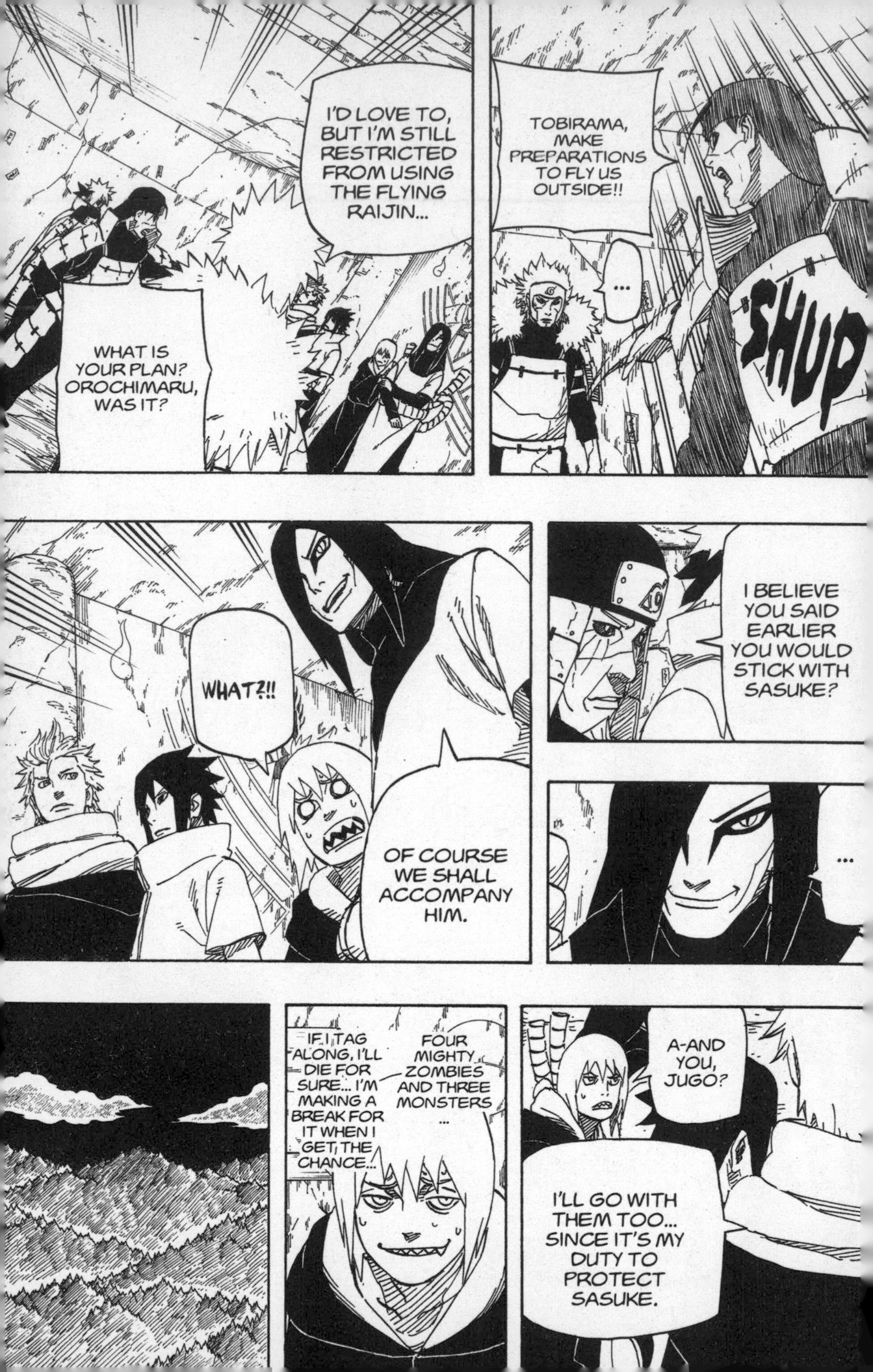
TOBIRAMA, MAKE PREPARATIONS TO FLY US OUTSIDE!!
...
SHUP
I'D LOVE TO, BUT I'M STILL RESTRICTED FROM USING THE FLYING RAIJIN...
WHAT IS YOUR PLAN? OROCHIMARU, WAS IT?
I BELIEVE YOU SAID EARLIER YOU WOULD STICK WITH SASUKE?
...
OF COURSE WE SHALL ACCOMPANY HIM.
WHAT?!!
A-AND YOU, JUGO?
I'LL GO WITH THEM TOO... SINCE IT'S MY DUTY TO PROTECT SASUKE.
FOUR MIGHTY ZOMBIES AND THREE MONSTERS ...
IF I TAG ALONG, I'LL DIE FOR SURE... I'M MAKING A BREAK FOR IT WHEN I GET THE CHANCE...

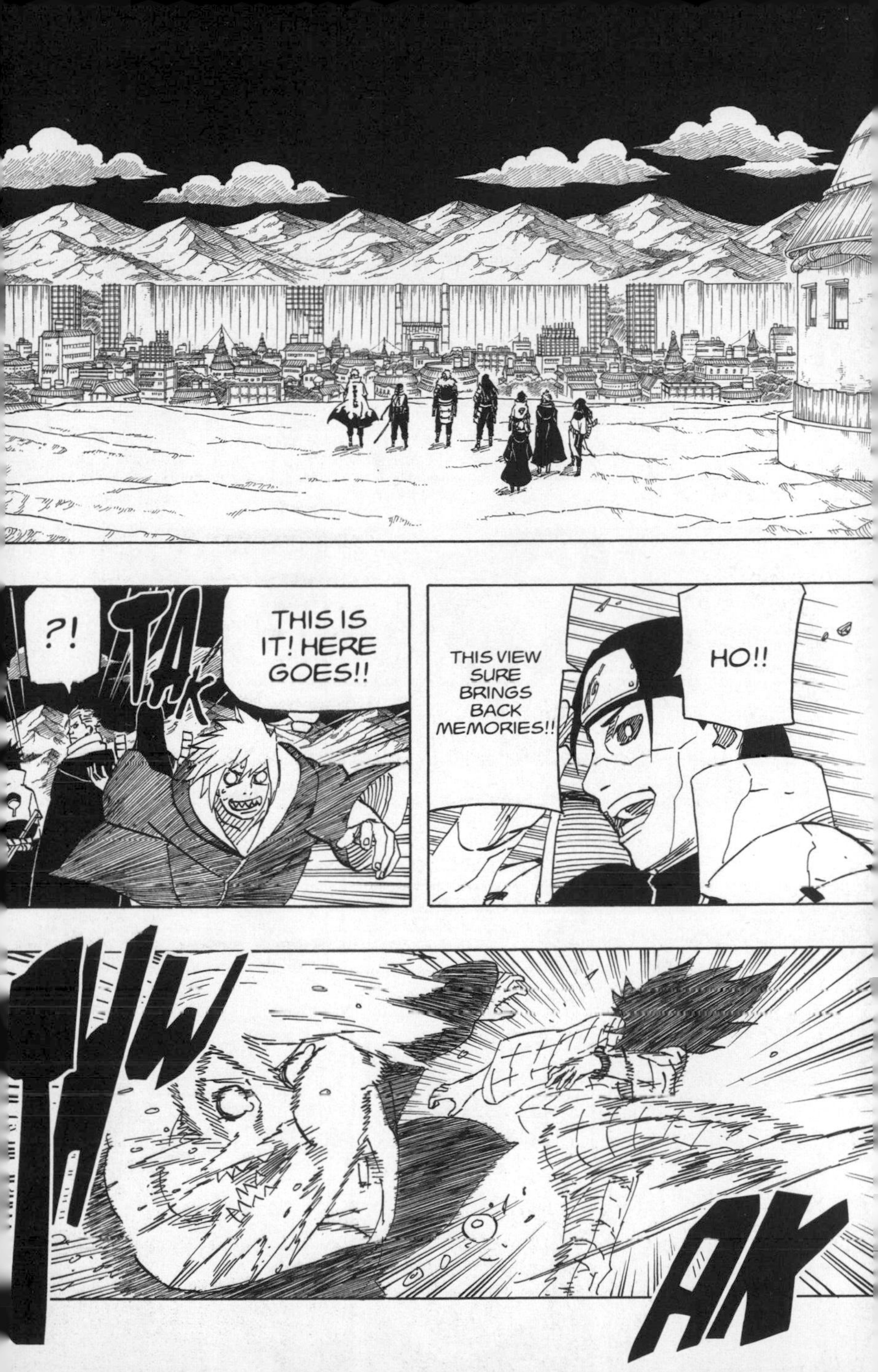
HO!!
THIS VIEW SURE BRINGS BACK MEMORIES!!
THIS IS IT! HERE GOES!!
TAK
?!
THWAK

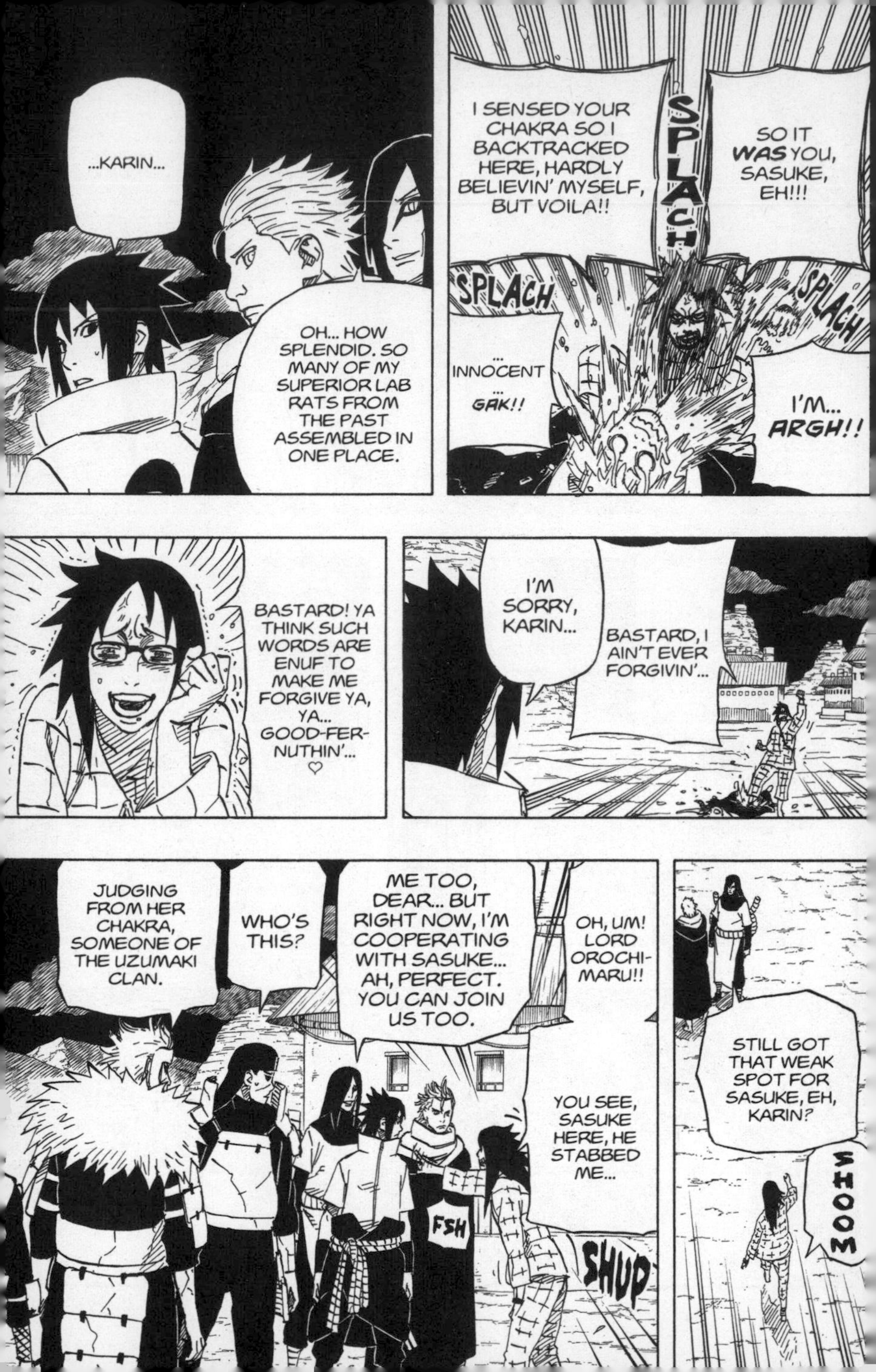
SO IT WAS YOU, SASUKE, EH!!!
I SENSED YOUR CHAKRA SO I BACKTRACKED HERE, HARDLY BELIEVIN' MYSELF, BUT VOILA!!
SPLACH
SPLACH
SPLACH
I'M... ARGH!!
... INNOCENT ... GAK!!
...KARIN...
OH... HOW SPLENDID. SO MANY OF MY SUPERIOR LAB RATS FROM THE PAST ASSEMBLED IN ONE PLACE.
I'M SORRY, KARIN...
BASTARD, I AIN'T EVER FORGIVIN'...
BASTARD! YA THINK SUCH WORDS ARE ENUF TO MAKE ME FORGIVE YA, YA... GOOD-FER-NUTHIN'... ♡
STILL GOT THAT WEAK SPOT FOR SASUKE, EH, KARIN?
SHOOM
OH, UM! LORD OROCHI-MARU!!
YOU SEE, SASUKE HERE, HE STABBED ME...
SHUP
FSH
ME TOO, DEAR... BUT RIGHT NOW, I'M COOPERATING WITH SASUKE... AH, PERFECT. YOU CAN JOIN US TOO.
WHO'S THIS?
JUDGING FROM HER CHAKRA, SOMEONE OF THE UZUMAKI CLAN.

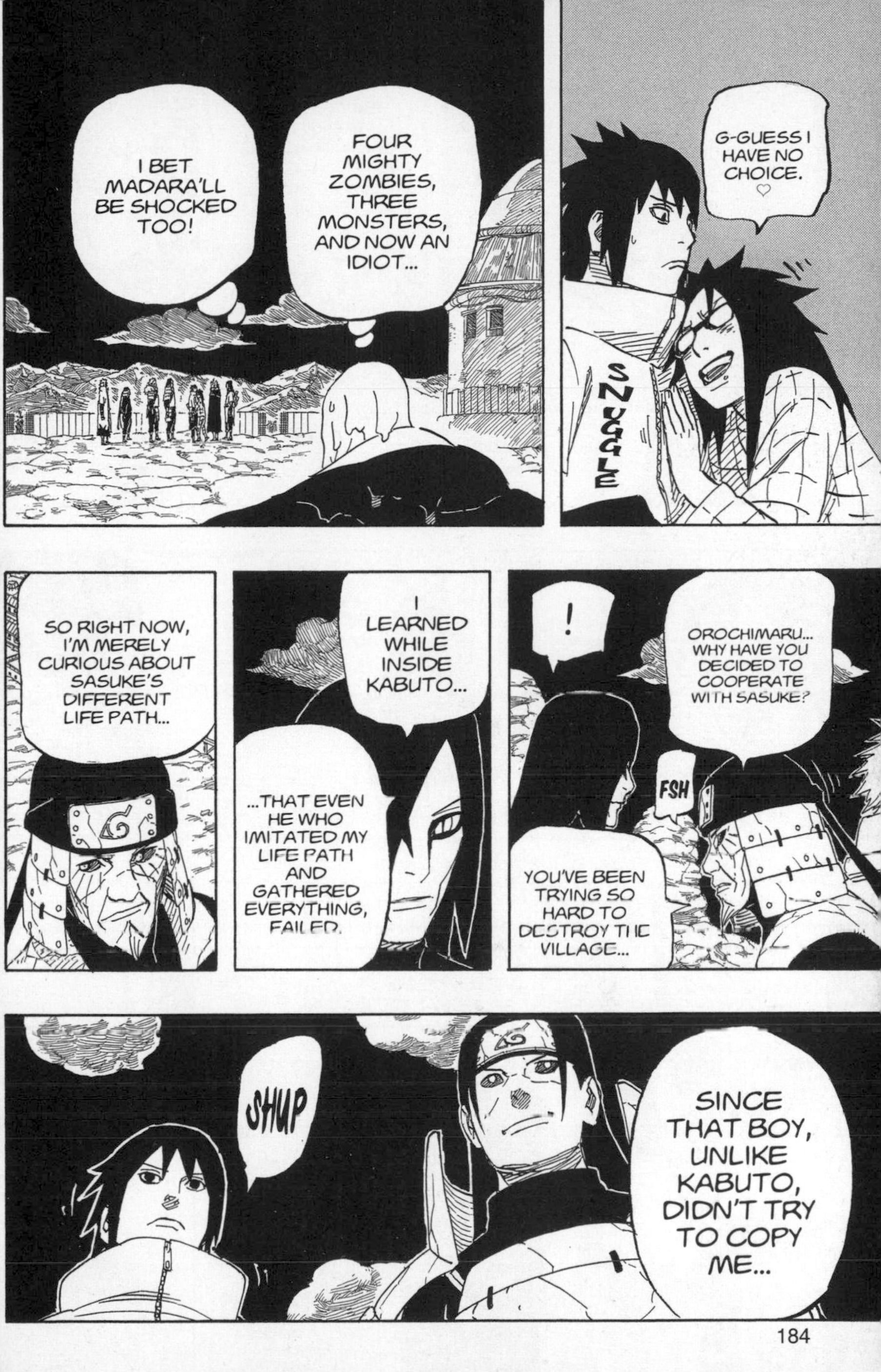
G-GUESS I HAVE NO CHOICE. ♡
SNUGGLE
FOUR MIGHTY ZOMBIES, THREE MONSTERS, AND NOW AN IDIOT...
I BET MADARA'LL BE SHOCKED TOO!
OROCHIMARU... WHY HAVE YOU DECIDED TO COOPERATE WITH SASUKE?
!
FSH
YOU'VE BEEN TRYING SO HARD TO DESTROY THE VILLAGE...
I LEARNED WHILE INSIDE KABUTO...
...THAT EVEN HE WHO IMITATED MY LIFE PATH AND GATHERED EVERYTHING, FAILED.
SO RIGHT NOW, I'M MERELY CURIOUS ABOUT SASUKE'S DIFFERENT LIFE PATH...
SINCE THAT BOY, UNLIKE KABUTO, DIDN'T TRY TO COPY ME...
SHUP

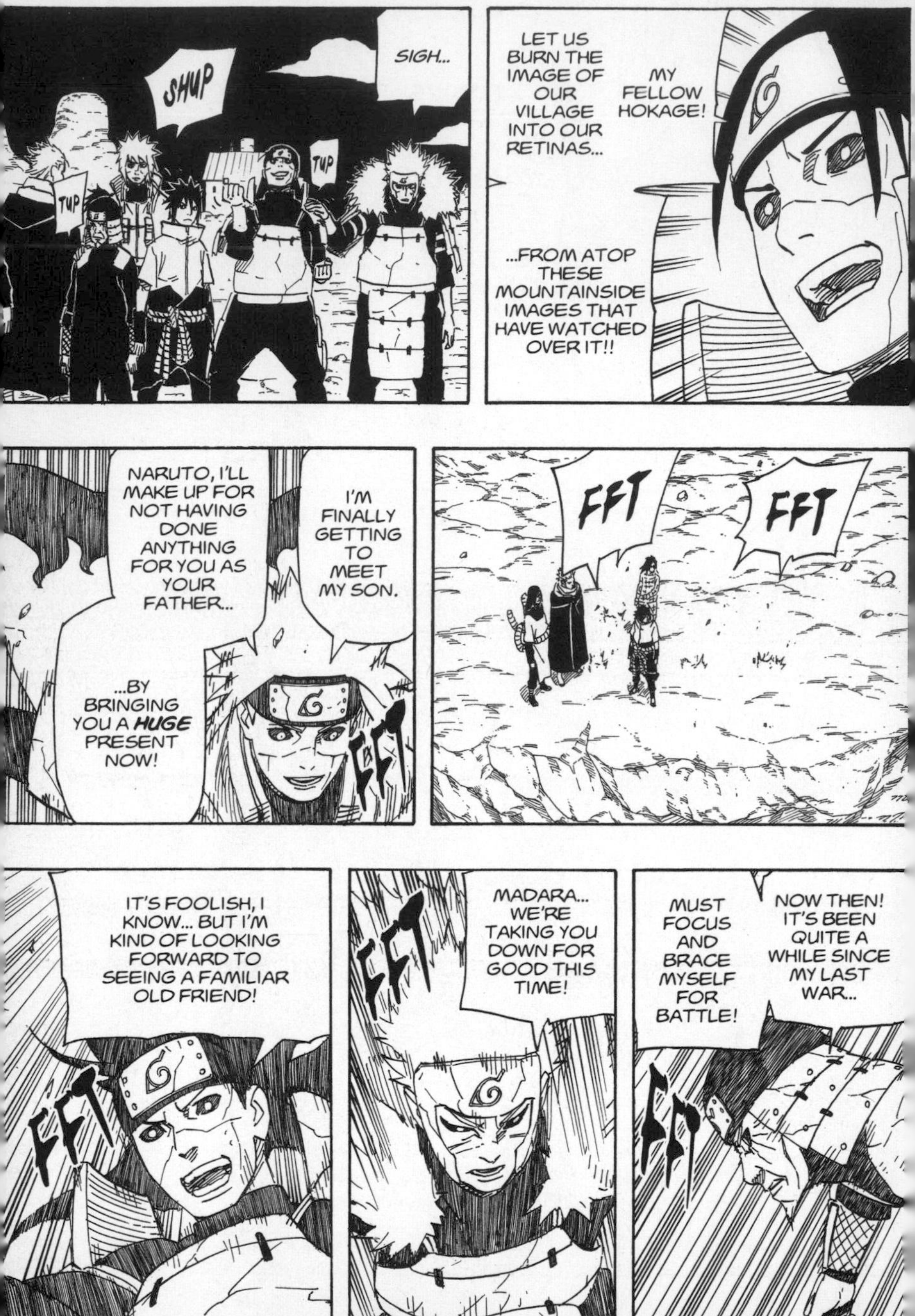
MY FELLOW HOKAGE!
LET US BURN THE IMAGE OF OUR VILLAGE INTO OUR RETINAS...
...FROM ATOP THESE MOUNTAINSIDE IMAGES THAT HAVE WATCHED OVER IT!!
SIGH...
SHUP
TUP
TUP
FFT
FFT
I'M FINALLY GETTING TO MEET MY SON.
NARUTO, I'LL MAKE UP FOR NOT HAVING DONE ANYTHING FOR YOU AS YOUR FATHER...
...BY BRINGING YOU A **HUGE** PRESENT NOW!
FFT
NOW THEN! IT'S BEEN QUITE A WHILE SINCE MY LAST WAR...
MUST FOCUS AND BRACE MYSELF FOR BATTLE!
FFT
MADARA... WE'RE TAKING YOU DOWN FOR GOOD THIS TIME!
FFT
IT'S FOOLISH, I KNOW... BUT I'M KIND OF LOOKING FORWARD TO SEEING A FAMILIAR OLD FRIEND!
FFT

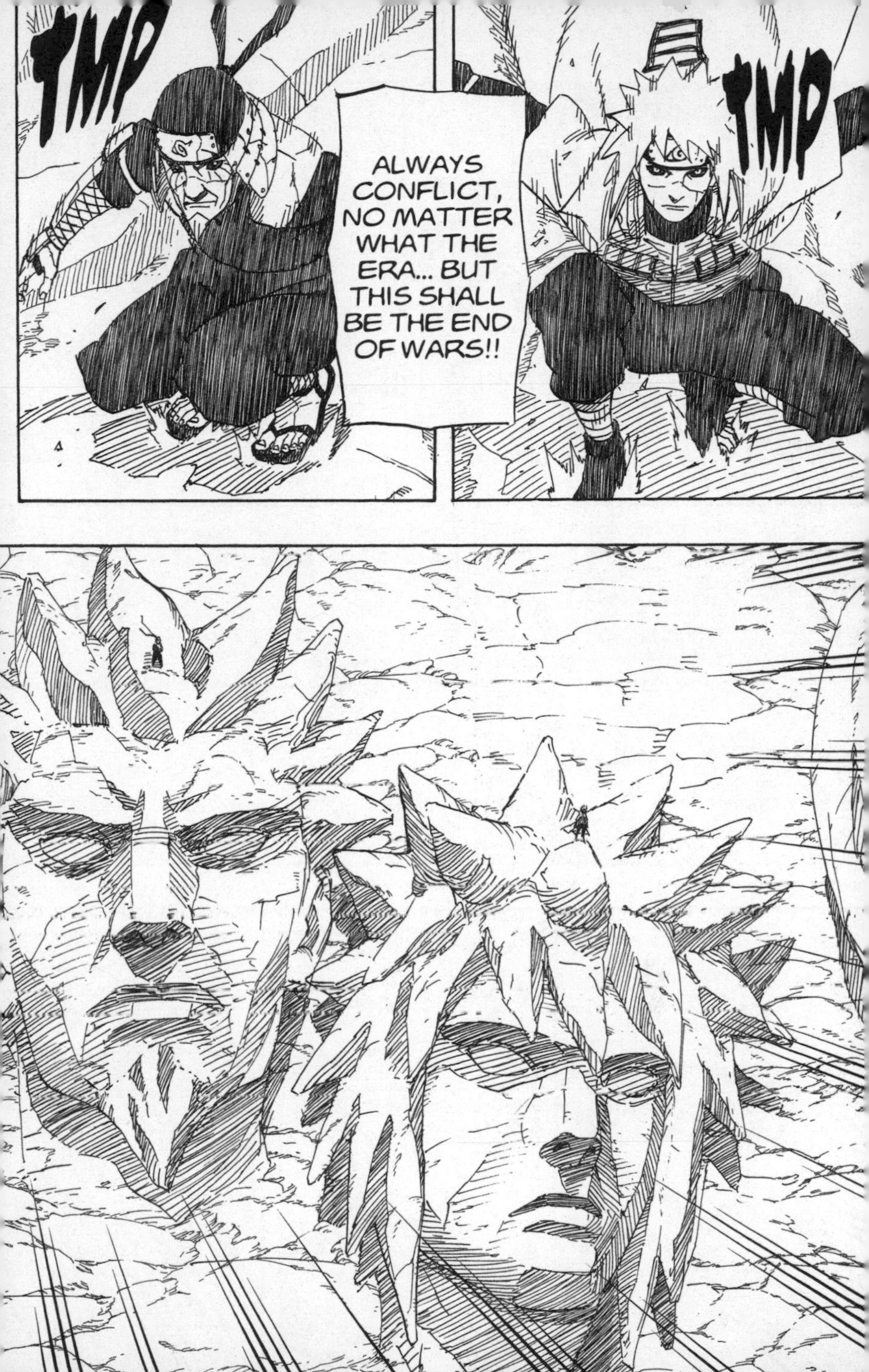
TMP
ALWAYS CONFLICT, NO MATTER WHAT THE ERA... BUT THIS SHALL BE THE END OF WARS!!
TMP

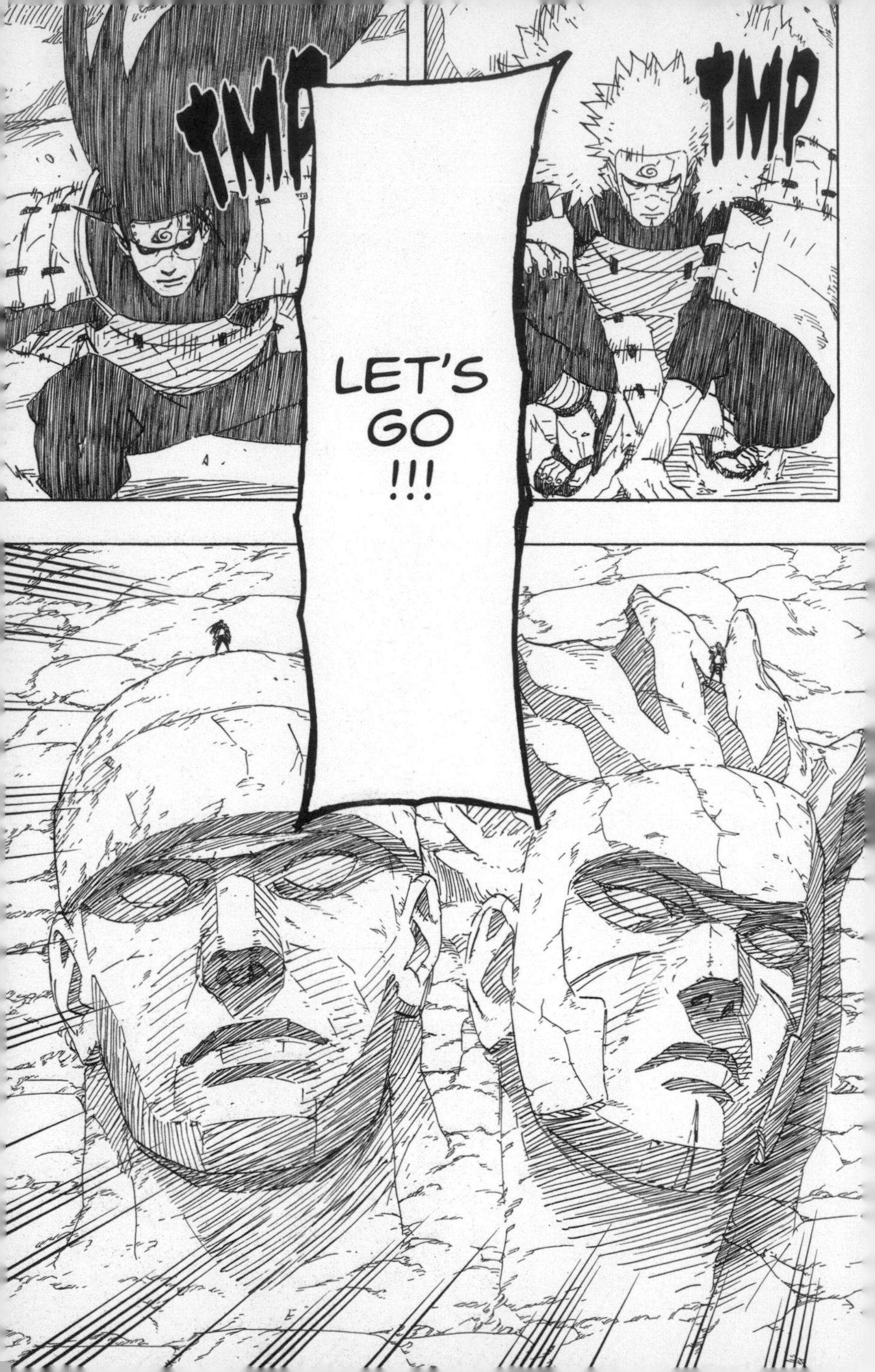
TMP
TMP
LET'S GO !!!

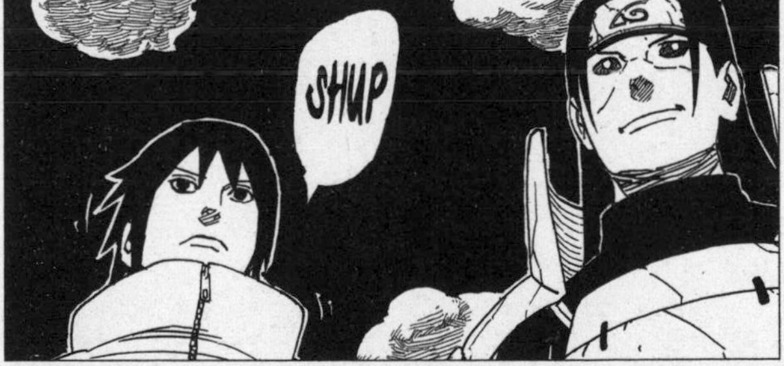
SHUP

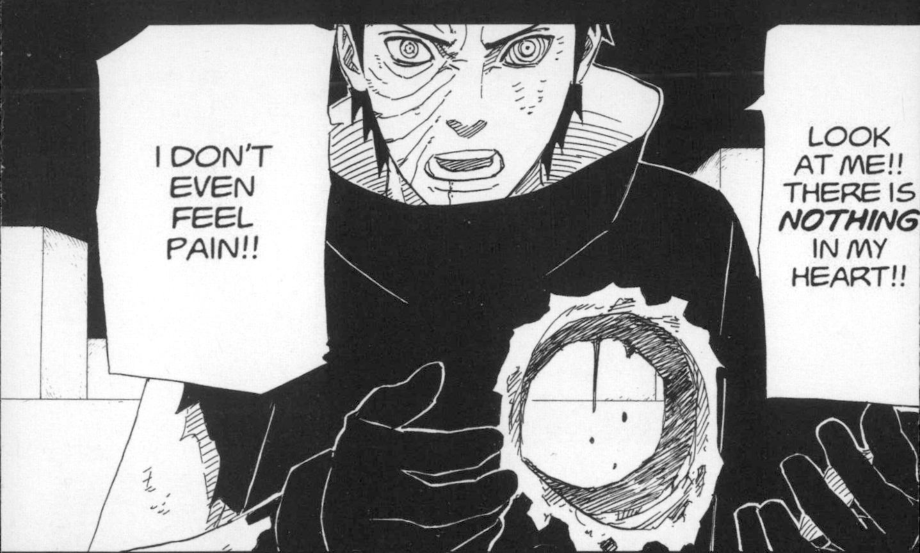
LOOK AT ME!! THERE IS *NOTHING* IN MY HEART!!
I DON'T EVEN FEEL PAIN!!

IN THE NEXT VOLUME...

SUPER REINFORCEMENTS

The four previous Hokage join the battle as the Allied Shinobi Forces gain the advantage for the first time. Kakashi will do whatever it takes to stop his old teammate, but Obito still has a few surprises in store for the ninja world!

AVAILABLE JULY 2014!

VIZMANGA

Read manga anytime, anywhere!

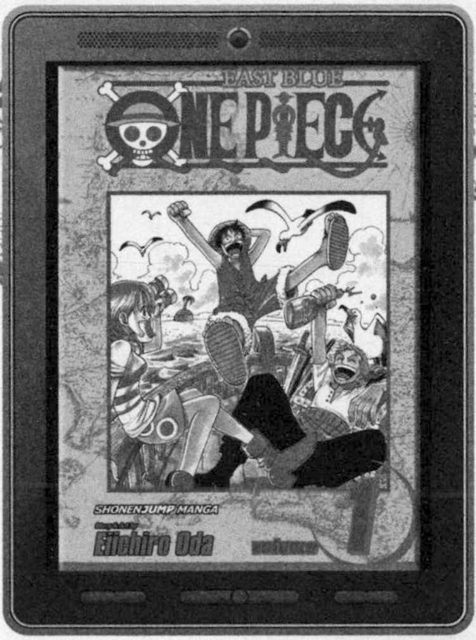
EAST BLUE
ONE PIECE
SHONENJUMP MANGA
Eiichiro Oda

rom our newest hit series to the classics you know nd love, the best manga in the world is now available igitally. Buy a volume* of digital manga for your:

iOS device (**iPad®, iPhone®, iPod® touch**) through the **VIZ Manga app**

Android-powered device (**phone or tablet**) with a browser by visiting VIZManga.com

Mac or PC computer by visiting VIZManga.com

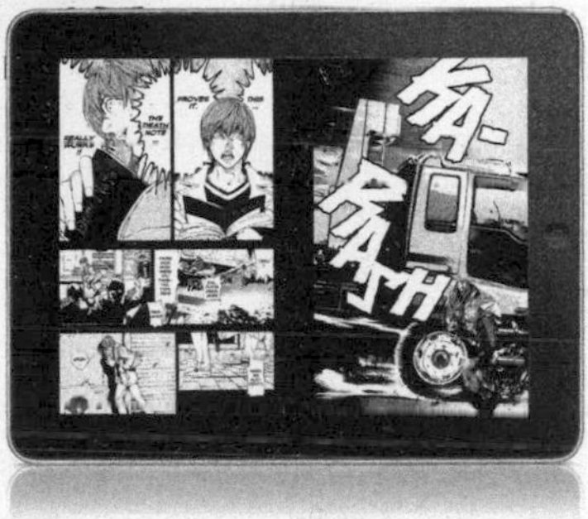

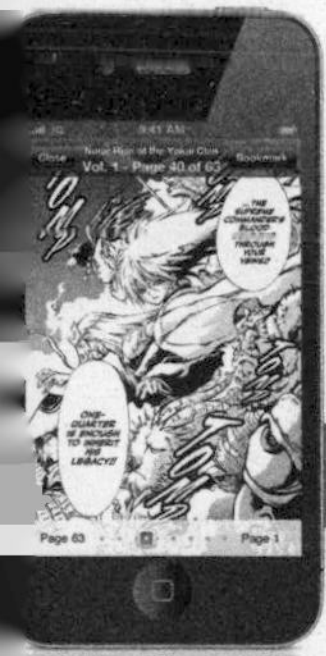

VIZ Digital has loads to offer:

- 500+ ready-to-read volumes
- New volumes each week
- FREE previews
- Access on multiple devices! Create a log-in through the app so you buy a book once, and read it on your device of choice!*

To learn more, visit www.viz.com/apps

*** Some series may not be available for multiple devices. Check the app on your device to find out what's available.**

RATED T+ FOR OLDER TEEN ratings.viz.com

viz.com/apps

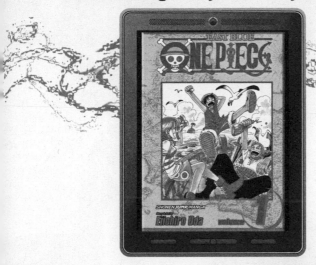

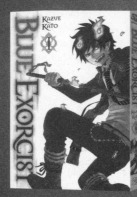

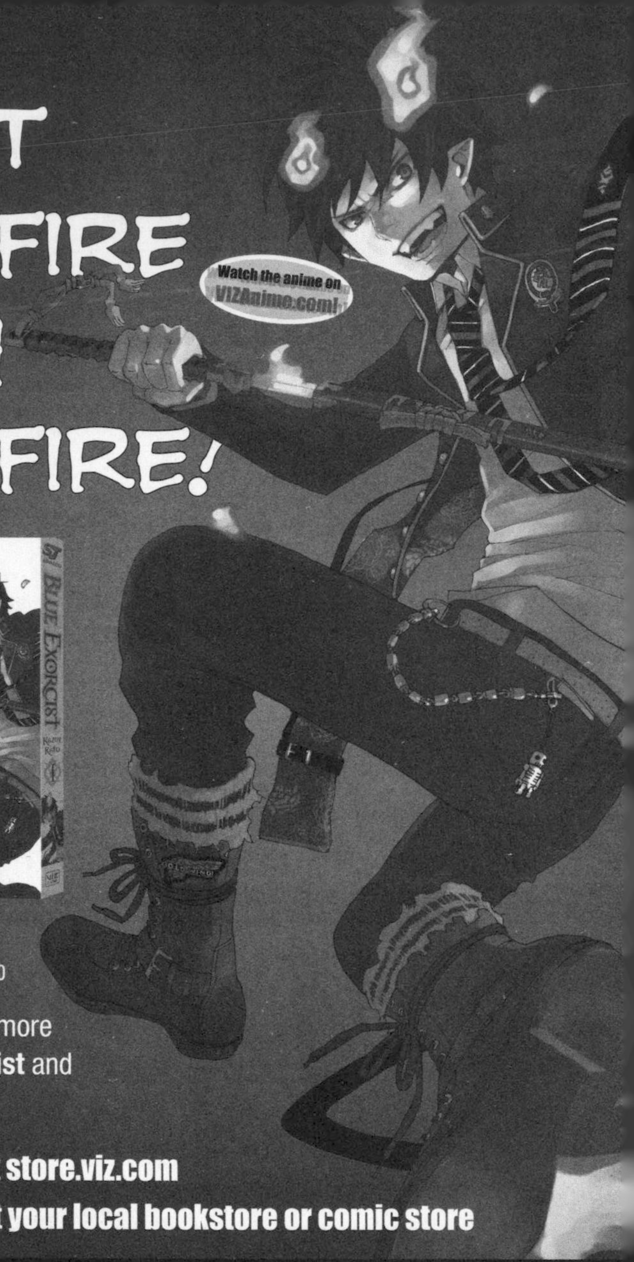

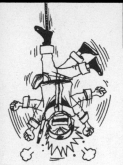

You're Reading in the Wrong Direction!!

Whoops! Guess what? You're starting at the wrong end of the comic! ...It's true! In keeping with the original Japanese format, **Naruto** is meant to be read from right to left, starting in the upper-right corner.

Unlike English, which is read from left to right, Japanese is read from right to left, meaning that action, sound effects and word-balloon order are completely reversed... something which can make readers unfamiliar with Japanese feel pretty backwards themselves. For this reason, manga or Japanese comics published in the U.S. in English have sometimes been published "flopped"—that is, printed in exact reverse order, as though seen from the other side of a mirror.

By flopping pages, U.S. publishers can avoid confusing readers, but the compromise is not without its downside. For one thing, a character in a flopped manga series who once wore in the original Japanese version a T-shirt emblazoned with "M A Y" (as in "the merry month of") now wears one which reads "Y A M"! Additionally, many manga creators in Japan are themselves unhappy with the process, as some feel the mirror-imaging of their art alters their original intentions.

We are proud to bring you Masashi Kishimoto's **Naruto** in the original unflopped format. For now, though, turn to the other side of the book and let the ninjutsu begin...!

—Editor

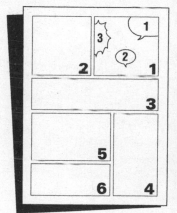